COST-BENEFIT ANALYSIS FOR EXECUTIVE DECISION MAKING

Alfred R. Oxenfeldt

COST-BENEFIT ANALYSIS FOR EXECUTIVE DECISION MAKING

The Danger of Plain Common Sense

amacom A division of
AMERICAN MANAGEMENT ASSOCIATIONS

Library of Congress Cataloging in Publication Data

Oxenfeldt, Alfred Richard, 1917–
  Cost-benefit analysis for executive decision making.

  Includes index.
  1. Decision-making. 2. Cost effectiveness.
I. Title.
HD30.23.095   658.4'03   79-14617
ISBN 0-8144-5490-9

First Printing

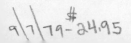

PREFACE

ALL OF US are fallible, but not equally so. Perhaps the least fallible are those who quickly acknowledge their errors and search out their source. (This is a tiny group.) Another group relatively free from error are those who have made many serious mistakes, admitted their errors (probably grudgingly and then only because they could not conceal them), and then earnestly tried to understand and eliminate the source of their errors. (This group is very small, but far larger than the first.) Most to be mistrusted and pitied are those who mistake good luck for skill. They probably lack the resilience to endure the inevitable big mistakes when they occur.

This book aims to reduce executives' errors. I offer as my main qualification to write such a book a long lifetime of mistakes. Almost anyone who knows the author well will testify to his numerous errors. (Controversy exists as to the speed and good humor with which he acknowledges his mistakes, however.) I offer as my second qualification my extreme outrage at these errors, which has pushed me to great efforts to find the causes of my mistakes and to seek remedies for them.

A long career as a business consultant has permitted me numerous opportunities to observe others in a decision-making role. The mistakes I have witnessed, and in some cases collaborated on, probably are easier for me to recognize and acknowledge than my own. In any event, I have been party and witness to many mistaken decisions by executives. Gradually I have learned some important ways to avoid many of these mistakes—or at least to substantially reduce their number.

This book distills my experience with executive decisions. It presents what I regard as the most effective methods of approaching decisions and the concepts and models that lead to valid decisions. It contains just about every important idea that I have learned, in a long career as professor and consultant, to improve executives' major decisions.

In deciding what to include in this book, I first identified those decisions by senior executives which they have difficulty with and in which they often make conceptual and other kinds of errors. I then searched my own training, reading, and experience for aids in making those decisions. The result is an arsenal of models, concepts, and computational procedures that come partly from economic theory but more heavily from behavioral science and decision theory. Many of the intellectual tools discussed here were drawn from the fields of statistics, accounting, market research, and operations research.

I have adapted and modified materials from those fields to develop procedures and approaches directly applicable to business problems. Most of the techniques discussed here are not new but are for the most part familiar ideas put to new uses, or they represent extensions and modifications of what is already known to business specialists. Still, the result of this selective and modifying process is a body of materials that implements a new concept of business economics. Although clearly a lineal descendent of the field launched by Joel Dean in 1951 in his path-breaking book, *Managerial Economics*, it differs in that it is focused heavily on operating decisions and depends much less upon economics for its intellectual sustenance.

This book includes only a modest amount of formal economic theory. Yet, I believe that it contains almost all of what modern economic theory can offer that is of significant value to business executives. I have presented the economic materials specifically to meet the needs of practicing executives, recognizing that some professional economists will be displeased because some of the intellectual rigor and elegance of the theory has been sacrificed for clarity. However, I have not knowingly omitted any complex or technical material that has important managerial application simply to spare the reader from hard thinking.

The interests and viewpoints of economists and businessmen are basically different. Consequently, it is largely coincidental when the writings of economists are directly relevant to business executives. For most executives, economists' writings usually require substantial modification; otherwise the executive must wade through much that is irrelevant to his needs to glean the fragments that do apply. Executives unfamiliar with the theoretical method often find the propositions of economics strange, if not patently false. When regarded as descriptive of reality (which they are not represented to be but which many nonprofessionals take them to be), they can be badly misleading.

This book does not compress all of economic theory that is of value or interest to business. Rather, it concentrates selectively on concepts and models that run counter to common sense or intuition. Emphasis is placed particularly on concepts and models that correct errors that are commonly made.

At many points in this volume the device of dialog is employed, not only because dialog is the stuff out of which much of life is fashioned, but also because executives must learn how to instruct others efficiently through conversation. Dialog is a powerful device for establishing that few demonstrably correct answers exist to business problems. Executives must settle for imperfect approaches, unreliable data, and highly speculative theories. Error and failure are universal facts of life with which executives must learn to live. These messages seem to come through much more clearly from dialogs than from traditional textual materials.

I received valuable help and good advice from Jonathan Schwartz, Robert L. Tebeau, L. Scott Miller, Anthony O. Kelly, and Martha Stodt. No words can fully express my gratitude for their assistance but I want to do what I can to acknowledge my debt to them.

Alfred R. Oxenfeldt

CONTENTS

Chapter 1

THE PRACTICAL VALUE OF ECONOMIC THEORY *or* THE UNRELIABILITY OF PLAIN COMMON SENSE

M ANY BUSINESS EXECUTIVES are impatient with theory, and with economic theory in particular. Apparently, they have had the embittering experience of studying highly complex theoretical material only to find it inapplicable to the concrete problems they face in business. They draw a sharp line between the theoretical and the practical. While quite understandable, this mistrust of theory can deprive executives of valuable ideas.

Economic theory can help greatly in dealing with important practical business problems. Indeed, common sense is frequently misleading in concrete business situations. Let us establish the validity of these two assertions with some simple but realistic illustrations.

Consider a firm that was exploring the advisability of introducing a machine to do mechanically what it had been doing by hand. After studying the situation closely, its executives decided that the undertaking would be profitable if a relatively trouble-free machine could be developed for less than $2 million in research and development. Its research people and engineers assured top management that there was a good chance of coming up with such a machine for less than that amount, and the project was authorized. After a year of work, $2 million was spent but a satisfactory machine was not invented.

The research people reassured top management that they had made great progress and were certain that they could produce the desired machine with an additional expenditure of under $1 million and probably in the vicinity of half a million. A committee of executives set up to study the matter decided to abandon the project. They concluded that it was certain to be unprofitable, since the $2 million already spent on research and development was all the company was justified in spending to exploit the profit opportunity.

A simple economic concept—"sunk costs"—would have led any hard-headed business executive to reach the opposite and correct conclusion.

Consider the XYZ Corporation, a large factory in an industry that was plagued with excess capacity. It was approached by a company that produced machinery for making XYZ's product. The latter company demonstrated convincingly that newly introduced machinery could turn out the product at substantially lower cost than the old equipment owned by XYZ. Its salesmen argued that the corporation should modernize itself to become more efficient and more profitable. Management rejected this argument on the grounds that, since it already had excess facilities, anything it paid for new equipment was a waste.

It may be contrary to plain common business sense to buy plant and equipment in the face of excess capacity, but it does often make dollars and cents. Fairly simple economic reasoning explains why and when it may pay to do so. Every executive should be able to construct an arithmetical model to demonstrate how a hypothetical company with excess capacity could increase its profits (or reduce its losses) if it scrapped its machinery and replaced it with more efficient equipment.

One last example should drive home the point that economic concepts often are needed as an antidote to "common horse sense." An independent businessman had been in business for many years and believed that he was "doing pretty well." He offered to take his son into the firm when the latter graduated from the Columbia University School of Business. The son, who had many job opportunities, asked to see the firm's financial records for recent years. After examining the records, he told his father that he had decided against entering the business. He explained that the way he figured it, the company was actually losing money. His father protested, pointing out that one of the best accounting firms had prepared the company's financial statements, which showed a net profit of $75,000—a return of about 10 percent on net worth.

The son explained his conclusion along the following lines: His father was drawing a salary of only $35,000 from the business, although he had recently refused a position with a large corporation that would have paid $65,000 annually plus sizable fringe benefits. Also, if his father sold the business for its book value of $750,000 (less any capital gains tax)—which he had every reason to believe he could do—and invested the proceeds in safe securities, he could obtain about a 7 percent return, plus the added security that comes from greater diversification. The son thus concluded that the firm was actually losing money rather than making $75,000, since it failed to include one important cost, what the father could have earned on the proceeds of a business sale, and greatly understated another, the value of the father's services.

The father expressed great annoyance with the newfangled theory his son had been taught at Columbia and promised to teach him sound business principles if he would come into the business.

Who should teach whom what in this situation?

The foregoing examples—which are not farfetched or exotic—suggest that certain key economic concepts are very powerful and lead to unexpected conclusions when applied to concrete business problems.

What makes a concept valuable? First, as implied, the concept should have broad applicability. Second, in a substantial number of cases it should lead to different decisions from those that would be reached through common sense alone. Third, it should apply to decisions concerned with quite different subject matters. Fourth, the concept should be nonobvious; its value increases as it runs counter to common sense or to intuitive judgments. Finally, it should not be an idea that one would learn in the ordinary course of affairs.

A number of concepts that meet these criteria are listed below. The list is based on discussions with executives in diverse industries.

Incrementalism, as it applies to both costs and revenues.
Resource allocation and the equimarginal principle.
Opportunity costs.
Decision costs—as distinct from other cost concepts, especially full-costing.
Market structures and competition.
Utility analysis.
Principle of diminishing utility.
Demand elasticities.
Economies of scale.
Principle of variable proportions.
Trade-offs and conflicting objectives.
Financial objectives—interrelationships among long- and short-run profits, dividends, and overtime.
Present value and discounted cash flow.
Uncertainty and subjective probabilities.

Once an aspiring executive knows these concepts, he resembles someone who has memorized many words in a foreign language but doesn't know the grammar and cannot retrieve vocabulary at the speed with which words are spoken. Such a person usually cannot communicate his thoughts and only occasionally will even recognize the subject under discussion. To use a foreign language, one must have mastery—that is, have almost instantaneous access to what he has learned plus an equally speedy ability to recognize what is relevant to the situation at hand. More specifically, one requires a *command over* what one knows; *knowledge* itself is not nearly enough, except in the contrived environment of the classroom and for the purpose of taking examinations.

Assuming that the reader has studied the list of key concepts and read tracts discussing what they mean, what can he do to gain command over them? First, he must meet them again and again, preferably in dissimilar circumstances. His goal is to be able to use them intuitively—an ambitious goal that represents a highly advanced state of command over ideas. Second, he must actively employ the concepts: he must decide which concepts are applicable and actually use them to arrive at a specific decision. In short, it is through repetition and continued application that one acquires mastery. Almost by definition, mastery is gained slowly, but one may expedite the process by continued reuse and review of the fundamental concepts.

Recognize, further, that mastery of fundamental nonobvious concepts rarely is total. Those who teach and apply the same idea again and again usually understand it better and differently each time. They can apply it more widely and effectively with added experience with the idea. Mastery is a relative concept.

Many subordinate economic concepts arise in any treatment of real-life problems. In the chapters that follow, they should not be allowed to interfere with the reader's concentration on those concepts listed above. Our aim will be to apply the key concepts in a variety of dissimilar situations so that readers may gain command over these concepts and confidence in their ability to apply them.

Chapter 2

DECISION MAKING: TOOLS, APPROACHES, AND STYLES

A LMOST ALL EXECUTIVES make decisions about people—how to handle their supervisors, their peers, and their subordinates. Executives also request allotments of funds and decide how to spend the funds assigned to them; they prepare written financial budgets and budget the time of their personnel and themselves. Beyond such decisions, which are common to virtually all senior executives, are various decisions needed to perform specialized job responsibilities. Although executive decisions cover an enormous range of subjects, they have many characteristics in common.

Major decision problems involve many variables.

Many of the business forces surrounding the decision are unstable.

The factors operating in any business situation are likely to be interrelated.

Every business decision involves a situation that is unique.

The data describing influential forces are usually scanty and of poor quality.

Most decisions affect rivals, who may take various counteractions.

There is limited time to reach a decision.

In most situations, decisions must be made without an opportunity to test their effectiveness.

This list is not meant to suggest that executives are helpless in the face of new problems. However, it is true that almost no business decision has a single demonstrably correct answer. Perhaps more than anything else, aspiring executives must reconcile themselves to a search for the best or most satisfactory solution, rather than the "correct" solution. The best decision must be defined as the most reasonable one at the time it is made, rather than as the one that turns out to be correct possibly because of unexpected developments.

Aids in Making Decisions

Tens of thousands of executives wrestle with complex business decisions every day. Many intellectual tools have been developed to assist them in this struggle. Let us list these aids, recognizing that some are designed to deal with highly specialized problems while others have broad applicability.

The main general sources of assistance in solving complex business problems are (1) an understanding of the main steps in the decision process, (2) information, (3) basic concepts, (4) models, (5) research techniques, (6) computational techniques, and (7) computing equipment.

UNDERSTANDING THE MAIN STEPS IN THE DECISION PROCESS*

It is possible to present a brief sketch of the decision process. The first step in the solution of any problem is to identify it. As a second step decision makers must decide what they are trying to achieve. The third step involves considering all factors—controllable and uncontrollable—that will influence the decision. Clearly, it is infeasible to think through every conceivable alternative; to attempt to do so would be a waste of time. Thus a crucial part of this step is to isolate the most promising courses of action for closer scrutiny. This process requires creativity in devising workable solutions that are not obvious, and also requires quick rejection of impractical solutions. The final step in decision making, the selection of the "best" alternative, consists of matching the outcomes of the various alternatives against the firm's objectives.

Beyond decision theory, as outlined here, three other subject areas contribute to an understanding of the decision process: (1) the literature dealing with problem solving,† (2) materials discussing research

---

* For a brief but highly competent summary of decision theory, see David W. Miller, "The Logic of Quantitative Decisions," in Abraham Shuchman, ed., *Scientific Decision Making in Business* (New York: Holt, Rinehart & Winston, 1963), pp. 313–332. See also Alfred R. Oxenfeldt, David W. Miller, and Roger A. Dickinson, *A Basic Approach to Executive Decision Making* (New York: AMACOM, 1978).

† See in particular the discussion of decision making in business by William Newman and Charles Summer, Jr., in *The Process of Management* (Englewood Cliffs, N.J.: Prentice-Hall, 1964), pp. 253–341.

methodology—in particular, the steps in the design of a marketing re-search project (see Chapter 6 for a detailed discussion), and (3) the psychoanalytic literature, which isolates the many forces that can work against a purely rational decision.*

Information

The information relevant to a decision should describe the existing situation fully and accurately so that the executive at least knows what problem he is trying to solve. It should also indicate what happened under the most analogous situation of which there is record. (Some of the information may bear upon what is being planned by other firms in the industry.) Of course, the most useful information is that which indicates the outcome of alternative actions the executive might adopt.

Basic Concepts

The term "concept" includes a wide variety of mental constructs, ranging from imaginative models of complex situations to simple distinctions. Basic concepts are abstract general ideas that are aids in thinking.

Models

Models represent a higher order of ideas than do concepts. Their purpose is to indicate how various factors work in combination to determine particular phenomena and thus to help in understanding and solving specific problems. (See Chapter 4 for a full discussion and illustration of models.)

Research Techniques

The amount of information that can be brought to bear on a business problem depends heavily on the research methods available. Many techniques have been developed for collecting information that assists in executive decisions.

Computational Techniques

It is possible to possess a wealth of relevant information, be master of the pertinent concepts, be adept at the decision process, and still be incapable of reaching a correct decision because of an inability to use the information at hand. The meaning and implications of information are rarely obvious;

* The literature on this subject is vast, and not oriented to business decision makers, of course. A brief but penetrating discussion of the defense mechanisms that prevent people from dealing realistically with problems is presented by Calvin Hall in *A Primer of Freudian Psychology* (New York: World Publishing Company, 1954).

information must be distilled before it yields its full message. A variety of techniques have been developed to help executives wring out the implications of data that would otherwise be hidden from them.

COMPUTING EQUIPMENT

Spectacular developments have taken place in the speed with which information can be retrieved and processed. These developments make it possible to apply information to business decisions that could never have been gathered or processed in time before. What is more promising—and we already have concrete examples, not merely hopes for the future—is the use of computers to improve the quality of decisions themselves by taking account of a large number of variables, computing interrelationships among the variables, and permitting a testing of many alternatives.

Of the seven aids to executive decision listed here, basic concepts and models probably are the most valuable. But even with these aids senior executives can rarely make decisions in which they have complete confidence. More important than the tools discussed are personal skills that substantially improve executives' decision-making ability. They can learn how to approach decisions and can develop styles that add greatly to the validity of their decisions.

Decision Approaches

Two basic approaches can be taken to decisions: the first is intuitive; the second is explicit. As defined here, all intuitive decisions basically are similar. Explicit decisions, however, cover a huge range; adding to the confusion, they usually include some intuitive elements. Let us look at these two approaches, with particular attention to when each would be appropriate.

THE INTUITIVE APPROACH

Almost all our decisions are based on unconscious thinking. Typically, we face an issue or stimulus and a reaction quickly floats up to consciousness, often in the form of a specific answer. That is, we form a judgment almost instantaneously. Usually, we act on that judgment. Thus we make most of our decisions without knowing how they were arrived at; we don't know what information, inferences, or deductions entered into them. When we decide this way, we are relying on intuition—the unconscious thought processes of the brain.

Are we wise to rely on decisions arrived at in this manner? Can we give credence to conclusions reached by a wholly mysterious process?

These questions can be dismissed on the grounds that the process "seems to work," that judgments made in this way seem to be correct most of the time. And when we look at certain kinds of decisions—for example, those made while driving an automobile or reacting to sudden emergencies—the validity of intuitive judgments seems to be high. Unfortunately, we lack an accurate measure of the validity of intuitive judgments in other types of decisions—those made by executives, parents, military leaders, diplomats, and so on.

What specifically do we want to know about our unconscious thought processes? We surely want to know how intuitive judgments are formed—how the unconscious brain works. We want to know how much value to attach to such judgments. When are they most reliable? Under what circumstances are they most distorted? What can be done to increase the validity of intuitive judgments? How do such judgments compare with the judgments we would reach if we took considerable time and employed sophisticated analytic techniques? How does our ability to make valid intuitive judgments improve, if at all, with practice? What kinds of practice help most? Does the acquisition of conscious decision-making skills improve unconscious decision-making skills? If so, how does this come about? How great are the differences among individuals in their intuitive skills? Are people who make good intuitive judgments in one sphere likely to make good intuitive judgments in all others?

We lack answers to most of these questions, for a variety of reasons: The answers apparently are not the same for different individuals; that is, the intuitive capabilities of individuals vary widely. We often do not know even after the event what answers are correct, unless we confine ourselves to definitional-logical-mathematical problems. A person's intuitive judgments about mathematical problems may have more or less validity than his or her intuitions about empirical problems. The validity of an individual's judgments varies with the emotional content of the problem. Individuals vary in their command of sophisticated decision-making approaches and skills, that is, how conscious of and concerned they are with decision making as a process and the techniques they understand for handling difficult issues.

In other words, any appraisal of the general validity of intuitive judgments would be very misleading if it included certain areas of high validity and others of very low validity. Unless studies of intuitive judgments deal with (1) different kinds of judgments and decisions, (2) different degrees of emotional involvement, (3) individuals possessing different degrees of intellectual interest in decision making, and (4) different degrees of skill and high-powered decision-making techniques, we cannot know whether to rely on intuitive judgments in particular situations.

Despite the enormous difficulty of appraising the validity of intuitive judgments, some broad generalizations can be made:

- Conscious and unconscious judgments are made by the same organ—the brain. We would therefore expect some rough equivalence in the ability of an individual to make both kinds of judgments.
- In spheres where individuals have a great deal of experience—as in driving automobiles—the validity of intuitive judgment is generally very high.
- Intuitive judgments are not highly consistent in their validity for most individuals, because of differences in mood, fatigue levels, emotional involvement, and so on.
- What a person cannot judge validly on a conscious basis, given time to do so, he cannot judge validly on an unconscious basis—unless he has had vast personal experience with the phenomenon.
- The ability to make intuitive judgments improves somewhat with practice, but mainly with greater experience with the phenomena about which judgments are made.
- An individual usually feels more confident of certain intuitive judgments than of others. The validity of intuitive judgments seems to vary with the confidence one has in them.
- Some individuals are extremely talented and consistent in making intuitive judgments, while most persons have limited ability.
- Few judgments are either purely conscious or purely intuitive, since even conscious thinking is a highly intangible and mysterious process. The spectrum of processes by which judgments are formed is extremely wide, and a huge gulf separates the highly intuitive from the careful, conscious decision.

What implications do these generalizations have for the average person? For the executive as a professional decision maker?

Most individuals can escape from relying on their own intuitive judgments only by relying on the intuitive judgments of others—by delegating decision-making responsibilities or following the advice of others. Even then, they usually depend on their intuitions to select the individuals to whom they delegate responsibility or whom they seek out for advice.

Every executive should make strong efforts to become sensitive to and informed about his skills and performance with intuitive judgments—in different spheres. How well does he compare with others in forming intuitive judgments? In what areas are his judgments usually better than average? In which are they worse? Under what circumstances does he perform best and when is he at his worst? Such self-diagnosis is not easy but is extremely valuable. Sometimes a close associate can give us valuable information and insights about our strengths and weaknesses.

An executive should work at developing a conscious and explicit approach to decision making in order to contrast the results reached with intuitive judgments and to improve unconscious judgments by increased competence with conscious judgments.

It is also important to make careful, objective analyses and evaluations of subordinates and colleagues on the very issues on which one assesses one's own performance, for only then can one delegate and seek advice wisely.

The Explicit Approach to Decision Making

By definition, all decisions that are not approached intuitively are dealt with "explicitly," even though such decisions usually contain many intuitive elements. Explicit approaches cover a wide range, from the simple listing the pluses and minuses of a contemplated action to the use of elaborate mathematical or econometric models. Similarly, they include reliance on scraps of dubious evidence as well as elaborate and costly research studies. Since the explicit approach to decision making represents so many highly dissimilar things, one must be most specific about the particular explicit approach that is under discussion.

Toward this end, we shall classify explicit approaches to decisions according to the amount of information used; whether the decision is made by an individual or by a group; whether the decision was defended in writing; and whether a formal mathematical model was used. Table 2-1 presents a schema for classifying approaches to business decisions.

Table 2-1

A Classification of Explicit Decision Approaches

		Uses voluminous information		Uses moderate information		Uses little information	
		Uses mathematical model	No mathematical model	Uses mathematical model	No mathematical model	Uses mathematical model	No mathematical model
Group decision	In writing	1)	5)	9)	13)	17)	21)
	Not written	2)	6)	10)	14)	18)	22)
Individual decision	In writing	3)	7)	11)	15)	19)	23)
	Not written	4)	8)	12)	16)	20)	24)

Let us direct our attention to cell 1, the most elaborate approach to decision making; we would term this approach "management science." It is most explicit, employs mathematical-econometric models and techniques, and makes heavy use of empirical data; it takes a written form and involves the efforts of more than one person. How does this approach compare with intuitive decision making? How much more or less effective is it than the approach described by cell 24? Will management science always produce better decisions than pure intuition? What pitfalls ordinarily beset such decisions?

Management science and decision making. A few propositions will help to avoid misunderstanding. First, a decision maker can employ many different approaches to the same decision—and when the decision is important it would be wise to do so. Usually, executives form intuitive judgments before they have completed a management science study, and often before they even initiate one. When such a study produces a different conclusion from that arrived at intuitively, executives face dilemmas. (Later, we will explore appropriate behaviors for such situations.) Second, skills in management science techniques apparently differ as much as—or more than—skills in intuitive decision making. Third, management science techniques used by naive analysts often produce nonsensical results; conversely, sophisticated management scientists do not advance naive conclusions. They recognize when management science techniques are inappropriate and use them only when they fit the situation.

Some management specialists hope that management science techniques will be applicable to much higher-level executive decisions than is the case at present. With the passage of time, improvements and refinements have been made in operations research techniques; a breakthrough could occur so that major management decisions will be made by mathematical techniques. But that situation certainly appears a remote possibility to many business specialists.

Whatever the potentialities of management science, it is clear that executives must employ an explicit approach to their most important decisions. Even if they are prepared to rely solely on their intuitions, their colleagues and employers rarely will do so. Explicit approaches offer several important advantages: first, they permit decision makers to review their thinking after they have formed a judgment to see whether they have gone astray. Second, the decision makers can obtain the suggestions and criticisms of others on specific elements in their decision. Third, an explicit approach gives the decision maker a place to start—some concrete issue on which to focus. Without an explicit approach, decision makers would probably seek much more information than they require and waste considerable time in worry for lack of specific questions on which to focus their thoughts.

The more developed explicit approaches to decisions include the following elements:

Identification of the objectives involved in the matter at issue.
Identification of the difficulty or opportunity under consideration.
Structuring of what one knows about the phenomenon involved in the decision under consideration—model building.
Identification of alternative actions available.
Identification of the effects of each attractive alternative.
Evaluation of the most attractive alternatives.
Selection among the attractive alternatives.

Some explicit approaches combine or omit some of these elements. As a consequence, they will suffer some loss in validity. Still, circumstances may not permit an executive to devote the time and resources required to perform each step, and he will be forced to pick those on which to concentrate his attention. No single approach is suited to all executives, to all situations, and to all decisions.

Decision Style and Executive Decision

Executives can employ the most suitable approach to their decisions, apply the best models and appropriate concepts, use relevant, accurate, and voluminous information, and still make poor decisions. Beyond valid approaches, models, concepts, and information, executives require certain personal qualities and behaviors if they are to make valid decisions. Mainly, they need an effective "decision style." By this term, we denote qualities closely linked to basic personality traits that strongly influence an executive's behavior in a decision-making setting.

Take the example of extremely inflexible, close-minded, and biased executives. They can, and most likely will, reach mistaken conclusions frequently, however well informed they are about models, concepts, or approaches and even though they possess considerable factual information about their problems. Similarly, executives who avoid decisions, feel impelled to make them very rapidly, or fail to avail themselves of the good advice available to them will perform far less well than decision makers with opposite traits. Their style will prevent them from deciding as well as their knowledge of concepts, models, approaches, and facts would permit.

What personal qualities and characteristics are particularly helpful for decision makers? And how should they behave with respect to decisions, especially important ones? These questions are essential matters for executives and aspiring executives to consider in depth. Accordingly, they will be discussed here, albeit superficially. Mainly, we will limit ourselves to lists of desirable personal qualities and behaviors.

The following lists present the personal qualities and behaviors usually desired in executive decision makers. These lists have no firm empirical foundation but represent a rough consensus of executive and business specialist opinion. Clearly, the qualities and behaviors desired will vary according to whether one is making decisions about clothing styles or major financial investments for an insurance company. Figure 2-1 presents a scale which individuals can use to identify the main characteristics of their decision styles and probable strengths and weaknesses.

PERSONAL QUALITIES DESIRED IN EXECUTIVE DECISION MAKERS

- Objectivity: wants to reach a correct decision rather than seem smart or prove he was right in the past; tries hard to avoid effects of personal bias.
- Flexibility: prepared to alter his views on any subject without requiring overwhelming evidence.
- Tolerance for risk: accepts danger of mistake and failure without trauma.
- Nondefensiveness: willing to admit errors.
- Tolerance for ambiguity: can form judgments in spite of conflicting information and paucity of information.
- Patience with detail: will examine relevant data with care, even if much time is required.
- Logical powers: can sense inconsistencies; will try to reason his way through complex issues.
- Imagination: can generate alternative solutions; generally feels a dissatisfaction with existing answers.
- Resilience under pressure: can endure tension without losing perspective.
- Maturity: has had considerable worldly experience; possesses emotional stability not necessarily related to chronological age.

BEHAVIORS DESIRED IN EXECUTIVE DECISION MAKERS

- Takes time to decide when time is available, rather than rushing through decisions.

Figure 2-1. Dimensions of a decision style.

	Speed of decision	
1. Slow	_____	Fast

	Requests advice	
2. Never	_____	Almost always

	Receptivity to advice	
3. High	_____	Low

	Objectivity	
Highly 4. emotional	_____	Highly objective

	Attention to detail	
Very 5. impatient	_____	Patient with detail

	Desire for factual evidence	
6. Strong	_____	Little interest

	Willingness to delay decisions	
Anxious to "get decision 7. over with"	_____	Willing to deliberate at length

	Ability to decide in face of limited information	
Unable to make 8. a decision	_____	Quite willing to decide

	Liking for decision making	
9. Enjoys	_____	Dreads

	Independence of judgment	
Swayed 10. by anyone	_____	Not swayed by anyone

	Explicitness of method	
Highly 11. intuitive	_____	Fully explicit

	Readiness to delegate decisions	
Quite 12. willing	_____	Very reluctant

	Time horizon of decision	
Preoccupied with the 13. immediate	_____	Concerned with long run

	Performance under stress	
Badly 14. impaired	_____	Performance improves

	Anxiety about decision after it has been made	
Feels great stress until outcome 15. is known	_____	Concentrates only on present decision

How to use this scale

1. Compare yourself with the person whose decision-making behavior you *know* best. If you are equal to that person in the particular dimension, place an X in the middle of the line. If you are diametrically opposite, put an X at the end of the line close to the word that describes you. For example, if you are much slower at making decisions than the other person, put an X near the word "slow" on dimension 1. Connect the X's by a line.

2. In the same way, compare yourself with the person whose decision style you *admire* most. Connect the X's with another line.

3. Decide, after examining these lines (profiles), what changes you want to make in your decision style. Then, give thought to how you hope to bring such changes about.

- Reviews decisions with others before taking action, when opportunity exists.
- Conducts post-mortems of decisions, especially when they turn out badly.
- Doesn't agonize over decisions once they have been made.
- Monitors past decisions to determine whether underlying assumptions were valid.
- Asks for advice from people who might have something to contribute.
- Accepts good advice when it is offered.
- Delegates decisions or parts of decisions when he is not well qualified to make them.
- Learns from errors instead of expending energy on defending them.
- Exposes views to competent people who are likely to disagree with them.
- Deliberates and broods before making decisions, when the opportunity exists.

We have now listed the main personal qualities and behaviors that characterize effective decision makers. Are these in the same category as approaches to decisions and the so-called tools for and aids to decision making? More specifically, can these be learned? Can and should executives try to change their personalities to become better decision makers? Should they change their behavior?

Exceptional people can change some of their fundamental characteristics—with great effort and some outside help—and do so even fairly late in life. Most people apparently cannot do so and may not want to. But with effort just about everyone can modify his *behavior* in desired directions. And much of what is to be gained from personality change and growth can be obtained from changed behavior, without any alteration of basic personality. For example, people can curb their impatience and tendency to decide quickly and can even adopt a procedure which requires delay and a re-examination of the issues; they may routinely solicit advice, as a standard operating practice, even though—indeed, just because—it is contrary to their nature to seek help from others.

Much is to be gained by knowing one's strengths and limitations as a decision maker in all possible respects: in the tools that are needed, the approaches that might be employed, in personal characteristics, and in decision style. By learning one's weaknesses and obtaining help from others to remedy them, executives can avoid the greatest penalties of their limitations. Moreover, they can capitalize on their strengths; in addition, they can put their strengths at the service of their colleagues, who will then be more likely to do the same for them.

Is there a single best approach to executive decisions? A single best decision style? A best set of decision-related behaviors? The answer to all three questions is emphatically negative. The approach to a decision that is used should match the nature of the decision itself and the circumstances surrounding the decision.

THE NATURE OF THE DECISION

Earlier, the difficulties that often confront executive decision makers and the factors that make their decisions complex were discussed. Certainly, the complexity of a decision should influence the approach taken to it. Other characteristics are also important. Table 2-2 presents a classification of executive decisions constructed for the purpose of selecting a suitable approach. The type of decision indicated by cell 1 represents the most difficult for an executive: it is unfamiliar, complex, involves high stakes, and he has little time to deal with it. If all characteristics but the availability of time were the same and the executive had much time to reach a decision, one would expect him to employ a relatively elaborate approach like those designated by cells 1 and 3 in Table 2-1. Similarly, if an executive faces a quite familiar and simple issue, possesses much time, and only low stakes are involved (cell 36 in Table 2-2), he can afford to employ a casual and highly intuitive approach.

Table 2-2

A CLASSIFICATION OF EXECUTIVE DECISIONS

Type of problem	Stakes	Highly complex		Moderately complex		Quite simple	
		Little time	Much time	Little time	Much time	Little time	Much time
Very unfamiliar	High	1)	7)	13)	19)	25)	31)
	Low	2)	8)	14)	20)	26)	32)
Somewhat familiar	High	3)	9)	15)	21)	27)	33)
	Low	4)	10)	16)	22)	28)	34)
Very familiar	High	5)	11)	17)	23)	29)	35)
	Low	6)	12)	18)	24)	30)	36)

THE CIRCUMSTANCES SURROUNDING THE DECISION

Decision approaches differ according to the circumstances surrounding the issue. In particular, such circumstances as the following should affect the choice of approach: time available, resources available, visibility of the decision, personalities actively involved, and policy constraints. These circumstances require little elaboration. Surely one must expect the availability of financial resources and time to limit a choice of approach to decisions; similarly, one recognizes that group decisions require compromise. Especially if persons of high rank have strong preferences and strong aversions regarding method, these must be honored. And organization policy may rule out certain approaches. For these reasons, decision makers in large organizations do not select their approach to decisions solely on the basis of merit.

One major conclusion follows from the foregoing discussion: decision makers must be flexible. They must have a wide repertoire of behaviors and must be able to behave differently as the occasion requires. They should be familiar with many approaches and know to what kinds of decisions they are best suited. They should likewise know the aspects of their personality that often result in errors and know the remedies for those weaknesses. Finally, they should understand their customary decision-making behavior and the consequences of that behavior. In sum, they must know and understand the significance of their personal qualities; they should be able to diagnose the needs of specific decision situations; and they should select the specific combination of approach, behavior, and style suitable to the case at hand.

The following dialog applies the concepts discussed in this chapter to a real-life situation.

Decision Approaches: A Dialog

Ben Printz is the major owner of a chain of large retail music stores in a metropolitan center. The city has been afflicted by extreme price cutting for almost two years. During that period Mr. Printz's stores and most others have lost business and market share to two large aggressive price cutters. These two chains do not offer as wide a selection as Mr. Printz and other large retailers; also, their stores are less attractive, do not have skilled, courteous sales help, and keep customers waiting. Still, their low prices have enabled them to acquire a sizable share of the record business in a very short period of time.

Mr. Printz has been in the retail business all his life and in the music business for over 20 years. Although not formally trained in business and management, he has been a careful student of business and has squeezed out all that is to be learned from his personal experience.

Mr. Anchor is a college professor and marketing consultant who specializes in decision making. He met Mr. Printz in connection with a special assignment and was very impressed with his decision-making skill and native intelligence. He was particularly anxious to learn how a successful intuitive decision maker would react to more formal, structured approaches to decision making.

The dialog is a partial summary of their discussion.

MR. A: I'm not disagreeing with your recent decision to cut prices sharply, Ben. You're much better informed about conditions in your market than I'll ever be. But I'm questioning your approach to such a major decision. It seems to me that it's very risky to act on decisions reached by your intuitive-judgmental approach; furthermore, it doesn't do much to develop your subordinates.

BEN: I don't know what you mean by that—I gave this decision a lot of careful thought. I spent weeks thinking about this major price move before I made it. I discussed it many times with my partner and our senior executives. It seems to me that you're complaining because I didn't write it all down in detail.

To tell you the truth, I don't know what you would have me do different, except maybe for writing it all out. I have all the relevant facts available; I can't even think of other facts I would want if they could be had for the asking. Certainly, I worried a great deal about this decision before I made it. What more could I do?

MR. A: That seems a fair question. As an outsider to your industry, I'm not likely to approach your decision in a very efficient manner. Still, I'll accept the challenge and suggest the way that I believe this kind of decision should be reached. But remember, I'd expect to do a much better job if I were familiar with the industry and had made similar decisions in the past. I feel a little like a new auto driver who has to make decisions in heavy traffic.

The first thing I'd do is diagnose the current situation. I'd ask myself whether and why I must make a decision *now*. What that means is, I'd pinpoint what seems to be going wrong that I'd be able to change for the better. And, what is closely related, I'd make very explicit what objectives I was pursuing. In this case, these two steps wouldn't be too difficult, but they're not as simple as they appear.

BEN: Seems clear to me that there's a strong need to make a decision in the very near future. These two big price cutters have cut sharply into my business for over a year now, and they've hurt the record business generally by pushing prices to a new low level where *all* retailers can barely survive. I'm serious when I say that we may not be able to survive. I had hoped that after they gained a foothold they would charge reasonable prices; instead, they're sticking with these low prices—even though they can't be making any money at these prices. So my goal is to deal with the price cutting by these two competitors so that I'll be able to pay my bills. I'm well·aware of the problem and my objectives. In other words, I've certainly taken the first two steps you mentioned.

MR. A: Well, yes and no, Ben. I see a substantial difference between what you just said and the way I'd deal with these first two steps. But you may think I'm just quibbling. Sure, your problem is caused by the emergence of two large price cutters who threaten to grow larger and cut further into your sales even while pushing down your unit profit margins. But the underlying problem may be quite different from what appears on the surface. It may not be these two competitors that are the real problem but the fact that several manufacturers are taking active measures to increase the number of retailers—especially if they will cut prices. The manufacturers may expect to get substantial increases in sales volume because of their low prices and the greater exposure of potential customers to records. So my diagnosis would differ from yours—but that may not result from a difference in approach.

And, on the subject of objectives, your goal might be to create an acceptance by both manufacturers and retailers of a long-range attitude toward the industry that includes the economic interests of all parties involved in the record industry. You'll never find this a really profitable business to be in if the record manufacturers ignore their own dependence on retailers and have no concern for retailers' long-run economic interests. Similarly, retailers have to recognize that record manufacturers and recording artists are entitled to strive for wide exposure and large sales. In other words, your goal might be to persuade the various factors in this industry to act with wisdom and restraint for their own long-run benefit.

BEN: That all sounds great and you may be viewing this problem in a more searching and thoughtful way than I am. But I have to deal with these two price cutters before I'm hurt even more than I've suffered already. My immediate goal must be to either drive them out of the business altogether or force them to raise their prices so that all of us can survive. I can't undertake a missionary role of getting all factors in the industry to adopt an enlightened long-run viewpoint.

Maybe that's the difference between us—I'm emphasizing my short-run goals and you're stressing the long-run goals. Right now, I want to ensure that I'll survive the short-run crisis I face.

MR. A: We don't disagree about that. But you should start by identifying your long-run goals because they may imply particular short-run actions. In other words, I'd certainly grant the urgency of dealing with the price cutting situation you face. But your long-run goals might require that you tolerate it for a little longer. I don't know how I'd come out on that issue—I'm just trying to explain how I'd approach this problem and not claiming to offer the right answer.

The point is that what I would decide to do if I were in your shoes would be a direct result of the way I described the problem and the goals I set for myself. Of course, I might end up doing just what you would do. However, since my approach requires me to be explicit and to formulate my objectives clearly, it should substantially reduce the risk of my pursuing a mistaken or partly mistaken objective.

BEN: Are you suggesting that I am mistaken in trying to reduce the inroads that these two price cutters are making into the whole market, including my share of the business? Unless this situation changes soon, I will be in deep financial trouble and should get out of this business altogether. I've just got to do something about these price cutters. Don't you agree to that, at least?

MR. A: Yes and no. Sure, they're hurting you badly. But any change in your prices now might make things even worse for you. In some situations, nothing will improve matters; any action you take would make things worse. But, more to the point, your best solution might be not to lower your prices and put added price pressure on these two price cutters but to complain to the manufacturers from whom they're getting their merchandise and probably easy credit terms; it could be the manufacturers who are fostering the situation and who might be best able to remedy it, at least to some degree. After all, you don't want to go to great cost and disrupt the record market further to push these two competitors out only to find the manufacturers are helping several others to enter the business.

BEN: Right. What you say makes some sense, but we now seem to be discussing content rather than approach. You claim that I'm pursuing the wrong objectives, not that I don't have clear objectives.

MR. A.: Sure, you're clear that you want to get rid of the price cutting problem—so you do have clear objectives in that sense. My point is that approaching the problem as you did, you were bound to formulate your objectives more loosely than if you adopted a systematic, formal, and structured approach. Different results flow from doing things in a written, explicit, and systematic manner. It leads to a different answer in many cases, simply because of the difference in approach. It offers real advantages—but it might also have some disadvantages.

BEN: I can't judge the advantage of your approach until you describe what you would do. You seem to be suggesting that I should try to persuade the record manufacturers that they are short-sighted in facilitating the operations of new retailers—rather than hit out at the price cutters directly. Maybe I could do both. Just show me where you would go from your statement of the problem and your stated objectives.

MR. A: Okay, but I feel uncomfortable suggesting answers when I know so much less about your industry than you do. But maybe we could apply my approach together. I'll indicate what I think we should do and then you help me to do it. It seems to me that your next step would be to identify all the things you might do to get the record manufacturers and most of your competitors to recognize the long-range damage to the industry from current conditions. Let's list what those actions might be.

I can see several obvious things: Talk to the manufacturers at the highest levels to find out what they intend to do and to let them know how you feel; talk to representatives of your trade association and have them protest to the manufacturers; and issue a statement of your views to the industry through a statement to the trade press. Aren't there other things you might do?

BEN: I could talk to some other large retailers who are being hurt along with me to have them bring some pressure on the manufacturers. I'd have to be careful to avoid discussions that could cause antitrust problems. But mainly I'd need to know what to suggest to them. There is no point to telling them that they have a price cutting problem; I'm sure that their infant children know about it, it is so serious. The question is, what might we retailers do?

MR. A: You know the answer to that much better than I. Let's skip that step for a moment, if you don't mind. Let's assume that you have come up with three possible actions to suggest to your fellow retailers; you would want to decide which of the three to favor. How would you forecast the effects of these three possible actions?

BEN: That's a strange question. The answer seems obvious. I'd just ask myself what would happen if we did thus and so.

MR. A: I figured you would give that answer. And here's where your approach and mine really diverge widely. Let me explain what I'd do and see how it compares with what you actually did in estimating the effects of your projected price reduction. First, I'd start by making a list of the key parties involved in this industry—starting with sources of talent at one end. My list might be pretty long; it would include the different kinds of middlemen in the industry as well as the major customer segments. Once I had identified these, I'd ask myself how each contemplated action would affect each one of those interests.

BEN: Could you be more specific? I'm not sure I understand what you would do. First, indicate some other parties involved in this industry. Then, how would you figure out what effect any action would have on that party?

MR. A: I can answer both questions very quickly: Some of the parties in the industry that you should give serious thought to are the manufacturers of records, their exclusive distributing companies, rack jobbers, "one-stops," discount department stores, large specialty retailers of records, and your major customer segments—the heaviest buyers, whoever they may be.

As to figuring out what effect any action would have on each party, that is something that a person with your experience would do much better than I could do. But my point is that a systematic approach will force you to touch many bases before arriving at a decision—though it is still possible that some bases would be missed.

BEN: In my discussions with my colleagues as well as in my thinking about the problem, I'm sure that I gave attention to all those parties you mentioned. But I can't show you in writing what I thought. And to be frank, I couldn't tell you this minute where I came out with all my thinking about the various parties. Maybe that is your point.

MR. A: It is in part. I claim that a systematic and explicit manner of approaching decisions increases the probabilities of getting a good answer. It doesn't guarantee a good answer, but at least you will end up by knowing just what you did and did not think about. And you would be able to compare your reasoning with that of others—like your colleagues. They would be able to see it down in black and white.

BEN: Your method would certainly be good for the paper industry; it sure would require lots of writing. But would I really reach a different and better conclusion?

MR. A: Let me see if I can demonstrate quickly the advantage of my approach. In justifying your decision to lower prices sharply, you said that you expected to increase your profits. That must mean that you expect a very large increase in sales volume. Isn't that so?

BEN: Yes, I anticipate a quick increase in sales with the new prices to about double what they would be at the old prices. With that sales increase, my profits should increase between 25 and 30 percent.

MR. A: I can understand that arithmetic but it gives me serious problems. Where do you expect this increase in volume to come from? Will it all represent additional sales of records in this market? Or will your higher sales mean lower sales for the other retailers in the city? I'd be particularly interested in how much volume you expected to attract away from the two price cutters.

BEN: Well, I didn't really break down the expected sales increase in that way. But I'd say that some of the increase would be entirely new business.

MR. A: About how much would you expect to be new business? 75 percent, 50 percent, 25 percent, or 10 percent?

BEN: I don't know, maybe 25 percent—it could be as much as one-third.

MR. A: Then 67 to 75 percent of the increase in sales you expect would come from your competitors? Which of them would be hit hardest by your price cut? Do you think you would take from all of them fairly equally?

BEN: I'm not sure, I wouldn't even know how to find out—so how could I know? But I'd guess that most of my customers are highly price-conscious and also look for a very wide selection. Only a few very large metropolitan retailers offer anything comparable to what I offer. They would be the hardest hit, I would expect.

MR. A: If I understand your thinking, you expect a 67 to 75 percent increase in your sales at the expense of a few competitors. I assume that each of them would be hurt significantly. And the competitor that was hurt most—I doubt that the few you have in mind would be hurt equally—would really have a sharp cut in sales and profits.

BEN: What profits? Most of them were losing money before I cut my prices. That's right—one or two of the largest retailers situated within a mile or so of my stores might really get hit badly. Come to think of it, one is already on the ropes financially. I wonder whether he'd be able to last.

MR. A: Would you expect him to just accept the loss of business and go bust?

BEN: I see your point. Of course not! He'd know perfectly well why he was losing business and to whom. He'd have to cut prices also.

MR. A: And if he as well as you cut prices, what would happen to your other competitors' sales?

BEN: Okay, I admit that it was useful to examine the effects of my price change on different types of retailers. I should have gone down the road you followed. But I might still have felt obliged to cut prices because I just couldn't let things go on the way they have been going. Maybe everyone—including the manufacturers—has to recognize the crisis conditions existing in the industry and do something about it.

MR. A: It could be. But I'd again want to see whether and how the main manufacturers of records would be affected by your price move. It could be that they'll be delighted with the 25 to 33 percent increase in your sales volume—to begin with. And they'll also have the higher sales that will result from your competitor's price cuts. Again, I'm not saying that your conclusion is wrong; I'm questioning your approach.

BEN: I must say that I now have a question in my mind as to whether I did the right thing. If I'm not too old or rigid to learn new tricks, I may study what specialists in decision making say. I hope it's more helpful than most of the stuff I've read about how to be a better manager.

Chapter 3

RESOURCE ALLOCATION AND COST-BENEFIT ANALYSIS

EXECUTIVES make two types of decisions that are fundamentally economic in character. (Virtually all decisions have some economic ingredient.) The first type will be termed "comprehensive," "coherent," or "integrative" decisions and represent sets of decisions rather than single decisions. Comprehensive decisions require the decision maker to select combinations of actions out of a huge number of possibilities and to determine how far to pursue each of them. The main comprehensive decisions made in organizations are budgets and plans.

The second broad type of executive decisions will be termed "single" or "ad hoc" decisions. These are usually occasioned by the unexpected occurrence of a problem or the emergence of an opportunity. Here the executive deals with a single decision, largely in isolation.

Both types of decisions are discussed in this chapter. Not surprisingly, they have much in common; in particular, both pursue the economic goal of "optimum allocation of resources." In layman's language, that means they try to use the decision maker's resources where they do the most good. This one economic goal may be said to override and embrace all others.

This chapter examines the nature of resource allocation as well as the basic logic involved in approaching both comprehensive and single decisions. The logic underlying comprehensive decisions is embodied largely in the so-called equimarginal principle; the logic underlying single decisions is that of cost-benefit analysis.

Optimum Resource Allocation

Resources are being used most efficiently when the excess of output (ends, desires, goal attainment) over input (resource use, costs, sacrifices) is at a maximum. (Indeed, we ordinarily measure efficiency in all things by the ratio of output to input.) What, then, is required for efficient resource use? What must individuals, executives, or government planners know and do to get the most out of what they have—and thus minimize deprivation?

Efficient resource use requires a clear identification of ends or goals, knowledge of what resources are available, and knowledge of how those resources can best be used to produce what is desired. (Implicit in such knowledge is an understanding of existing technology.) Although other information is needed, the foregoing are the most crucial items. Thus, if one knows what he wants, what he has to work with and how the things he has might be used to make the things he wants, he can, after very careful calculation, allocate his resources in a way that will produce a maximum of what he wants.

People allocate resources to different uses all the time and on many levels. An individual allocates his resources when he decides how to spend the next five minutes, what to order at a restaurant, how much time to spend reading different articles in the newspaper, and the like. Similarly, a nation allocates its resources, however indirectly, when it formulates budgets and establishes rules that govern business activities—taxes, antitrust regulations, tariffs, interest rates, and so on. Nations engaged in detailed economic planning allocate their resources when they set output goals for individual industries and when they set social and cultural goals.

Executives employed by large enterprises usually attempt to utilize the resources under their control in the most efficient way. In other words, almost all decisions by executives affect resource allocation, and they seek maximum output relative to input of resources.

HOW RESOURCES ARE ALLOCATED IN PRACTICE

Executives typically use concrete measures of both input and output; these are dollar amounts of costs and outputs. Of course, some inputs and outputs are intangible and, though usually translatable roughly into dollars, they do not initially and directly take the form of dollars. Still, unlike the general economic planners or individuals allocating time or energy, business decision makers have the benefit of fairly concrete measures of input and output. The more common methods employed to allocate resources are as follows:

- Set priorities. Find the most important activity and do that "to the full"; then do the next most important activity "to the full"; and so on.
- Do everything in the same proportion. Determine what you want of all things and cut back each in the same proportion, depending upon how much the resources can produce.
- Assign traditional percentages of your resources to each use. Stick to the proportions that prevailed in the past.
- Decide on an ad hoc basis. Decide each issue separately as it arises rather than view all needs and all resources as a coherent whole.
- Keep on doing what you have been doing until it becomes clearly unsatisfactory.

These methods do not require much information, which may explain why they are so widely used. But it is not surprising that they rarely produce a valid decision in complex and volatile environments.

Let us examine the first of these methods—setting priorities and filling the most urgent priority first in full, then filling the next most urgent priority in full, and so on. This approach was employed in the distribution of scarce materials during World Wars I and II and provides a dramatic example of the allocation process. As supplies of vital raw materials (such as steel, nickel, or molybdenum) became scarce during the early stages of the armament program, companies producing vital armaments were given priorities—preference with supplies over all other buyers. Those producers were able to meet their needs in full before others could obtain any materials. The priority system was quickly refined to distinguish between more and less urgent users so that some obtained AA priorities, others received A priorities, still others received B priorities, and so on. This arrangement finally had to be abandoned because it became very clear that some of the items produced by those holding the highest priorities were not as vital to the war effort as things that other firms without any priority would produce.

The fatal flaw of the priority system is explained by the principle of diminishing marginal utility, which holds that the value (benefit, gain, pleasure) that a nation obtains from added units of product will decline as it has more of it—during any given period of time. Accordingly, added tanks, guns, ships, and planes are less valuable as the nation has more of them; and as the output of such things as garbage pails, pots and pans, and tools for the repair of appliances is curtailed, their value rises. At some point, the nation gains more from using scarce metal to make items for civilian use than to make military items. And within either category (military or civilian), as more of the most essential item is made, its value declines, so that it becomes advantageous to shift to the next most essential item. In fact, one usually should not really speak of any item as being more or less essential than another, because its essentiality depends on its present availability. Water is of negative value in a flood and of enormous value in a drought. The principle of diminishing marginal utility is the core of the equimarginal principle.

The Equimarginal Principle and Comprehensive Decisions

The economist contends that to allocate resources efficiently one must apply the "equimarginal principle." This method of resource allocation is much more complicated than those listed above; it requires a great deal of information and involves complex processing of that information. Accordingly, it requires some explaining.

The equimarginal principle incorporates a rationale that explains how to get maximum output from the use of any particular quantity of resources. Similarly, this logic indicates how to produce any given output with minimum resources. Although the information required to apply this principle fully is rarely available, the logic is powerful and helpful. The following hypothetical example, although highly oversimplified, indicates how the principle should be applied.

Consider a management that is deciding how to divide its marketing budget among three activities: advertising, personal selling, and customer service. Table 3-1 shows the effects on the firm's expenditures on sales, all occurring during the following year in an even stream. Observe that the table indicates a decline in the "marginal productivity" of each marketing activity beyond some point. That means that added efforts to produce

Table 3-1

EFFECTS OF DIFFERENT MARKETING OUTLAYS ON UNIT SALES

	Increase in output (in unit sales)		
Outlay	Advertising	Personal selling	Customer service
0	500	500	500
$1,000	500	500	500
$2,000	700	800	650
$3,000	900	1,050	800
$4,000	1,100	1,250	950
$5,000	1,250	1,400	1,100
$6,000	1,400	1,500	1,200
$7,000	1,500	1,550	1,250

output (here, sales or customers) of a given size or cost add progressively less to output. That is, beyond some point the extra output for each "effort" or dose of resources becomes smaller than the last. To greatly simplify the exposition without doing violence to the concept, we will assume that the firm must make its outlays in $1,000 lumps.

Observe that with a $1,000 outlay for any of the three activities, the sales of the company would be the same—500 units. That similarity in sales results from the fact that sales would not be affected at all by an expenditure so small on any of those activities—they have not gotten over the threshold. Beyond that point, outlays on the different marketing activities yield dissimilar amounts of added sales. The equimarginal principle calls for dividing the additional lumps—in the following way:

The first lump goes to that activity that yields the greatest increase in sales; in this case, it would go to personal selling, for that sum would increase unit sales by 300 units—the difference between sales of 500 and 800 units. The second $1,000 lump would again go to personal selling, for it would add 250 units of sales to the total—the difference between 800 and 1,050—which is more than could be obtained from any other use. The third lump could go to either personal selling or advertising, both of which yield 200 unit increases in sales. (In the case of advertising the increase is from 500 units to 700.) This process would continue in the manner described until the entire marketing budget was allocated. If done in this manner, the *last* $1 of outlay would add the same amount to total sales in all three activities. (That result would be more easily demonstrated if our illustration dealt with $1 outlays rather than with outlays of $1,000.)

When resources are divided among alternative uses in this way, the result is a larger total of output than could be obtained in any other way. That is, if one shifted a "lump" of resource from one activity to another, the output (sales in this case) would decline.

The equimarginal principle helps us think constructively about the allocation of all forms of resources: money, time, energy, affection, etc. Specifically, the principle directs decision makers to consider shifts of small lumps of resources from one use to another and estimate whether the shift will improve or worsen their situation. Although this approach seems simple-minded, it can help mightily in uncovering gross errors.*

Budgets and plans embody the chief comprehensive decisions made by individuals and organizations. To prepare them requires an extremely

* In the foregoing hypothetical example (Table 3-1), we assumed that we know the effect of expenditures for advertising, personal selling, and customer service on the firm's sales in units. That rarely is the case, though valid decisions clearly require such information.

broad perspective involving an awareness of all feasible alternative actions and of all available resources. The decision maker's goal is to make the best possible match between the two. Underlying such decisions is a weighing of alternative possibilities and a mental shifting of resources from one potential use to another and an estimation of the effect. This process cannot feasibly be replaced by a series of individual decisions. Accordingly, the conceptual basis for comprehensive decisions is different from that employed to make single decisions, even though both pursue the same goal—the optimum use of resources.

Comprehensive decisions like budgets and plans usually represent a set of many hundreds, if not more, of interrelated separate choices. Little wonder that they are so difficult. They are complicated by another factor: generally, many individuals must participate in the planning and budgeting process. The individual responsible for preparing a plan or budget must depend upon other people. These usually possess highly specialized knowledge and they alone can estimate what is needed for their activity and what will be gained with different investments of resources. The objectivity and competence of such individuals generally varies. Consequently, persons responsible for budgets and plans cannot regard requests for funds by different executives as equally valid. If budget requests from all "claimants" totaled, say, 12 percent more than the resources available, the budget director would be unwise to simply cut every request by 12 percent. That procedure would penalize the careful and reward the greedy. To avoid crude measures like equal percentage cuts for all, the budget director must gain a familiarity with the individual activities for which the funds will be used.

Single or Ad Hoc Decisions and Cost-Benefit Analysis

Most business decisions arise unexpectedly and must be made in a relatively short time, in contrast to the decisions embodied in plans and budgets, which usually are prepared according to a regular time schedule. Single decisions are, of course, constrained by a firm's plans and budgets; but to a considerable degree, they also stand alone. For example, a speedy decision must be made when one of the firm's production lines produces an extraordinarily large percentage of rejects and those responsible cannot uncover the cause; or, sales in an important market are persistently below plan; or, someone has turned up an interesting product opportunity that might be exploited in several different ways. Single decisions also involve more major concerns: Should we add a new product to our line? Should we introduce a new production process now or await further technological improvements? Should we develop a training program for executives to eliminate certain errors that plague our operations? Should we float a new security issue or borrow from private sources?

Business decisions have a common structure and many common characteristics. An understanding of this structure and these characteristics will help an executive to formulate decisions in ways that facilitate valid results.

One of the mainstays of single decisions is cost-benefit analysis. The essence of cost-benefit analysis is simple and obvious: the "worth" of any action, project, investment, or strategy equals the excess of the benefits it yields over the costs (sacrifices) it entails. Consequently, to pick the best of the alternatives available, a decision maker should estimate the net benefits to be obtained from each and pick the one offering the greatest net benefits. What could be more simple and logical?

But to apply cost-benefit analysis to important decisions, a business executive must resolve several profoundly vexing issues, which arise because the business environment is extremely complex, volatile, and unpredictable. The issues to be resolved in any major decision are as follows:

- What effects of an action should be included in its cost, and what effects represent benefits?

  Benefits occur when one gains an objective; costs are incurred when one loses an objective.

  An executive should include only costs and benefits that result from the decision action—not some average or standard amount computed according to formula.

- How can an executive deal with the uncertainty of the effects of each alternative action? Of course an executive can make a "best forecast," but it is obvious that many outcomes are likely enough to occur to justify consideration.

  In major decisions, these different outcomes should be identified explicitly and their implications explored—in particular, the amount of injury they might cause the organization.

- How can an executive value the effects of an action, especially its intangible effects?

  This problem has two parts: (1) How to identify the significant effects of the action. The "solution" consists of gaining a thorough understanding of the phenomenon, and that requires the use of valid models. (2) How to value those effects in a specific context.

- How can an executive take account of the fact that the effects of an action occur at different points in time—years apart?

This problem has a relatively simple but still tricky solution: it is to state all effects as present values.

- How can an executive take account of organization policy, limited resources, the prejudices of persons with strong influence in the organization?

    Constraints on a decision maker's choices may sometimes be overcome; but they should be identified, and the cost of overcoming them should be reckoned in the total cost of the relevant projects.

These issues will be discussed briefly in the following sections so that readers may gain a preliminary understanding. They are developed in considerable depth in the balance of the book.

THE CASH-FLOW MODEL OF A BUSINESS ACTION

Executives propose actions or strategies only in the expectation of achieving some benefit. (The term "benefit" and its synonyms "gain," "satisfaction," "reward," "revenue," are used almost interchangeably to denote the attainment of objectives in whole or in part.) More precisely stated, executives expect to achieve a *net* gain from their actions, since obtaining a benefit almost invariably requires some sacrifice. The objective of maximum net gain may be linked to the objective of optimum allocation of resources. If a firm makes decisions that yield a maximum of net benefit, it will be using its resources very efficiently. Indeed, an executive will often find occasion to apply the equimarginal principle to individual decisions within the broad framework of cost-benefit analysis. That is, in deciding what to do about a particular problem, a decision maker must allocate his time to different facets of the decision; and he must put together an action program consisting of several parts among which he will try to allocate resources according to the equimarginal principle.

Accordingly, individual business decisions usually require a firm to expend money and other things in the expectation that it will recover more than it expends. Although both expenditures and benefits take nonmonetary as well as monetary form, it will simplify matters greatly to view alternative actions initially as having only monetary consequences.

The monetary benefits and sacrifices involved in most business actions can be viewed as streams that extend through time. They can be described by the size, duration, evenness, and certainty of these money streams.

Clearly, most business decisions give rise to a series of expenditures rather than a single outlay at one point in time. For example, if a firm replaces a machine, it must not only pay the price of the new one but also the costs of repair and maintenance as they occur. When a firm undertakes an advertising campaign, it makes payments at different times for the design, research, and execution of the advertising material itself and for the media by which it is communicated. When a business enters a new market or adds a new product—or does almost anything—it makes a stream of outlays rather than a single expenditure. If there is a typical pattern, it is that outlays usually are heaviest near the beginning of a business action and become quite light toward the end. Figure 3-1 presents a configuration that might be considered fairly typical; of course, the time scale would be drastically different for, say, the acquisition of a new plant and for the holding of larger inventories.

The money benefits that a firm derives from its business actions also take the form of a stream, rather than a single receipt of funds. These usually occur over so long a period that the passage of time may be a significant factor in the decision. The configuration of receipts over time usually is quite different from that for outlays; ordinarily receipts start at a low level, rise to a moderate level (moderate compared to the size of outlays at their peak) and then stabilize roughly for a while before they begin to decline. Both receipts and expenditures would actually be irregular rather than smooth and even as shown in Figure 3-1—they occur at intervals and in lumps rather than in a regular and continuous stream.

The information presented in Figure 3-1 can be combined to describe the *net* inflow or outflow of funds (Figure 3-2). The outlays in each period are subtracted from the cash inflows to arrive at the net figure. Figure 3-2 also shows the initial capital required to carry out the action in question. Initial capital requirements represent the amount of funds which the firm must possess before it can undertake a project; roughly speaking, that means the excess of disbursements made in the initial stages of the project over receipts up to the time that receipts exceed outlays. Beyond this amount, one would ordinarily add a sum to cover contingencies.

Thus far, three dimensions of business actions have been mentioned: the amount of capital required to put it into effect; the outlays and receipts involved during each time period; and the time duration of the money flows. The many and complex factors that determine the receipts and outlays in any specific case will not be explored; they vary enormously from case to case. Other aspects of business actions require discussion, however. These are uncertainty, the constraints on executive decisions, possible threats to "survival"—the risk of "ruin"—and the importance of intangibles.

An analysis of a decision that takes all these aspects into account is far more complex than is suggested by the patterns of cash flows. To handle

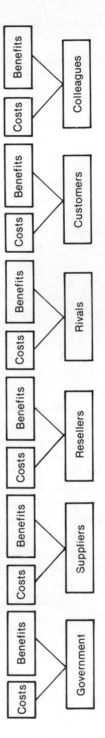

Figure 3-1. Receipts and expenditures per year for typical business decision.

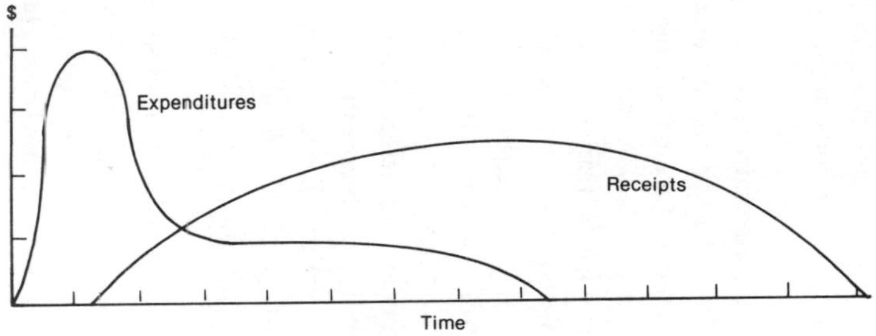

Figure 3-2. Net flow of funds.

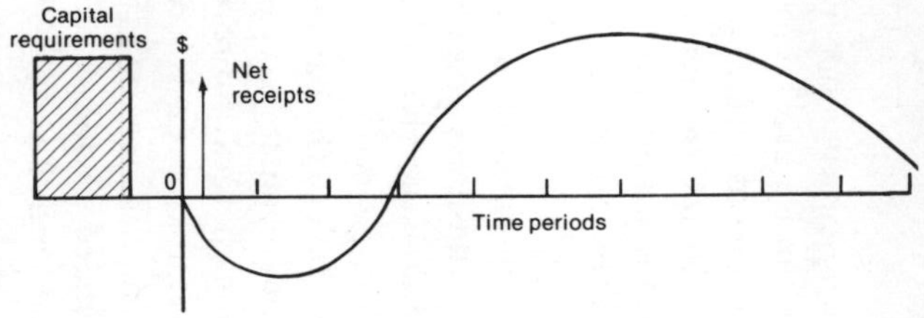

Figure 3-3. A consequence net structure of a decision alternative for strategy 1.

much of this complexity, the so-called consequence net framework can be used. A very simple version is presented in Figure 3-3.

The box labeled Strategy 1 represents one of several actions under consideration by the decision maker. He will try to identify all significant consequences of that action, both favorable and unfavorable, and will evaluate them. He would do the same for all alternative actions under consideration.

In the consequence net, the favorable and unfavorable consequences are associated with particular "parties to the business process." In almost all cases, the consequences of business decisions involve colleagues, ultimate customers, rivals, resellers, suppliers, and government. Accordingly, the consequence net would list the effects on each of the parties to the business process expected from each strategy being evaluated. Once listed, a price tag (representing cash flows or accounting charges and revenues) would be placed on each one. By this procedure, the executive can compare the benefits and costs for each party to the process for each time period. The consequence net structure can be extended to locate the favorable and unfavorable consequences by time periods and thus describe the net favorable or unfavorable consequences over the life of the project.

The consequence net structure emphasizes the identification of all significant consequences of any action under consideration. By directing the decision maker to consider possible favorable and unfavorable consequences vis-à-vis all parties to the business process and to separate tangible from intangible and short-term from future consequences, it should prod the executive's thought processes and reduce the danger of complete omissions or oversights.

The decision maker would be wise to translate the information sorted out by the consequence net into cash flows by various time periods. Beyond that, he would also want to take explicitly into account the intangible consequences of his decision, which usually will not take a cash form for a long time, if ever.

Table 3-2 presents another structure for assembling the information collected to prepare a cost-benefit analysis. In concept, it is directly related to the consequence net structure; instead of taking a hierarchical form, it consists of a tabular arrangement, which is much easier to prepare and manipulate.

UNCERTAINTY—A CHARACTERISTIC OF ALL BUSINESS ACTIONS

No executive can forecast either his outlays or income streams accurately over the life of an investment; he cannot even forecast with confidence the value he will himself place on money over the life of the invest-

Table 3-2

PROPOSED STANDARD FORM FOR ESTIMATION OF BENEFITS AND COSTS

Source	Benefit	Cost	Estimated Amount	Comments

1. *Ultimate Customers*
 Tangible behavioral benefits
   Added unit sales
   Higher price
   Better product mix
   Favorable word-of-mouth
   Other _____
 	
 Intangible attitudinal benefits
   Brand awareness
   Product knowledge
   Brand preference
   Increased desire for product
   Other _____				

2. *Resellers*
 Tangible behavioral benefits
   More distributors
   Better quality distributors
   Lower distributor margins
   Greater sales support
   Hold larger inventories
   Perform more functions
   Other _____
 	
 Intangible attitudinal benefits
   Loyalty to manufacturer
   Open to suggestions from manufacturer
   Willing to forgo immediate profits for
     long-run gain
   Other _____				

3. *Rivals*
 Tangible behavioral benefits
   Follow the industry "leader"
   Refrain from immediate strong retaliation
   Retract price cuts
   Participate in industry trade association
   Raise prices when costs increase
   Desist from price cutting when demand
     falls temporarily
   Other _____				

Table 3-2 (continued)

Source	Benefit	Cost	Estimated Amount	Comments

Intangible attitudinal benefits
   Trust rivals
   Be prepared to grow slowly rather than
     disrupt industry
   Be willing to help when you are in trouble
   Adopt a long-range view of the business
   Other _____
 	
   _____				

4. Suppliers
Tangible behavioral benefits
   Charge low price
   Provide premium quality
   Give preference when supplies are short
   Hold large inventories
   Provide information about technology
     and rivals
Intangible attitudinal benefits
   Feel friendship for the firm and its
     executives
   Try to help firm rather than take
     advantage of its weaknesses
   Trust firm to be fair
   Other _____
 	
   _____				

5. Colleagues
Tangible behavioral benefits
   Help other division's programs work
   Lend assistance when the firm is in need
   Trust firm to be fair
   Other _____
 	
   _____
 	
Intangible attitudinal benefits
   Develop affection for your division
   Give help quickly and in friendly way
     when asked
   Trust the division's fairness and honesty
   Other _____
 	
   _____				

Table 3-2 (continued)

Source	Benefit	Cost	Estimated Amount	Comments

6. *Government*
Tangible behavioral benefits
  Withdraw regulation
  Warn rather than punish
  Subsidize rather than constrain
  Other _____
 	
  _____
 	
Intangible behavioral benefits
  Trust your firm more than others in the
    industry
  Desire to help your firm
  Be prepared to give advice and valuable
    inside information
  Be accessible when information is
    requested
  Other _____
 	
  _____				

ment. How, then, can he hope to evaluate the courses of action open to him and process uncertain outcomes to reach a concrete decision?

The two chief sources of uncertainty faced by a decision maker in assessing courses of action are (1) lack of knowledge of the true "state of nature" and (2) an inability to forecast the precise effects of his actions because of incomplete knowledge and understanding.

States of nature represent conditions beyond the control of the decision maker that influence the outcome of his actions. Examples are the state of international relations, interest rates, general business conditions, the industry level of demand, the number of firms operating in the industry, technological developments, or the availability of credit. By their very nature, these conditions are unknowable with certainty and yet have a significant effect on many business actions. Accordingly, a forecast of the revenue and cost implications of major actions must be based on informed guesses about the state of affairs that will prevail. The executive must estimate the outcome of each of his alternatives under each relevant state of nature; he must also estimate the likelihood of each state of nature and know *how* each state of nature would affect the outcome of each action he might adopt.

Let us be more specific. Each of the alternative actions considered by an executive gives rise to a series of potential flows of receipts and outlays; for each of the various states of nature that are relevant, the decision maker would expect a different flow of income and outlay. For example, one of the actions under consideration by a decision maker might be the acquisition of a new machine to produce a special part that the firm was currently buying from a supplier. One state of nature deserving consideration is that the personnel employed to tend this complex machine would prove to be imaginative and skilled (N_1); another is that they would be very much the opposite (N_2); another possible state of nature is that the employees would be somewhere between the first two extremes (N_3). In each of the three cases, the flow of expenditures and benefits from the purchase of the machine would be quite different. Figure 3-4 depicts three different patterns of *net* income resulting from the purchase of this machine, each representing the best forecast of the outcome of the action under different states of nature.

The foregoing line of reasoning can be extended one more step if we use a "decision matrix." This notational device expresses in convenient form the following information: (1) states of nature; (2) alternative strategies; (3) likelihood of each state of nature; and (4) the outcome of each action under the various states of nature. Table 3-3 presents a very simple decision matrix. In effect, each cell in a decision matrix expresses the net benefits to the firm over the full life of one alternative for one state of nature. In order for a decision matrix to be used, the information contained in the curves representing flows of outlays and receipts over the life of a business action must be collapsed into a single number.

Since the decision maker does not know which state of nature will come to pass, he should assign a probability to each one that expresses his view of the likelihood that it will occur. Termed "subjective probabilities," they express the decision maker's views, and presumably reflect all of the evi-

Figure 3-4. Patterns of net income flows.

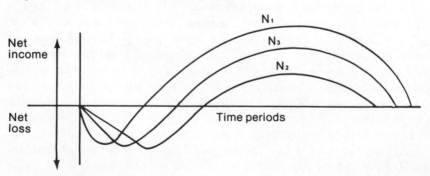

Table 3-3

A HYPOTHETICAL DECISION MATRIX

States of nature		N_1	N_2	N_3	N_4
Probability of each state of nature		.4	.3	.2	.1
Expected net benefit of each action:	A_1				
	A_2	X			
	A_3				

dence available to him. Rarely could he prove the validity of these probabilities, however.

The outcomes of any business action are uncertain for a second reason beyond ignorance of the state of nature that will prevail. Even if an executive is fairly sure he knows what state of nature will come to pass, he cannot know for sure what outlays and revenues will accompany his actions. *We simply do not know enough to forecast accurately the costs and revenues resulting from any complex business action.* Consequently, an executive's estimates of the cost and revenue implications of any course of action under a specified state of nature must take the form of a frequency distribution. That distribution would identify several outcomes as well as the probability that each will occur. (See Table 3-4.) Refer back to the decision matrix in Table 3-3 and take any of its cells—say, X, which represents the outcome of action 2 (A_2) and state of nature 1 (N_1). Underlying the single outcome that we find in that cell might be a frequency distribution similar to the one described in Table 3-4.) Several defensible techniques might be employed to translate such a frequency distribution into a single figure: a

Table 3-4

FREQUENCY DISTRIBUTION

Outcome (profit)	Probability	Expected value
$100,000	.2	$20,000
75,000	.5	37,500
60,000	.2	12,000
50,000	.1	5,000
		$74,500

weighted average (termed "expected value"), the most likely outcome, the median, and the midpoint.

The steps involved in computing the contents of each cell in a decision matrix deserve some clarification. Recognize that each action carried out under some assumed state of nature will give rise to a stream of costs and benefits over time, as was explained. To take account of the value to the decision maker of present funds over future funds, this stream is translated into "present value" (discussed later in this chapter). Inasmuch as the decision maker does not understand fully the effects of his actions under any assumed state of nature, his forecast must recognize several possible different streams of costs and benefits. That is why one would expect the content of each cell to take the form of a probability distribution. Once this distribution is established, it too can be compressed into a single figure— for example, by substituting for the distribution its weighted average. Thus far, we have explained how the contents of *each cell* in the decision matrix might be computed. Now, let us see how a single value could be computed for *each action*, for A_2 in Table 3-3, for example.

Let us assume that the correct value for the cell marked X is $74,500, as computed in Table 3-4. We can now assume figures computed in the manner described for the other three cells along the line marked A_2. These would be the best estimate of the outcome of that particular action under different states of nature. Table 3-5 presents hypothetical results for the action A_2.

Another simple step is required to compress the figures presented in Table 3-5 into a single estimated worth of action A_2. It consists of weighting each of the cells by the probability that each corresponding state of nature will occur. Accordingly, the figure of $74,500 is multiplied by .4; the figure of $98,000 in column N_4 is multiplied by only .1, because it is only one-fourth as likely to occur as N_1. By weighting the other expected values by .3 and .2, respectively, one arrives at an estimated worth of action A_2 of $76,200. The decision maker presumably would compare this

Table 3-5

ESTIMATED WORTH OF BUSINESS ACTION A_2

	State of nature				Estimated worth of action
	N_1	N_2	N_3	N_4	
Probability of state of nature	.4	.3	.2	.1	
Expected value	$74,500	$82,000	$60,000	$98,000	$76,200

number with estimated worths for actions A_1 and A_3, and select the strategy with the highest estimated worth.

The process by which the executive should estimate the outcome of each action before making his decision is complex. However, the greatest difficulties have not yet been considered. Much of the inescapable difficulty results from the fact that the future is uncertain and business decisions relate to the future. Any more simple view of decisions is assuredly erroneous.

CONSTRAINTS ON THE DECISION MAKER

An executive cannot choose freely among all theoretically possible alternatives. The most attractive may be unfeasible because of barriers which are either unique to the firm or quite general—such as legal barriers. Among the more important of the *unique* limitations are the following:

- A lack of financial resources to carry out the proposed program on the desired scale.
- A lack of skilled personnel required for efficient execution of the proposed program.
- An incompatibility of the proposed strategy with company policy.
- A risk of creating organizational strife because of internal power alignments.
- Greater risk of loss than owners-management are prepared to tolerate because it endangers their "control."

These constraints are self-evident. Firms have limited resources and capabilities, and the goals of influential managers dictate what will be considered acceptable. A decision maker must be sensitive to these limitations and not waste his time or resources in exploring wholly unfeasible alternatives that might be extremely attractive for some other firm. On the other hand, limitations and constraints rarely are completely fixed and immovable. Added resources can be acquired and the possession of an attractive alternative itself may afford access to both liquid funds and even managerial talent. Also, attitudes of management and owners can be altered with tact and talent. Sometimes it is possible to change attitudes by demonstrating what they cost. Nevertheless, an executive must count the cost of efforts to bring about such changes and should be realistic about the probability of achieving success. In any event, his assessment of each course of action open to him must take explicit account of the many constraints on a free selection.

IMPORTANCE OF THE DECISION—THE DANGER OF "RUIN"

Another dimension of business actions might be termed the "threat to survival." Some decisions involve trivial choices: neither the firm nor the decision maker's position would be affected significantly by the results of the choice made. At the opposite extreme, an adverse outcome of the decision could threaten the very survival of the enterprise or the tenure of the executive—or both. Such vital decisions need not be particularly complicated—the difficulty of decisions is not highly correlated with their importance. However, they will understandably receive far more attention than routine and trivial decisions. Typically, such vital decisions pose severe tests to emotional stability, for their importance is likely to be unnerving to the decision maker and increase the likelihood of error. Moreover, the importance of a decision is not always measured by the amount of money directly involved. Some decisions are just more visible than others, partly because they may have generated controversy. Some gain their importance because they affect intangibles which are valued highly, even though they do not directly or indirectly correspond to large sums of money.

DETERMINANTS OF OUTLAY AND INCOME STREAMS

As indicated, business actions give rise to a stream of benefits and sacrifices. The shape of these streams reveals the scale, duration, average level of receipts and outlays, and evenness of the receipts and outlays associated with that action. What factors, in general, affect the outlay and income streams associated with business actions?

Factors determining the shape of outlay streams. The scale of an action—whether it involves very large sums or minor amounts—obviously influences the contours of its outlay stream. Not all scales of operation are equally efficient—the building of a new plant, the size of an advertising campaign, or the number of executives to be given special management training will have different levels of efficiency. The forces that economists describe as "returns to scale" favor the selection of particular scales of expenditure for any given action. Returns to scale reflect the specific technology involved; sometimes the scales of expenditure are very large.

The time pattern of outlays resulting from business decisions often reflects forces of inertia. Some business actions simply maintain former levels of activity, for example, continue advertising at the same level. Other business actions penetrate a new and higher level of effort. For example, a firm may train its salesmen in new skills; to do so requires, initially, overcoming their disinclination to engage in studies and fear of failure in a new challenge. These factors can only be overcome at cost. Once inertial forces like these have been overcome, progress can be made at relatively low cost. It is far less costly to maintain skills at a level already attained than to develop them.

Technology largely dictates the timing and magnitude of outlays. Certain costs are involved, for example, in the preparation (including market research) of an extensive advertising campaign, with payments to talent and media; these reflect the forces of technology as well as payment practices in the business affected. Similarly, the payments associated with the purchase of a machine are largely dictated by forces beyond the control of the decision maker, who, in taking a specific action, would take into account technological factors as well as banking and industrial practices.

The level and shape of the outlay stream are also affected by the fluctuations in prices that must be paid. For example, expected changes in wage rates, the cost of power, taxes on real estate, and similar items can significantly affect outlays during periods of inflation.

Factors determining the shape of income streams. A business's income is ultimately derived from the firm's customers; their responses to its efforts to win patronage and the responses of its rivals largely determine what income the firm will receive. Five factors strongly affect the shape of income streams that accompany business actions:

- The threshold. To achieve any benefit from an action, it is necessary to make efforts on a scale sufficiently large and prolonged so that it is perceived by the audience to which it is directed. Lesser efforts will have virtually no effect.
- Diffusion. The influence of many efforts to inform and persuade customers has a cumulative effect, for as more people are reached, each person affected becomes a source of information for others.
- Reinforcement. One influence may be powerful simply because, and only when, it builds upon and thus reinforces another that accompanies or preceded it. An advertisement may greatly strengthen the influence of a salesman selling a product; alone, neither the advertisement nor the salesman might have much effect.
- Decay. The tendency of any effort to wear off with the passage of time unless it is replaced or maintained is known as decay.
- The responses of rivals. Firms often can frustrate the actions of their rivals, though usually at some cost to themselves.

A COMPARISON OF INCOME AND OUTLAY STREAMS

Many business decisions involve fairly similar streams of income and outlay. Their attractiveness cannot be judged without careful calculation, especially if the outlays and incomes are obtained at different times. Difficulties in comparing income and outlay streams result mainly from the fact that they reflect payments at different points in time.

The value of income to anyone depends partly upon when it is received. For example, $100 received ten years from now is not equal in value to $100 received right now. If one had the $100 now, he could invest it; in ten years, he would possess substantially more than $100. Or, more to the point, if a firm received $100 now it could reinvest it in the business and possibly earn a very high rate of return; if it received $100 ten years from now it could not now make use of the funds. Hence, this vital conclusion that one must take account of the timing of cash inflows and outflows to determine their worth.

Let us consider an example. Assume that a particular project would involve four cash outlays and four cash inflows as described in Table 3-6, columns 1, 2, and 3. The total of cash outlays is substantially less than the cash inflows, but they occur at different times. Our task is to place a value on the outflows and inflows to determine the worth of that project to the firm. We would then compare that project's worth with that of other projects under consideration. To reach that end, we will translate each cash outflow and cash inflow into its "present value." Specifically, we will ask ourselves how much it would be worth today to receive the various cash inflows and how much it is worth to us to pay out the cash at different times in the future. (If we need not expend $100 until ten years from now, we can use those funds for ten years in our business or invest them on the outside to produce income. Consequently, an outlay of $100 ten years from now costs us less than $100 now.) The first time one meets this idea,

Table 3-6
A Hypothetical Set of Cash Inflows and Outflows*

Time period (1)	Outlay (2)	Income (3)	Net income (4)	Discount factor† (5)	Present value (6)
1/1/77–12/31/77	$1,000,000	0	−$1,000,000	1.0	−$1,000,000
1/1/78–12/31/78	300,000	400,000	100,000	.870	87,000
1/1/79–12/31/79	200,000	600,000	400,000	.756	302,400
1/1/80–12/31/80	100,000	800,000	700,000	.658	460,600
1/1/81–12/31/81	0	200,000	200,000	.572	114,400
Totals	$1,600,000	$2,000,000	$ 400,000		−$37,600

* Inflows and outflows were treated as if they occurred on the first day of this year.
† A discount rate of 15 percent is assumed.

it seems both strange and even objectionable. However, it is one of the most important and useful ideas applicable to financial decisions.

Tables are available which express future receipts of income in present value equivalents. To use such tables, the decision maker must select the appropriate discount rate—that is, the value of money to him (or "the cost of capital") and must know the time at which the cash inflow or outflow is expected. For example, he might try to determine the worth of $1.00 received ten years from now if he assumes a discount rate of 15 percent. Table 3-7 shows the appropriate discount factors. The answer given by the table is .247, meaning that, on the assumptions made, $1.00 to be received in ten years is worth less than 25 cents now, and $100 to be received in ten years is worth $24.70 now.

One can process all outlays and income flows from a project by this technique to arrive at a single figure. (We shall refer to this procedure as "translating all cash flows into their present values.") That figure would describe the difference between the present value of cash inflows and out-flows after they had been translated into a comparable form. The appro-priate calculations for the data presented in Table 3-6 are shown in col-umns 4, 5, and 6 of the same table.

The worth of a set of cash outflows that occur over substantial time periods depends strongly upon the discount rate by which it is adjusted. The appropriate rate to use in specific situations raises vexing questions, which will not be discussed here. It is important to recognize, however, that a shift in rate may alter the ranking of alternatives quite markedly.

Observe that the total of cash outflows in the example described by Table 3-6 was $1.6 million and the total of inflows was $2 million. After these figures were adjusted for the time at which the inflows and outflows took place (that is, expressed in current values) the worth of the project proved to be negative. That is, it would not earn a 15 percent "cost of capital." In our example, management judged the value of capital to be 15 percent—that is, it could earn that rate of return or more from other projects.

TANGIBLE AND INTANGIBLE SACRIFICES AND BENEFITS

Broadly speaking, the sacrifices that a firm makes are the reciprocal of its objectives. For example, a firm that seeks security makes sacrifices when it assumes risks; if its owners seek an easy life they incur sacrifices when they suffer tension or when heavy demands are made on their time. A firm makes mainly financial sacrifices and does so when it gives up its assets—whether by giving up cash or by suffering a reduction in the value of other assets like inventories, plant and equipment, accounts receivable, and the

Table 3-7

PRESENT WORTH OF $1

Year	1%	2%	3%	4%	5%	6%	7%	8%	9%	10%
1	0.9901	0.9804	0.9709	0.9615	0.9524	0.9434	0.9346	0.9259	0.9174	0.9091
2	0.9803	0.9612	0.9426	0.9246	0.9070	0.8900	0.8734	0.8573	0.8417	0.8264
3	0.9706	0.9423	0.9151	0.8890	0.8638	0.8396	0.8163	0.7938	0.7722	0.7513
4	0.9610	0.9238	0.8885	0.8548	0.8227	0.7921	0.7629	0.7350	0.7084	0.6830
5	0.9515	0.9057	0.8626	0.8219	0.7835	0.7473	0.7130	0.6806	0.6499	0.6209
6	0.9420	0.8880	0.8375	0.7903	0.7462	0.7050	0.6663	0.6302	0.5963	0.5645
7	0.9327	0.8706	0.8131	0.7599	0.7107	0.6651	0.6227	0.5835	0.5470	0.5132
8	0.9235	0.8535	0.7894	0.7307	0.6768	0.6274	0.5820	0.5403	0.5019	0.4665
9	0.9143	0.8368	0.7664	0.7026	0.6446	0.5919	0.5439	0.5002	0.4604	0.4241
10	0.9053	0.8203	0.7441	0.6756	0.6139	0.5584	0.5083	0.4632	0.4224	0.3855
11	0.8963	0.8043	0.7224	0.6496	0.5847	0.5268	0.4751	0.4289	0.3875	0.3505
12	0.8874	0.7885	0.7014	0.6246	0.5568	0.4970	0.4440	0.3971	0.3555	0.3186
13	0.8787	0.7730	0.6810	0.6006	0.5303	0.4688	0.4150	0.3677	0.3262	0.2987
14	0.8700	0.7579	0.6611	0.5775	0.5051	0.4423	0.3878	0.3405	0.2992	0.2633
15	0.8613	0.7430	0.6419	0.5553	0.4810	0.4173	0.3624	0.3152	0.2745	0.2394
16	0.8528	0.7284	0.6232	0.5339	0.4581	0.3936	0.3387	0.2919	0.2519	0.2176
17	0.8444	0.7142	0.6050	0.5134	0.4363	0.3714	0.3166	0.2703	0.2311	0.1978
18	0.8360	0.7002	0.5874	0.4936	0.4155	0.3503	0.2959	0.2502	0.2120	0.1799
19	0.8277	0.6864	0.5703	0.4746	0.3957	0.3305	0.2765	0.2317	0.1945	0.1635
20	0.8195	0.6730	0.5537	0.4564	0.3769	0.3118	0.2584	0.2145	0.1784	0.1486
21	0.8114	0.6598	0.5375	0.4388	0.3589	0.2942	0.2415	0.1987	0.1637	0.1351
22	0.8034	0.6468	0.5219	0.4220	0.3418	0.2775	0.2257	0.1839	0.1502	0.1228
23	0.7954	0.6342	0.5067	0.4057	0.3256	0.2618	0.2109	0.1703	0.1378	0.1117
24	0.7876	0.6217	0.4919	0.3901	0.3101	0.2470	0.1971	0.1577	0.1264	0.1015
25	0.7798	0.6095	0.4776	0.3751	0.2953	0.2330	0.1842	0.1460	0.1160	0.0923
26	0.7720	0.5976	0.4637	0.3607	0.2812	0.2198	0.1722	0.1352	0.1064	0.0839
27	0.7644	0.5859	0.4502	0.3468	0.2678	0.2074	0.1609	0.1252	0.0976	0.0763
28	0.7568	0.5744	0.4371	0.3335	0.2552	0.1956	0.1504	0.1159	0.0895	0.0693
29	0.7493	0.5631	0.4243	0.3207	0.2429	0.1846	0.1406	0.1073	0.0822	0.0630
30	0.7419	0.5521	0.4120	0.3083	0.2314	0.1741	0.1314	0.0994	0.0754	0.0573

Table 3-7 (continued)

Year	11%	12%	13%	14%	15%	16%	17%	18%	19%	20%
1	0.9009	0.8929	0.8850	0.8772	0.8696	0.8621	0.8547	0.8475	0.8403	0.8333
2	0.8116	0.7972	0.7831	0.7695	0.7561	0.7432	0.7305	0.7182	0.7062	0.6944
3	0.7312	0.7118	0.6913	0.6750	0.6575	0.6407	0.6244	0.6086	0.5934	0.5787
4	0.6587	0.6355	0.6133	0.5921	0.5718	0.5523	0.5337	0.5158	0.4987	0.4823
5	0.5935	0.5674	0.5428	0.5194	0.4972	0.4761	0.4561	0.4371	0.4190	0.4019
6	0.5346	0.5066	0.4803	0.4556	0.4323	0.4104	0.3898	0.3704	0.3521	0.3349
7	0.4817	0.4523	0.4251	0.3996	0.3759	0.3538	0.3332	0.3139	0.2959	0.2791
8	0.4339	0.4039	0.3762	0.3506	0.3269	0.3050	0.2848	0.2660	0.2487	0.2326
9	0.3909	0.3606	0.3329	0.3075	0.2843	0.2630	0.2434	0.2255	0.2090	0.1938
10	0.3522	0.3220	0.2946	0.2697	0.2472	0.2267	0.2080	0.1911	0.1756	0.1615
11	0.3173	0.2875	0.2607	0.2366	0.2149	0.1954	0.1778	0.1619	0.1476	0.1346
12	0.2858	0.2567	0.2307	0.2076	0.1869	0.1685	0.1520	0.1372	0.1240	0.1122
13	0.2575	0.2292	0.2042	0.1821	0.1625	0.1452	0.1299	0.1163	0.1042	0.0935
14	0.2320	0.2046	0.1807	0.1597	0.1413	0.1252	0.1110	0.0985	0.0876	0.0779
15	0.2090	0.1827	0.1599	0.1401	0.1229	0.1079	0.0949	0.0835	0.0736	0.0649
16	0.1883	0.1631	0.1415	0.1229	0.1069	0.0930	0.0811	0.0708	0.0618	0.0541
17	0.1696	0.1456	0.1252	0.1078	0.0929	0.0802	0.0693	0.0600	0.0520	0.0451
18	0.1528	0.1300	0.1108	0.0946	0.0808	0.0691	0.0592	0.0508	0.0437	0.0376
19	0.1377	0.1161	0.0981	0.0829	0.0703	0.0596	0.0506	0.0431	0.0367	0.0313
20	0.1240	0.1037	0.0868	0.0728	0.0611	0.0514	0.0433	0.0365	0.0308	0.0261
21	0.1117	0.0926	0.0768	0.0638	0.0531	0.0443	0.0370	0.0309	0.0259	0.0217
22	0.1007	0.0826	0.0680	0.0560	0.0462	0.0382	0.0316	0.0262	0.0218	0.0181
23	0.0907	0.0738	0.0601	0.0491	0.0402	0.0329	0.0270	0.0222	0.0183	0.0151
24	0.0817	0.0659	0.0532	0.0431	0.0349	0.0284	0.0231	0.0188	0.0154	0.0126
25	0.0736	0.0588	0.0471	0.0378	0.0304	0.0245	0.0197	0.0160	0.0129	0.0105
26	0.0663	0.0525	0.0417	0.0331	0.0264	0.0211	0.0169	0.0135	0.0109	0.0087
27	0.0597	0.0469	0.0369	0.0291	0.0230	0.0182	0.0144	0.0115	0.0091	0.0073
28	0.0538	0.0419	0.0326	0.0255	0.0200	0.0157	0.0123	0.0097	0.0077	0.0061
29	0.0485	0.0374	0.0289	0.0224	0.0174	0.0135	0.0105	0.0082	0.0064	0.0051
30	0.0437	0.0334	0.0256	0.0196	0.0151	0.0116	0.0090	0.0070	0.0054	0.0042

Table 3-7 (continued)

Year	21%	22%	23%	24%	25%	26%	27%	28%	29%	30%
1	0.8264	0.8197	0.8130	0.8065	0.8000	0.7937	0.7874	0.7813	0.7752	0.7692
2	0.6830	0.6719	0.6610	0.6504	0.6400	0.6299	0.6200	0.6104	0.6009	0.5917
3	0.5645	0.5507	0.5374	0.5245	0.5120	0.4999	0.4882	0.4768	0.4658	0.4552
4	0.4665	0.4514	0.4369	0.4230	0.4096	0.3968	0.3844	0.3725	0.3611	0.3501
5	0.3855	0.3700	0.3552	0.3411	0.3277	0.3149	0.3027	0.2910	0.2799	0.2693
6	0.3186	0.3033	0.2888	0.2751	0.2621	0.2499	0.2383	0.2274	0.2170	0.2072
7	0.2633	0.2486	0.2348	0.2218	0.2097	0.1983	0.1877	0.1776	0.1682	0.1594
8	0.2176	0.2038	0.1909	0.1789	0.1678	0.1574	0.1478	0.1388	0.1304	0.1226
9	0.1799	0.1670	0.1552	0.1443	0.1342	0.1249	0.1164	0.1084	0.1011	0.0943
10	0.1486	0.1369	0.1262	0.1164	0.1074	0.0992	0.0916	0.0847	0.0784	0.0725
11	0.1228	0.1122	0.1026	0.0938	0.0859	0.0787	0.0721	0.0662	0.0607	0.0558
12	0.1015	0.0920	0.0834	0.0757	0.0687	0.0625	0.0568	0.0517	0.0471	0.0429
13	0.0839	0.0754	0.0678	0.0610	0.0550	0.0496	0.0447	0.0404	0.0365	0.0330
14	0.0693	0.0618	0.0551	0.0492	0.0440	0.0393	0.0352	0.0316	0.0283	0.0253
15	0.0573	0.0507	0.0448	0.0397	0.0352	0.0312	0.0277	0.0247	0.0219	0.0195
16	0.0474	0.0415	0.0364	0.0320	0.0281	0.0248	0.0218	0.0193	0.0170	0.0150
17	0.0391	0.0340	0.0296	0.0258	0.0225	0.0197	0.0172	0.0150	0.0132	0.0116
18	0.0323	0.0279	0.0241	0.0208	0.0180	0.0156	0.0135	0.0118	0.0102	0.0089
19	0.0267	0.0229	0.0196	0.0168	0.0144	0.0124	0.0107	0.0092	0.0079	0.0068
20	0.0221	0.0187	0.0159	0.0135	0.0115	0.0098	0.0084	0.0072	0.0061	0.0053
21	0.0183	0.0154	0.0129	0.0109	0.0092	0.0078	0.0066	0.0056	0.0048	0.0040
22	0.0151	0.0126	0.0105	0.0088	0.0074	0.0062	0.0052	0.0044	0.0037	0.0031
23	0.0125	0.0103	0.0086	0.0071	0.0059	0.0049	0.0041	0.0034	0.0029	0.0024
24	0.0103	0.0085	0.0070	0.0057	0.0047	0.0039	0.0032	0.0027	0.0022	0.0018
25	0.0085	0.0069	0.0057	0.0046	0.0038	0.0031	0.0025	0.0021	0.0017	0.0014
26	0.0070	0.0057	0.0046	0.0037	0.0030	0.0025	0.0020	0.0016	0.0013	0.0011
27	0.0058	0.0047	0.0037	0.0030	0.0024	0.0019	0.0016	0.0013	0.0010	0.0008
28	0.0048	0.0038	0.0030	0.0024	0.0019	0.0015	0.0012	0.0010	0.0008	0.0006
29	0.0040	0.0031	0.0025	0.0020	0.0015	0.0012	0.0010	0.0008	0.0006	0.0005
30	0.0033	0.0026	0.0020	0.0016	0.0012	0.0010	0.0008	0.0006	0.0005	0.0004

like. These represent sacrifices because owners of a business seek profits, which are made possible by increases in a firm's assets.

Intangible costs represent another class of sacrifices by firms or business executives. Intangible costs (and intangible benefits also) are of two types: one class ultimately assumes a monetary form; the other forever remains intangible. An example of the first type is the loss of consumer or retailer goodwill as a result of an action taken. This action would not immediately and directly reduce sales and income, but in the first instance would alienate some consumers and retailers. In time, however, the alienated consumers and retailers would buy less—and thus tangibly affect the firm.

Some intangibles represent business ends in themselves; that is, they are what we will term "ultimate objectives." These intangibles will not assume a tangible form; they will not affect the firm's financial costs or revenues. Still, they are the firm's objectives, and any gain or reduction in them is to be considered in making a decision. Examples for some business owners are power, prestige, and social contribution. Accordingly, any business action that would enhance the owner's power, for example, should be credited with a benefit of equivalent value—even though this power would not add a cent of revenue over the firm's life.

It is difficult, even frustrating, to assign quantitative magnitudes to intangibles, even if we understand why we are valuing them. Nevertheless, some general rules are available that will guide decision makers in valuing intangibles. First, it is necessary to express both the inflow and outflow streams in comparable terms; a mere listing of cost items and benefit items will not lead one to a valid decision. Second, intangibles represent major factors in many business decisions and therefore cannot be ignored. One must attempt to value them; by ignoring them one places a zero value on them, and that is manifestly wrong.

Below is a selected list of important intangible sacrifices and benefits that arise in business decisions:

- Improved brand image—or damage to brand image.
- Better labor morale—or worse labor morale.
- Improved relations with middlemen—or deteriorated relations with middlemen.
- Greater *esprit de corps* among executives—or damaged *esprit*.
- Better relations with regulatory authorities—or damaged relations.
- Improved managerial skills—or lessened skills.
- Increased shelf or other display space in resellers' stores—or reduced space.

- Wider knowledge of the brand's special product features—or less knowledge.

It should be clear that such consequences of business actions must not be ignored, because they affect the extent to which a firm will achieve its objectives. And in valuing intangibles, decision makers should relate them to the ultimate effect they will have upon the success of the firm—rather than value them by some absolute standard.

Almost all intangibles are intermediate or instrumental goals or costs, rather than ends in themselves. An illustration of this proposition may be illuminating:

A firm is contemplating an advertising campaign designed to raise the esteem with which the firm's management is regarded by potential customers. Tests show that this advertising campaign has this desired effect. A majority of the firm's top executives support the campaign arguing that it will be advantageous for the company to have its management skills admired by prospective customers. (They surely get satisfaction from having their skills extolled in public media.) The value of such an advertising campaign depends on the effects of a higher regard for a firm's managerial skills on the sales of its products. Actually, a high regard for the management of a supplier could make some potential customers fearful of being outwitted with the result that some prospective customers would avoid dealing with the firm. Thus, the advertising program might run counter to the attainment of the firm's goals. Even though it would appear that "it would be nice" to have people admire the way the firm is managed, what appears a valuable intangible benefit would, in such a situation, represent a tangible cost. Of course, management could consider the pleasure of being highly regarded a valuable ultimate goal—but the owners of the firm probably would not want to pay to bring it about.

Executives generally adopt one of the following extreme positions toward intangibles: (1) they ignore them altogether; (2) they assume that intangible costs and benefits are exactly off-setting—cancel each other out; (3) they treat them as the dominant considerations and ignore the tangibles. The only logically defensible policy is to identify potential intangible consequences of contemplated actions, explore their nature and size in the specific situation to determine whether they affect the attainment of the firm's goals, and value them in money terms solely according to their expected effects on the firm's goals. In making such calculations, the decision maker must recognize that the intermediate effect—the intangible result—may occur but yet not affect the firm's success.

Unfortunately, we know relatively little about the connection between many apparently desirable intangible results and a firm's goal achievement. Many conditions that superficially appear beneficial actually have little or no effect upon the goals that a firm's management pursues.

Although no rigid rules can be set down for the valuation of intangible benefits or sacrifices, two lines of approach suggest what is ordinarily involved. Assume that some action is under consideration that would worsen employee morale for some time; how should this effect be assigned a numerical value? The first approach would be to estimate the cost to the firm in the form of increased labor turnover, higher absenteeism, and high production and administrative costs arising from a decline in effort expended by employees. (Higher employee morale could have a similar effect; contented workers sometimes are inefficient workers.) So, the value assigned would be the sum total of expected adverse monetary effects. The second approach would be to estimate the cost that the firm would be forced to incur to restore employee morale to the level from which it had fallen. A decision maker would explore both of these approaches and use that value which was lower, for he presumably would decide whether to accept the decline in morale or to correct it, according to which course was least costly.

Summary and Conclusions

A business decision involves a choice among alternative courses of action. To make such a choice, the decision maker must evaluate each alternative and determine what it will contribute toward the achievement of the firm's objectives. To make such an evaluation, he must estimate, at least mentally, the stream of benefits and sacrifices that each action would entail. His task will be greatly complicated by the uncertainty that surrounds most business decisions. This uncertainty results partly from a lack of knowledge of the pertinent outside conditions that will prevail when the action is taken and will influence its outcome; it results even more from one's limited knowledge of the consequences of one's actions.

Another difficulty in estimating the stream of benefits and sacrifices associated with each action results from the fact that they occur at different times. Since money in the present is more valuable than money in the future—because it can be put to work to earn more money—each important outlay or receipt must be converted into its "present value."

Even after an executive has computed the present value of each alternative action, he faces added difficulties. He must take into account the constraints upon his decision. Many of these appear trivial and usually are vexing, for they are results of lack of objectivity or personal vanity or ambitions of other members of the firm. A decision maker can only hope to estimate the cost to the firm of failure to adopt the best alternative and hope that he can deter unwarranted opposition in this way. Of course, some constraints cannot be overcome. What is theoretically the best decision may be a foolish choice if the firm lacks the resources to carry it out efficiently.

A major difficulty in evaluating many business actions arises from the need to assign quantitative values to their many intangible costs and benefit consequences. Clearly, intangibles deserve consideration in any decision, and every effort should be made to assign realistic values to them; however, a reliable basis for computing those values is not usually available.

Chapter 4

MODELS

OUR DECISIONS cannot work out well unless we understand the phenomena involved in our choices. That is why we turn to others when faced with decisions requiring technical knowledge that we lack. Understanding a phenomenon consists of knowing the elements it is composed of, what each element does, and how the parts fit together. It is what we mean when we say that we know how a clock, a faucet, a lock, an individual's circulatory system, or a camera works.

Clearly, "knowing" varies widely in degree. If we mistakenly believe that we know or understand something fully, we are at one extreme of knowing—a position that is most likely to cause error. At the opposite extreme is full understanding of a phenomenon—an uncommon condition that contributes mightily to good decisions. We take this second extreme to mean the possession of a valid "model" of the phenomenon. But what is a model?

Model Defined

A model is a simplified replication of reality that identifies its main components and indicates how they are interrelated. The following are the key elements of a model:

- It is a simplified version of a more complex reality; the degree of simplification varies according to the use for which it is intended.
- Its purpose is to illuminate a real-life phenomenon; some simplification is required for ease and clarity of understanding.

- Although simplified, the view of reality presented by a model does include its main elements and their interrelationships; simplification occurs by omitting nonessentials.
- The model depicts reality for a particular purpose and a particular audience; the best model for one individual or one purpose might be quite different from what another person would find most helpful, or that the same person would find illuminating in thinking about the same phenomenon for a different purpose.
- A model is an intellectual tool, a device that assists in the thought process. Its value therefore is to be assessed primarily by the validity of the conclusions or decisions to which it leads.
- A model can be expressed in a wide variety of media.

The Inescapability of Models

Everyone who thinks uses models. (Blindly following memorized rules is not considered thinking one's way through a decision.) One cannot reach conclusions by facts alone, even though we all know people who take the position that "the facts in the case dictate the solution to a problem." They are distrustful of theories and typically begin their analysis of any problem by "gathering all available facts." One reason that many people place a high value on facts is the history of scientific discovery, which can be viewed as a cemetery full of defunct theories. Some trace the demise of most theories to the collection of facts that disproved the prevailing theories and suggested new ones. Theories, then, are seen as "soft" and facts as "hard." Fine. But how do we know which facts are relevant to an issue unless we have some theory about it? Most data are ambiguous and rarely have meaning unless illuminated by a theory. Executives often possess enormous bodies of data about such things as costs, sales, and labor productivity, and still may not understand the forces that determine fluctuations in costs and quality of output. Consequently, they make poor decisions about those issues, even though they possess voluminous information about them.

On the other hand, a theory may not suffice to solve real-life problems. Sometimes, a fact is the crucial element in a decision, as in the following example. A firm finds that its packaging material is becoming wet and losing strength, with the result that much of its output is damaged in transit to customers. In this situation certain theories are fairly obvious: the moisture must come from either inside the package or outside; also, other packaging materials may not be weakened by equal amounts of moisture. To these theoretical propositions the decision maker must add some facts. By factual analysis, it might be determined that the difficulty stems from the highly humid plant environment. However, this circumstance would be very costly to correct. A change in packaging material would overcome the difficulty without substantial cost.

Little wisdom is required to reach the conclusion described. On the other hand, if we wished to explain why and how the high humidity in the plant arose and how it weakened the structural strength of the packaging material, we might have considerable trouble. The facts in this hypothetical case were crucial only because we already possessed a satisfactory theory. As decision makers we need most what we don't yet possess. If we have a valid theory, we need data; if we have data and lack a theory, we mainly need a good theory. We actually require both.

Thus executives facing difficulties cannot run them down simply by gathering enough data. Facts alone will settle few issues. Instead, the solution of problems and the making of decisions inevitably require an understanding of the phenomenon that includes both facts and theory—a model.

Effects of Deficient Models

Models help us understand how things work. Most people need models in situations involving complex appliances. When a complex appliance ceases to operate and we open it up, most of us are totally baffled by what we see and cannot think usefully about correcting the difficulty. Lacking even slight understanding of the appliance, we cannot possibly make valid decisions about how to repair it.

A related example involves our first exposure to an unfamiliar phenomenon. In that situation, we look for a parallel in our experience. For example, when the average American observes a cricket match for the first time, he usually is bewildered. Most try to find similarities to baseball—the sport they know that involves bats and balls. Given the major differences between baseball and cricket, most Americans never do understand cricket. Thus a major obstacle to understanding results from having a misleading or inappropriate model.

Individuals sometimes are torn between two conflicting models, as in the following incident. I visited France in December 1962, when the French currency was shifting from the "old franc" to the "new franc." The old francs were worth only one percent as much as the new. For a while, both old and new francs circulated side by side. On arrival at the airport, I found myself with some crisp 5-franc notes (each worth $1 in U.S. currency) and with some dirty copper coins that said 20 francs. The coin apparently was worth four times as much as the note, to judge by the number of francs each represented. However, when I started to tip the porter who handled my baggage, I felt strongly that something was wrong. I could not bring myself to select a coin or note to give the porter; I felt almost in a panic and started to walk first in one direction and then in another. My view of a currency system is one in which crisp notes are much more valuable than dirty coins; my view of the number system is one in which 20 francs are four times as valuable as 5. This conflict between two models made me incapable of taking action. I ended up by holding out my money to the porter and asking him to take a fair tip.

Situations often arise in which several persons who are equally well informed express different views about the same subject—as usually happens in business. Imagine a conversation among four mothers who are discussing what they would do about a troublesome child in the playground "if the child were theirs." One favors a rigid regimen of discipline: "Just let him step out of line and I'd let him have it until he learned." Another prescribes more parental attention and love: "Just show him that he need not be naughty to get the attention of his mother, and he'll behave like any other five-year-old." A third takes the position that "just lay down the rules without emotion and administer punishments that are in line with the offense and as much as possible tied to the offense." The fourth simply states that "some children are born good and others are difficult to handle from birth." These four mothers had considerable experience with five-year-olds and were equally acquainted with the situation and child involved; yet all presented dissimilar views on how to handle a troublesome child. They prescribed very different remedies for precisely the same situation because they had different models of child behavior.

Although the proposition advanced is not spectacular, it is vital: *the conclusions that one reaches reflect the general views one holds of the subject under consideration rather than the facts one possesses.* If a businessman makes a decision about how, when, and where, to advertise, he is simply applying his theories about how advertising works to a specific fact situation. Accordingly, the validity of his decisions will depend upon the validity of his theories—that is, the validity and depth of his understanding.

The Difference Between Theories and Models

Technically, all theories are models; however, many models are not theories. The term "models" is applied very widely and often indiscriminately. Theories have a clearer and more circumscribed meaning, though they too take varied forms.

Typically, theories express a relationship between two or more variables under carefully defined circumstances. One fairly pure type of scientific theory takes the following form: "X is a particular function of Y, if one controls for temperature and humidity." Most scientific theories are much more complex than this, involving a large number of independent and controlled variables. In some cases it is possible to state a theory in precise quantitative terms. Such theories indicate just how much a single unit change in each of the independent variables will affect the dependent variable.

Other scientific theories are far less quantitative and represent speculations or hypotheses that are consistent with available evidence. The theory that the personality can usefully be divided into the "id," "ego," and "superego" and the theory that protons and neutrons and other subatomic particles have particular shapes and properties are illustrative of this class of scientific theory.

Both classes of scientific theory are descriptive of empirical realities; they may simplify reality by "controlling for" some complicating circumstances. Still, their purpose is to permit prediction as well as to contribute understanding to some phenomena. It need hardly be observed that scientific theories can be mistaken; often they are stated in loose and general form and simply reflect the meager understanding we possess of the phenomenon about which we are attempting to theorize. Theories emphatically need not take a mathematical form, although scientists understandably strive to develop that type of precise theory.

Models can illuminate relationships, but they do many other things as well. They mainly indicate how things fit together and explain how they function so that we know better how to cope with them or forecast their behavior.

Are Models or Theories Really Necessary?

Anyone who thinks is employing models or theories—or both; and those models largely dictate our decisions. However, many successful executives maintain that they hold no theories and are even critical, if not contemptuous of highly theoretical people. Although they see a sharp contrast between a hard-headed man of affairs and a theorist, their success in business depends primarily on validity of their theories and the skill with which those theories are applied.

Many business executives who hold valuable theories—judged by their ability to grasp what is happening and to cope with it—reach valid conclusions but cannot state their theories or explain their line of reasoning. Regrettably, many of the most successful people in business—and doubtless in many other fields as well—cannot communicate fully their understanding so that others might be enlightened by them. Sometimes they can be helped to articulate their theories. Mainly, we are forced to infer their theories from the decisions they make.

It is important that executives state explicitly the theories that underlie their judgments. In the process they will usually uncover flaws that otherwise would pass unnoticed. Although many already successful executives cannot offer explicit statements of their theories, their effectiveness probably would grow if they could communicate their theories to others. After all, one cannot place high confidence in a person's predictions, even one's own, unless he knows the basis on which they rest. In addition, an executive's ability to make use of what he understands presumably expands when he gives it a clear structure and exposes it to a conscious critical examination by himself and others. Certainly he cannot instruct his subordinates or associates and improve their understanding unless he can articulate his views.

We thus have reached some vital conclusions: facts alone will not settle issues; some theory or model of the phenomenon is needed to make sense of any facts and to identify the relevant facts. Executives—scientists of a kind in their particular line of business—rely upon the validity of their theories. Although their theories can take any of myriad forms, they should be explicit. Unless an individual knows just what his theories are, he cannot match them against the available evidence to test their validity. Moreover, by making them explicit, he can invite others to evaluate them—a process that usually helps to strengthen and clarify them.

Forms That Models Can Take

Generally, models can take any form that is illuminating to the user and helps him to reach valid conclusions. Individuals are so different in their thought habits, knowledge, and viewpoints that one would not expect everyone to regard any given phenomenon in the same way. We certainly cannot say much with confidence about the form of a person's models when they are "in his head." On the other hand, when we discuss phenomena with businessmen (or academic specialists in business) we can learn what form their models take when they are made explicit. We find that the forms are varied, almost unlimited.

The following discussion, describing the more important types of models that executives use, is highly selective and suggestive rather than definitive. It is argued that models need not be highly refined, structured, and mathematical. Anything that illuminates by simplifying and identifying key elements and their relationships is a legitimate model; to demand highly structured models and forgo the use of any other kind would be seriously misguided. To strive for and prefer structured mathematical models does not require that we ignore all others—a posture adopted by some business specialists.

THE MODIFIED ANALOGY

An important and valuable type of model is the modified analogy; very likely, most of our first models of any phenomenon take this form. Subsequently, we often replace analogies with other, more special-purpose models. Analogies are the most useful devices for illuminating and giving at least a crude structure to a new and mysterious phenomenon. Teachers constantly use analogies when more direct efforts to explain something unfamiliar fail.

In the field of business, one finds many useful analogies. For example, advertising has been likened to propaganda designed to alter attitudes and to education that is intended to transmit information. Efforts to improve labor morale may be considered similar to courtship in some respects; individual items in a firm's product line may be considered analogous—for pricing purposes—to members of an athletic team; the behavior of firms in many markets may be said to resemble the actions of "have" and "have not" nations in international politics.

The critical role of analogies in the learning process and in scientific discovery is only now becoming recognized.* We can understand what is new to us mainly by building upon what we already understand, that is, by applying what we do know to things that we don't understand. More specifically, we apparently come to understand something that is new to us by first likening it to some phenomenon that we understand quite well. We then seek out and specify the differences between the familiar, understood phenomenon and the new one. In that way we arrive at our model of the new. This process has been termed the "displacement of concepts."

CHECKLISTS: A PRIMITIVE TYPE OF MODEL

The checklist usually contains a catalog of factors to be considered in the course of making a decision. While it is intended to guide a decision maker's behavior by telling him what items to consider, it also conveys a crude picture of the phenomenon about which he is trying to make a decision. Especially for persons who know very little about it, a list of all the factors that influence a phenomenon that one is trying to understand

---

* See Donald Schon, *The Displacement of Concepts* (New York: Barnes & Noble, 1963) for a clear and insightful discussion of this process with extensive illustrations from man's intellectual history.

can be extremely illuminating. For example, a list of the main parts that make up an automobile or the human body would provide a helpful beginning toward understanding how they work. Rather than an exhaustive list of the component parts, a selective list, indicating the main components would be particularly illuminating at the start to persons who knew nothing.

Such a list would be even more helpful if it grouped items in some relevant fashion. For example, the components might be grouped according to similarity of function: the key systems in an automobile (ignition, electrical, combustion, steering, braking, and so on), or in the body (nervous, skeletal, circulatory, muscular, gastro-intestinal, respiratory, and so on), with the chief parts or organs involved in each. Even a crude checklist that grouped items according to their importance—the extent to which they influenced the phenomenon in which one was interested—would illuminate the unfamiliar far more than a random list.

Checklists are primitive, especially when they are exhaustive, and therefore they may bewilder rather than enlighten. Moreover, they do not indicate relationships among elements, though by simple grouping they can move somewhat in that direction. Most checklists are nevertheless far more illuminating than no model at all; sometimes our understanding of certain phenomena is so limited that all we know can be transmitted best in this form.

STRUCTURED MODELS: ORGANIZATION CHARTS, MATRIXES, FLOW DIAGRAMS

Relationships can usually be conveyed effectively by abstract visual structures. In the field of business, a limited number of structures are widely used to convey relationships. For example, the organization chart and related devices (like pyramids) convey the notion of level—indicating the superior and the subordinate, the general and the specific. Thus, these devices do not simply indicate what elements are involved but indicate where they fit into the picture; they position elements in a way that a simple list cannot.

Flow diagrams vary widely in their complexity, but usually contain the key features of an organization chart and also show sequence and priorities. Lines varying in thickness, texture, solidity, or color can be used to designate the nature of the role played by different parties or steps in a process; the addition of arrows and other elementary devices (dots, underlines, and the like) can contribute additional dimensions and illumination. Mainly, flow diagrams are used to provide models of processes like planning, production, scheduling, and communicating.

The matrix is one of the most simple, flexible, and powerful models for illuminating important phenomena. A matrix permits the arrangement of factors in space to show how their interaction affects a phenomenon. For example, to explain the nature of firms in a market, one might hypothesize that their behavior and influence is determined mainly by two factors: their age and their size. On that basis, one might develop a matrix which would permit one to identify different "types" of firms—ranging from the large old firm to the young small one—each believed to be different in their effect on, say, prices, product innovation, or expenditures on advertising. (See Table 4-1.) One could indicate in each cell of the matrix the behavior and influence expected of firms with the corresponding combination of characteristics.

Iconic, Analog, and Symbolic Models

Models replicate the real world by various devices, as has been stated. Iconic models—such as scale models, globes, or photographs—resemble the reality they are intended to replicate. They ordinarily are far smaller than that reality and permit the viewer to perceive it from a new and illuminating perspective.

Analog models, such as thermometers, and graphs of quantitative relationships, represent one real-life phenomenon by another. They are ordinarily more simple, clear, and easily manipulated than the reality. Consequently, they make it easy to describe relationships among variables and facilitate the analysis of those variables. They provide convenient tools for simulation, permit new approaches to problems, and may yield fresh perspectives.

Symbolic models are limited to those that employ mathematical or logical symbols—though iconic and analog models may be considered symbolic also. Symbolic models possess the particular virtue of being amenable to mathematical manipulation.

Table 4-1

A CLASSIFICATION OF FIRMS FOR PRICE ANALYSIS

Size of firm	*Old*	*Middle*	*Young*
		Age of firm	
Large	Price leader		
Medium			
Small			Aggressive, undisciplined

This review of models, admittedly incomplete, suggests the following conclusions:

- A model builder has a very large number of media in which to express his view of a real-world phenomenon.
- Some media are better suited to model building for particular phenomena than are others. They vary in their flexibility and in the number of different variables they can easily depict.
- The medium used to represent a phenomenon may truly become its message in some cases. Particular types of models incorporate a style and a particular way of viewing the underlying phenomenon. (For example, economic theory's reliance on geometric models could not but help lead economists to stress those variables that are amenable to geometric treatment and to de-emphasize those that are not.)
- As particular types and styles of models become widely used in any field of study, most people translate their own models into the commonly used medium. However, one is well advised to express his models in several different forms in the hope of achieving new freedom, power, and insight from the variety of viewpoints.
- Some individuals develop special skills in incorporating information about a complex phenomenon in an insightful and clear manner. One can anticipate the emergence of specialists in model building.
- Quite as important as clarity and insightfulness, the form of a model must be selected for its power—the ability to handle a large number of variables, amenability to processing by mathematical methods and the computer, and ability to incorporate dynamic elements.

We have advanced a theory about the function of theories in decision making. It asserts that the mind forms simplified views about the outside world—which we call models—and then bases forecasts and decisions upon them.

How Models Are Produced

When we explore how people form their models—whether consciously or unconsciously—we are asking how people achieve understanding. More specifically, through what process do we come to understand new and unfamiliar phenomena?

The mind must build on what it already understands. Accordingly, we can be fairly certain that *the first step in the process of acquiring understanding consists of transferring what we already know to what is new and unfamiliar.* Almost always, *this process involves analogies.*

With an analogy as a base, one can—perferably with help—*search for elements in the analogy that do not apply and the elements that should be added or modified* to increase the resemblance between the analogy and the new phenomenon. In this process, the learner comes to comprehend the new phenomenon more fully. He can interpret his experience with it better and apply his new understanding retroactively to questions that troubled him in the past.

Many decision makers who understand thoroughly the phenomenon at the heart of a problem cannot put that understanding in the form of a useful and explicit model. On the other hand, lacking understanding, one should not even try to build a model. Useful models cannot be built in ignorance. A model builder requires two essential elements: a thorough understanding of the phenomenon, and an ability to express relationships—that is, to simplify and to create a structure. Neither alone will produce useful models.

How Models Are Used in Decision Making

Decision making clearly is a mental process, although it can also be carried out by rote memory or by following rules. (For example: an executive might decide to threaten to take the franchise away from any distributor who falls behind quota three quarters in a row.) Decision making involves many high-level mental faculties, especially when an unfamiliar and complex difficulty is faced. Logic, memory, analysis, evaluation, imagination, association, intuition, and other mental processes may be involved. Accordingly, any careful discussion of decision making requires some view of how the brain functions in the process (even as a careful student of the piano should be familiar with the anatomy and function of the hand as well as the construction of the piano).

When people think—that is, try to figure something out, as opposed to remember—they apparently "work on" (process or think about) internal counterparts of the outside world. That is, they develop constructs— something in the mind that they believe represents what they wish to think about; they then work on that internal construct to reach conclusions that they will apply to the outside world.

We may say that the brain is simulating—working on a representation of reality, rather than on reality itself. This simulation process is involved in all high-level mental activity and occurs quite unconsciously. Although we assume that the mind is somehow working on or reasoning about the outside world itself, a little reflection suggests that the brain can only process things within itself.

For example, imagine a top-level executive who receives a report from several associates that one of his subordinates, a factory manager, was seen in a semi-intoxicated condition in the office on three separate occasions during the preceding two weeks—confirming a vague impression that the executive had formed in one brief meeting with him. The factory manager has had a brilliant record during his eight years with the firm and was being groomed for a top-level post. The executive's associates ask what action he plans to take.

In this situation the brain could perform in a variety of ways. First, it could return an immediate answer—perhaps to the effect that the factory manager should be called in straightaway and given a firm but friendly admonition to mend his ways, or that the matter should be taken under close observation. When the brain produces suggested remedies in this way without revealing its process of production, we call the mental process "intuition" or "judgment." But if the brain returns no answer automatically, the following process, described in terms of an analogy, is likely to take place. The brain will place on its workbench (so to speak) a representation of a man with the main characteristics that the supervisor believes the factory manager to possess—proud, reserved, emotional, reasonable, intelligent. It then conducts some experiments to explain why such a person would suddenly start drinking to excess and to explore such a person's reaction to measures that might be taken to stop his drinking.

Our executive would typically end up with one or more theories about the cause of his subordinate's drinking and about how best to deal with each one of them. In exploring possible remedies, he might mentally experiment with a heart-to-heart talk, a reprimand, a threat, fatherly advice, advice to visit a psychoanalyst, or conversations with the man's wife, to see how the man on the brain's workbench would respond to each of those strategies. Clearly he could not do all these things to the actual manager; he could only do them to his internal construct of the man.

The validity of the executive's conclusions from such experiments or simulations will depend heavily upon the accuracy of his internal construct of the outside man. Also, it will depend upon the ability of his brain to manipulate this internal construct, that is, to conduct valid simulations. Brains clearly vary widely in both the validity of their internal representations of the outside world and in their ability to process them in some meaningful way. If they are emotional, unobjective, illogical, both their internal representations of reality and their processing of them will be faulty and their conclusions will be erroneous.

This view of the brain's functioning represents a piece of mental equipment—a model—that might help the reader understand how his own brain functions. We are communicating with the reader's brain about his brain—an exceedingly difficult form of communication; most brains apparently treasure secrecy about their mode of operation.

Decision making is a mental process which reflects and depends on the working of the brain. The brain works by constructing an internal version of the outside world; it conducts experiments, makes detailed examinations of, and reasons about that internal version of the outside world. Its conclusions reflect that internal version rather than the actual outside world; the validity of its conclusions depends largely upon whether these internal representations accurately mirror the outside world. For example, if the *internal* factory manager responds favorably to a heart-to-heart talk but the *actual* factory manager does not, the brain has produced a mistaken decision.

Thus, the validity of our decisions depends upon our perception and understanding of reality. Good decisions require good models, and the caliber of our decisions reflects the quality and validity of our models.

A model is helpful if it indicates relationships not recognized before and eliminates elements and discards relationships that were mistaken. For a model to do these things, it must be valid—that is, reflect the reality reasonably well. It must incorporate the key elements and identify the main relationships operating, and it must be in a form that is readily intelligible to the user.

Assume that we are confronted with a complex problem about which we are not very well informed. We want to learn something about the problem, and we recognize our inability to cope with it. We have available in a book or a report something that purports to be a model of the phenomenon around which the problem revolves. The model is expressed in a medium that is readily intelligible; or, at least, it presents no major barriers that we must overcome. How would we use a model under those circumstances?

First, we would try to internalize the model, make it part of our intellectual property. We would try to visualize the interplay of the elements depicted in the model, to understand why the elements in the model were represented in a particular way. For example, why is one element considered prior in time to another? Why is the relationship between this and that proportional (linear)? Why are the elements independent of one another or interdependent? What important things have been omitted?

In this process of internalizing the model, we presumably see the phenomenon in a new light. And if the model is essentially valid, we should gain in power to cope with the problem at hand. Simply put, the model would enable us to understand much better the thing we are trying to control. Even more simply stated, models teach us things we didn't know about phenomena we need to understand. What makes them particularly valuable teaching tools is their simplicity, their clarity, their concreteness, their emphasis on the essential, their parsimony and relevance. A good model is the result of heavy investments of thought and understanding with great attention to effectiveness of expression.

Given the manner of their construction, one must not expect the full import of most models to be immediately obvious. They require study in the usual case, even though many do immediately illuminate a phenomenon considerably—especially for someone who was imprisoned by a mistaken model. In other words, the internalizing of a model—adopting it as one's own—is time-consuming and sometimes quite difficult. The difficulty is particularly great for those who are relatively inflexible; those who hold viewpoints or adopt approaches which they cannot relinquish.

The internalizing of a model usually requires that we try to apply it to concrete situations, most often an actual problem faced in the past. We can then simulate with the help of the model. For example, we can change the value of one key ingredient and see how the model would forecast its effects. In other words, we can use the model to isolate the features of a situation and explain how the situation would be altered by a change in one of its elements.

The more such applications we make of a model, the more elements we change in our simulation of a real event, the greater our familiarity with the model and our understanding of the phenomenon. Some phenomena are highly complex, and we cannot hope to understand them quickly and painlessly; no simple medium can convey the many variables and intricate relationships that exist among them. To understand those phenomena will necessarily require great time and effort; sometimes it will require the learning of particular notational systems, possibly a review of mathematics. But even then the model will frequently represent a very speedy and parsimonious way of acquiring or deepening our understanding of a baffling reality.

Some models can provide a structure in to which we can pour information to develop factual diagnoses and even remedies. For example, a mathematical model that accurately explains sales might be "solved" to determine what factor was "missing" and caused a low level of sales. The diagnosis would immediately point to the remedy in such a case. The number of such models is not great, especially for phenomena involving human behavior—including the behavior of rival firms, government regulators, voters, and similar groups. They do exist in substantial numbers in the physical sciences and in such fields as engineering, production, physical distribution, where our understanding of the forces operating is fairly great, partly because those forces are stable.

The use of a model involves a vital decision: whether it is truly applicable to the problem at hand—perhaps with modification. Even a very useful model represents only a base on which the decision maker can build, usually by adding variables to take account of special features in the situation. By providing the base on which to build a more complex but applicable replication of a problem, the model can make a major contribution to a better decision. Rarely, however, can a model give a decision maker a complete and valid picture of the real-life situations with which he tries to cope. Overwhelmingly, a model represents a structure which yields insight as it permits us to add elements and possibly delete and modify others to arrive at a reasonably valid picture of the situation under study.

The application of a model is a highly active process. The model user cannot simply act as a sponge, absorbing what is there. Rather, the model will usually demand special efforts to break out of a habitual way of thinking about a phenomenon. After a change in viewpoint and mastery of the model, the decision maker must invariably search out missing ingredients and make modifications that will transform the model into a workable and valid replication of a real situation.

Assessing the Value of Individual Models

Any model that adds to a decision maker's understanding is of value because it should contribute to better decisions. But a model which illuminates for one may not do so for another individual. Accordingly, the evaluation of models is highly subjective.

There are several questions to ask about the usefulness of any model:

- Can it be understood and applied without lengthy preparation and practice?
- Can the model incorporate many variables, if desired?
- Does the model permit the introduction of changes over time?
- Does the model permit easy incorporation of interdependencies among some of the variables?
- Does the model permit visualization as well as mental conception?

Once a model has been put to use, a decision maker can ask more personal questions, such as these: Has it permitted me to identify sources of difficulty and to forecast the results of outside events or my actions as well as the models I have been using up to now? If I were to continue to use this model, would it provide greater illumination than other models with which I am now more familiar? Does it get the job done? How does it compare with other tools that I might use?

If time and resources permit, an executive confronted by a vital problem usually would benefit from using several models and comparing their effectiveness. In applying different models, an executive can usually learn something from the very differences among them; a comparison of the variables they include and the relationships they posit will be illuminating in itself in most cases.

As a practical matter, individuals tend to evaluate models on the basis of the results the models can produce. Unfortunately, results will vary more with the individual's familiarity with the model and the amount he can add to it, rather than with the intrinsic power of the model itself. The reluctance to discard familiar models and master new ones can greatly impair an individual's decision-making powers.

Important Models for Business Decisions

Executive decisions deal with a wide spectrum of phenomena—from the psyches of employees and customers to methods of charging depreciation against assets. Consequently, the number and variety of models that might be applied to business problems is enormous. However, two models are of particular value to executives because of their wide generality—that is, they can be applied to a number of apparently dissimilar problems.

THE INVENTORY MODEL

Let us examine first the so-called inventory model. This was originally developed to determine how much of specific items a firm should hold in inventory—and thus to determine how much of them to order and when.

The problems associated with inventory levels vary with the particular item, but the issues relevant to inventory levels are mainly of two kinds: (1) the costs incurred by adding to (or reducing) inventory levels, and (2) the benefits gained by adding to (or reducing) inventory. After sorting out all the costs and benefits of changes in inventory levels, one can hope to estimate that point at which the net benefits are greatest. In other words, inventory levels represent a condition of opposing costs. The more a firm has in inventory of a particular item, the fewer sales it will lose and the fewer customers it will alienate; on the other hand, the larger its inventories, the greater its carrying costs, space costs, and deterioration in inventory value owing to spoilage, outmoding of style, and other factors. The problem of setting the optimum inventory level in specific units then becomes one of quantifying the benefits and the costs within an uncertain setting—that is, when the seller does not know how much will be sold and when it will be sold, and he cannot be certain of how long it will take to obtain delivery from suppliers.

The inventory model invites the decision maker to identify and quantify the added costs and benefits that result from adding to inventory. Figures 4-1 and 4-2 suggest the logic underlying the inventory model. Figure 4-1 sets down the more important added benefits and costs that result from adding a given number of units of a particular item to inventory. It shows that both costs and benefits are affected. They are not affected equally by an increase in inventory, so that at some point—that is, when holding given quantities of the item—further increases in inventory will add more to costs than to benefits.

Figure 4-2 represents much the same thing as Figure 4-1 but in a different format. It shows the effects of increasing the size of an inventory for an item. Line B shows the costs, which include the costs of carrying charges and of space, deterioration, and the like. Line A describes the benefits. By holding larger inventories the firm will experience fewer lost sales and lower levels of customer dissatisfaction, and will receive greater quantity discounts. What we see is that certain costs and benefits rise as the size of inventory increases while others decline. Line C measures the difference between the benefits and costs. The point at which the difference between benefits and costs is at a maximum is the optimum size of inventory.

The logic of an inventory model applies very well to decisions about optimum size of the labor force for a firm, cash balance requirements, and even the optimum investment in machines for a firm. In all cases, holding larger inventories of anything (merchandise, workers, cash, machines) increases certain costs; and with larger inventories, the executive is better able to meet future needs and contingencies—and reduce the costs resulting from unexpected needs and contingencies. These two sets of factors must be weighed and balanced against each other.

The foregoing is a gross oversimplication of inventory models, which are themselves simplifications of reality. This discussion tried to illuminate a nearly universal problem—balancing costs against benefits. There are costs and gains connected with almost everything. At some point, the gains relative to the costs are at a maximum. That is the point at which an executive will aim.

The Portfolio Model

Another very general model is the portfolio model. In its most common application, portfolio theory is used to select securities for addition to a portfolio. Typically, it is assumed that the goals of the portfolio managers

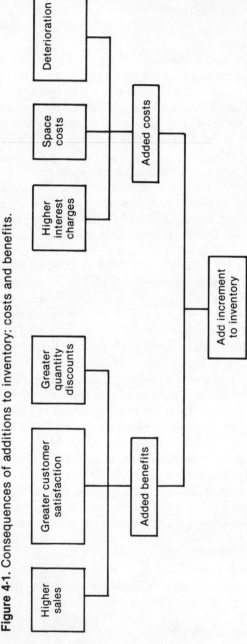

Figure 4-1. Consequences of additions to inventory: costs and benefits.

Figure 4-2. Net benefit from holding different inventory levels.

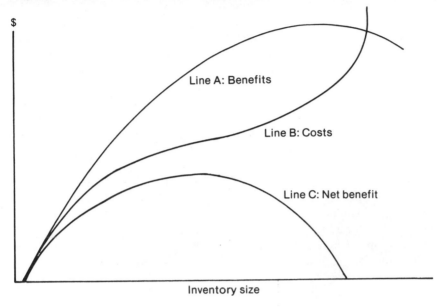

Inventory size

are to maximize return and minimize risk. When an asset is evaluated using the portfolio concept, not only are its independent risk-return characteristics examined but the question raised is: How will the addition of this asset affect the risk-return composition of the portfolio as a whole?

Assume there are two stocks being examined; each independently has the same return and risk characteristics. However, one stock goes up when the total or overall portfolio goes up and down when the portfolio declines, whereas the other moves in exactly the opposite direction. Viewed independently, both stocks are equally desirable; they have equal return and risk. On a portfolio basis, however, the *second* is *preferable*. It provides the same rate of return as the first stock and its counterbalancing variance will reduce the overall risk of the total portfolio, something the first stock will not do. Recognize that the addition of the stock reduces the decline in rate of return on the downside, but reduces the gain on the up-side.

Portfolio theory is not limited to the financial sphere. It has application in personnel, marketing, and a variety of other areas. Assume a manager has decided to hire another clerk. Of the two applicants, Mr. A is slightly less qualified than Mr. B. Should the executive therefore hire Mr. B? The answer should depend in part not only on the separate qualifications but on how well they will fit with their co-workers. Assume the office hours normally run from nine to five; however, many customers would call in orders until 6 P.M. if given the opportunity. Mr. B, like all the workers currently employed, wants to work from nine to five so he can use convenient public transportation. Mr. A, on the other hand, lives nearby ànd for personal reasons would welcome the opportunity to work from ten to six. Therefore, viewing the office as a portfolio of people, each with different abilities, interests, and preferences, Mr. A may be the more desirable candidate.

In the marketing area, portfolio analysis can be a very useful tool. Suppose a supermarket is considering which products it should put on weekend special. Should it lower the price on coffee or detergent? If coffee is selected, coffee sales are expected to increase store profit $600 over the weekend. If detergent is chosen, the increased profit contribution will be only $375. Should coffee be chosen? On an independent basis perhaps it should. However, because people would buy more detergent, they also may buy more mops, bleach, starch, and related goods, causing the net profit contribution to exceed the profitability of the coffee special.

Again, this description of the portfolio model and the examples represent great oversimplifications, but the essential idea should be clear—that actions should not be evaluated solely on their independent merits, but rather on their impact on the firm as a whole within a particular context.

Summary and Conclusions

We have seen that thought requires models; models incorporate and convey understanding. It is wise to make models explicit and compare several models of the same phenomenon before making important decisions.

Models take many forms, most of which are highly personal to the individual using them. Usually they embody analogies to those phenomena with which the individual is most familiar. Models are largely built in stages by transferring knowledge from a familiar subject to one that is unfamiliar and then altering and refining the transferred material. Most models start as transferred analogies. Models in the form of mathematical equations represent the ultimate stage in the development of a model. In only very few situations does a business executive have available to him useful mathematical models.

Models are highly compact and therefore may not easily be absorbed and mastered; usually their value and power become evident to the user only after considerable practice and familiarity with them. Most people err by sticking to familiar relatively weak models rather than reorienting their method of conceptualizing a problem, for the latter is arduous and one does it poorly at the start.

Model building is a relatively specialized ability; still, no matter how great one's model building ability, his models will have little worth without deep understanding of the phenomenon being modeled. Combined with that understanding, skill in the building of models can produce clear, flexible, and powerful models that persons unskilled in model building could not approach.

The medium in which a model is expressed exerts a strong influence over the adaptability of that model to specific problems. Almost invariably, a model must be extended, refined, and even revised in order to apply it to a concrete problem.

Skill is required to select among alternative models as well as to apply the best of available models. Once a decision maker recognizes that he is constantly selecting and manipulating models, he will become conscious of what he is doing and rather quickly develop greater proficiency in doing it.

Models: A Dialog

To further understanding of how an executive might develop a model to help with a specific decision, we present an imaginary dialog between an executive (Joe) who possesses deep understanding of a phenomenon based on long years of insightful experience but who knows nothing about model building and a specialist in model building (Bill) who knows little about that phenomenon. They have just started a discussion in an effort to develop a model for a particular decision that is under active consideration.

BILL: Well, Joe, as you know, our goal is to produce a model that will help us to explain and correct our poor sales record in Milwaukee—and in other cities when they arise.

JOE: Yes, I know and I'm curious about this experiment that I allowed myself to be talked into. In the past, Bill, I've handled perhaps a hundred situations in which sales in some market were poor. In most cases, I've done pretty well—or so my bosses through the years have believed. In no instance have I felt the need to produce a model.

BILL: Yes, I know and can appreciate your doubt about the need for this enterprise; however, I hope that you will give it a conscientious try. You'll surely find the result interesting; at least you will learn what specialists in model building do for a living.

JOE: That's reassuring. Of course I'll help as much as I can to produce a useful model to solve this problem. Let me remind you, Bill, that our sales haven't actually declined in the Milwaukee market. We've only had a drop in the proportion of our company's total sales that took place in Milwaukee. Total sales in that market were about equal with last year's, but we expected a 7 percent increase.

BILL: That's not likely to cause us any trouble. At the start, we'll assume that the same forces are operating, whether sales fall in absolute terms or fall relative to sales in other markets.

JOE: Are you saying that there is no difference between a model to explain a decline in sales and to explain a disappointing increase in sales? How could one know that in advance?

BILL: I'm not saying that there is no difference but we may end up with that conclusion. Our first model is likely to take a fairly general form, at least at the start. By virtue of its generality, it may apply to many situations.

JOE: I think I understand what you said, but I'm not sure. What troubles me is that when you speak of general models, I constantly come back to the fact that the source of a business problem and the remedy for it usually are anything but general. An executive must know the specific details involved in that situation and deal with them in concrete and detailed terms.

BILL: Yes, I know that; but we must work our way up gradually to a highly detailed and specific view of the situation we are trying to understand. We will be wise to start by developing a broad and general model that sets down the main forces that influence sales and then, in steps, make that model more complex and specific—until it incorporates all that you know and believe about the forces that could keep sales from coming up to expectations.

JOE: That helps.

BILL: Good. As a start, I'd suggest that we try to explain a disappointing level of sales rather than to explain the actual level of sales that occurs.

JOE: I'd opt for doing what is easiest. If we could construct our model to explain below-expected sales, we might then explain such sales by a below-expected level of *total* demand or below-expected levels of advertising, or more-than-expected numbers of competitors and such things.

BILL: You are very much on target, Joe. Let's do it that way at the start, at least. We will deal with far fewer factors if we explain why sales are below expectations than if we try to explain the absolute level of sales.

JOE: How about the factors I mentioned a moment ago: I'd expect sales to be lower than expected if we actually did less to move the merchandise than we had intended to do—or if our competitors did more to push their sales than we anticipated.

BILL: That's very reasonable; in a minute, I'll ask you to list the things you may have done less of or that competitors may have done more of than were expected. Now I want to ask you a difficult question: What other problem or process does this question of explaining sales below expectation remind you of—is there anything that is analogous to it in your opinion?

JOE: That *is* a tough question.

BILL: Let me try again. As you spoke, I thought of a parallel to the problem that we're discussing. I see a scale: on one side are the things your firm does to promote sales; on the other are the things your competitors do. Now, you expected your firm and your rivals to put particular amounts of sales effort on the scale and therefore expected some particular balance on the scale. If unexpected things went on one side of the scale, they would either be offset by things on the other side or would change the balance. That is a model to explain the relationship between actual and expected sales. Now, can you think of any analogy like that which conveys your picture of why sales fall below expectations?

JOE: Frankly, I'm hard pressed to find a better way of visualizing that phenomenon than the scale. Does your experience suggest any other analogies?

BILL: Yes. I can think of a few, but they essentially say what the scale model says and not as well. For example, I could compare your sales experience in a market to the position that your son attains in his class. His class standing will reflect his efforts in class, in doing homework, and his native ability, along with the efforts of other students in the class.

JOE: That's interesting and a little more illuminating than the scale analogy for me. Shouldn't we move on to more specific ideas about what might explain why sales were below expectations?

BILL: Good idea. Let's now set down the most simple, universally applicable model. It may be called a dependent-independent variable model. We start with the phenomenon that we want to explain—in this case, sales below expectations; we call this the dependent variable. Then we list the things on which it depends—these we call the independent variables; some people would call them causes.

JOE: I see what you are doing. This approach should be applicable to almost any phenomenon you are likely to meet because it is wholly free from content; whereas the scale notion implies some of the processes at work, this dependent-independent variable model just helps to organize your thinking; it doesn't really say anything or inform you in any way.

BILL: That probably is true of any tool that is almost universally applicable. What we seek, of course, is an understanding of what will help you with your particular problem of sales below expectations in Milwaukee. To attain that end, we must know many specific things about your particular situation. What would be true for appliances would not be true for detergents or liquor sales. The more our model incorporates the forces that operate in your particular markets, the better it will help you to understand and solve your problem. We cannot settle for a simple general model.

JOE: I can see that. Shouldn't we move along and try to identify the factors that might cause sales to fall below expectations for a major appliance in a market like Milwaukee? Is that your message?

BILL: Yes, it is. Now, what are the most important factors that operate in such markets to influence your sales performance with major appliances—measured against sales targets?

JOE: First, I must admit that our sales targets are not equally difficult to attain in all markets; we try to get some people to "stretch" more than others. In other words, we have two sales targets—the one we set down, partly as a motivating device; the other is not written down but several sales executives have it clearly in mind.

BILL: So, one explanation for sales in a given market falling below target is that the target was set unusually high. Is that right?

JOE: Yes, but that does not apply in this case. Sales in Milwaukee were below our unwritten as well as our written sales targets.

BILL: Fine. What, then, do you see as the forces that result in sales below a realistic sales target? And be very specific about what they are at this point. This is where your contribution to our model will be greatest. You can draw on your long business experience and suggest factors that might be operating to depress sales. I certainly could not do that.

JOE: Okay. If asked why sales in a market sometimes fall below expectations—where our expectations were realistic to start—I'd have to mention the following kinds of causes: First, our competitors are cutting prices. Usually, if that were to happen, our people would fairly quickly learn of it and take counter-measures—but not always.

BILL: That is very helpful; just for the record, I'd want to treat separately the cutting of prices by retailers and by distributors.

JOE: That's all right with me, but I'll just ramble on. Another common reason for disappointing sales has been some notable success by a competitor. He may have developed a superior product feature or have stumbled onto an effective national advertising campaign that attracted attention. A few years ago our major competitor got his hands on a strong national TV program and hurt us in most markets. And whenever a competitor adds a new product feature that we don't yet have, we suffer in sales for awhile.

BILL: Remember that we are trying to explain why sales are unexpectedly low in particular markets; that would seem to confine our interest to factors that are not national in scope. But don't let that bother you. I'd prefer to have you just "ramble on," as you call it. You're doing just fine.

JOE: I've really implied most of the things I'd want to mention. In a local market if our distributor or retailers were to let up on their efforts to push our products, we'd show poor sales results. A strike or a closing down of a key retail account would show up in diminished sales. Or, if our distributor were to deliver sets that were not carefully inspected before being shipped, we'd possibly have lots of customer complaints that would hurt sales. I don't know whether you want me to go on; I could list many additional ways in which our distributor and retailer might hurt us. Should I do that?

BILL: At this point, maybe only suggest some other factors that might make sales disappointing; we are likely to come back to the failings of retailers and distributors again before we are finished.

JOE: Let's shift to advertising, which seems to influence appliance sales pretty strongly. If our competitors were to increase the weight of their advertising, we'd be hurt. Or, if our retailers and distributors were to cut down on their advertising, I'd expect our sales to fall. Of course, apart from "weight" of advertising, the quality of it—its ability to attract attention, to awaken interest in our products or the desire to buy—is very important.

BILL: What I've gotten so far is that such factors as price (at retail or to retailers), weight of advertising and its content, the various things that retailers and distributors might do to satisfy or displease customers, their service activities and the like are the main factors that influence sales. I don't want you to list everything you could possibly think of, because our model must be selective. We want an accurate, but simplified picture. Of course to produce such a picture you generally create a complex picture and then drop out some things as being relatively unimportant.

JOE: Could you set down a model that would incorporate what I've said already so that I can see what a dependent and independent variable model would look like?

BILL: Sure, that's easy. Here it is: level of sales equals f. That is, level of sales is a function of relative price, relative weight of advertising, relative impact of advertising appeals, relative support of retailers, sales efforts of own distributor, relative attractiveness of product features, relative appeal of product design, et cetera.

JOE: I can see the logic and value of that kind of model. Why don't we settle for it?

BILL: We could probably do a lot worse, but how could we tell whether we have developed a really good model until we have examined others? Often, one stands out far above the rest.

JOE: I'd be interested in any other "standard" types of models you can tell me about—like the independent-dependent variable type.

BILL: I have only a few standard approaches that are likely to fit most situations. For example, one can usually model a situation as an input-output system.

JOE: That sounds very high-falutin'. Will I be able to understand it?

BILL: You can get the basic idea without much trouble, even though it isn't easy to define a system.

JOE: I've read a few definitions and found them very fuzzy. Mainly, I get the impression that a system is like a machine with a series of parts that work together to make the thing work. I frankly think of a system as a refrigerator with a compressor, electric motor, and other parts that combine to make things cool.

BILL: That isn't a bad start. As I define it, a system consists of elements that combine to perform some particular function, with each part having a special task. A complex machine, like an auto, has many subsystems—like the electrical systems, the braking system, the combustion system, and so on.

JOE: The human body represents a more complex system, I'd think. It has a gastro-intestinal system, the circulatory system, the respiratory, nervous system, et cetera.

BILL: Right; now let's talk about this notion of inputs and outputs in systems. Each of these systems takes something in and, after it "does its thing" it puts something out.

JOE: I see the general idea, but let's apply it. In the case of a refrigerator, the thing that is put into the system would seem to be electrical power and what comes out is "cooling."

BILL: Right. Let's then see what happens when one tries to explain a disappointing level of sales as an input-output system. Would you like to give it a try?

JOE: I'll see what I can do with it. The input of the system includes such things as our sales efforts and those of our rivals and the demands of customers, let's say; the output consists of our sales and competitors' sales. The system itself takes these sales efforts and consumers' demands and turns them into customers' responses—actions of purchase or nonpurchase.

BILL: That's a very good answer as a start. But the key question to raise is whether that view of the matter is useful; does it help you to understand why sales fell below expectations and possibly suggest what you should do about the problem you face in Milwaukee?

JOE: I wouldn't be able to answer that offhand. Frankly, I didn't get the feeling that I was describing a system. In other words, it isn't clear to me just what is working on the inputs to produce the outputs. What is our system in this case? Is it firms in this industry? Is it the "market"—whatever that means?

BILL: That's a good question; I'd expect the system to be what you believe turns the inputs into outputs; it might be a combination of things including the manufacturers, the retailers, distributors, and customers, or it could be "the market," and maybe even more than these. If that were the case, our system would have many elements, each of them fairly complicated.

JOE: Well, that is what we should expect. After all, our dependent-independent variable model did refer to distributors, retailers, customers, and to what we and our competitors do. If that is the case, presumably our input-output system should include those elements. Isn't that so?

BILL: Yes, it is. Not all models would include precisely the same ingredients; but one would expect them to include the same key ingredients.

JOE: I'd like to know what other standard approaches you know; I found the first two very helpful and I think I could use them to advantage. If you have others, I'd sure like to know what they are.

BILL: Let me see, we've talked about looking for analogies, the dependent-independent variable approach and the input-output system. The last I can suggest is the "noun method."

JOE: That sure sounds odd. What do you mean by the noun method?

BILL: I know of only one other person who uses this method—the man who told me about it. It goes this way; you characterize the phenomenon you are trying to model by a noun. In our problem, we are talking about disappointment, frustration of goals, failure to achieve one's objectives—these nouns or noun phrases describe pretty well the failure of a firm to achieve its sales goals.

JOE: Okay. I can see how those nouns do describe our Milwaukee situation, but how does that help to develop a model?

BILL: In several ways. First, as you string out these nouns, you often find that they clarify the essence of the phenomenon; that is, this method could direct your attention to the heart of the matter. In this case, for example, it is that you had goals or expectations that were not realized;

the nouns also convey the impression that your failure is due to your own shortcomings or the strengths of your rivals.

JOE: I'm not sure that I got all that from these nouns, but proceed. What other ways do you benefit from this stringing out of nouns?

BILL: Well, it mainly suggests analogies. For example, failure to attain one's objectives suggests a military analogy. I'd expect that military men have a whole set of models that would help us to understand a firm's failure to achieve its sales goals; or, those models would at least help military men to see such a problem with great clarity—because they face that kind of situation very frequently.

JOE: I'm afraid that I'm not really getting the whole message. I can see this rattling off of a string of nouns as being suggestive, but it can hardly be said to produce a model.

BILL: That's true enough, but don't knock the method until you have given it a try. You see, what it gets you to do is search for the key mechanism or processes that are involved in the phenomenon that you are trying to illuminate with a model. What is more, you do it with one or a few words that carry lots of associations and connotations that are suggestive, as a minimum; and often they will direct your attention to key aspects of the phenomenon that might otherwise be overlooked. After all, a list of nouns is very easy to handle; it takes little time to string them out—especially with the help of a thesaurus.

JOE: I'd like to change the subject if I may. We've been talking about how to produce models, but you've alluded several times to the fact that a number of widely used models already exist right now. Wouldn't one of them meet our needs in this case?

BILL: I doubt it. I have been referring to models developed and used mainly by so-called management scientists and operations researchers. Those models are amenable to mathematical expression and to at least an approximate mathematical solution.

JOE: That would certainly seem to be an advantage. But I'd expect them to be one form or another of what we called a dependent-independent variable model. Am I right?

BILL: I'd say you were, at least in principle. That fact helps to drive home an important point: models have essentially the same logic and meaning whether expressed in mathematical or nonmathematical form.

JOE: Although that may be true, clearly a mathematical model is more useful than one that is only qualitative.

BILL: It is difficult to argue with that position, but you may be setting up a straw man. When you don't understand a phenomenon well enough to express the relationships among the variables in mathematical form, you just cannot have a useful mathematical model. In most cases—even with business problems—we are in that situation; we cannot express in quantitative terms the relationships between the determining factors and the dependent variable with which we are concerned. Take our problem of the failure to achieve our sales goals in Milwaukee. Could we state the relationship between weight of advertising, relative price, appeal of advertising messages and sales, relative to plan, in quantitative terms?

JOE: No, we've tried to do that sort of thing many times—or at least our market research department has—but without success. Oh, I see now. That means we are merely left with our old friend, the dependent-independent variable model. It identifies the factors that determine the extent of our sales achievement without stating them in numerical terms. If we could quantify those relationships, then possibly we could explain why sales were disappointing.

BILL: That is true, but we probably would not need a mathematical model for that purpose. If we knew, for example, that the Milwaukee distributors were making less effort to sell your product, or that your advertising appeals were ineffective or obnoxious, we would have our answer, without any mathematical statement being necessary.

JOE: That's a good point. Our diagnosis of the trouble needs only an indication of the factors that we should examine. But we would need a mathematical model if we wished to predict the result of any behavior we might adopt.

BILL: For certain kinds of action, such a model would help—assuming that we could develop a valid model of that kind. However, what we would need more than anything else would be some bright ideas about how to motivate our distributor, or some clever ideas for a better advertising campaign. We need good ideas more than we need formulas for making forecasts. And, if we are dealing with bright ideas, almost by definition, we are dealing with something whose effects cannot be forecast accurately.

JOE: This discussion certainly has been an eye-opener to me. First, I see that nonmathematical models serve our needs, or at least the most important ones, most of the time. Second, I realize that we cannot have valid mathematical models for most of the problems that I'm concerned with—like sales, personnel, advertising, distribution, product design problems, and the like. Mainly, I am getting the impression that as a business executive I mainly need models that will help me understand such things as human nature, people's prejudices, associations, aspirations, fears, and such. If I really understood what people were truly like, I could probably diagnose most of my difficulties and dream up clever ways of overcoming them.

BILL: That is quite a set of conclusions you drew there. I agree with you, but I'm not absolutely certain that we are right. Certainly I have no doubt that a decision to employ mathematical models or none at all is a serious error. Any model that helps us understand a phenomenon better is useful. Even if it is in the form of a checklist or an analogy—no matter what its medium of expression.

JOE: My untutored opinion may not be worth much, but I agree completely. I certainly have found this discussion very stimulating and illuminating. But, frankly, I still have some question about the applicability of what we discussed to my sales problem in Milwaukee. I'd like to make a suggestion.

BILL: Fine, what is it?

JOE: I'd like to tie what was said into a tight knot; I'd want to test its applicability by setting down the different kinds of models we thought might be useful. Then I'd want to show how they would be of help to an executive like myself; that would mean, indicate what I would understand or do differently from what I would have done if I were not exposed to different models. I'd also want to compare the different models and see how to assess the value and validity of any model. And I'd like to see how you put a model to use once you have it.

BILL: That is a tall order, but very worthwhile in my opinion. I'd like to point out some of the difficulties that we would face if we tried to do those things. First, we really cannot know anymore what you would have done. Our discussion probably has contaminated your innocent mind. If those models we discussed actually help you to understand the determinants of sales performance, you will have gotten that help and probably not recognize that fact. Especially in business, when you teach someone something he didn't know, he often sincerely feels that he knew it all along.

JOE: I'll accept that fact. Maybe we could use as our benchmark the kinds of things that we actually did—or said in our memos—in past situations that we faced like the one in Milwaukee.

BILL: That is a good idea, but a difficult one to make applicable. Let me mention some other difficulties. We only discussed different kinds of models in sufficient depth to indicate their fundamental nature—and did not really try to develop any one of them to the point where it might be useful for an operating executive. So, we'd only be assessing rather primitive models, rather than the kind we could develop and would want to use.

JOE: That's a fair comment. Maybe we should select two or three and really develop them thoroughly. Once we've done that, we could assess their value, compare them, and illustrate how they might be put to use.

BILL: If you like, we will do that. However, it would not really be possible to generalize on the basis of even that kind of experience. In the first place, we would be limited to assessing your particular tastes in models—those which reflect your individual working and thinking style. One must expect, moreover, that you would gain in facility with the development and use of models with practice. So, I am not persuaded that our experiment would permit you to do what you apparently want to do—assess the value and ways of working with models—in general. Still, I would like to continue the process of making you a model builder and model user, and your suggestion would be an excellent way to proceed.

JOE: Have you any more difficulties to record? I'd suggest that we carry our analysis of models a little farther building on what has been said up to this point.

BILL: Fine. There is one other point. We could not possibly appraise the nature and value of mathematical models on the basis of what we have in mind. To include them in our purview would involve us in very elaborate and costly efforts to gather and process data.

JOE: I can understand that, and I deeply regret it; I'd like to get a clear idea of what one gains and what one might be required to give up in using a quantitative model. I know that the striving for quantification is all the rage in business generally and in marketing in particular. However, I've seen no examples of concrete applications of mathematical models that permit me to appraise them with confidence.

BILL: We might be able to satisfy you on this score without doing it in connection with the Milwaukee problem. But you cannot hope to examine a representative cross-section of all mathematical models; exposure to one could only suggest some of the problems faced and the methods used to overcome them when one uses such models. It could not permit you to generalize about them. The value of models surely varies enormously.

This dialog has been carried forward far enough to indicate the essential nature of models and to differentiate the understanding that is incorporated into a model and the specialized skill of model building itself. Of course, the dialog was contrived; one is not likely to find many such pairs of executives working together to produce a model.

Chapter 5

MEASUREMENT, INFORMATION, AND FORECASTING

W HEN we make decisions that must be exposed to others, we usually strive for concreteness—we try to identify all significant elements entering into our analysis, assign concrete magnitudes to them, make our assumptions and logic explicit, and describe our computational techniques so that they can be replicated. This emphasis on concreteness and quantification raises some fundamental methodological issues. For example, how far can executives go toward valid decisions on the basis of information alone? What phenomena can be measured and what cannot be? How accurate must measurements be to be useful for decision purposes? How can executives best deal with qualitative phenomena that are considered unmeasurable—like distributor loyalty, employee morale, customer trust, and retailer resentment of past poor service?

A major issue divides specialists in business these days: the validity and applicability of quantitative techniques. A few believe that most top-level decisions will soon be made by essentially quantitative methods; most business specialists believe that quantitative methods will rarely be relied upon to make major business decisions. Many, however, believe that *parts of* most decisions can be made by quantitative methods. Underlying these divergent viewpoints are different assumptions about executives' ability to obtain the information they require and to measure and forecast essential business phenomena.

This chapter deals with the topics of measurement, information, and forecasting as they relate to business decisions. Each will be discussed separately for simplicity and clarity, even though all are interrelated: without some kind of measurement, information is of little use; without information, forecasting is haphazard guesswork.

Measurement and Executive Decisions

If a person from a primitive tribe were taken to a crowded supermarket, his observations would be totally unlike those of the store manager's. Each would attend to different things. The manager might observe the level of traffic, the speed with which customers were being checked out, the places of highest congestion. The visitor might notice the level of noise or the quality of the air in the store. Each might not even perceive what the other focused on.

Before we can have information or even perceive reality, we must carry out a process analogous to measurement. That is, we must select some aspects of reality to observe and then record something about them. In our example, the store manager's observations were essentially quantitative: the level of traffic means the number of shoppers—total customers less nonbuyers like young children and accompanying spouses; speed of checkout means the number of shoppers whose purchases were totaled each hour at each counter and at all of them together. Actually, few managers will measure these quantities numerically. Rather, they will usually note whether store traffic is "very heavy" or "lighter than usual"; they will see the checkouts as being either "in fine shape" or "causing trouble." Although the manager might not think he is making measurements, he is indeed doing so; and it is rough measurements of just this type that underlie most business decisions.

WHAT IS MEASUREMENT?

Technically, measurement is the process of ascertaining the quantity of some attribute of a phenomenon. For example, we can measure a single attribute of people—their height. The measurement process would require a definition of height—it might deal with the posture of the person being measured, whether or not the person is to wear shoes, whether the distance to the top of the hair or the head is to be taken as height, and so on. Once height is defined, then a unit of measure would be selected—like inches or meters. Finally, we would apply the unit of measure to the persons to measure their height. Our culture abounds in such familiar measurements: weight, time, distance, temperature, humidity, rainfall. The field of business also has its common measurements: sales (in units and dollars), market shares, profit before taxes, profit after taxes, net income, current ratios.

As it happens, many phenomena entering into executive decisions are not traditionally measured. For example, few supermarket managers measure their traffic, except in the casual manner described. One should question whether most phenomena of clear relevance to executive decisions can be measured at all. Can one measure the loyalty of a manufacturer's dealers and distributors to his brand, labor morale, the quality of the product offered to customers, the quality of service delivered, the aggressiveness of rival firms, the ability of employees to perform well under stress?

Before we determine whether something can be measured, we must know the purpose of the measurement. What do we seek to measure and why? What do we mean by distributor loyalty to a manufacturer, by labor morale, and so on? These represent concepts in the observer's mind; they may have no external manifestations. If that is the case, they probably cannot be measured. On the other hand, one may define distributor loyalty to mean the investment by a distributor of his own funds in such things as the manufacturer's signs, and his willingness to forgo current profits in order to change price in the way the manufacturer suggests. On the basis of such a definition, measurements could be made. But is one really measuring distributor loyalty in employing that definition? Thus, to measure most nontraditional phenomena, one ordinarily must define the concept and then identify the indicators or external manifestations that reflect this concept. One can only measure the latter, which may be only imperfectly related to the concept to be measured. The indicators must reflect the concept to be quantified fairly accurately if the executive's decisions are to be valid.

Let us examine a highly intangible concept that was given clear definition, the indicators specified, and the results put to managerial use. This example shows that, with ingenuity, one can at least roughly measure a highly intangible notion. An investigator wanted to measure the self-indulgence of those who were buying his brand and compare it with that trait among persons who bought his closest competitor's brand. He wanted to test the hypothesis that customers for the two brands were significantly different, because if there was a difference, he believed that the way he marketed his brand should capitalize on it. He defined the concept of self-indulgence as a placing of very high value on avoiding effort or pain and a readiness to make substantial sacrifices of other valued things—like money and self-esteem—to avoid them.

What actions or conditions are manifestations of self-indulgence? This investigator thought of persons in his own acquaintance whom he regarded as self-indulgent. What did they do that made him regard them thus? His answer indicated that these people would frequently take cabs, or would decide to stay home from work, or were unwilling to forgo a good time in order to help out a member of the family or a neighbor. The investigator then framed questions which revolved about such behaviors and tested them on a group of persons he knew well. Their responses separated the individuals into three groups: self-indulgent, self-denying, and middle-roaders. More to the point, in every case the responses placed the individuals where he would have put them. He then used his questions to study persons who bought different brands of the item he produced and learned that his customers were indeed substantially more self-indulgent, on average, than those buying rival brands. That is, the use of his indicators showed them to differ significantly in self-indulgence.

With this information, the firm's marketing team made a series of decisions about how to package, promote, and price his brand that they would not have made otherwise. They were pleased with the results of their decisions.

This example is quite unusual in several respects. Many firms could not capitalize on the knowledge that their customers were more self-indulgent than most customers. Also, the definition of the concept and the indicators used were ingenious. However, this case history reveals the benefits and possibilities of measuring things that most businessmen would dismiss as unmeasurable.

For every such success story, there are many failures. Intangibles are difficult to measure and almost impossible to measure precisely. But one can sometimes learn very valuable things from fairly rough measurements.

Precise measurement is almost always difficult and costly. Fortunately, it is rarely essential in business decisions. Indeed, if an executive were choosing between two alternatives that are almost exactly equal in attractiveness, he probably could not measure well enough to identify the better of the two. However, *if the difference between them is so slight, it doesn't matter whether the better one is chosen.* For example, if we were choosing between two industrial designs for a product which really were equally attractive, we would benefit little by determining which of the two really was the better. What we mainly need to do is separate alternatives that are significantly different. For that purpose, our ability to measure ordinarily is adequate.

A common bias that exists among information gatherers is to seek accuracy and precision for their own sake. Sometimes this bias is useful; however, it is badly misplaced in most business situations. Executives must decide in individual cases how accurate their information must be to meet their particular purpose. The best information available to them usually is admittedly low in quality.

How can highly qualitative phenomena be measured? Can we really measure the relative attractiveness and effectiveness of different advertisements? Can we measure the relative competence of two prospective employees? Can the relative profitability of two style ideas be determined? The answer to these questions is, assuredly, yes. That means we can get approximate answers to those questions that meet our needs reasonably well. With effort, ingenuity, and expense, we can often get strong indications—or moderately reliable measurements—on such issues.

Executives unfortunately cannot know all they want and need to know. They should:

- Be as clear and precise as possible in defining what they seek to measure.
- Make unorthodox and crude measurements when they are the best that can be obtained under the circumstances. They should be prepared to develop their own concepts, manifestations, and units of measurements.
- Refrain from measuring when the results will not alter their behavior.
- Recognize the inevitability of some error and inaccuracy in measurement.
- Refrain from seeking precision for its own sake.

Information and Business Decisions

Many decision makers believe that their decisions should be based primarily on solid facts. They seek information very diligently on almost every issue potentially relevant to the decision at hand. In part, their view of information's role in decisions may reflect an intellectual conviction based on extensive experience. Considerable evidence suggests that an individual's personality strongly determines the extent to which he relies on factual information for decisions. For some, the display of factual information is a ploy by which they seek to establish expertise and thus gain in persuasiveness. Other decision makers seem almost indifferent to information. They behave as if they can just figure out the best decision largely on the basis of logic and by applying the relevant concepts. They exhibit a high tolerance for ambiguity and uncertainty.

Few executives seem to hold a middle position in this issue; almost all seem to have at least a weak prejudice. I side with the second group. I have found that careful formulation of the problems and a sorting out of issues cut information requirements enormously—though rarely to zero.

Since decisions differ enormously, generalizations about the role of information in effective decision making are pointless. What an executive must know is *when* to gather information; *what* kinds to seek; *how* the process should be accomplished; and with *what degree of accuracy*.

What Is Information?

A sharp distinction is usually made between data (or facts) and information. Data represent statements which may be true and accurate but which must be processed—made relevant to a specific problem—to become information. Two processes are required: selection—separating the useful from the useless (for the specific purpose) and the irrelevant from the pertinent, and interpretation—drawing inferences or more general propositions that are supported by the data but which may not be obvious.

Persons with their heads full of facts may have little or no information. Indeed, such people often perform relatively poorly in problem solving and decision making, not because facts lead to wrong conclusions but because facts alone are not nearly enough to reach conclusions.

Even carefully processed facts are rarely a sufficient basis for problem solving and decision making. Information is only one ingredient—generally a vital one—but rarely the most vital.*

Purposes Served by Information

What good will a decision maker get out of specific information in a particular situation? How can it help him? If these questions are answered carefully in advance, a decision maker is not likely to go astray. That is, he won't spend large amounts of money and time to obtain and interpret information that seems useful and interesting but really cannot help him to make a decision.

Information can serve five general purposes in a decision-making context. It can help to describe, explain, predict, evaluate, and discover or innovate. Let us sketch these potential uses of information to make concrete what information can and cannot do for a decision maker.

Description. Decision makers need to know what is going on in order to determine whether something is going wrong and learn whether environmental conditions are changing. Descriptive information is generally the least difficult to obtain and involves relatively less interpretation than other kinds. Paradoxically, it frequently is the most costly to obtain, because accuracy to small tolerances frequently is required to detect significant incipient changes.

Explanation. When we use information to explain phenomena, we are dealing with the extremely complex issues of causality and association. To establish causes often is extraordinarily difficult, but that is one of an executive's responsibilities. He is expected to know what factors influence significantly the phenomena he manages. For example, if he is a sales

---

* This issue is dealt with on a somewhat deeper level in the discussion of models in Chap. 4.

manager, he should know what factors influence the behavior of ultimate customers, resellers, and salesmen—as a minimum. To do that, he must be able to explain how environmental changes—that is, changes in general business conditions, tax rates, competitive activity, compensation arrangements—affect customers, distributors, retailers, and salesmen.

To gain such understanding, an executive must draw conclusions from experience, on the basis of information about what happened in the past. He need not employ formal (statistical) methods to achieve understanding; some persons can apparently do so on the basis of a combination of high native ability and extensive experience. On the other hand, with considerable data at hand, an executive can sometimes achieve far better understanding by employing formal techniques. Such techniques can also indicate to what extent it is possible to understand and explain the phenomena under consideration, and thus suggest the validity of forecasts.

The use of information for explanatory purposes is perhaps its most valuable application to decision making. By explaining phenomena, information contributes directly to model building.

A statistical technique that uncovers causes. To see why many believe that business phenomena can be explained by statistical techniques, we will sketch the rationale of statistical techniques and consider the difficulties in applying one such technique to business decisions.

In this illustration, our goal is to explain our firm's sales in its major product/regional market. Specifically, we want to know what factors explain—that is, account for changes in—sales of widgets in Atlanta, our largest market. As knowledgeable executives, we have some hypotheses about the factors that determine sales of our product.

Assume that we believe the following factors affect our firm's sales of widgets in any market: (1) relative price, (2) relative promotional activity, (3) relative appeal of our style/design, (4) total sales in the market—which might require a separate explanatory effort, (5) number of retail outlets carrying our line, and (6) number of salesmen we have calling on distributors and retailers in the market. With these prior beliefs, we set about explaining our actual sales in Atlanta on the basis of these factors.

If we have good factual information about these six factors, we could make a "multiple correlation study." That means, operationally, that we could employ a well-established statistical technique in a thoroughly routine fashion to produce what is called an estimating equation:

Sales units = 115,750 − 2,400 relative price + 1,630 relative advertising
　　　　　　　+ 940 index of style/design appeal + 4,200 number of retail outlets
　　　　　　　+ 2,700 number of salesmen + .2 change in total industry sales

This equation actually describes *past* relationships. But if the conditions of the past prevail in the future, the estimating equation would predict the future as well as describe the past. That could be "very well" or "miserably" or anywhere in between. It is possible to describe numerically how well the estimating equation accounts for past levels of sales by computing the "standard error of estimate."

Multiple correlation analysis can be extended under ideal conditions to do even more than these impressive things: it can produce "partial coefficients of correlation." These measures explain the separate influence of each factor. Accordingly, we can determine the relative effect of each of our six factors on sales.

What do executives require in order to determine the kinds of causal/explanatory relationships we have described? First, they must have *accurate* data for their firm for some *extended period* on all the items believed to be related. (Correlation studies can also be based on "cross-sectional" data for the most recent period for which data exist. For example, they could be built on data for prices, advertising outlays, and number of retail outlets in the 112 metro U.S. markets for the period July 1, 1978, to December 31, 1978.) Second, their data must describe a period of time during which the relationships among the factors remained quite stable and consistent. Almost all statistical techniques treat all data as if they come from an unchanging universe. Third, the alleged causal factors must represent genuinely related economic forces rather than specious influences— relationships that are apparent but not real. That is, the executive must not accept nonsense correlations.

The conditions set down are not easily met. Most firms operate in a volatile environment. The influences at work and their effects apparently change substantially over moderately short periods in many industries. Moreover, the more factors that are tested together, the greater the number of statistical observations required to get a reliable result. In the hypothetical case we have been discussing, one would require annual data for at least a 25-year period; but few if any metropolitan markets for consumers' goods are fairly stable for so long a period.

Consequently, even if an executive has extensive and accurate information about the past, statistical techniques cannot produce reliable conclusions about causal relationships. Nevertheless, they do permit an executive to squeeze out whatever causal implications exist in the data in a systematic and objective manner. They at least provide a base on which an executive might build his own view of existing causal relationships.

Prediction. To forecast, we must understand the phenomenon about which prediction is to be made. That means that one should be able to explain it much as an estimating equation might. Indeed, as already indicated, most estimating equations are computed for purposes of prediction.

The subject of forecasting is vast, and we shall barely scratch the surface here.* Some points that deserve particular emphasis are listed below.

- One should distinguish passive from active forecasting. The first deals with environmental forecasts—predicting things that one cannot affect but to which one must/can adapt. Active forecasting aims to predict the consequences of the decision maker's actions, for example, the effect on sales—and other factors—of a particular sales promotion.
- Some forecasts are based on formal techniques, while others are completely qualitative and intuitive.
- Forecasts, like plans, yield their greatest benefits in the preparation, and not in the final result. Forecasts can help an executive greatly, even though they are not correct.
- Most formal forecasting techniques are based on one of the following assumptions:

    Past relationships will endure.

    The current situation will persist into the near future—that is, tomorrow's weather will be like today's.

    The emergence of new conditions can be observed. If we examine the present situation very closely, we can detect early beginnings of future developments.

Evaluation. Most executives evaluate their major activities if it is feasible to do so. A few types of evaluation are standard operating practice: periodic evaluations of employee performance are almost universal, as are measurements of sales performance against a sales quota. Apart from these widespread evaluation procedures, executives evaluate important activities whenever they get clues that something may be amiss or because a long time has elapsed since the previous evaluation.

Underlying any evaluation is a standard against which an activity can be measured. Sometimes, as in employee evaluations, the standards are subjective and rest mainly on comparisons with other employees doing similar work. (This standard cannot readily be applied to most executives inasmuch as their functions usually are unique.) Evaluations of individual salesmen, distributors, and sales divisions rest mainly upon numerical measures of potential sales. But, what standards can be used to evaluate a research and development department? A sales training program? A pub-

---

* The final section of this chapter discusses the most important forecasts made by business organizations: the business outlook and sales forecasts.

lic relations department? An executive development program? An advertising department?

Most standards employed are based on past performance by the same person or organization or on current performance by other comparable persons, units, or organizations. Another, more qualitative, approach sometimes taken is to ask what might reasonably have been achieved under optimum work methods and other conditions. A person or organization might rate high by the first two standards but poorly by the third—one may perform substantially better than others and still not nearly attain his potential.

Most evaluation studies involve the following elements: An appraisal of alternative standards of evaluation, which sometimes requires the development of a new standard; the collection of information that would serve as a standard, which often involves getting inside information about other firms; and a comparison of the person or organization to be evaluated with the standard.

Innovation. Few people would regard invention as a form of information. Nevertheless, researchers are sometimes asked to collect bright ideas, suggestions, proposals, or hypotheses. If successful, these studies can help executives mightily with their decisions. From time to time, some managements make major efforts to gather innovative ideas. However, despite a substantial increase in formal organized efforts to gather new workable ideas, their number remains tiny.

What is special about innovation studies is that the researcher does not seek a representative sample but one that is purposely very unrepresentative. Information for such studies is gathered from the most highly informed and imaginative people that one can persuade to participate in the study.

Classifying information into the five distinct types described above can in itself help executives to define and appraise their information needs. Generally speaking, one describes, explains, and evaluates in seeking better ways of doing things and to predict outcomes. Executives predict partly so that they can select among alternatives; they also predict (as in the case of sales and general business conditions) in order to take actions suited to the conditions anticipated. In other words, descriptive, explanatory, and evaluation studies serve primarily as the basis for prediction and invention. Such studies have trivial value unless they assist in prediction and in selecting appropriate actions.

An Executive's Informational Goal: Response Data

The type of information that an executive needs above all others combines all five of the types we have discussed. It starts with the actions that the firm might adopt (based on experience and invention), describes what happened when such actions were taken in the past, and tries to explain how they might work. On the basis of such explanatory studies, predictions are made by using some kind of statistical estimating procedure.

Most executives may be likened to engineers who operate a control panel containing many levers. Their responsibility is to manage those levers to attain the objectives set down for them. To perform his duties, the engineer mainly needs to know what happens if he moves each of the levers in particular ways—that is, he requires what we call response data. He wants to know the response of customers, suppliers, rivals, employees, junior executives, and others to the actions he might take. He has many choices: he can move each lever up or down or sideways. And, he can move certain levers *in combination*.

This analogy between an executive and an engineer managing a control panel highlights the need to know the connection between the actions or decisions he might take and the organization's objectives. But the analogy is deficient in two significant respects: It implies that the executive knows all the activities (levers) under his control, which sometimes is not the case, and that his decisions are only concerned with *how much* of an action is taken rather than *in what way*. Actually, most executives' actions have content as well as quantity. For example, the effectiveness of most advertising campaigns depends at least as much on what message is communicated as on the frequency or weight of the messages.

How can an executive learn the connection between his activities and the benefits achieved by his organization (and/or himself)? We have referred to this connection as the functional relationships of controllable variables; these include the effects of separate actions as well as those taken together. The answer surely calls for an executive to learn what happened in the past when similar actions were taken.

No one would deny that most decisions by executives revolve about and imply conclusions about the functional relationships of their controllable variables. We must ask how and how much executives can learn about them if they use the best methods available to them. Can they determine from a careful analysis of the past the effects of actions taken in the future? Does history repeat itself? Will past relationships obtain in the future?

Some business phenomena, mainly those in the areas of production and logistics, are quite constant over time; others are far less stable, with market-related matters usually the most volatile. Still, no field totally lacks order and continuity; the future of all fields bears some resemblance to their past. Therefore, an executive will want to learn fully what relationships existed in the past and how they were changing. Having learned what he can about the past, he will then do what he can to take into account changed circumstances in the future.

The techniques of formal statistics accurately summarize past relationships to the extent that accurate and full descriptions of the past are available. Correlation studies of past experience yield quantitative statements of the effects of the controllable variable on outcomes related to the decision maker's goals. We can also measure the consistency and validity of such relationships *in the past*.

Correlational studies yield valid results only if the years included in the study include data that are homogeneous—that is, if the same forces operate in essentially the same manner throughout the period. The same requirement applies to cross-section correlations: the forces operating in all the different geographic markets should be the same. Those requirements are rarely completely met for business phenomena that executives make decisions about. However, they may be met to a sufficient degree to provide useful, though imprecise, results. The decision maker often must choose between using highly suspect information or none at all.

Executives must be very hard-headed in deciding what information to collect and how accurate the information must be to meet their needs. Whereas in some scientific contexts, knowledge and exactitude are sought as ends in themselves, great precision rarely is required for decision making; rather, it represents an extravagance. Executives must seek information only for utilitarian purposes.

When to Collect Additional Information

What information should a decision maker seek? His objective clearly is to improve his choice. That means that the information he collects should either help to devise a choice—suggest potential actions that otherwise would go unrecognized—or dictate his choice among present alternatives. Before gathering information, executives should confirm that the information gathered could affect their decisions and actions. Studies that are interesting but have no chance of affecting anyone's decision because company policy or top management prejudice forecloses any change are essentially worthless.

What specifically might an executive do to determine what information would help him reach a valid conclusion, determine how accurate the information should be to meet his needs, and appraise the value of specific items of information? The following steps are recommended for these purposes:

- Set down the items of information you believe are required to reach a decision.

- Assume numerical values for each item. Make your assumptions reasonable.
- Set down the decision or conclusion you would reach if you obtained those results.
- Determine whether you actually require added information to reach a decision.
- If so, assume reasonable values for the added information and set down your decision.
- Continue this process until you are confident that you have identified all the information needed to support a decision.
- Drop each piece of information on the list, one at a time, and see what decision you would reach without it. If the decision is not altered, drop that information requirement. You would by this process have eliminated unnecessary or redundant information.
- Alter each assumed value by approximately 30 percent, one at a time. Set down the conclusion you would reach. First raise the assumed value, then reduce it from the original value. Observe in each case whether your conclusion would be altered by changing the assumed values and whether the change is significant in the valuation you place on any alternative.
- Determine in this process what items of information have the greatest effect on your valuation of an alternative. That is, determine which items, if changed only slightly, would have major effects on your valuation.
- Examine each item on the list of required information individually and decide whether you already possess sufficient information of the required accuracy.
- Decide which of the others it would be desirable to study, taking account of the cost, the likely validity of the results, and the probability that the results would affect the decision reached—that is, would the dominant decision maker accept results that differed from his present convictions?

The procedure outlined ordinarily demands exacting thought and sometimes considerable time. However, it represents a highly systematic method of reaching a decision as well as a method of determining information requirements. The time required to reach a decision after information has been gathered is greatly reduced if this procedure is carried out, and the decision reached is more likely to be valid.

Gathering information can impose heavy costs in ways other than direct outlays for collection. Information collected may be incorrect and lead to mistaken conclusions. Frequently, information is collected that one could know in advance is almost as likely to be wrong as right. Once collected, such information is treated as if it were valid. The firm would be far better off if everyone recognized that the answer to a particular question was not known.

Executives should recognize that information collection can easily become an excuse for postponing decisions, a substitute for careful thinking, and a costly way of merely satisfying curiosity. If an executive wants to know some fact accurately—like the number of units of an item he will be able to sell next year or the price at which he will sell his output—he is likely to fail. The information required to know such things with accuracy simply does not exist. Any gains in accuracy he can add to the information he already possesses ordinarily would involve large expense, for he must study larger samples or conduct more market tests.

To minimize the need for information, a decision maker could determine the sales volume he requires to make the project under consideration profitable—that is, if sales were above specified levels he would decide in favor of the project. These quantities could be determined largely on the basis of logic combined with estimates of his costs. Given the relevant cost data, he might find that he needs sales of at least 25,000 units and a price of at least $75.00. He might already possess enough information to make those figures seem easily attainable or out of the question. He need make no further search for information.

Forecasting and Executive Decisions

More than any other kind of information, executives require forecasts, or predictive studies. Their decisions are carried out in the future, when circumstances may differ greatly from the present. Accordingly, executives require two chief informational inputs: a forecast of the future environment; and a forecast of the effects of their actions—that is, functional relationships—in the environment. Thus, forecasting is crucial to effective decision making.

Although all business decisions involve forecasts of costs and benefits, many of which must be made by the decision maker, two kinds of forecasts are made routinely in most firms to be used by decision makers as inputs into many of their decisions. These are general environmental forecasts and forecasts of unit sales, and we shall discuss them specifically once we discuss what it is possible to forecast.

What Business Phenomena Can Be Forecast?

Very few persons can accurately forecast the outcome of horse races or the movements of the stock market; those who do for a while usually run into long dry spells that can culminate in bankruptcy. On the other hand, astronomers are remarkable forecasters; chemists and production specialists do a highly consistent job of forecasting what will happen when ingredients are mixed in test tubes and vats or when materials are processed through a factory. Clearly, some phenomena can be forecast far more accurately than others and far more successfully under certain circumstances than under others. We are interested to know whether and when a particular phenomenon can be forecast accurately.

Factors that facilitate forecasting. Two major circumstances determine the accuracy of forecasts: (1) the stability of the environment in which the phenomenon operates—for example, whether the test tubes and vats are clean, or whether the machines are in good operating order, and (2) the forecaster's understanding of the forces that influence the phenomenon. These factors are interrelated: when the environment is stable, it is often easy to learn the effects of the forces that are operating. Conversely, attempts to understand the effect of individual factors in a highly dynamic, volatile environment usually fail.

If executives deal with things whose effects they understand very clearly, like the operation of a well-developed familiar machine, they can accurately forecast the number of units that will be turned out in an hour. On the other hand, if they are trying to forecast the effects on sales of a change in style, or a change in advertising theme, or the effects of a new executive's appointment on the morale and productivity of a division, they are dealing with partially understood (and possibly misunderstood) phenomena and therefore cannot predict their effects accurately. If a firm makes such changes in a volatile environment, its forecasts of their effects are likely to be highly inaccurate.

The foregoing discussion suggests two important questions: What are the outward manifestations of a stable environment? When is one trying to forecast unfathomable forces and when are they predictable? It is easy to fall into circular reasoning: when forecasts have been accurate, one may take that fact as proof that the firm operates in a stable environment and that the forces being forecast are quite stable. A record of consistently accurate forecasting strongly suggests that those conclusions hold for the past. However, executives must be prepared to find, as many executives have found in the past, that what was forecast quite accurately for many years suddenly behaves in a wholly unexpected manner.* As economies mature, the unexpected becomes increasingly likely.

Things that appear far too complicated to forecast sometimes prove to be predictable with high accuracy. Witness the success of astronomers

---

* One of the best-known examples of a sudden breakdown in a forecasting method is that of the New York Telephone Company's ability to predict telephone usage. The breakdown occurred in the 1960s.

already cited. It is the stability of a phenomenon over time—as is the case with physical forces—that largely accounts for our surprising success in prediction despite great complexity.

To return to the question of what business phenomena can be forecast, we can say roughly that matters related to production and logistics are most amenable to the use of formal statistical forecasting techniques and are likely to be quite valid. Forecasts of market and personnel phenomena are likely to be least valid because the environments in which personnel and marketing actions are taken are quite volatile, the forces operating are highly complex, and some of the forces do not remain stable over time.

Clues to our ability to forecast. If an analysis of historical developments does not uncover consistent patterns in a phenomenon, we must assume that we cannot predict it. Even if we do find some consistency and regularity in past developments, we cannot be certain that they will endure. On the other hand, we should assume that the future bears some resemblance to the past. If fairly consistent patterns have held for several years, those patterns are not likely to be erased or reversed suddenly and without some signals that a major change is taking place.

Let us, then, assume the following fairly common situation: After exhaustive research, a forecaster has found a modest degree of regularity in a phenomenon's recent behavior. That is, the forecaster finds that the phenomenon he is trying to predict does not behave randomly and chaotically. However, his forecasting "equation" or system does not give him highly accurate predictions. In other words, he has something to contribute to a forecast, but cannot forecast accurately. Moreover, he recognizes that current circumstances and those expected in the near future differ from those in the past. Consequently, his ability to forecast is lower than his ability to explain what happened in the past. How do forecasters function under such circumstances?

Most forecasters base their forecasts on the assumption that past conditions would continue into the future, even though they recognize that conditions have changed. They then adjust that prediction to take account, however roughly, of the expected changed conditions. To do that, the forecaster will try to identify the forces that are now operating that did not before or that do not operate in the same way as before. He would ordinarily hold some opinion about whether the newly operating forces increase or reduce the result and whether their effect is large or small.*

The adjustments described are highly qualitative. Two expert executives would not make the same adjustments. Still, statistical forecasts can

---

* The forecaster should also be aware of and adjust for factors that were not included in the statistical forecast but that deserve to be included. These would be treated much as are forces that did not operate before.

be adjusted and almost always should be. Indeed, an executive must question the validity of any statistical forecast that has not been adjusted in the manner described.

Forecasts of the general environment and unit sales. Few generalizations hold for all industries and firms. It is an unusual business that operates in a stable environment that changes in a consistent and predictable manner. Precise forecasts of their relevant environments therefore are partly flukes. Environmental forecasts must be at least partly qualitative and subjective if they are to take account of changed circumstances or omissions from the statistical estimating equation.

Forecasts of a firm's unit sales are likely to be even less reliable than forecasts of general business conditions or even of total industry sales. To understand why that is so, let us indicate the elements that must enter into a firm's sales forecasts. A firm's sales depend almost entirely on three sets of circumstances: first, variations in general business conditions—few industries are unaffected by what happens in the total economy and more especially in the areas in which they operate; second, developments in the specific industry that will affect total industry sales; third, changes in the individual firm's market share—that is, its share of total industry sales. All three of these influences on a firm's sales are difficult to forecast. Although offsetting errors in forecasts of these three elements might occur, no strong reasons would lead one to expect errors to be compensating rather than additive. So the forecaster of sales has three opportunities to go astray in his forecasts.

Despite the perils suggested, most firms do rely upon environmental forecasts made by professional forecasters (forecasts made by outside experts) and they do almost always prepare and make use of sales forecasts. They have little choice, because almost all their most vital decisions—how much to produce, what to buy, how much to borrow, and the like—rest upon a forecast of their firm's sales, which in turn are affected by what happens to the economy generally.

How accurately do firms forecast sales? We can forecast the answer to this question with great confidence: it varies widely from product to product, firm to firm, and time to time. Nevertheless, top management has no choice but to make sales forecasts. What it can choose, however, is how much effort and resources to devote to its environmental and sales forecasts.

WHEN AND HOW CAREFULLY TO FORECAST

A forecast need not be accurate to justify the effort and to meet the decision maker's needs. Executives are wise to forecast if the results improve their decisions enough to cover their forecasting costs. That is, a forecast should be made if it changes a firm's behavior so that its costs fall or revenues rise enough to offset the costs of producing the forecast. Moreover, the firm should make greater efforts if the added accuracy of the forecast affects the firm's actions enough to produce net revenues in excess of the cost of the greater efforts. Forecasts are like any other activity of business—they must meet the test of a cost-benefit analysis.

There are several good reasons to believe that "accurate-enough" environmental* and sales forecasting is generally possible:

- All events and conditions have underlying causes. Things do not happen without reason.
- By careful analysis, specialists usually can identify the chief factors that affect the environments and sales with which executives are concerned.
- These causal factors are usually moderately stable in their effects over substantial periods of time.
- A careful analyst can often determine the approximate effects of the more important factors influencing the environments in which he operates.

How to Use Forecasts

Executives should know what to expect of forecasts made by others and understand how to use them. Are we raising an artificial issue? Shouldn't a decision maker use a forecast as if it were correct? After all, doesn't it represent the best estimate available to him? What does or should a forecast represent?

To approach answers to these questions, let us consider a hypothetical business executive who has received from his firm's forecasting department an industry sales forecast stating that sales in the following year will be between 10 and 11 million units if the price is about $5 per unit and if other conditions remain essentially unchanged. What can the executive take such a statement to mean? How could the executive use this forecast?

A few propositions should help us to get ahead with these questions.

---

* Firms need not make their own forecasts of the general economic environment. Very commonly they can obtain, often with little or no cost, a highly professional forecast of general business conditions and of the level of activity in major sectors of industry and even in their particular industry. On occasion, they can obtain forecasts of conditions in individual metropolitan markets from outside sources. When such forecasts are available from others, the task of decision makers is to search them out, learn how they were made, evaluate their past performance, and then employ them as inputs in their decisions if they appear useful.

A variety of outcomes (sales levels) are possible.

The best informed person could not possibly estimate the exact level of future demand. Due to the action of many forces, some not even knowable and most beyond the control of the firm, the forecaster cannot know with certainty what will happen a year hence.

The range of possible outcomes varies widely from subject to subject. When the phenomenon forecast is highly repetitive and the forecaster has extensive information about it, the range usually will be narrow. When it is unfamiliar and unique, the range will be very wide.

The possible outcomes are not equally likely.

It may be wholly reasonable to expect a level of sales (at a price of $5.00) to be as low as 7.5 million, in the event, for example, of a sharp business recession or the development of a competitive product, or as high as 14 million, if general business improved and if a new feature of the product caught on quickly. However, the probability of selling 7.5 or 14 million units is far smaller than the possibility of selling say, 10 million units.

There is no single number that exactly and fully characterizes an entire schedule of all possible outcomes and their likelihood of occurrence.

The average (weighted by likelihood of occurrence), termed "expected value," of all sales outcomes may be 10 million units. However, that number does not convey the same information as a listing of all outcomes and their likelihoods.

In effect, the foregoing three propositions dictate that a forecast take the form of a probability distribution. In the hypothetical case we are exploring, it might be as follows:

Outcome (millions of units)	*Likelihood of Occurrence (probability)*
Below 7.5	1 in 25
7.5 to 8	2 in 25
8 to 9	3 in 25
9 to 10	4 in 25
10 to 11	5 in 25
11 to 12	4 in 25
12 to 13	3 in 25
13 to 14	2 in 25
Above 14	1 in 25

Other propositions might be added to explain the basic nature of forecasts and the best way that executives can make use of them:

Decisions often must take account of extremely high or low values, which may be quite unlikely, as well as of the most likely outcomes.

An executive should want to know particularly about any situation that would injure or threaten the existence of his enterprise, even if it is unlikely. Some outcomes are so damaging that decision makers will avoid them if it is possible to do so. Conversely, executives are understandably interested in taking advantage of any opportunity to "make a killing."

The most probable outcomes do not necessarily group closely around a single and central value; the three or four most likely outcomes sometimes are very different.

A very low level of demand or a quite high one may be the most likely outcome. (This conclusion holds even more for the demand for the output of a single firm than for an entire industry.) Often a result close to the middle is unlikely to occur.

Accordingly, we must interpret the forecast of industry sales of 10 to 11 million units as follows: the most likely level of demand next year, if price were around $5, is between 10 and 11 million units, but there is a good chance that demand will be substantially higher or lower. As originally stated, the forecast did not indicate the range of possible outcomes and their likelihood of occurrence. Consequently, the decision maker could not take them into account.

An inspection of the probability distribution above reveals a commonplace but paradoxical situation: the most likely outcome is quite unlikely. That is, the chances of sales between 10 and 11 million units, in the example cited, are about one in five. In other words, the chances of sales being between 10 and 11 million units are only one-fourth as great as their being outside those limits. Consequently, a businessman who based his decision on the prediction that demand would be between 10 and 11 million units (a wide range in itself) would almost certainly be in error.

One finds an unfortunate tendency among many executives who use forecasts made by others to push their forecasters to take a stand, requiring them to forecast a single specific outcome. They defend this pressure on the ground that otherwise they will be forced to make the forecast themselves; and, since the forecaster is more qualified than anyone to estimate the most likely outcome, he should do so. Beyond that, they want the forecaster to assume responsibility for his single-point estimate. Such pressure on forecasters deprives executives of the full distribution of possible outcomes and limits them to only a fraction of the information that the forecaster can provide.

The implication is, then, that an executive must not base his decisions on a single best guess about the future. It is both possible and generally

necessary to make decisions that take into account several possible outcomes. But can a business go in several directions at once? Can it prepare,
simultaneously, for very high and very low levels of demand?

Almost everyone would agree that executives should devise programs of
action that take account of more than one potential outcome, if they can.
Sometimes there is little they can do but acknowledge that they are likely
to be operating on the basis of a mistaken forecast and therefore are very
alert to signals that they should alter course. However, they often can take
precautionary actions. For example, an executive recognizes that with
sales levels below certain limits, his firm would suffer such financial re-
verses that its credit standing would be seriously injured; and, with still
fewer sales, it would be forced to bankruptcy. On the other hand, he also
recognizes that with high sales volumes, the firm would have an opportunity to earn profits that would permit it to substantially reduce its production costs and even to enter new fields. What might the firm do to avoid
disaster and to be ready to capitalize on a bonanza should it develop?

To protect against bankruptcy, it might send a salesman to South Amer-
ica or the Middle East, or elsewhere, and arrange to unload 3 million units
at prices somewhat above the firm's out of pocket costs in the event that
domestic sales turned out to be very low. The salesman's cost could be
regarded as a form of insurance that the company purchases because of an
existing threat to its existence. Conversely, since the forecast indicates that
demand might be as high as 14 million units and yield huge profits, the
firm might take an option on additional production facilities and supplies.
Or it could hold relatively large inventories of raw materials and components. These arrangements would also represent a form of insurance. In
this case, it would be against having a bonanza slip through its fingers.
This example is a gross oversimplification, but it does make the point.
Executives must be prepared to find that their forecasts are substantially
wrong and must ready themselves to change their course quickly.

MONITORING FORECAST DEVELOPMENTS

If an executive understands the rationale underlying the forecast he is
using, he will know on what developments the forecast rests. That is, he
will know what potential developments could do most to invalidate it and
the most doubtful factors in the future. As a result, he could systematically
monitor particular developments. He would know what kinds of changes
are likely to occur, in what direction, and by what amount.

Beyond that, he would be wise to think through *in advance* and select the
actions to take in each contingency. No executive should be taken by
surprise because, say, sales are either higher or lower than were forecast; he

should have a plan for what to do when sales substantially exceed or fall short of the forecast. The competent executive is not necessarily one who can prepare good forecasts or who can identify a good forecast when he is offered one. (Good and bad forecasts often look equally persuasive.) Rather, he knows what to be on the lookout for and what contingency actions to take.

Summary and Conclusions

Decision making requires far more than the collection and interpretation of information. Indeed, the factual content and basis of most important executive decisions is surprisingly small, and forecasts are the main raw material of which decisions are made.

Many executives either are overwhelmed by a flood of facts or frightened into avoiding decisions because they lack information. Some executives have both reactions, since the flood of facts does not provide the information they desire. A gap is inevitable between what information executives desire and what they can possess.

The collection of information is widely regarded as a relatively routine process requiring the application of tested and proved methods. Such is not the case. Especially in business, opportunities abound for the development of insightful approaches to data gathering. With skill, effort and imagination, one can quantify almost anything *usefully*, if not precisely.

Information has five main uses: it describes, explains, predicts, evaluates, and produces discoveries. To have worth, information must be able to alter behavior. Frequently, rough approximations are sufficient to meet a decision maker's needs, for he is required to pick the best of several alternatives and *not* to determine precisely the value of each.

Much of value often is learned in the conduct of research, even when the results are inconclusive or wrong. Especially is this true of studies aimed at establishing functional relationships or other forms of response data. Unfortunately, the basic data required to establish functional relationships rarely are adequate to support highly valid results. Still, they do help to fill the information void and add to understanding, even though they do not explain or solve anything fully.

A competent executive knows what information would help him, has ideas about how to get it, knows how to interpret and apply the results. He also is able and willing to make decisions when he has little or no reliable information.

Forecasts rarely are very accurate, whether they are of individual costs and benefits, of general business conditions, or of sales. But, decision makers have no alternative to forecasting; their actions rest on or imply forecasts—whether they are explicit and systematically prepared or unconscious. Many phenomena can be forecast usefully, but error is almost guaranteed. A competent executive wants to know the various outcomes that may occur and how likely they are to happen. He will prepare contingency plans and monitor developments so that he can tell early whether the forecast is holding, and if not, in which direction it errs and to what degree.

The Bremil Company Price Program: A Dialog

The Bremil Company, whose home office is located in the Midwest, is a large producer of major household appliances and of "brown goods"—TV sets, radios (including automobile radios), and high-fidelity phonographs and tape decks. Its annual sales are over $100 million.

The conversations reported here took place between Art Williams and Ted Jarret. Art Williams is Bremil's vice-president of sales; he has spent his entire business life with Bremil—all the years since he obtained an MBA with honors from an Ivy League school. Ted Jarret is the associate director of sales, reporting directly to Williams, and is also well trained in business. He worked for two other large national corporations before joining Bremil about seven years before this conversation occurred one morning in Art's office.

The conversation revolves around a recommendation made by Bill Craig, the vice-president of marketing, to whom Art Williams reports. He has proposed that Bremil make substantial price adjustments in order to spur lagging sales of refrigerators. The adjustments proposed represent approximately a weighted average change of 10 percent, but would vary widely from model to model.* Craig's recommendation is based on a report by his assistant, Ken Smith, a recent addition to his staff.

ART: Who made this silly estimate of what we'd sell if we go ahead with our program to reduce prices by an average of 10 percent? It's been a very long time since I got so upset at a report prepared in this company.
TED: Frankly, I only scanned the report, so I wouldn't want to take a strong position on it either way. But it didn't strike me as being bad at all. I was impressed by the obvious erudition of the author.
ART: I'd call it downright incompetent. Who ever heard of an executive

---

* More will be said about price elasticity of demand in Chapter 13, where this dialog is continued. For present purposes, note that price elasticity measures the responsiveness of unit sales to changes in price and does so in an unusual form. It indicates the percent change in sales that is associated with each 1 percent change in price. Accordingly, a price elasticity of 1.2 means that a 10 percent drop in price would result in a 12 percent increase in unit sales.

for an industrial company forecasting the results of a price program by applying a statistical measure of the price elasticity of the demand for his product?

TED: Hold on a minute. After all, when you forecast the results of a price reduction, you're dealing with price elasticity of demand—no matter what you call it.

ART: I'm not even willing to concede that. When a firm reduces price, the result depends on many things, like the way its rivals respond, and the way potential customers interpret the price reduction.

TED: That's true. Sometimes customers buy less of a product following a price cut because they take the price reduction as evidence that most customers have lost interest in the item—as if something were wrong with it.

ART: Well, those are only a few of the things that the writer of this report neglected to consider. If you dig behind all of his general discussion, you'll find that he just used a figure on the price elasticity of demand to grind out a forecast of sales after the new prices go into effect.

TED: But one way or another, the question the report deals with is, how will unit sales respond to a change in price; by definition, that is clearly a problem in the price elasticity of demand—it concerns the responsiveness of unit sales to changes in price. Isn't that so?

ART: Look, Ted, forget the textbook definitions. I thought that we were speaking as business executives with a concrete problem to solve, not as schoolboys trying to get a good grade on our report cards. I expected this report to identify, illuminate, and predict the effect of factors we have to consider before going ahead with the projected changes in our prices. Would you seriously suggest that we should measure price elasticity and then use that measure to forecast the results of charging different prices?

TED: Well, as a matter of fact I don't know of any firm that forecasts the results of price moves in that way—though that was the method that my economics teachers seemed to recommend. But if that isn't the way to make such forecasts, how is it generally done? Show me a better way.

ART: You sound as if you might have written this report yourself. If so, I'm sorry to hurt your feelings, but I think it represents a real disservice to the company.

TED: Come off it, Art; you know perfectly well I didn't write that report. But the young new MBA who did prepare it interviewed me in the course of preparing the report, so I guess that makes me a collaborator, or an accomplice.

ART: I sure wouldn't brag about that if I were you, but I don't want to make this a personal issue. Still, I'm really upset, and even a little worried, when a report like this gets circulated. It represents a point of view and approach to our problems that is becoming highly fashionable, even though it seems almost childlike in its simplicity and sometimes leads to absurd conclusions. One of the things that upsets me is that the approach is always presented so piously under the banner of pure science.

TED: I'll admit that Ken—the guy who wrote the report—didn't seem to know very much about our business, or about pricing problems either, for that matter. On the other hand, he did seem very well trained in most business subjects. He clearly has covered much of the literature on price elasticity of demand. To tell the truth, I felt a little inferior to him when we talked—not that he put on airs at all; he just knows so many things that I don't know.

ART: Yes, I'm sure he does, but about what? Would you entrust your job to him? Maybe he knows what many equally uninformed economic theorists have written about price elasticity. But how does that relate to what would happen if this company were to lower its prices by an average of 10 percent on its products in two months, as has been proposed? Do you think management theorists deal with the same problems we executives have to cope with? Do they really consider the forces that operate in our world? Can we apply much of what they say or recommend to our problems?

TED: Yes, I think so. I certainly would contend that price elasticity of demand deals with the very questions that we are wrestling with. That concept formulates the problem of how price affects sales in a way that may be different from the way we usually discuss it, but it is the very same problem. I must be missing your point. How does our present problem differ from a problem in the price elasticity of demand?

ART: Maybe I'm stating my position poorly; I'm sorry. Sure, we want to estimate the effect of lowering price on sales, and technically, that constitutes a problem in price elasticity of demand. But Ken, if that's the author's name, has used an approach that I consider wholly inapplicable to our problem. I think that his approach won't work with a concrete operating problem like the one he was asked to discuss.

TED: Are you arguing that we can't measure price elasticity accurately? Or are you saying that when we do measure it, we get a result that can't be applied to concrete problems—like this one—because it is based on false premises, or is too simple and ignores the most important factors operating in the market place? Sure, no one can measure anything perfectly, and no forecasting tool is infallible. Or could it be that you feel threatened by the newer and more scientific approach to management that the report seems to employ? Are you afraid that these young people will show us up, that our days are numbered, and that we'll be working for them before long?

ART: I don't like growing old any more than anyone else does; and I guess it doesn't make me feel too good to find that some young kids fresh out of school know lots of things that I don't. Still, I don't think that the strength of my feelings comes from fear or jealousy. I think my reasons for being upset by this report are quite realistic and have to do with whether these young people will help to run this business better or actually drag it down. At the moment, I get the impression that some of them are a menace.

TED: It's hard to see how their education could hurt. After all, they have learned some things that we weren't taught when we went to school; these things have been developed quite recently. To the extent that those new developments are applicable to our problems, we should be grateful to have such people around.

I consider it very important that these newly hired young people be encouraged to use new scientific approaches. One reason I'm so anxious to have us hire them is that they'll teach us better ways of doing things. It's important for us not to intimidate them so much that they're afraid to take a position that we consider unorthodox.

ART: That all sounds very sensible and I would seem a dinosaur to attack that position, but in this instance, I see how that policy might cause considerable harm. Just for the moment, assume that this guy Ken was as wrong-headed as I have been saying. Look at what has happened. We got a report that is far off the mark. It was necessary for us to reach the conclusion that it is mistaken, which takes a lot of time. We even run the risk of hurting some people's feelings in the course of discussing such a report. And when we're all finished, we still don't know whether to make the price change. We may therefore end up by delaying or not making the move simply because of the time we wasted considering this report.

TED: You certainly are exaggerating the damage caused by such reports. After all, a lot is likely to be learned in discussing this kind of report, even though the report itself may be wrong.

The bigger danger is that some people might be intimidated by the razzle-dazzle and accept the results, which you assure me are badly mistaken. That's really a serious risk. But I still want to know what is so obviously wrong-headed about measuring the price elasticity of demand and applying the measure, as in this case.

ART: I'd be glad to tell you; and I might mention that this won't be the first time that I'll have paid my disrespects to the usefulness of price elasticity of demand. I wrote a critique of a report about 18 months ago that might sum up my views better than I could do it here and now. Why don't I send it to you, and then we can discuss the matter sometime next week over lunch.

TED: Great, send it around and when I've read it, I'll call you.

Here is the memo that Art sent to Ted that same day:

To: William Craig
From: Art Williams
Subject: JIM CLARK'S REPORT ON PROPOSED PRICE REDUCTION

Since I disagree completely with the conclusions that Jim Clark reached and think he is way off the mark, I am setting my thoughts down in writing to insure that I state them clearly and effectively. (You might want to distribute this memo to the others who will be present at our meeting on Thursday to discuss Jim's report.)

If Jim's conclusions are correct, then it is only by wild accident and the fact that he has made many off-setting errors. The approach he has employed to assess the impact of the projected price reduction seems wholly inappropriate—even though it might receive an A+ from a professor of economic theory and is clearly the work of an intelligent person. However, to judge by his report, the author is wholly innocent of any knowledge of industrial pricing.

I shall set down my objections to this report—mainly, a critique of the approach employed—in the form of a list. If my points are not clear, I'll elaborate them at the meeting.

1. The author has applied a computation of the price elasticity of demand for the entire industry to our individual firm. This use of an elasticity measurement is inappropriate unless all firms exactly match our price change on all models. Yet, nowhere in the report does Clark deal explicitly with the responses of our rivals—clearly an essential determinant of the effect of our price change on sales. (Incidentally, I would not expect all of our competitors to respond at the same time in the same way and to the same degree.)

2. It is far from clear that the price elasticity of demand is the same for all firms in any market, especially in our industry. Remember that we have not tried particularly to appeal to the price-sensitive customer, whereas J & M and the ARISTO do feature price appeals. I'm not at all sure that the elasticity number that Clark has ended up with takes account of such differences in marketing approaches.

3. As you know, we do not intend to alter the prices of all models by the same amount. I'm not aware of anything that Clark did to take account of the dif-

ferent way we will be handling individual models. We made great efforts to make our cuts where they would be most visible, and least painful to us. I'd expect the effects of the cuts to depend on how successfully we make them appear to be larger than they really are—something that an elasticity measure surely would not get at.

4. As you well know, most of our sales are concentrated in six markets, five of which are east of the Mississippi River, whereas about half of *all* sales are made on the other side of the river. As I understand Clark's method, his computations of price elasticity reflect the experience of the entire industry. If we use that kind of result, we are assuming that each market is like the national average in its responsiveness to price change. That assumption may be valid, but I don't think it is.

5. We mean to advertise this price reduction pretty heavily—by our standards. Consequently, the effects of our advertising must be added to the expected effect of the price change itself. The combined effects of the price reduction with substantial added advertising might be very different from the total of their separate effects. I am referring to the very strong possibility that price and advertising are synergistic in such situations.

6. We must worry about whether the effect of our price reduction will be to steal future sales from ourselves, rather than divert sales from our rivals. (I'm not claiming that such "stealing" will be the only or even the main effect, but I'd want to be sure that it was taken into account.)

7. Clark is using a computation of price elasticity that was made a few years ago by a graduate student who wrote a thesis dealing with demand conditions in our industry. I simply raise the question of whether customers' sensitivity to price changes is the same now as it was four years ago—even assuming that it was a valid measure for that time.

In short, I see many grounds for objecting to the method that Clark employed to forecast the effect of our contemplated price change on unit sales. He has completely ignored the reactions of our rivals, the differences to be expected in the reactions of the various segments that compose our market, the effects of our advertising, the problem of whether, who and how many of our present and prospective customers will even perceive the price change, and what interpretation they will place on it. Accordingly, I recommend that we either commission another study or just take a consensus of opinion and let it go at that.

Five days later at lunch . . .

TED: Those are very telling points in your memo—and all of them apply equally well to Ken's report. One thing that surprised me, though, was that you didn't stress the difficulty of measuring the price elasticity of demand. In other words, your criticisms would hold even if it were possible to get an accurate measurement of what happened to sales in the past when price was changed.

ART: Not exactly. You see, the price elasticity of demand may be fairly unstable over time. So even if you could measure what it was last year, the measurement might not apply to this year. And since it is so difficult and costly to make a price elasticity study, these studies probably are made very infrequently—even by those few firms that do make such studies.

TED: That's not my understanding of the situation. I understood that the price elasticity of demand is very stable over time so that there is no need to recompute it often. And with computers available, once you have made a good study of price elasticity, which would be tough and costly, I admit, you would have prepared the ground so that you could update your calculations relatively easily.

ART: You may be right about the cost of computing the elasticity of demand *if* you have developed a valid model and technique and have arranged for a flow of data. But that is quite a set of "ifs." In any case, I'm sure that in some industries the data are very costly to collect; also, it is difficult and expensive to collect information on the prices of different brands, sales—by models, and such factors as customers' attitudes and their knowledge of price. But even if cost and difficulty of computing price elasticity were not problems, why would you expect it to remain quite constant over time?

TED: Well, I'm sure I read somewhere that it was—though like most things I've read about price elasticity, it probably referred to a few major agricultural products and maybe petroleum. But why would you expect the reactions of customers to price changes to shift from one year to the next?

ART: Remember that we're concerned with both customers' and competitors' responses when we try to predict the effects of our price changes on our sales. And on that score I think you'd agree that our competitors—and even we ourselves—do not always respond in the same way to price changes by other firms.

TED: That's right. Uusally what we do depends on which other firms make a move, how much we need extra business—which is largely related to the excess capacity we have—and the like.

ART: But even then we don't always respond in the same way. Sometimes we wait to see how much of an effect our competitors' price change will have and at other times we almost beat them to the punch.

TED: I guess that I'd agree that our rivals' responses aren't consistent over time, at least in this industry. But don't you think that customers probably respond to changes in prices in much the same way from one year to the next?

ART: I wonder about that. Sometimes buyers view a price reduction as evidence that the product isn't popular and the manufacturer is hard-pressed to get rid of it, rather than as a chance to buy a bargain. It's strange, but when you reduce prices at certain times, most customers take the reduction as the first sign of a series of price declines to come and wait for bigger price reductions.

TED: That's true. But would you say that these differences in customers' interpretation are greater this year, say, than they were five years ago?

ART: I'd make two points on that issue. First, I think we are getting more clever about the way we present our price changes to customers so that we can more often obtain the interpretation that we want—though still not always. Second, since our purpose is to forecast the effects of the projected 10 percent price reduction, then it's not useful to employ a measure that includes the effects of such conflicting interpretations by customers which get kind of averaged out. Our forecast should be based on what we expect to happen in this case—on the particular interpretation we expect most customers to make.

TED: That's a sound point. Even though it's tough to do, we must judge what interpretation customers will make in this particular situation.

ART: Our research shows highly diverse customer responses: almost always you find some customers responding to a price reduction by rushing to grab the lower price before it disappears while others expect further reductions, and postpone purchase—some just decide that they don't want the product any more because it no longer seems as good as they once believed it to be.

TED: But do you have some reason for expecting the proportions in these categories to shift?

ART: Yes, as I already suggested, we're getting more skillful in getting customers to make the interpretation of our price changes that we want them to make. But a couple of other factors probably have changed the way customers respond to price movements now as compared to the past—the effect of inflation and the threat of recession.

TED: That's true. Those developments have made many customers highly sensitive to price, and that's how some so-called experts explain much of the popularity of new food discount stores.

ART: I don't know about that; discounters have been very popular long before this inflation in several other fields.

TED: You've certainly raised enough questions in my mind so that I wouldn't want to assume that customers' responses to price changes would be the same over long periods of time.

ART: Good. I really can't prove that customers' responses to price changes are very unstable, but we have to be prepared to learn that they are.

TED: If that's the case, and I just conceded that it seems to be, then the methods used to measure the elasticity of demand are very suspect. Mainly, they rest on data covering a span of years in which the forces operating in our market were not constant. In other words, you're suggesting that several different "universes," not one, may have been combined together in statistical measurements of demand elasticity.

ART: Absolutely right. That is only part of the measurement problem—though it is a fatal flaw in itself. The methods used to measure elasticity assume that the responsiveness of customers to changes in price will be the same at different levels of price—whether they are relatively high or low. I would question that assumption about as much as the stability of customers' responses to price changes over time.

TED: Well, it's clear that you don't trust measurements of price elasticity—at least for industrial products.

ART: That's right. For one thing, every elasticity study I've seen applies to an entire product—not just to a single brand. An elasticity figure might reflect a stable pattern of interaction among all firms in the industry—where such stability existed. However, even if the pattern were stable over time, the elasticity figure would tell us nothing about our particular position in the industry—that is, what the price elasticity of demand was for our firm.

TED: Then how do you even measure price in such cases? Do you take an average of all brands' prices? If so, do you weigh them equally? Or do you give overwhelming weight to the lowest-priced offering, since that would seem to have a greater effect on unit sales than does the price of higher-priced brands?

ART: Frankly, I don't really feel competent to answer some of those questions. But what I said holds, quite apart from these questions. If the price elasticity of demand for our products is about 1.5, that means really that if all sellers lowered price by 10 percent that would result in a 15 percent rise in unit sales. But what does that tell us about what would happen if we alone lowered price by 10 percent?

TED: It seems clear to me that it would result in much more than a 15 percent increase for us—we'd not only share proportionally in the increased total industry sales of 15 percent but we'd get lots of people to buy from us rather than from competitors.

ART: Right! That is just what I meant. The effects of any price change by one firm on its sales depends very heavily—you might even say it depends most—on how rival firms respond to the change. If they are doing very poorly, they'll probably be sensitive to the risk of losing business; if they can't handle the business they are getting, they probably wouldn't react to a competitor's price cut.

TED: I see the point. Their reaction would depend upon the situation in which they found themselves. So individual firms might well respond differently.

ART: That's my expectation. I just don't have enough information to justify my generalizing on the subject. What I really want to do is emphasize several key messages that need to be driven home around here.

TED: Such as?

ART: What I'm stressing are the conditions of diversity that appear in all markets—different kinds of customers which we now call different customer segments; different items in a product line; different competitive conditions in different regional markets; differences that occur over time in customers' responsiveness to a price change—here I'm pointing out that the initial reactions of customers to a price change might be very different from their ultimate reactions; and even differences in the ways individual competitors respond to any price change.

TED: Are you implying that we can't generalize about anything?

ART: No, but I'd say that we usually generalize on much too broad a level. I'm selling the need for middle- or low-level generalizations that take account of important differences of the kinds I mentioned. You just can't deal effectively with most things if you treat them as if they were all like the average.

TED: But as a big business selling ultimately to literally hundreds of thousands of customers, we certainly can't treat each individual separately and specifically.

ART: You're absolutely right. We must find ways of dealing with the diversity of customers, of geographic markets, of rivals, of surrounding circumstances, and so forth, that take account of major differences and ignore minor ones. At least that's my position. It isn't easy to sell, maybe because I don't understand it well enough to see all of its implications.

TED: If I understand you, and I'm not sure I do, then you're raising a most vital and general issue. I'm always upset by talk around here about how our customers do this or like that or object to something else. Every study I see shows that customers do and like and object to different things. We seem to be mired in "average" thinking.

ART: That's the very disease I'm trying to attack. I guess that my main objection to the use of price elasticity is that it is sicker with the disease of "averagism" than most other things we do. Well, that gets us far off the subject. You said that you had questions about a few of the points in my critique of Jim Clark's report. I'd be interested to know what they are.

TED: I do have one more question about your critique of Jim's report. You talk about the fact that we don't emphasize price in our advertising and in general try to feature quality and special convenience features. In your opinion, does that mean that we'll get more or less response from a price cut than our competitors?

ART: I'd say less. However, I'm not sure of that, but I'm sure that our present customers would not react the way that price-sensitive customers would. The tricky question is whether we could, by a price reduction, attract a whole new class of customers. We probably have very few price-conscious customers and you'd wonder why we'd expect to appeal to customers wanting quality, design, service and convenience by offering them lower prices—rather than by giving them more of what they want.

TED: That's very good thinking that I've not heard before. If we lower price here, presumably it is in the expectation that we'll attract the price-sensitive customer. I wonder whether we won't even injure the believability of our quality and service claims by our price cut. Most people associate lower price with less quality.

ART: I'm not sure that I know the answer to that question and it really gets us off the subject of price elasticity—and how customers differ in their sensitivity to price appeals. I'm just making another application of this vital diversity principle that I stated a little while back. But maybe we can discuss this problem some other time. . . .

Chapter 6

EXECUTIVE DECISION MAKING UNDER UNCERTAINTY

E XECUTIVES CANNOT PREDICT precisely the consequences of their actions. As a result, their decisions are never demonstrably "right." In that respect, executive decisions differ from solutions to mathematical problems and puzzles. Moreover, executives usually do not know, even after the event, whether the answer they obtained is the best they could have found under the circumstances.

One cannot judge the correctness of a decision by its outcome. Because of plain luck, some poor decisions turn out well. Conversely, carefully and wisely made decisions frequently turn out badly because of developments that no one could have foreseen. Although executives cannot know whether their decisions will be right, they must approach decision making in a manner that should produce the most valid decisions they can make under the circumstances.

The executive is not alone in making decisions although unable to forecast outcomes. All decisions face the future and are therefore, to varying degrees, uncertain. The major decisions of life—the selection of a mate, a career, a lifestyle, or a community; the decision about whether and how many children to have—incorporate very high levels of uncertainty. What we say about executive decision making is applicable to personal decisions as well.

Our purpose in this chapter is to determine how to cope with uncertainty as it arises in such decisions as whether to add or drop an item from the product line, whether to carry out an executive training program, how to modify the distribution structure, and what kind of advertising program to adopt. Most discussions of uncertainty focus on finance and relate to investments in listed securities. Those discussions are relevant to what is said here, but they emphasize aspects of the subject that are less important for operating decisions.

Uncertainty Defined

Uncertainty means an inability to predict accurately. As it applies to business decisions, uncertainty means that decision makers cannot forecast what will happen if they select any of the alternatives among which they are choosing. Uncertainty varies widely in degree; sometimes executives' forecasts of outcomes represent almost wild guesses; at other times, their estimates are virtually certain to be within a few percentage points of the actual outcomes.

Uncertainty is often contrasted with risk; the two terms are also used interchangeably by many writers. Later in this chapter, we will give our own special meaning to "risk," but until that point both terms will be used to denote an inability to forecast precisely the outcomes of ones actions.

Uncertainty is a harsh reality that executives must face without becoming either paralyzed or unnerved by it. Some executives enjoy uncertainty and regard it as a challenge. These are usually the happiest if not the most successful executives. Uncertainty is a threat as well as a source of opportunities. Fortunately it is a condition that executives can do something about.

The Chief Sources of Uncertainty

Why cannot executives forecast outcomes of their actions? The problem is not that they lack the time and money to collect information. No one, however much time and money he devotes to the task, can precisely forecast most business phenomena. (Executives usually cannot even obtain precise information about what happened recently.) Nor does the problem result from a lack of forecasting skill. Uncertainty reflects the nature of the phenomena with which executive decisions are concerned. They are highly complex and are influenced by many factors, none of which are precisely predictable. These influences include:

- The general economic environment.
- Developments in their particular line of activity.
- Developments in particular geographic markets.
- The behavior of many parties to the decision, usually colleagues, ultimate customers, rivals, suppliers, resellers, and government regulatory agencies.

Executives really do not know how their actions "work" for several reasons: (1) Mainly when they take actions, they do several things at once rather than one thing at a time; they carry out programs rather than single-dimensional actions. (2) Their actions will be taken in environments that are different from the environments in which those actions were taken in the past. (3) Their future actions will ordinarily have a different "content" than their past actions. (4) The parties affected by their actions change. They "learn" and therefore are likely to respond differently in the future than they did in the past.

Given the enormous complexity and unknowability of factors that enter into executive decisions, it is not surprising that precise forecasts of the outcomes are impossible.

What Decision Makers Can Do about Uncertainty

As suggested, executives must reconcile themselves to uncertainty. As one author puts it, they must "plan on uncertainty."* It just will not go away, even if they collect every last shred of available information.

Up to this point, we have emphasized what executives cannot do and know. But they do know something, often quite a lot, and can learn more about what is likely to happen. Executives never make decisions in total ignorance. They know general orders of magnitude, as a minimum; usually they possess considerable general background information and much scattered detailed knowledge. Most important, they often understand the forces that affect the outcome of their actions. (That is, they possess valid models.) Also, they usually have access to some others who know more than they do. What decision makers can do about uncertainty is *make full use of what they know and can readily learn*—even though they cannot forecast the outcomes of their actions.

Perhaps the best starting point for decision makers who want to take explicit account of uncertainty is to decide specifically what they want to know. Of course, they want to know the outcome of each alternative they are considering, so that they can simply pick the one that gives them the most of what they seek. But since it is impossible to know the outcomes, they must fall back on what they *can* know.

What, then, would they want to know that *is* possible to know? What information would help them most? How can information about an uncertain future be organized in a manner that would help executives most to make decisions? It is suggested that executives should process the informa-

* For an excellent analysis of uncertainty in public policy decisions see Ruth P. Mack, *Plan on Uncertainty* (New York: Wiley Interscience, 1971).

tion, impressions, logic, opinions, and guesses available to them into a particular structure. When the scraps of evidence, opinion, guesses are so structured, the executive can choose based on full use of what is available to him. Even then, he must expect to be wrong from time to time—and perhaps often. But without a systematic approach like the one described below, his errors would be numerous.

The executive should try to describe in a convenient structure the different outcomes that may come to pass. The particular outcomes that interest the decision maker are those that relate to his goals. If he is concerned solely with rate of return on investment, then the structure should indicate the different ROIs that may come to pass and the probability of each outcome. If he seeks from his decision an increase in sales support from his distributors, his structure should be built around the effects of each alternative on distributors' support for his product line. Whatever his goals, he should recognize the possibility of more than one outcome from each alternative he is considering and should not consider the different outcomes equally likely. Table 6-1 presents a probability distribution for two different projects, alternative 1 and alternative 2. The table clearly describes a condition of uncertainty. It shows that the best the executive can do is identify the different outcomes that may occur if he were to select either alternative 1 or alternative 2; and it shows that these outcomes are not equally likely. The columns labeled Probability state the likelihood of the different outcomes in an unambiguous way that has become conventional. It shows the number of chances in 100—in the considered opinion

Table 6-1

Probability Distribution Showing Outcomes and Their Likelihood

Potential outcomes (return on investment)	Probability	
	Alternative 1	Alternative 2
Over 30%	.02	.01
25–30%	.10	.06
20–24.9%	.25	.35
15–19.9%	.45	40
10–14.9%	.10	.08
5–9.9%	.05	.06
0–4.9%	.02	.02
Some loss	.01	.02
	1.00	1.00
Worth to decision maker	?	?

of the executive—that the particular result will come about. For example, the likelihood that alternative 1 will produce a return on investment between 20 and 24.9 percent is .25, or 25 chances in 100.

Even if an executive is able to put the scraps of information, opinion, logic, and guesswork into such a structure, he faces difficult problems. His next task is to decide how much his firm should be willing to pay for a project that offers the potential outcomes described in Table 6-1. The purpose of organizing the executive's information in this way is to focus his analysis on his highest-level goals so that he can assign a worth to each of the alternatives.

Let us sketch why the particular structure outlined should meet the decision maker's needs. When described by probability distributions of all relevant outcomes, each alternative resembles a lottery. The various outcomes are analogous to prizes and the probabilities are similar to the number of prizes. (Although this analogy is helpful, it is not exact. Actually, only one outcome—prize—will come to pass, whereas most lotteries do pay many prizes. Still, lotteries allow only one prize for each ticket, so the analogy is fairly close on that score.) The chief point urged here is that the value of a lottery ticket—or a project with many possible outcomes—is affected by all the prizes that one might win—even though at most one can win only one prize.

We are now ready to raise a series of specific questions about how an executive should cope with uncertainty. In particular, we want to explore how best to construct a probability distribution, and how to attach a worth to such probability distributions so that the worth of different projects can be compared.

CONSTRUCTING A PROBABILITY DISTRIBUTION

To construct a probability distribution, let us take as an example an executive who has narrowed his choices to a few alternatives. He has estimated, however roughly, the costs and benefits of each alternative, and is sensitive to the particular benefits he seeks and the sacrifices he wishes to avoid. In other words, he has been thinking about the outcomes that are of particular concern to him. After he reduces his choices to a manageable number, he presumably will be able to attach a worth to each alternative, make careful forecasts of their outcomes, and then reach his final decision.

The ability of an executive to forecast anything, discussed in Chapter 5, depends on his understanding of the processes involved in his actions combined with his skill in processing and interpreting whatever information is available to him. Let us consider a simple example to see what is involved in a forecast.

An executive is trying to construct a probability distribution for a project which calls for the addition of a new item to his firm's line of offerings. He sees the outcomes as dependent on the following factors: the total revenue he will obtain from this item over several years in the future, plus any additions of net revenue resulting from increased sales of other offerings in the firm's line, less any reductions in net revenue due to reduced sales of the firm's other offerings. In turn, he would see the total revenues obtainable from the new item as depending upon its unit sales, its average unit price, and its average unit cost.

With this general model as a start, he tries to identify the determinants of the sales of such a new item, the factors influencing its unit costs, and its price. His thoughts necessarily range over such matters as: How many and what kinds of distributors and retailers would carry the item, and how much sales support would they give the item. (That is, would they advertise it? Would they tell their salesmen to push it? Would they give it visibility in the store or the catalog?) How will competitors respond to his firm's offering a new item? What might be the possible effects of the new item on the prices the firm's suppliers charge for raw materials and components? How might the firm's employees and their union officials respond to the new item?

To give clear direction to his analysis of the problem, an executive should structure his information/guesses/forecasts in the light of the factors listed above. He should identify what has been called the determining variables or leverage factors.* In many business decisions these are the same set of four factors: unit sales, unit price, unit cost, and total investment. It is usually wise for the decision maker to construct separate probability distributions of these items or of factors which underlie them. (The more that an executive pushes behind factors to examine their determinants, the more thorough but complex his analysis.) From those distributions he usually can construct descriptions of the outcomes in which he is interested for they determine return on investment.

Subjective Probabilities and Guessing at Outcomes

One approach to the construction of probability distributions is to start with a list of outcomes which includes *all* possibilities. (Observe, for example, that Table 6-1 includes all possible outcomes.) The task is then to

* See David Hertz, "Investment Policies That Pay Off," *Harvard Business Review*, January–February 1968, p. 98. Hertz refers to leverage factors as "factors that will influence the key variables determining future costs and revenues. For example, capacity will influence sales volume; timing of market entry will influence price; and so forth."

assign probabilities to each outcome. That can be done by helping the decision maker to formulate the information and opinions that he possesses into an estimate of the probability that an outcome will come to pass. Let us illustrate again.

Assume that our decision maker decides to work with the four factors listed above and starts to estimate all possible unit sales outcomes. That requires him to include categories that contain all outcomes above a particular level and below another. His task then becomes one of "guessing" the likelihood of each group of outcomes. In making his guesses, he presumably will draw on everything he knows, believes, and can reason his way to. It is a well-established fact that almost every executive is willing to make such guesses and will feel pretty strongly about the validity of his guesses. (See the final section of this chapter for methodology.)

It is this last point that is crucial: whether for good or ill, most decision makers hold convictions about the likelihood of different outcomes. Resistant at first to the idea that they can estimate the probability of different outcomes, they are usually quick to oppose suggested probabilities. In the course of doing so, they find that they can forecast probabilities within rather narrow ranges. Especially if aided by a skilled interviewer, executives can develop probability distributions which accurately reflect their views—which may be highly inaccurate, of course. Unfortunately, their views often are not stable so that if interviewed by the same person a few days later, they might alter their estimates substantially. One must therefore ask how much reliance to place on such estimates; perhaps a more important question is, should one not repeat the process until the decision maker has narrowed his estimates to a small range?

Is there anything an executive can do to improve his estimates of probable outcomes? Clearly, the acquisition of better models, more and better information, and the devotion of more time to thinking through the problem would make an executive's estimates of the probability of different outcomes more valid and stable. Also, he might delegate the construction of particular probability distributions to colleagues who are far better informed than he.* It might be supposed that by doing these things, a decision maker would narrow the range of possible outcomes, thus reducing the uncertainty he faces. Although that supposition probably holds in most cases, added information and study sometimes uncover more extreme outcomes than were originally foreseen. One cannot always reduce the range of significant outcomes by added research and analysis.

---

* The final section of this chapter discusses methods of obtaining subjective and intuitive information from oneself as well as others for the purpose of risk analysis.

Risk vs. Yield

Executives face varied options when they choose among alternate projects. Some projects combine high yields with high risk. Others offer modest yields with modest risk. Opportunities offering both high yield and low risk offer no difficulties to a decision maker. Decision makers presumably evaluate each opportunity by balancing the desire for high yield against the overall chance of achieving it. That is, they "trade off risk and yield."

What is involved in a trade-off between risk and investment? How is it done? Surely, the first step is to define terms and explore how each is to be measured so that they might be traded off.

Risk, according to Webster, is "the possibility of loss, injury, disadvantage or destruction." When a decision maker takes a risk, he exposes himself to such possibilities, for he does not know the outcomes of his alternative choices. The degree of our knowledge of outcomes is to be seen in the range of outcomes we consider likely. For example, if we believe that the chances are 90 in 100 that a project will earn profits somewhere between $150,000 and $155,000, then we say that it is not risky; conversely, if the chances are 90 in 100 that a project will produce something between a $100,000 loss and $300,000 profit, then we say that the second is far more risky. Risk is associated with the variability and range of potential outcomes.

We must ask whether it is possible to summarize a full probability distribution of outcomes by one number that measures yield and another that measures risk. Can one develop a single "true" value for yield and for risk; or, is any measurement valid only for a particular individual at one point in time? We have already described, in Chapter 3, "expected value" as a useful measure of the worth of a distribution of outcomes, but it is not the only one and not the best in many situations. A world of differences separates a useful measure from one that is truly valid. The worth of a distribution of outcomes cannot be stated accurately by a single number and rarely by two.

The Measurement of Risk

Considerable disagreement prevails about the measurement of risk. Specialists nevertheless agree on two propositions: (1) some measure of the range of possible outcomes is needed for each period, and (2) those outcomes must be evaluated in the light of the expected returns on all of the organization's other projects. That is, individual projects do not have independent riskiness. A project risk must be assessed in the context of an overall portfolio—composed of all of the projects that the firm undertakes.

The prevailing view among specialists holds that the best measure of risk is the standard deviation. This statistical term describes the variability of a distribution around its mean so that approximately 65 percent of all observations lie within one standard deviation of the mean and 95 percent lie within two standard deviations. Granted that the standard deviation measures variability, it does *not* measure risk. The standard deviation treats favorable outcomes—those above the mean—the same as unfavorable ones. But when executives try to avoid risk, it is only the adverse outcomes that deter them. Accordingly, a decision maker must define and measure risk in ways that treat differently the negative and positive deviations from the mean of the distribution.

The standard deviation would be a satisfactory measure of risk if distributions of outcomes were symmetrical, that is, if each positive outcome were offset by a roughly equal negative outcome. However, such symmetry is unlikely in most projects that come before executives for decision. Proposals for actions that executives pass upon are enormously varied and one cannot generalize about the nature of their distributions with confidence. However, a large class of projects has a fairly clear maximum possible loss—which roughly equals the sums put up to carry out the project. The favorable outcomes of those projects often are extremely high, though such outcomes are not highly likely. Specifically, a project may involve a maximum potential loss of $10,000 but offer potential profits as high as $200,000 with an average return of, say, $45,000. So, one quite important class of projects has distributions of outcomes with long "tails" in the positive direction—which violates the assumption of symmetry. In short, no evidence shows that the distributions of outcomes for most projects are symmetrical. For that reason, the standard deviation fails as an accurate measure of risk. Risk must be measured solely with reference to what the individual decision maker regards as unfavorable outcomes. Recognize that favorable outcomes enter into the computation of expected values and are weighted in the same manner as unfavorable outcomes.

This trade-off between risk and yield is depicted visually in Figure 6-1. Line A shows a project with very variable outcomes; Line B shows one that has a very narrow range of possible outcomes. Both have the same expected value. In Figure 6-2, Line C shows a project whose expected value and variance are higher than those of the other project, Line D. The trade-off issue deals with the question, "How much of expected value should we give up to get how much of a narrower range of outcomes?" In Figure 6-1, A clearly is more risky than B; given the same expected value for both, B would be preferred by most decision makers. No trade-off is involved in this decision. The choice depicted in Figure 6-2 offers the

Figure 6-1. Equal return but unequal risk.

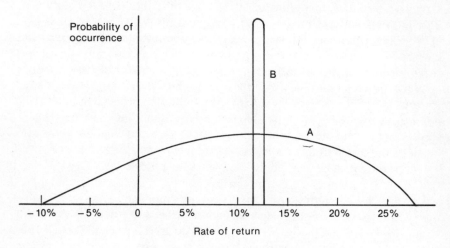

Figure 6-2. High risk, high return vs. lower yield, smaller risk.

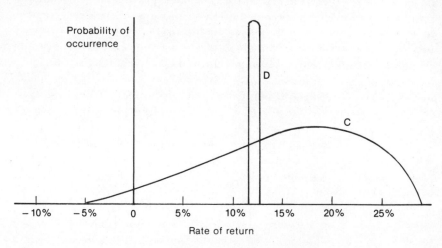

decision maker the option of taking a substantial risk of unfavorable outcomes to get an attractive expected value or of settling for a modest rate of return where the most unfavorable outcome is "not bad." Here the executive must ask how much yield he is willing to give up for safety—the trade-off question.

Why is there usually a trade-off between risk and yield? The reason is that most people dislike uncertainty and must be rewarded if they are to assume it. Although that proposition is valid as a general rule, some persons welcome risk rather than try to avert it. Consequently, it is impossible to devise a general measure of risk that represents the views of all decision makers.

Let us then return to the question of how we can measure the riskiness of projects and develop trade-offs (which really represent a rate of exchange between risk and yield) for individual executives. We have agreed that risk denotes the unfavorable potential outcomes of a project. Our starting point might then be an enumeration of outcomes that most executives would consider unfavorable. Certainly, one would find differences among individuals, but the following outcomes deserve considerations:

- The most unfavorable outcome with a probability of, say, 1 in 100 or even 1 in 50. We can call this the "worst that can happen." Even worse things could occur, but are exceedingly unlikely.
- The probability of a loss as great as, say, X dollars, where X equals a sum that would create dismay among top management.
- The probability of some loss.
- The probability of an outcome below the "cut-off rate of return"—the minimum rate acceptable to top management.
- The probability of an outcome below the rate of return that was forecast for this particular project.

These potential outcomes would not be equally significant to decision makers and should not be given equal weight in their measure of risk. As we can now recognize, the impact of unfavorable outcomes usually increases disproportionately with their size and should receive greater weight in the decision maker's calculations. For most people, it is the large negative outcomes that represent risk—those near the top of the list given.

Using the list above as a guide, a decision maker could construct an index of risk in order to compare the riskiness of projects. The index would be computed on the basis of the particular outcomes he wishes to take into account; they might include all five in the list, plus others, or they might include only one or two. Once he has constructed a procedure for measuring risk, he could then establish a trade-off between expected value and risk as measured by his particular index. In that way, he could make selections among projects on a systematic and explicit basis.

In summary, we conclude that risk varies from person to person. Each executive must define it for himself—and presumably it would vary over time. As defined here, risk refers only to unfavorable outcomes. (Favorable ones are taken into account in measuring expected value.) Measures of variance measure risk only if the projects being compared have identically shaped distributions of outcomes (they need not all be "normal" distributions). To trade off risk against expected value, one must measure risk in a prescribed manner and decide how many points of risk one will accept to gain an extra percent of expected value.

MEASURING THE WORTH OF A PROBABILITY DISTRIBUTION AT ANY POINT IN TIME

One way to approach decisions which have uncertain outcomes is to evaluate their worth directly. Let us start with simple examples and work our way toward more complex cases. What is the worth of a distribution of outcomes involving the tossing of a coin? That is, how much would an individual be willing to pay to participate in the gamble? That distribution has two outcomes: victory and loss. We will assume that victory means getting $1 and loss means getting nothing. What would a rational person pay to play that game—once?

On intuitive grounds, we see the worth is about $.50. If the individual is a risk averter, the amount will be slightly less than $.50. On the other hand, if he is a risk seeker, the worth of the gamble will be a bit more than $.50. In either case, the amount willingly paid would be quite close to $.50.

Let us now take a similar gamble which also has only two outcomes: a gain of $10,000 and a zero outcome. What would a rational person pay for the right to play that game?

Many people would not want to play a game that could inflict serious financial wounds, although they might also make a major "killing" if it turned out to be successful. They would not see a $10,000 gain as offsetting to a $10,000 loss, if both were equally likely. If we applied the logic of the coin toss with payoffs of $1 or zero, at first glance it appears this gamble would be worth $5,000. This is not the case. Few individuals would be willing to pay that much in order to play. (Some would be happy to do so, usually those of large financial means and those who enjoy taking risks.) The reason that few persons would be willing to pay $5,000 to play this game is that the pain of losing a substantial amount of income is far greater to most people than the pleasure from winning an equal amount of income. To win $10,000 gives pleasure, indeed, but not enough to offset the pain of a loss of an equal amount. The economic principle that explains this phenomenon is the principle of diminishing marginal utility (discussed in Chapter 3), which holds that the utility (satisfaction, value, worth) of added income declines as we have larger amounts of income. If our income is, say, $8,000 per annum, another $1,000 of income would add greatly to our total satisfaction. If our income were, say, $50,000 per annum, another $1,000 of income would add far less to our total satisfaction—though it would have some worth.

This notion of worth is what economists describe as utility—the want-satisfying ability of money and other things. Now, we wish to ascertain the worth to us of a probability distribution with many outcomes, some positive and others negative. We now recognize that we must be concerned with more than money outcomes. We must translate outcomes expressed in monetary terms into outcomes expressed in units of utility or worth. So, we must establish a table which indicates how many dollars equal how many "utils."* This table would be different for each individual and furthermore vary over time.

Let us start with some base. We might agree that an outcome from an investment that yielded $100 was worth 50 utils; we then ask, what would be the worth of an outcome of $500, $5,000, $50,000? And what would be the worth of losses of $100, $500, $5,000, $50,000? For most people, the higher the outcome—say the $50,000 outcome—the greater the ratio of dollars to utils. We started with a ratio of 2 dollars to 1 util; with a $50,000 outcome, the ratio might become 5 to 1—making a $50,000 outcome worth 10,000 utils. When we examine the losses, we would expect the ratio of dollars to utils to fall sharply. For example, at a loss of $100, the ratio might become 1 to 1. A loss of $50,000 might shift the ratio of dollars to utils sharply so that each dollar of loss is worth 20 negative utils. In other words, a loss of $50,000 would have a worth of one million negative utils. Figure 6-3 describes the relationship between money and utility when dealing with outcomes of different size.

What the foregoing discussion implies, then, is that in valuing a probability distribution—which is expressed in money—a decision maker should translate the individual outcomes into utils; these can then be totaled. At that point, he can value in dollars the total net utils represented by the probability distribution—for executives invest dollars, not utils.

The steps in valuing a probability distribution of decision outcomes—termed a utility analysis—are as follows: (1) Establish for the decision maker the relationship between dollars and utils; (2) translate the probability distribution of dollar outcomes into a total of utils, by multiplying the number of utils for each outcome by the probability of each outcome; (3) total the figures obtained in step 2, and (4) determine the dollar value of

---

* This procedure is analogous to adjusting a temperature reading for the windchill factor. The adjusted figure expresses how the air really feels.

Figure 6-3. Diminishing marginal utility of money.

that number of utils from the relationship between dollars and utils established in step 1. The simple example in Table 6-2 will clarify these calculations, which are less complicated than they seem.

The worth of 3,900 utils can be determined approximately from the table, which indicates that an outcome of $10,000 is equal to 4,000 utils. Accordingly, an expected outcome of 3,900 utils is worth close to, but below, $10,000.

A few propositions can be stated about the relationship between dollars and utils that might be helpful:

- If the sums involved are small, the ratio between utils and dollars for any individual will not change much over an entire probability distribution and there is little point in making a utility analysis under such circumstances. If a large organization is involved, the sums can be large and the ratio between utils and dollars will not change much—and a utility analysis will not lead to different results from those obtained by dealing solely in dollars.
- The relationship between utils and dollars partly reflects the decision maker's appetite for or aversion to risk; this can vary widely among

individuals. Also, it can vary substantially for the same person over time.

- The task of preparing a statement of equivalencies is formidable; ordinarily an executive requires help from specialists to prepare such a statement.
- Some questions can be raised about the validity of expressing outcomes in equivalent utils without also taking account of the probability of that outcome. In other words, neither outcomes nor probabilities may be independent factors, especially when one is dealing with extreme outcomes.

The discussion of utility analysis has been technical and complicated, especially for those to whom these issues are new. These difficult subjects have been introduced here because executives must be familiar with the concepts and procedures discussed, since they take positions on these issues often without recognizing the implications of their choices.

The concept of utility has been discarded by the younger generation of economists largely because it cannot be measured accurately, but because of other difficulties as well.* However, the fundamental issue discussed here, about which economists agree completely, namely the nonproportionality of money outcomes and worth to or impact on the decision maker, can be formulated without employing the utility concept. To do so, however, is far more cumbersome and less illuminating to most people than the exposition adopted here. Indeed, almost all current writers on uncertainty

Table 6-2

DETERMINATION OF THE WORTH OF A PROJECT VIA UTILITY ANALYSIS

Outcomes	Probability	Outcome expressed in utils	Utils times probability	Ratio of $ to utils
$50,000	.1	10,000	1,000	5 to 1
$25,000	.4	7,000	2,800	3.6 to 1
$10,000	.3	4,000	1,000	2.5 to 1
0	.1	−1,000	−100	—
$55,000	.1	−10,000	−1,000	−.5 to 1
			3,900 utils	

* For a criticism of the utility concept and a clear presentation of the arguments in favor of reformulating the theory of choice to avoid its use, see Vivian C. Walsh, *Introduction to Contemporary Microeconomics* (New York: McGraw-Hill, 1970).

in economic decisions have leaned heavily on the principle of diminishing utility.

The plain fact must be faced that, with minor exceptions, the worth of everything declines beyond some point—and often very sharply—the more one has of it at any time. That fact explains why executives must not base certain of their decisions solely on expected money outcomes.

Table 6-3 classifies executive decisions for the purpose of determining whether or not to make a utility analysis. Observe that the decisions which warrant such an analysis involve both large sums and a large amount of negative variance—that is, they pose the possibility of a wide range of unfavorable outcomes.

Executives obviously cannot carry out elaborate risk analyses for all their decisions. What is more, they should not, even though almost all business decisions involve considerable uncertainty. Risk analysis is costly and time consuming and should be made only when the expected benefit exceeds the estimated cost. Surely one would not make a risk analysis for a decision involving a selection among alternative suppliers of typewriter ribbons. Still, one probably should make a very careful risk analysis of a choice among three drugs which cost no more than typewriter ribbons. The importance of decisions is not determinable simply from the sums involved. Rather, their importance reflects their potential outcomes, including nonmonetary effects, and especially their negative variance (see Table 6-3).

To discuss risk analysis in greater detail, let us examine the procedure that a decision maker trained in risk analysis would use in choosing among

Table 6-3

CLASSIFICATION OF DECISIONS FOR PURPOSE OF DECIDING WHETHER TO MAKE A UTILITY ANALYSIS

Sums involved	Amount of negative variance		
	Great	*Moderate*	*Tiny*
Very large	Give the "full treatment"	Utility analysis may be justified	Expected value, median, or modal value sufficient
Medium	Utility analysis likely to be justified	Utility analysis may be justified	Expected value, median, or modal value sufficient
Small	No special treatment required	No special treatment required	No special treatment required

alternatives involving precious and devastating outcomes. This is the so-called full treatment that a project could receive, for an executive should know everything he might do if it were imperative that he do the best possible. Following are the steps involved in giving projects the full treatment for uncertainty.

1. Develop the different potential outcomes of each project under consideration and their probabilities in a probability distribution.

• Make a separate distribution for each relevant time period—ordinarily a year—and for each ultimate objective.

• State the potential outcomes in terms of the highest-level objectives under the decision maker's control. Preferably, they would represent the firm's ultimate objectives.

• Select the leverage factors upon which the probability distribution will rest. Pick the level at which outcomes can be estimated with greatest validity.

2. For each probability distribution of ultimate outcomes, develop a utility analysis. Recognize that the firm's ability to tolerate loss will change over time, so that the translations of money outcomes into utils might be different in different years. Recognize also that in trading off money and utils, the firm is conducting a whole portfolio of activities with which the one in question would be combined; do not treat the separate projects in isolation. The result of this complicated set of processes would be a single figure representing the dollar equivalent of the utils to be obtained from the project.

3. Adjust each such figure for the pure rate of interest to translate it into its present value. In this way, take account of what is given up by receiving money in the future rather than in the present.

4. To this figure, which has already been adjusted for risk in step 2, apply a risk premium to take account of the risk of the decision maker's death before receiving the rewards of the investment and to cover the contingencies of errors in forecasting his personal needs, in predicting the future environment, and so forth—all of which are hazards that arise in placing a value on future income. The pure rate of interest does not place a value on these considerations.

TREATMENT OF RELATIVELY UNIMPORTANT BUT RISKY DECISIONS

Most of the decisions made by business executives represent relatively minor choices among alternatives which involve considerable uncertainty. How should they handle such decisions?

To help an executive decide what to do about uncertainty, we can classify business decisions according to three major characteristics: the scale and scope of the decision—by which we mean the dollars at risk, the level in the organization at which the decision is made, and the range of potential outcomes of the decision. Table 6-4 indicates the classification system that emerges from the combination of these characteristics. A fourth characteristic, whether or not the decision is purely financial, will be included by confining our discussion to nonfinancial decisions. Financial decisions are defined here as those involving the selection of listed securities for a portfolio as distinct from a business activity like an advertising promotion, or the addition or dropping of a new item in the product line.

Before discussing the treatment of relatively unimportant decisions that embody substantial uncertainty, we should remind ourselves that this chapter deals only with one aspect of decisions—the fact that their outcomes are unpredictable. We will therefore consider relatively simple decisions lest we be overwhelmed by combining the complexity of risk analysis with a complex decision.

We should recognize at the outset that decisions low down in an organization and of a small scale (cell 6 in Table 6-4) often pose serious hazards. For example, defective minor supply items or small components that fail can ruin a run of costly product or can close down a production line; defective dyes can ruin thousands of yards of expensive carpeting. Similarly, the hiring of an employee who is emotionally disturbed, dishonest, or otherwise disruptive can demoralize an organization and cause prized employees to leave. Consequently, considerable danger of damaging outcomes must be reckoned with at almost all levels of an organization. How

Table 6-4

A Classification of Nonfinancial Decisions for Purposes of Risk Analysis

	Large scale		Medium scale		Small scale	
	High in organization	Low in organization	High in organization	Low in organization	High in organization	Low in organization
Outcomes over broad range	1)	4)	7)	10)	13)	16)
Outcomes over modest range	2)	5)	8)	11)	14)	17)
Outcomes over narrow range	3)	6)	9)	12)	15)	18)

NOTE: This table is similar to Table 6-3, but it differs in that it distinguishes decisions made near the top of the organization from those made well below the top.

can top management arrange that persons low in the organizational hierarchy deal with the uncertainty element of their decisions—recognizing that they are not likely to be familiar with risk analysis or the equivalent?

Surely the answer is that top management must decide which decisions made at low levels in the organization involve substantial risk. That step is the starting point. Then, top management must decide how the different kinds of risky decisions can best be made by persons unschooled in risk analysis. Top management has the following options:

- It could establish procedures which lend support to the employee and which give top management some review and check on the decision. For example, it could prescribe that all new hirings must be processed by the personnel department, which would give applicants tests and check references carefully.
- It could require that whole classes of decisions—such as dismissals of employees, or refusal to accept delivery of supplies that appear defective—be checked with the legal department.
- It could require that certain decisions be referred to superiors.
- It could set down operating rules which represent top management's own solutions to certain issues. For example, it could require that inventories of a given size be maintained, and that only suppliers that meet certain tests for reliability be used as major sources of supply, and the like.

In all these instances, the risk element of a decision will have been decided by someone relatively high in the organization or at least specialized in handling risk-laden situations. To achieve this result, top management must identify such decisions and prescribe procedures by which they are to be made.

What is lacking from the procedures listed above is that the actual decision maker does not contribute all that he might to the decision. Very possibly that person knows a good deal that others cannot know and it might improve the decision to involve the decision maker—at least to the extent of asking him to identify the extreme outcomes. Such involvement of the decision maker would moreover have independent benefits: it would presumably lead the decision maker to monitor events and thus perceive signs of trouble earlier than otherwise; and it would help him understand why certain decisions require the involvement of others.

What else can top management do to insure that subordinates handle risk in the optimum manner? Beyond what has been said, top management could require executives to do the following:

- Provide information or estimates of the different outcomes that enter into the firm's risk index, discussed earlier.
- Identify the factors that could cause the unfortunate outcomes to come about.
- Establish monitoring arrangements, so that an adverse outcome is discovered at the earliest possible time, thus minimizing loss.
- Indicate actions that might be taken to limit the damage of the unfortunate outcomes.

We will not discuss the other types of decisions identified in Table 6-4. Although we have dealt with only one type and a relatively extreme type, we have raised the more central issue that executives face in handling risk in their day-to-day decisions.

Potential Protective Actions Where High Risks Are Assumed

Let us now deal with the very frequent situation in which an executive has made a decision that involves high risk; he recognizes the adverse outcomes that might ensue and their likelihood—and even knows what factors will determine whether those outcomes will come to pass. What might he do to minimize the injury of an unfortunate outcome? First, he should search out possible actions that would reduce the loss due to the unfortunate outcome, should it occur. One clear example of this approach is to take insurance against the adverse outcome; another is to engage in "hedging."* Unfortunately, these options usually are not available. Other approaches to minimizing injury caused by unfortunate outcomes depend upon the nature of the hazard faced. For example, if the hazard is that a new item that the firm is introducing may not sell as expected, the firm might make arrangements in advance to dispose of surpluses in distant markets, perhaps abroad, and be ready to move quickly should domestic sales of the item be very low.

In addition to identifying the circumstances that would bring about the adverse outcome, and establishing monitoring arrangements, management should establish *in advance* what we call trigger points, which would indicate when the action is to be considered a mistake that must be corrected as quickly as possible. If, for example, the disaster feared is that competitors will take a particular counter action to its price move, then just as soon as, say, three customers report that competitors have taken that action, the firm would consider its decision a mistake and take all preplanned correc-

---

* For a brief discussion of hedging as a method of reducing risk, see W. W. Haynes, *Managerial Economics: Analysis and Cases*, rev. ed. (Dallas, Tex.: Business Publications, Inc., 1969), pp. 543–544.

tive measures. If the misfortune feared were very low dealer acceptance of a product, then management might indicate the specific sales levels that must be achieved during successive intervals for the program to be continued.

Although decisions that have unfortunate outcomes cannot be completely avoided, their impact can be minimized by facing them frontally. It is not enough to hope that they will not come to pass. When faced directly, misfortunes can be uncovered in their incipiency and ameliorated before they do even greater damage.

For its part, top management should set down its own requirements for projects. These requirements should include the following: the minimum acceptable rate of return—the cut-off rate of return; the maximum risk it is willing to take of a specified loss—of say, $100,000 for example; the maximum risk (that is, the probability) of any loss at all of the project. With such guides clearly specified and explained, projects would not be presented to top management that otherwise now consume considerable attention.

The Need for a Decision Rule

A decision rule is a prescribed procedure for making choices. It is established before the analysis is undertaken and is to be followed whatever the outcome. Unless committed in advance to a rule, decision makers may ignore the results of their analysis and rely on hunch. Experience shows that the temptation can be very strong to rely on one's intuitions in many specific cases. Decision rules force decision makers to adopt an objective and well-informed procedure that will protect them against impulse and emotion.

What decision makers need mainly is a valid procedure for placing a value on a probability distribution so that they will be able to rank alternatives and know the maximum they should pay for them. Several important propositions have already been developed on that subject that can be summarized as follows:

If the sums involved are small, and no serious damage can result from the decision, then the worth of a probability distribution may be taken to be its expected value—the outcomes weighted by their probabilities. This rule is based upon research in which trials were made from distributions that were known—balls drawn from an urn. Under these controlled experimental conditions, the best approximation to the results of the drawings was the weighted average.

Where large sums are involved and the probability of severe damage or actual ruin is significantly large, then a decision maker must apply utility analysis. Such analysis requires the use of "translators" or "equivalencies" between dollar outcomes and utils. These equivalencies incorporate—but in no explicit manner—a trade-off between yield and risk. How risk is handled in the process of utility analysis is extremely difficult to articulate, but it is a valid process.

Each important decision is unique. The decision maker consequently cannot be considered to be making the same kind of decision over and over—like a person betting on the proportion of red and black balls picked from an urn in many trials. An executive therefore cannot assume that the law of large numbers operates. The decision maker must be considered analogous to someone drawing balls from many urns, each with unknown and different proportions of balls of varied colors. What decision rule, if any, is appropriate for such a situation?

The issue is exceedingly complex and specialists do not agree. However, it appears that a decision maker should apply some rule, rather than make ad hoc decisions. *If he varies his rule, it should be before rather than after he makes his analysis.*

Obtaining and Using Intuitive Information

Decision making under uncertainty requires extensive use of subjective, or intuitive, information, such as the identification of outcomes and the assignment of numerical probabilities to alternative outcomes and forecasts; this information is developed usually in the absence of significant quantitative data. Accordingly, this final section of the chapter explores methods of extracting such information from oneself, and from others. What we refer to here as information is based on undistilled material in the unconscious memory of individuals; usually it appears to the possessor of the information as a general impression.

Executives ordinarily know a great deal about the phenomena they manage, but they may have very little detailed numerical or systematic information about them. The information they do possess, even though undistilled and nonnumerical, represents an invaluable potential resource for decision makers, especially when the gap in their formal information requirements is great. Practice and skill are required to make good use of this valuable resource.

Before discussing the procedures for uncovering such unconventional information, let us be clear about what that information may be. We are not referring to information which executives possess and do not wish to disclose. Rather, we are concerned with obtaining from informed individuals some information that they do not realize they possess. Usually, they will be cooperative enough but have little confidence in their impressions; at least, they don't want to be blamed or criticized if they turn out to be mistaken. Sometimes an unexpectedly large body of quite reliable information can be extracted from an executive; occasionally, one obtains a set of very strong convictions. On the other hand, sometimes very little can be obtained, even though the person has had extensive experience that would ordinarily produce considerable information and strong impressions.

In almost no case will executives already possess in their subconscious memory *all* the information they require to make the decisions they face. Almost always, they must make an effort to gather additional information for any significant decision at hand. Even then, after making special data gathering efforts, it is rare indeed for executives to possess such complete and formal information that they have no need for intuitive judgments. Invariably, they face a gap between what they know and what they need to know. They must fill this gap with subconscious information, with guesswork, with logical reasoning, or with a combination of all these means.

In the following discussion, it is suggested that when executives possess extensive relevant experience, their intuitive forecasts, assignments of probabilities, and judgments—if arrived at in a careful, systematic manner—may be more valid than elaborate statistical analyses and costly market research studies. Virtually every quantitative study will incorporate several arbitrary assumptions, intuitive judgments, and logical jumps. Accordingly, let us now examine how one might gather subjective information and guard against distortions that might destroy its validity.

MEANS OF OBTAINING INTUITIVE INFORMATION

What measures might executives employ to plumb their own minds and to extract the intuitive views of others? How might they employ specialists to help with this task? In our discussion, we will first discuss means of obtaining as much intuitive material as one can and then turn to methods of avoiding the distortions that often afflict intuitive judgments.

Assume that an experienced executive is making a vital business decision and is prepared to devote considerable time and financial resources to that decision. He finds that he cannot obtain the factual data he requires to forecast the tangible and intangible outcomes of the strategies he is trying to evaluate. Therefore, he seeks to dredge up whatever useful information he can from his own unconscious and to obtain similar material from those colleagues whose views he values highly on the problem at hand.

Extracting intuitive materials from oneself. Some people can learn a good bit about their unconsciously held views by talking to themselves. This method of plumbing one's unconscious improves with practice—and usually requires a place where one can be alone. Other people find that they can get their best insight into their unconscious views by discussing the subject with someone with whom they feel completely secure, like one's dearest friend, one's mate, or a business associate. As long as the mental "censors" are removed, many people apparently can stimulate a flow of judgments to their consciousness; occasionally, they can get at the basis for those judgments as well. Talking to oneself and talking things out with others are not mutually exclusive; both deserve a try when one faces major decisions. Better said, they are worth several attempts on different occasions; one cannot always get this process started; and one is much more productive at uncovering unconscious materials at certain times than at other times.

One can extract intuitive materials from oneself in a more straightforward manner, by putting down in writing the questions to which one seeks answers. These might be individual forecasts or assumptions about present conditions—like what consumers are now doing or seeking, or the condition in which the executive's rivals find themselves. Also, the executive should list the ideas and concepts that are troubling him—for example, should certain items be included or excluded from costs for this particular decision? or, Should orders on one's books for a present model that would be withdrawn when a new model is introduced be counted as a cost of the new model? In any systematic and explicit approach to decision—which is clearly required if the decision is major—a decision maker should identify what he needs to know to reach a conclusion that will attain the level of accuracy he seeks.

Having once listed such questions and issues, the decision maker restates them with some precision and clarity, allowing space alongside each item to record his views. More specifically, he follows each question with three columns; in one he sets down his view of the most probable result—what he considers the best or most likely answer. In the other columns, he indicates the highest and lowest outcome with a probability of 10 percent. He further indicates whether he believes the distribution of outcomes to be skewed or highly centered around the midpoint, mono-modal or bi-modal. (These questions would be asked—and answered—only by executives who were trained to think in terms of underlying distributions of data.)

In response to this set of questions, the decision maker sets down his views and seals this set of answers in an envelope. Some time later, perhaps in several days, he again sets down his thoughts on each of these questions, using the original questions now arranged in a different order. When he has done this, he compares his two sets of answers, identifying the questions to which he has given quite different responses. He then constructs a new schedule using only these questions. After a day or so, he makes another set of estimates. He continues this process until he has reached conclusions which he feels reflect his best thinking.

Thus, by talking aloud to himself, or talking to a good listener, and by setting down his questions and answers at different times, a business executive can hope to uncover his intuitive judgments. The more he does these things, the more he will usually make explicit the reasoning underlying his judgments. In this process, he may arrive at some hypotheses that could be tested, or at least compared with the impressions held by others. In the absence of other and better data, the executive must rely on such answers as he obtains from this process; after all, they represent his best thinking. But an executive rarely must rely solely on his own thoughts.

Extracting intuitive materials from others. As suggested, a decision maker could send to others a copy of the questions he has asked himself. From whom should he try to obtain information, and how might he obtain the most complete, candid answers to his questions?

Identifying those whose views should be solicited generally is not difficult. The decision maker should search his list of acquaintances for individuals whose views on the questions and issues he has raised would influence his own decision. That is, he should limit the list to individuals who are particularly well informed on those issues and whose views he respects. (He might send different questions to each individual, according to his view of the particular competences of each.)

No wholly satisfactory method exists for insuring complete, candid responses, but some guides may help. First, the decision maker must make certain that all questions will be clearly understood by all parties; if questions are vague, it is likely that respondents will provide answers that seemingly are to different questions. Second, he should insure that it is possible to give short answers to the question; most executives' time is valuable so that brevity becomes a special virtue. And third, the decision maker should insure anonymity with respect to everyone but himself. The answers to some questions may call for very controversial material; consequently, anonymity may help reduce executive inhibition.

These limited guides can be helpful, but many questions must be answered before the decision maker can be confident that he is tapping a large percentage of the intuitive information available from others. For example, does one use the same methods to obtain information from superiors as from subordinates? Does one do the same with insiders as with individuals from outside the firm? Below are other questions that are germane to obtaining subjective information from others.

- Under what circumstances should one attempt to obtain intuitive material from executives in person? Does the "mood" of the respondent affect his answers very much? If so, what kind of mood would one want them to be in when they are interviewed? Should one interview them in the office, over lunch, or at the club?
- If one solicits information under the promise of anonymity, how could one make such a promise believable? Should one ask an individual to put his views on the record?
- Should one give others an opportunity to revise their responses? If so, how many opportunities should they be given?
- When should one obtain information in person and when in writing?
- Should one obtain only "answers" or should one request reasons for the answers?
- To what extent and when should one try to stimulate their thoughts by giving them information about or reminders of similar situations, by providing relevant background and the like?
- Should one give them advance notice of the issues that you will question them about (whether in person or on paper does not matter), or should one question them without prior notice?
- What incentives should one offer to obtain cooperation from colleagues? From individuals outside the firm?

Obtaining Intuitive Materials That Are Free from Major Distortion

In the process of obtaining intuitive information from himself and from others, the executive must take measures to insure that it is of high quality. The next section discusses the factors that distort intuitive information as well as some methods of counteracting them.

Avoiding distortion of information obtained from oneself. It is impossible for an executive to recognize all the influences that may bias and distort his intuitive judgments. Two common sources of distortion deserve special mention, however. First, most people suffer from a strong tendency to overvalue recent experience. Recent events apparently receive undue weight simply because they are more prominent in our memories. As a result, executives tend to generalize mainly on the basis of recent experience and tend to underutilize more appropriate data stored from earlier experiences.

The second common source of bias is the tendency to overvalue the unusual and unique. This source, like the first, occurs mainly because the mind retains and retrieves only a limited amount of the total information accumulated from life's experiences; those incidents which are unusual, unique, and possibly exciting will be remembered more vividly and drawn upon far more than more routine experiences.

Two means of minimizing distortion are available to an executive. First, a checklist of sources of bias would enable a decision maker to evaluate his intuitive judgments in a particular case and reflect on whether or not a specific bias might be operating. For example, he can ask himself if recent experiences have unduly influenced his judgment. And, if so, he might reach back in his memory for other, less prominent experiences. Once he does this, he might want to modify his intuitive judgment.

The second major tool is the schedule of key questions referred to in an earlier section as a means of generating information about a problem. By constructing a series of questions that must be answered and then reanswering those questions more than once, an executive may avoid many sources of bias. It is to be expected that each time the decision maker reflects on a question he will recall additional experiences that bear on the problem at hand. Thus, the process that will generate a large quantity of information would appear to incorporate measures for protecting the quality of the data obtained.

Avoiding distortion of information obtained from others. When a person is asked to express his judgment on some issue, he may make a response that does not truly reflect his views. The kinds of distortions that take place vary widely with the circumstances under which such views are solicited, but several operate in most cases. They include:

- The tendency to tell people what they want to hear.
- The inclination to say things that seem smart and attract attention.
- The tendency to say what is safe and noncontroversial.
- The tendency to say what one believes is the "party line."
- The tendency to have one's judgment unduly influenced by something that happened in the recent past, or by some event that was dramatic but unrepresentative.
- The tendency to be intimidated by the views expressed by other persons who hold high positions.
- The tendency to be persuaded by persons who are strong communicators, but whose arguments may be badly flawed.

There is no one method or group of methods to insure that all these possible distortions can be avoided. There is a method of collecting intuitive data, however, which can help the decision maker to avoid some types of distortion that occur when collecting information from others. It is a method developed by "futurists."

Some of the most relevant thinking about the collection of intuitive material has been done by futurists—individuals who are deeply involved in making very long-range forecasts. Many futurists find that statistical techniques are unreliable for their purposes and have settled upon the collection of intuitive judgments as the best basis for most long-range forecasts. Out of that body of thought has emerged an approach to long-range forecasting termed the Delphi method, which mainly reflects the thinking of Ulaf Hellmer and Norman Dalkey. These men have been deeply impressed by the vulnerability of intuitive judgments to distortion and therefore reject the results of direct interpersonal discussion—committee, conference, task force, and the like. They have developed procedures which have received fairly extensive testing in recent years. These are outlined briefly below.

An individual or small group is assigned the task of conducting a Delphi study of a particular subject. Its first task is to identify and solicit the cooperation of individuals whose views on the subject would be most valuable. They then design and execute a questionnaire study consisting of the following steps:

Step 1: The first round of questionnaires is mailed to respondents, who are asked to submit answers to questions without elaboration or defense.

Step 2: The questionnaires having been summarized, the results are reported to the respondents. They are given an opportunity to revise their estimates; in addition, they are invited to comment on the results as reported. In particular, they are asked to express any opinions that would indicate why the highest and lowest estimates are implausible.

Step 3: These responses are summarized (not at all a simple mechanical task) and both the changed estimates and the opinions expressed are reported back to the respondents. They are asked to comment on the revised estimates and the opinions expressed. Also, they are offered an opportunity to revise their own estimates.

Step 4: Respondents are given a summary of the materials received in step 3 and asked to revise their estimates, if they so desire. Although further comment is not actively solicited, it is permitted.

The logic of this approach is clear: its purpose is to permit the kinds of interaction and stimulation that occur when individuals get together in person without allowing any individual to influence the others unduly. Although the method described will not overcome all the distortions of intuitive materials that were listed, it does represent a powerful attack on the most important of them. Experience with its use has been very reassuring, but still not by any means conclusive.

USING SPECIALISTS TO OBTAIN INTUITIVE INFORMATION

We know relatively little about the way that human intuition (the unconscious) operates; we know even less about how best to make the contents of the unconscious explicit so that it might serve as an input to conscious and explicit decision making. For that reason, specialists should be assigned the responsibility for collecting intuitive materials when they are needed. This section merely sketches some procedures that such individuals might employ and the qualifications that should be sought.

It will be assumed that the specialists assigned to collecting intuitive material would receive the full support of top management and that executives would know their functions and be given reason to respect their competence. These assumptions might not easily be met. Indeed, the notion that intuitive information can be collected by systematic procedures and is equivalent to and often preferable to the usual type of numerical evidence is not readily acceptable in many companies. Most executives hope that they will obtain reliable, "factual" information about the future when they often cannot describe or explain many things even on the basis of hindsight. Acceptance of the arrangements to be described requires that executives understand the futility of searching for reliable statistical methods to forecast phenomena which are not amenable to such techniques. Similarly, top management must demonstrate its respect for information based upon intuitive judgments of subordinates that are collected in the manner to be described.

Three main techniques are available to a staff specializing in collecting intuitive judgments for business decision: personal interview, questionnaire studies, and group discussion. Each of these can be conducted in a variety of ways. The specialists should be flexible enough to recognize the need for varied techniques and to come to know which techniques are best suited to the specific situations that arise.

In time, specialists presumably accumulate a list of persons whose views should be solicited on particular issues; they will know how best to motivate and reward them, and whether to obtain their views in writing, in personal interviews, or from group discussion. They have developed skills in formulating questions, summarizing responses, and securing participation, and they can even accumulate a track record on the individuals they use repeatedly as sources. Moreover, those individuals will in all probability become more facile in participating in such intuitive-data collection efforts and be able to provide large amounts of undistorted intuitive material.

An illustration. Assume that an executive has been trying to forecast the effect of assigning an additional regional salesman to a particular market for a three-month period both to stem the tide of lost sales and to obtain information about what is going wrong in that market. The executive's problem is to determine the most likely effects, both negative and positive, of this action. Recognizing the great difficulty of estimating the effect of adding a salesman to a territory, the executive decides to obtain the views of some colleagues who have had far more experience with this kind of situation than he. Accordingly, he has sent them the following communication:

> As you may know, we've been experiencing disappointing sales in Milwaukee for some time; frankly, we're not sure why sales have been so poor, but are assuming that our distributor is not devoting nearly as much time to the business as usual. Accordingly, we're considering assigning one of our experienced regional salesmen (probably Henry Stern) to work in the Milwaukee market for a few months mainly calling on our present retail accounts and working with the distributor's salesmen. He'll also try to open some new accounts if time permits.
>
> You are an old hand at such matters and know much more about the effects of putting an extra man in a market than I do. I'd therefore appreciate your help in making this decision. Would you therefore please answer the following questions to the best of your ability?
>
> You will not be quoted and only I will know your answers. I am soliciting answers from some other people and my report will only refer to the views of the group as a whole. Please be relaxed about this request. Just set down your best thoughts. If you want to explain or qualify your response, don't hesitate to do so.
>
> May I please hear from you within three days?
>
> I greatly appreciate your cooperation and would be pleased to reciprocate any time.

> Cordially,

QUESTIONNAIRE

The following questions seek your estimate of the effect of assigning an experienced salesman to the Milwaukee market for three months.

1. How do you think the contemplated action would affect the attitudes of members of the distributor's organization?
   Favorably _____   Unfavorably _____   Little, if at all _____

If you expect either a favorable or an unfavorable effect, please indicate the size of that expected effect.

Large _____   Moderate _____   Small _____

2. How do you expect the assignment of an extra regional salesman to the Milwaukee market would affect the attitudes of retailers carrying our line in that market?

Improve _____   Worsen _____   No effect _____

If you expect either improvement or worsening, please indicate the size of the expected effect.

Large _____   Moderate _____   Small _____

3. How would the assignment of a salesman affect the amount of sales support our line receives from retailers carrying the line?

Much more _____   More _____   Same _____

Less _____   Much less _____

4. Would this assignment of a regional salesman enable us to increase the number of retailers carrying our line? Reduce? Leave it unaffected?

Increase _____   Reduce _____   No effect _____

5. How do you think our sales in Milwaukee will be affected by the contemplated action? Compare them with what you believe they would be if no extra salesman were added. Please estimate the effect on sales separately for three months after the salesman begins to work in the territory and for six months after.

Effect of added salesman on retail sales of our Milwaukee market

In three months (per month)	*In six months* (per month)
Most likely change _____% up	Most likely change _____% up
_____% down	_____% down
Worst outcome (10% chance of that outcome or something worse)	Worst outcome (10% chance of that outcome or something worse)
_____% up	_____% up
_____% down	_____% down
Best outcome (10% chance of that outcome or something better)	Best outcome (10% chance of that outcome or something better)
_____% up	_____% up
_____% down	_____% down

6. Would you expect the regional salesman to have a stronger favorable effect on large or on small retailers?

On large retailers _____   On small retailers _____

Would you please volunteer your reasons: _____

_____

_____

7. Do you believe that this regional salesman will be able to uncover the chief cause of our sales difficulty in Milwaukee?

Yes _____   No _____   No opinion _____

Our executive received seven responses to the foregoing questionnaire; everyone to whom it was addressed responded, and in addition he had his own two responses. The first thing he did was to discard his first set of responses. He requested his assistant to summarize the results, and these are shown below.

Question

#1   Favorably, 6;   Unfavorably, 0;   Little if at all, 2;
      Large, 4;   Moderate, 1;   Small, 1

#2   Improve, 7;   Worsen, 0;   No effect, 1;
      Large, 4;   Moderate, 3

#3   Much more, 3;   More, 3;   Same, 1;   Less, 1

#4   Increase, 5;   Reduce, 0;   No effect, 2;   No answer, 1

#5   *In three months*   (average of all responses; 1 said that the effect
      would be reduction in sales)
      Most likely change, +4%;   Worst outcome, 0;
      Best outcome, +7%

      In six months   (average of all responses)
      Most likely change, +6.5%;   Worst outcome, +1.0%;
      Best outcome, +11.0%

#6   On large retailers, 2;   On small retailers, 6

#7   Yes, 5;   No, 1;   No opinion, 2

Processing Intuitive Information into Decision Inputs

Once our business decision maker has accumulated a body of intuitive material from himself and others, he must process this material into a form that will contribute most to valid decision.

First, he must decide how much weight to give the responses of others when they differ from his own and whether he wishes to give equal credence to all others, even though he assesses their expertise quite differently. Second, he must determine whether he wishes to evaluate the individual answers by looking at their underlying logic and consistency. (Such supporting material should be collected if such an evaluation is contemplated.) Third, he must decide whether to employ an arithmetic average of responses or the modal or median response. It is essential that the decision maker commit himself on these issues *before* he has completed the data collection process lest he end up by underutilizing the responses of others.

The processing of intuitive information of the type that would be collected in our hypothetical example is not much different from the processing of statistical data. In both cases, one screens information for accuracy, adjusting or discarding what seems to be atypical or the result of human error. One would use intuitive data as if they had been obtained by a market research study, in this case taking account of the fact that error could arise from the misperceptions and unrepresentative experience of executives rather than, say, housewives.

One technical point deserves brief mention: the translation of a few estimates into frequency distributions of possible outcomes. In our hypothetical questionnaire study described earlier, the executives were asked to estimate the sales impact of adding a regional sales manager to the Milwaukee market for three months. The estimates (one for three months and another for six months) were summarized—presumably using the measure of central tendency prescribed by the executive—and showed three values. One is the "most likely outcome"; the other two show the amount that had one chance in ten of being exceeded and the lowest level to which sales might fall with a probability of one in ten. From these three numbers, a decision maker might want to construct a full frequency distribution—that is, determine the likelihood of intermediate levels of sales and assign a correct probability to them. He will, in effect, try to reconstruct a full frequency distribution from a few points.

This method of reconstruction requires an understanding of the characteristic shape of distributions of such sales effects; that is, are they normally distributed? Are they highly or flatly peaked? Are they skewed to the right or left, if indeed they are skewed? Specialists in gathering and processing intuitive information could assemble the data required to reach conclusions on these questions.

Of course, a decision maker might be content to forgo the refinement achieved by employing a frequency distribution of possible outcomes and settle for the use of his "best guess," or "most likely outcome." The point is being urged here that the use of such refined decision-making techniques is certainly not precluded by the procedure employed here. Indeed, a market research study of potential customers does not produce any probability estimates; these must be constructed either by the researcher or by the executive. The methods available for doing this are highly subjective and not tied directly to the data collected in the survey.

CONCLUSIONS

The approach to intuitive information described here has not been tested; to the author's knowledge only one of the specific tools described, the Delphi forecasting procedure, has ever been applied to business problems. Yet despite this lack of empirical verification, the approach does seem sufficiently promising and free of risk to justify its use. And if most of the tools involved do realize their potential, the approach can go far to reduce the present agony of choice that confronts businessmen when they make major decisions. If nothing else, its use should help to reduce executive anxiety by providing a reasonable procedure to replace the worry and procrastination to which executives are prone when making complex decisions.

Whatever the value of this particular method of generating intuitive information, executives should acknowledge that the lack of information does not itself explain the great uncertainty they feel when making complex business decisions. To a large extent this uncertainty reflects the inadequacy of the models that the executive has available to him. Without adequate models, the full value of information cannot be realized. Thus, the executive must recognize the existence of both an *information gap* and a *models gap*. Having done so, he can make a maximum effort to bridge those gaps by the systematic generation, refinement, and processing of qualitative materials. Executive intuition "in the raw" is highly suspect and could result in very serious error. The use of careful procedures to obtain intuitive material, on the other hand, may open up a valuable source of information, concepts, and models that will restore executive intuition to good standing in both the business and the academic community.

The Management of Uncertainty: A Dialog

The Sylvan Corporation manufactures a line of small appliances (clocks, toasters, coffee-makers, electric knives, electric can-openers, and the like) and is among the five largest corporations in that field. It is moderately profitable, and its management is strongly committed to "profitable growth." Last year, its rate of return on investment was 14 percent after taxes—its highest return since 1951.

The finance committee of the corporation assembles capital investment projects at quarterly intervals, and the major screening of projects takes place in the fall, in conjunction with the annual planning process. During the winter, spring, and summer, the finance committee is permitted to invest approximately 20 percent of the company's estimated investable funds (about 40 percent are invested during the fall). In the event that the projects brought forward fail to consume the allotted resources, they are carried over to the next period.

The finance committee has set a "cut-off rate of return" of 20 percent on investment for the coming year—an increase of 2 percent over that of the preceding year. Underlying this change was the consensus that investment opportunities were improving and the conviction that the higher rate of interest prevailing in the economy should be reflected in the company's cut-off rate. During the spring the projects brought forward for consideration by the committee all carried an estimated rate of return in excess of 20 percent. The total amount of investable funds required to implement all these projects was almost double the funds available.

Ordinarily, the finance committee would array the projects in the order of their expected rate of return and go down the list until the funds available for investment were exhausted. However, Mr. Roe, a new member of the committee, protested against this system on two scores: First, he said that he mistrusted the estimated rates of return and thought the committee should develop a method to protect itself against the usual optimism characterizing such estimates. Second, he argued that the method did not in any way take account of the risk aspect of the investment alternatives.

The chairman of the committee debated both points. He pointed out that one function of the committee was to pass on the reasonableness of the estimates included in the projects. Second, the committee was expected to reject any investment that involved excessive risk. Mr. Roe granted the validity of the chairman's position but stressed that the committee's actions represented only a partial attack on the problems he had raised. He argued that the estimated rates of return were either accepted or rejected—but not revised; that is, if a proposal seemed unduly optimistic, the committee would reject it or send it back for re-estimate—but would not make its own estimate of the most probable rate of return. As he stated it, "None of the ROI figures we use represent our own estimates, but are the estimates of others that we cannot reject." With respect to the treatment of risk, his argument is best summarized in his own words:

> It does not make sense to distinguish between projects as if they either do or do not represent tolerable degrees of risk; acceptable risks may vary substantially and we should take such variations into account. What we want to do is find that combination of projects—a portfolio of investments—that best meets our objectives. Every portfolio might very well include some very risky small investments which had an extremely high expected rate of return, and some large, almost risk-free investments that promised less than our cut-off rate of return. I doubt that each investment should be considered on its own merits, without considering the other projects that the firm has adopted.

Mr. Cox, one of the most senior members of the finance committee, found these arguments interesting but not conclusive and raised a few questions. First, he asked how Roe proposed to make estimates of ROI that reflected the committee's views. Second, he wanted to know how they could select the combination of projects that would best meet the company's objectives. He was not sure that the committee would err if it considered each project on its own merits, rather than regard itself as "purchasing a bundle of projects"; however, he said that he did not know what particular actions or decisions that position implied. The following dialog ensued.

ROE: You asked what procedure we might use to pick the best projects available to us. The most important thing we must do is make our objectives very explicit. It is not enough to state that we will pick the projects with the greatest ROI because they vary in other respects— mainly in their riskiness; therefore we must specify our trade-offs between expected rate of return and risk of loss. After all, we want both high return and small risk of loss.

COX: Frankly, although I've heard a great deal about trade-offs and could explain them in general terms, I've never seen that concept made truly operational. Let's try to do it in this case, even if it takes a lot of time. As a start, would we all agree that the company should accept a risk of loss higher than average on an investment if the expected rate of return was extremely high?

ROE: I would certainly agree with that general statement, which implies a direct trade-off between risk and return on investment. Frankly, I've never worked through a concrete attempt to apply specific trade-offs between risk and ROI, but I think it's worth a try.

COX: What are you proposing—that we try to state specifically in concrete numerical terms how we would balance expected rates of return against risks of loss?

ROE: Something like that, but it's a much more complicated problem than you imply. After all, the term "risk" is very unclear and complex. What do we mean by risk? Is it simply the likelihood that we'll suffer some loss? Ths risk that we'll earn less than we estimated? That we'll go broke? Is it affected by the chance to make a killing? What does it mean?

COX: I'd suppose it means all of those things and more; surely you could argue that one element of risk is the probability of getting very high returns, though most people associate risk only with danger of loss. Your questions make risk seem almost too complicated to handle.

ROE: One way or another, this company has been handling it for years. We certainly have been screening investments for risk, without indicating what we mean by the term, or even what we were doing about risk. It would seem that risk embraces the entire probability distribution of possible outcomes of a project.

COX: Let me get this straight. Are you proposing that we examine what you call the entire probability distribution of each project's outcomes? Where do we get such a thing for investments that are unique and have not even been made? I'd love to examine such a distribution, but I wouldn't know how to find one.

ROE: Remember that you have been estimating the most likely outcomes for years. That estimate also applies to a unique investment that never has been made before. To call a spade a spade, it is simply our best guess. Why should we not make a distribution of guesses, rather than a single figure.

COX: I'm sure I don't estimate the most likely outcome. When I see an estimate of return on investment, I just assess its reasonableness; sometimes I feel it is very reasonable and conservative; most of the time I feel the guy is stretching things a bit, but not too badly.

ROE: Probably many other members of the committee react in the same way, but let's examine the matter more closely. Wouldn't you agree that each one of our potential projects has many possible outcomes rather than one? Isn't it true that we really don't know what will happen— what profit we'll make—if we carry out the project?

COX: Of course. I don't know what will happen, but I do know what I think will happen. Sure, some unfortunate things might occur—but then, some developments could transpire that would be very much in our favor.

ROE: So you do recognize that several—and possibly many—different outcomes are possible, albeit not equally possible. Wouldn't it help us to make the best choice of projects if we set down the different things we believe might happen—and how likely they are to happen?

COX: Of course it would, but we're back where we started; I'd love to have that kind of information, but I don't know where to get it. Are you suggesting that persons submitting projects should be required to submit such sets of estimates?

ROE: That wasn't my point, but I think it would be a good idea. In fact, we must wonder what the estimates mean that are submitted to us. Surely those proposing investment projects must recognize that many things might happen.

COX: I'd assume that these estimates represent the outcome that the proponent considers most likely. Many proposals have the word "expected" in quotes in front of "rate of return." I'd therefore guess that means it's the outcome the author expects to occur.

ROE: Actually the term "expected" rate of return has a technical meaning when it's enclosed in quotes. It isn't very fancy; it only means the weighted average of the different outcomes that one has identified.

COX: Are you saying that if I believe that three outcomes are possible for an investment—one of $100,000, another $150,000 and another of $300,000, the expected value would be in weighted average of the three? I don't see where the weights come in.

ROE: The weights used would be the likelihood that you attach to each of those outcomes. If you considered all three equally likely, you'd just take a simple average—which means that you give each of them equal weight. But usually different outcomes would not be considered equally likely.

COX: Say the middle one was twice as likely as the other two, which were about equally likely, what would I do?

ROE: You'd assign a weight of one to the low and the high figures and of two to the middle one. You'd multiply them out and divide the result by four—or $700,000 divided by four—which is $175,000. Actually, I'd do it by dividing 100 points over the four—25 to the low and the high and 50 to the middle one—and would get the same result. These weights are called "probabilities." But then, I'm sure that you know very well everything I've told you in the last few minutes. As I recall, you studied a fair amount of probability theory in college.

COX: Regrettably, I don't remember much of it. I once did study some decision theory in an executive training program, but never did get a solid grounding in the subject. I now recall what is meant by the "expected value" but failed to associate it with the term "expected rate of return." So you are suggesting that we require all proposals to carry a set of estimates rather than only one, is that correct?

ROE: That's right.

COX: The idea of requiring such elaborate guessing games doesn't intrigue me very much, but it's impossible to assess the idea without giving it a try. I have lots of difficulty with the proposal. For example, I wonder how we can hope to get concrete estimates out of the persons submitting proposals to this committee. Also, how precise would they have to be for such estimates to be usable? Wouldn't wild estimates hurt us rather than help us? And, what would we do if this group disagreed with the persons making proposals about the possible outcomes and their likelihood?

ROE: Those are fair and important questions and I certainly don't claim to have good answers to all of them. Let's discuss them. However, let's agree to withhold our verdict on the procedure until we try it often enough to become comfortable and skilled with it. You are really asking about what is technically called "subjective probability." You must have heard about this subject when you were exposed to decision theory.

COX: Yes, but I don't understand it very well. Maybe you can tell me enough so that I would be willing to use subjective probabilities.

ROE: I'll tell you what I know. Subjective probabilities represent estimates based upon the evidence available to the person making the estimates. It is what he believes, given all the information and arguments he knows; you might call it the answer that the "weight of the evidence" on the subject leads to—for him.

COX: That is still fuzzy. I would grant that anyone making a proposal—or even those reviewing proposals—have information and opinions bearing on the proposal. The decisions they make will of course reflect that information and those opinions; what beyond that are you saying?

ROE: I'm saying that it's possible to take what a person knows, believes, and expects and state it in a numerical form that makes it possible to subject it to statistical analysis.

COX: Well, that idea is not wholly unfamiliar to me and I accept the fundamental message. In other words, there are ways that one can process the views that an executive holds. What troubles me—and always has since I heard about Bayesian statistics—is whether an executive can express his guesses in any concrete and specific form. Are there ways of helping an executive to express his assessment of the weight of the evidence? Are there ways of improving the quality of his guesses?

ROE: Of course, you're likely to improve the quality of guesses by collecting more information, but I assume that we're not going to do that. It is possible to help an executive to squeeze out of himself what he knows and believes about a subject in a way that he usually could not extract for himself. And, it is possible to get him to express his views in a way that is unambiguous and easily manipulated by statistical techniques.

COX: That sounds complicated; I'd appreciate a simple example if you could cook one up in a big hurry. Could you take one of the projects before us at the moment and use me as your guinea pig? Go ahead and squeeze out of me some subjective probabilities. I doubt that there are any inside.

ROE: All right, take the project submitted by Bob Jones. Do you think it is likely to yield a return of 40 percent?

COX: Oh no, not a chance, in my opinion.

ROE: Do you think it will produce a return on investment of less than, say, 5 percent?

COX: No, I think it will make a good bit more than that.

ROE: Which is more likely—a return of 40 percent or one of 5 percent, would you say?

COX: I certainly don't know; I'd say they were about equally likely—no,

I'd say that a return of 5 percent is a little more likely than one of 40, but not much.

ROE: If you think the return is somewhere between 5 and 40, would you say it is about the middle—about 22.5 percent?—above that or below that?

COX: You're crowding me now; I can't shave half percentage points. I wouldn't be surprised if it were between 20 and 25 percent.

ROE: Okay. Would you say it would be closer to 20 or 25—or about in the middle?

COX: Closer to 25 percent, I'd say. Well, you sure did get me to say a lot of things about that project of Bob's that I never realized I even believed. I can very well see that in no time at all you could translate what I said, and the other things you could squeeze out of me, into some fairly concrete statement of probabilities.

ROE: Exactly. So, you see what we mean by subjective probabilities and how we might help others to dredge them out of their minds. Actually, many people can cross-examine themselves without any trouble to produce the same result. Have we said enough about that subject to move on? You recall, I hope, that my proposal was that the members of the committee should be concerned with many possible outcomes, not only the most likely one; and that the members should not only estimate the different outcomes but should also assign probabilities to them. Do you agree?

COX: I agree that we should give it a try often enough to reach a verdict based on enough experience to feel confident of our verdict.

*   *   *

ROE: Let's at least decide finally what we mean by risk and then see whether we can find a way of measuring the riskiness of individual projects.

COX: Fine. But instead of using a formal definition of risk, let's set down some hypothetical numbers for a project. We can assume that those numbers are the best we can develop for the project and try to measure the risk it involves.

ROE: Very good, but I think it would be better to take two hypothetical investments and develop hypothetical probability distributions for both; then we'd get a clearer idea of the problems faced in selecting between projects that vary in riskiness.

COX: I'd go along with that. Let's see, how about constructing examples in which one project is twice as risky as the other. Frankly, I don't know where to begin; you should remember that I'm no powerhouse in this probability business.

ROE: You're being very modest; I think you understand the concepts better than the rest of us put together, even though you may not remember some of the details of computation. What points on the probability distribution should we estimate?

COX: Shouldn't we aim for the entire distribution?

ROE: I don't think so; we'll have enough trouble getting a few key points. Our ability to estimate outcomes is quickly exhausted so let's concentrate on what is most important.

COX: That sounds reasonable; what do you consider the key points?

ROE: First, the extremes—the best and worst outcomes with a significant probability of, say, 1 in 100.

COX: I'd like to get that straight. That means you'd ask what are the best and worst outcomes you could expect with one chance in 100 of occurring. That certainly makes more sense than asking about the very best and worst single outcomes that could possibly occur.

ROE: There are other points on the probability distribution that we might try to estimate, for example, the chances that the project would produce some loss.

COX: I take it that we'd be including in that figure the extreme outcomes of which we just spoke. In other words, we'd be cumulating the frequencies of previous outcomes.

ROE: Yes, that's right; by doing that, we greatly simplify our task—though it still won't be simple. I'd like to propose another simplification so that the example doesn't get completely out of hand. Let's assume that the ROI refers to investments that last one year or less—so that we needn't get involved with the problem of discounting future income back to present value.

COX: That's fine with me; I want this kept as simple as possible. Other points on the probability distribution seem important to you?

ROE: I'd suggest that the "cut-off rate of return" is important—which for us would be 20 percent; another would be a really high return—like 35 percent.

COX: Good, I think that I understand the principle and even the specific suggestions. May I make a further proposal for simplification: at least for our hypothetical examples, let's use round numbers. Concretely, let's take the 1 percent extreme low case; the "some-loss" point; a return of 10 percent or less; a return of 20 percent or less; a return of 30 percent or less; a return of 40 percent or less; and the top 1 percent case. Let me see, that would give us a total of seven points.

ROE: Okay, I've got these set down on my pad and I'm ready to make up some figures for two hypothetical examples. Let's call them the "Safe" and the "Risky" projects. As you suggested, we'll try to develop numbers that make the second twice as risky as the first. But I want our objectives to be clear before we start playing around with numbers. As I see it, we want to be able to define risk and to measure it, and do so in a way that permits comparisons of individual projects.

COX: Right. Here are some numbers for the "safe" project. [See Table 6-5.]

ROE: Those figures should serve very well. I'd judge the expected value of this distribution to be somewhere between 20 and 30 percent ROI with the mode at 25 percent. Do you agree?

COX: Yes, I would. By the way, I have troubles with cumulative probabilities in this kind of problem. Could we translate them into noncumulative terms?

ROE: Let's try. I'm sure we'll be forced to make some arbitrary assumptions and crude interpolations. After all, we have only limited information about the full probability distribution.

COX: That's all right as far as I'm concerned. We don't need precision at this stage. Let's start. We see a 1 in 100 chance of a loss of 15 percent or greater. Let's not worry about how that 1 percent is divided among all outcomes below minus 15 percent and just say that they all occur at minus 15 percent. Is that all right with you?

ROE: Certainly, at least for the moment. Then we can move along to the next number which shows a probability of 3 in 100 of an ROI of zero or less; that means a probability of 2 in 100 of an ROI between minus 15 and zero. I'd suggest that we just put these probabilities at zero rather

Table 6-5

PROBABILITY DISTRIBUTION FOR "SAFE" PROJECT

Outcomes	Cumulative probabilities	Uncumulated probabilities
ROI below zero	.03	.03
ROI below 10%	.20	.17
ROI below 20%	.50	.30
ROI below 30%	.90	.40
ROI below 40%	.96	.06

Range: Lowest return with probability (cumulative) of .01–.15% ROI Highest return with cumulative probability of .01–.60% ROI.

than try to distribute them over the interval between minus 15 percent and zero.

COX: You're turning that probability distribution into a bar chart of sorts, I hope you realize. That's all right with me.

ROE: If we follow that line of thinking, we can easily fill out the next two items. We'd end up with a probability of .17 of a return between zero and plus 10 percent ROI; .40 probability of a return between 20 and 30 percent; and a .06 chance of a return between 30 and 40 percent ROI.

COX: That leaves the last figure, which we derive from the range. We saw that there is 1 chance in 100 of a return of 60 percent ROI or above. If we set that 1 percent chance at 60 percent, following our crude simplification, we then find that 3 percent of the outcomes lie between 40 and 60 percent ROIs—and let's just set that at 40, for simplicity's sake.

ROE: As long as we recognize that we are playing fast and loose with these numbers, you have my blessing to simplify the problem as much as you like. I mainly want to see what would be involved in taking this set of numbers and creating another set that represents a doubling risk. [See Table 6-6.]

Table 6-6

TWO HYPOTHETICAL INVESTMENT PROJECTS OF EQUAL SIZE BUT DIFFERING IN DEGREE OF RISK (INVESTMENT ASSUMED TO BE $6 MILLION)

Outcomes		Probability	
($)	%ROI	Cumulative	Uncumulated
"Safe" project			
$−900,000	−15%	.01	.01
0 or below	0	.03	.02
Under 600,000	10	.20	.17
Under 1,200,000	20	.60	.40
Under 1,800,000	30	.90	.30
Under 2,400,000	40	.99	.09
"Risky" project			
$1,800,000	−30%	.01	.01
0	0	.03	.02
1,200,000	20	.20	.17
2,400,000	40	.60	.40
3,600,000	60	.90	.30
4,800,000	80	.99	.09

COX: I'll feel better about doing that now that we have developed a frequency distribution that is in a familiar mold for me. It seems to me that what we must choose between is a doubling of either the probabilities or of the outcomes in our distribution.

ROE: I guess those are our choices if we want to double risk, but frankly this whole notion of measuring risk is new to me. When you think about it, we cannot possibly double our probabilities. If we did, we'd get a total of 200 chances in 100 for the listed outcomes.

COX: Yes, that's right; that wouldn't work at all.

ROE: Right. Then, let's try doubling the outcomes. If we did that, we'd get the following. [See Table 6-7.]

COX: Good, and we can just do the same thing with the uncumulated probabilities.

ROE: The table [6-7] now includes those figures, and permits us to see what is meant by a doubling of risk—or does it?

COX: If you examine the numbers, it becomes clear that we've done more than change risk; we've changed the expected value; the mode now is 60 percent ROI, instead of 30 percent. The weighted average is just about twice as large for the risky project—as for the safe one. We certainly did not want that result.

ROE: That's quite clear now. We have raised the expected value greatly, even while we have doubled the range. How would you describe what we did to risk?

COX: I'm really confused about what we did do and what connection all this has with risk. Clearly, we did not just alter risk while keeping the expected value constant. We have left up in the air what a doubling of

Table 6-7

PROBABILITY DISTRIBUTION FOR DANGER PROJECT

Outcomes	Cumulative probabilities	Uncumulated probabilities
−30% or less ROI	.01	.01
ROI below zero	.03	.02
ROI below 20%	.20	.17
ROI below 40%	.50	.30
ROI below 60%	.90	.40
ROI below 80%	.96	.06
ROI below 100%	.99	.03
ROI below 120%	1.00	.01

risk means. We certainly demonstrated that you cannot double risk of a distribution simply by multiplying all the outcomes by two.

ROE: Let's not be concerned with these numbers at the moment. Since our only purpose is to define risk, no definition of risk emerged from our trying to create a numerical example.

COX: Maybe we shouldn't try to define or measure risk as such. Isn't our goal to rank investments in a way that takes into account everything that prudent managers should consider? We have indicated that management should consider all outcomes, not simply the most likely one, or a weighted average of all of them; we have even decided that management should consider several outcomes of particular significance—like the chance of some loss, a 10, 20, 30, and 40 percent ROI. We have referred several times to the importance of the range. And, I would myself attach particularly heavy significance to the unfavorable outcomes.

ROE: In other words, you're saying that the unfavorable aspects of any investment project are what you have in mind when you think of risk.

COX: That's exactly what I'm saying. I think a prudent manager should consider all outcomes but should give far greater importance to the unfavorable ones.

ROE: What that conclusion means to me is that there is no one thing that represents risk, but a whole series of ingredients that compose risk. What's more, each individual may assign different values to the various ingredients. Would you agree with that?

COX: Certainly, risk is not a simple notion that can be measured directly or doubled in any straightforward manner. But I think we should remind ourselves again about our purpose, which is to rank investments rather than measure risk. We should be pretty happy about that, because we clearly have not come up with a way of measuring risk. On the other hand, I might be able to evaluate investments without too much trouble if I had the kind of information we concocted about the risky and the safe projects.

ROE: That's the point, I guess, so why don't we turn to that and measure risk for the moment? One of the things we might turn to later is the possibility of measuring risk by using the standard deviation of the probability distribution. Someone proposed that in something I read somewhere. After this discussion, though, I am pessimistic about its serving our purpose.

COX: Frankly, when I think of risk, I think of unfavorable outcomes. The existence of a chance of a return on investment of 120 percent does not make it risky to me—but more attractive.

ROE: Most people use the terms that way in ordinary conversation, but we want to be quite precise. If we want to discuss unfavorable outcomes and handle them specially, we could do that. But, you already said some time back that our choice of investment projects should take account of all outcomes, good and bad alike.

COX: True, but we surely do want to treat unfavorable outcomes with particular care, even while considering all outcomes. What I mean is that we should give special and great weight to unfavorable outcomes. It seems to me that we mainly want to identify and avoid projects with outcomes that would damage the future health of this business.

A Hypothetical Decision Under Uncertainty

The hypothetical case described below illustrates the method and suggests the value of processing probabilistic forecasts relevant to business decisions. The data, which can be prepared by clerical help, illuminate greatly the contingencies that the decision maker must take into account, thus contributing to better decisions. Clearly, any decision maker who insists on obtaining forecasts that are single values, ignoring the many other likely outcomes, is basing his conclusions on incomplete, scanty, and superficial information. Consequently, he is likely to reach a mistaken conclusion. As the illustration shows, there is no need to deny oneself the information contained in a forecast in the form of a probability distribution. Fairly simple procedures are available for processing such data so that they become directly applicable to an executive decision. However, the complexity of the analysis of these data is greatly increased, as one must expect, with the complexity of the underlying decision.

The Brill Corporation manufactures a staple office supply item. It produces only one product and is a leading producer in that field. Brill was founded in 1926 and has been moderately profitable since its formation.

Mr. Jones is executive vice-president, chairman of the executive committee of the corporation, and is the firm's chief executive officer. The other officers of the company are all junior to Mr. Jones in experience and age except Mr. Brill, president, who has given up virtually all operating responsibility. In effect, Mr. Jones has been running the company personally for about two years, while trying to develop the younger executives to a point where they will be able to relieve him of some of his present burden.

The budget and operating plan are being prepared for the year 1980, which includes, among other things, decisions about monthly output and cash requirements. Mr. Jones is persuaded that the proper procedure is to determine the volume of output and from that decision, combined with a sales forecast, compute cash requirements.

The controller's office has estimated, on the basis of a careful study, that the company would enter the new year with a finished goods inventory of 100,000 units, which management considers the absolute minimum it should hold. (Indeed, it would go on overtime—or even patronize its competitors—to build inventories up to that level if they were to drop below that point.) After the regular dividend is distributed at the end of the year—largely to members of the Brill family—and funds are set aside to pay the small federal corporate profits taxes for the year, the company will have a cash balance of $12,000,000, which the controller regards as his minimal needs.

The company's situation is such that its current assets and current liabilities would just about cancel out over most of the year. In no month can it expect a noticeable change in its cash position due to its receipts from notes and accounts receivable or its outlays for notes and accounts payable.

The controller has stressed the importance of "self-financing"—that is, deriving all the funds that the firm needs for operations from its sales. He points out that the banks might refuse to make a loan to the Brill Company, because of the tightness of the money market. If they did grant a loan, it would be costly and might also weaken the company's ability to borrow in the future. The controller placed a dollar value on the cost of borrowing, when pressed to do so by Mr. Jones, saying he would consider the sacrifice to the Brill Company of borrowing $10,000 to be worth about $4,000 per year and a loan of $25,000 or above to involve costs equal to about 75 percent of the amount of the loan. Also, Mr. Brill has made it clear that he disapproves of borrowing on principle and has always insisted that Mr. Jones adopt a plan that would not call for borrowing.

The Brill Company's product exhibits no consistent seasonal pattern of production or sales. Like others that produce only this staple item, the company makes strong efforts to maintain a uniform level of output throughout the year, except for the last two weeks in July, when the plant shuts down for a vacation. Consequently, Mr. Jones wants to select a level of output that he can maintain virtually unchanged throughout the year, though he is prepared to vary output if it should prove necessary.

The item that the Brill Company produces is fairly though not wholly standardized. Since it is purchased by businesses, unit sales are quite sensitive to small differences between Brill's price and that charged by others. Consequently, the Brill Company's price may not be out of line with the prices charged by its rivals and especially the largest firm in the industry. For many years, the Brill Company followed a policy of charging $12 a dozen less for its product than the largest firm. Both Mr. Brill and Mr. Jones agree that this policy should be continued, and for good reason, since experiments with other policies had proved to be very painful. An established price policy in the industry obliges sellers to adhere to quoted price for at least six months—and generally the same price prevails throughout the year. The reason for sellers' reluctance to change price is that price reductions are retroactive to the beginning of the year.

Mr. Jones therefore assumes that the Brill Company's price is determined by the prices charged by its rivals; also he has every confidence that price will exceed out-of-pocket costs. Consequently, he plans to produce as much as he believes the company can sell. (If price were below out-of-pocket costs, he believes that he would be forced to sell at that price for a while rather than risk the loss of customers to other suppliers.) In other words, Mr. Jones will simply estimate his sales at the expected price and produce that amount.

Mr. Jones has requested information on estimated cash outlays per unit during the coming year from the controller's office and estimates of prices and unit sales from the sales department. In his instructions to these departments, he made clear that he wanted a forecast of all potential outcomes as well as the likelihood of each; moreover, he has requested that the probabilities be expressed in numerical terms, even though he acknowledged that there exists no completely reliable method of measuring these probabilities.

He has received some forecasts (see Table 6-8) which Mr. Jones believes to be the best information on which he can base his decisions. Although he understands the difficulty of making such forecasts and the high likelihood of error, he believes he should treat them as if they were completely reliable.

As indicated, Mr. Jones plans to select his level of output first and then determine the cash implications of his decision. Presumably, if he finds them unacceptable, he will revise his output decision.

In some ways his output decision is greatly simplified by the fact that the Brill Company possesses considerable warehouse capacity for holding inventory far in excess of its present levels. Mr. Jones regards the use of this space as costless to the company. Consequently, the only harm that would ensue from production in excess of sales would be an immobilization of cash in subsequent periods. On this basis, Mr. Jones believes he can ignore the relation between his output decision and profits. As a result, he will base his production decisions on cash and other considerations.

Mr. Jones has been through this planning and budgeting procedure many times before and has routinized his decisions to a considerable degree. After a cursory examination of the forecasts he received—to be sure they were mutually consistent and did not seem to contain any gross

Table 6-8
PRICE FORECAST

Price	Probability
$59	.03
60	.08
61	.15
62	.17
63	.20
64	.20
65	.10
66	.05
67	.02

Table 6-9
PRICE AND SALES FORECAST (PROBABILITY OF SALES AT GIVEN PRICE)

Sales (in thousands of units)	Price								
	$59	$60	$61	$62	$63	$64	$65	$66	$67
400					—	.10	.30	.70	.85
500				—	.10	.20	.40	.20	.10
600			—	.10	.20	.40	.20	.10	.05
700	—	—	.10	.20	.40	.20	.10	—	—
800	.05	.10	.20	.40	.20	.10	—		
900	.10	.20	.40	.20	.10	—			
1,000	.85	.70	.30	.10	—				

Table 6-10
PROBABILITY OF GIVEN PRICE AND GIVEN SALES

Sales (in thousands of units)	Price									Total
	$59	$60	$61	$62	$63	$64	$65	$66	$67	
400					.0200	.0200	.0300	.0350	.0170	.1020
500				.0170	.0400	.0400	.0400	.0100	.0020	.1120
600			.0150	.0340	.0800	.0800	.0200	.0050	.0010	.1630
700		.0080	.0300	.0680	.0800	.0400	.0100			.1790
800	.0015	.0160	.0600	.0340	.0400	.0200				.1675
900	.0030	.0560	.0450	.0170	.0200					.1330
1,000	.0255									.1435
										1.0000

error—and a discussion of those forecasts with the people who prepared them, he has passed them along to a clerk in the sales analysis section.

Table 6-8 shows the price, sales, and cash outlay forecasts he received, and Table 6-9 indicates the probabilities of the various sales levels, *given* a price. (Note that the probabilities in each column add up to 1.00.) In Table 6-10, the probability of a given sales level *and* a given price are shown. These are obtained by multiplying the probability that the price will prevail by the probability of the given sales level at that price. The sum of *all* the probabilities in Table 6-10 is also 1.00.

The meaning of Tables 6-9 and 6-10 is not immediately apparent. Any number in Table 6-9 denotes the probability that if the price shown in the table were to prevail, the sales indicated to the left would be realized. For example, the number .70 at the bottom of the second column indicates that if the price turned out to be $60, the chances are 70 in 100 that 1 million units would be sold.

Table 6-10 was derived by combining Tables 6-8 and 6-9, thereby taking account of the likelihood that each price between $59 and $67 would prevail. Consequently, each number in Table 6-10 indicates the likelihood of the corresponding price and sales—without any ifs, ands, or buts. Thus, the number .0560 at the bottom of the second column indicates that there are 56 chances in 1,000 that the price will be $60 and the firm will sell 1 million units.

To be sure you understand what has been said thus far, try to answer the following questions from the information presented in Tables 6-8, 6-9, and 6-10.

If 700,000 units were produced, would they all be sold?
If 700,000 units were produced, would any sales be lost through insuffi-
   cient production?

The forecast of cash outlay per unit presented to Mr. Jones is shown in Table 6-11 and indicates the amount of cash the firm must expend to produce every unit of output. (These will be termed "cost" for the sake of simplicity.)

At Mr. Jones's request, the sales analysis division prepared tables that showed the cash flow implications of different output decisions, taking into account the different possible levels of sales, costs, and price. (Mr. Jones explained that he had to make an output decision and was interested in the consequences of each possible decision, knowing that he almost certainly would *not* sell precisely the amount that was produced.) Accordingly, the cash flow implications of each production decision were determined by the following steps:

Table 6-11

Forecast of Cash Outlay per Unit

Cash outlay per unit	Probability
$57	.10
58	.20
59	.40
60	.20
61	.10

1. For each possible output level (using intervals of 100,000 units) and for each unit cash outlay, a cash flow matrix was formed. Each of its cells indicates the cash flow that would occur with every possible price-sales combination. Tables 6-12.1 and 6-12.2 are two of these matrixes, and indicate the cash flows at different price-sales combinations for outputs of 1 million and 700,000 units with cash outlays per unit of $57. (Observe that the *gross* cash outflow would be the same for each table since it reflects the assumed output and the unit cash outlay; the net flow depends upon the volume of sales and price, which are allowed to vary.)

2. The "expected cash flow"—by which we mean the weighted average of all possible cash flows—for each cost/output combination was computed. That is, the data compiled in tables like 6-12.1 and 6-12.2 were weighted to indicate the likelihood that each cell would come to pass. (The corresponding cell of Table 6-10 was used to accomplish this weighting.)

For example, Table 6-12.1 shows what would happen to the firm's cash position if it were to produce 1 million units with a unit cash outlay of $57. If, say, it sold 600,000 units at a price of $65, it would suffer a net cash outflow of $18 million. (It would have outlays of $57 million—1 million units × $57—and receipts of $39 million—600,000 × $65.) We learn from Table 6-10 that the probability of this combination of prices and sales is .02. Accordingly, we would represent this cell which indicates the net cash outlay given 1 million units of output ($57 per unit cash outlay, and 600,000 units of sales at a price of $65) by the figure of −$360,000 ($18 million times .02). The same computation was made for all cells in tables like 6-12.1 and 6-12.2. In all, 35 such tables were prepared—for each of seven levels of output and five levels of unit cash outlay. These will be referred to as Tables 6-12.1 to 6-12.35.

All the cells were totaled to determine the expected cash flow for that output and cash outlay per unit. The totals for assumed outputs of 1 million and 700,000 units are presented in Tables 6-13 and 6-14.

Table 6-12.1

CASH FLOW (IN MILLIONS OF DOLLARS) ASSUMING OUTPUT OF 1 MILLION UNITS AND CASH OUTLAY OF $57 PER UNIT

Sales (in thousands of units)	Price								
	$59	$60	$61	$62	$63	$64	$65	$66	$67
400						−31.4	−31.0	−30.6	−30.2
500					−25.5	−25.0	−24.5	−24.0	−23.5
600				−19.8	−19.2	−18.6	−18.0	−17.4	−16.8
700	—	—	−14.3	−13.6	−12.9	−12.2	−11.5	—	
800	−9.8	−9.0	−8.2	−7.4	−6.6	−5.8	—		
900	−3.9	−3.0	−2.1	−1.2	−0.3	—			
1,000	+2.0	+3.0	+4.0	+5.0	—				

Table 6-12.2

CASH FLOW (IN MILLIONS OF DOLLARS) ASSUMING OUTPUT OF 700,000 UNITS AND CASH OUTLAY OF $57 PER UNIT

Sales (in thousands of units)	Price								
	$59	$60	$61	$62	$63	$64	$65	$66	$67
400						−14.3	−13.9	−13.5	−13.1
500					−8.4	−7.9	−7.4	−6.9	−6.4
600				−1.7	−2.1	−1.5	−0.9	−3.0	+0.3
700	+1.4	+2.1	+2.8	+3.5	+4.2	+4.9	+5.6	—	

Table 6-13

EXPECTED CASH FLOW (IN MILLIONS OF DOLLARS) AT EACH COST LEVEL, ASSUMING OUTPUT OF 1 MILLION UNITS

Cost	Expected cash flow	Probability of cost level
$57	−12.3	.10
58	−13.3	.20
59	−14.3	.40
60	−15.3	.20
61	−16.3	.10

Expected cash flow at output of 1 million units = −$14.3 million

3. The "expected" cash flow was computed similarly for each level of output. The results are shown in Table 6-15.

4. The best and worst cash flows are also indicated for each level of output in Table 6-15. These are obtained from matrixes like those in Tables 6-12.1 and 6-12.2. For example, Table 6-12.1 shows the best cash flow for an output of 1 million units to be +$5 million. (Recall that we assumed the lowest cost in constructing this matrix.) The worst cash flow at this output would occur if (1) costs were $61, (2) price were $64, and (3) only 400,000 units were sold. Cash outlays would be 1 million × $61, or $61 million; cash inflow would be 400,000 × $64, or $25 million, for a net cash outflow of $35 million. The probability that the cash flow would be −$35 million, if output were 1 million units, is then the probability that costs will be $61 (.10) times the probability that price and sales will be $64 and 400,000 units (.02), or .002—that is, one chance in 500.

5. Table 6-15 also shows that, for each level of output, either of two things might happen: sales might be less than production—inventory would increase—and production might not be sufficient to fill all orders.

Table 6-14

EXPECTED CASH FLOW (IN MILLIONS OF DOLLARS) AT EACH COST LEVEL, ASSUMING OUTPUT OF 700,000 UNITS

Cost	Expected cash flow	Probability of cost level
$57	−0.4	.10
58	−1.1	.20
59	−1.8	.40
60	−2.5	.20
61	−3.2	.10

Expected cash flow at output of 700,000 units = −$1.8 million

Table 6-15

SUMMARY TABLE

Output (in thousands of units)	Cash flow			Expected inventory build-up	Expected loss of sales
	Maximum	*Minimum*	*Expected value*		
400	+4.0	− 0.8	+ 1.5	0	317
500	+5.0	− 4.9	+ 1.2	10	227
600	+6.0	−11.0	+ 0.2	32	149
700	+5.6	−17.1	− 1.8	69	86
800	+5.6	−23.2	− 5.0	125	42
900	+5.4	−29.3	− 9.2	197	14
1,000	+5.0	−35.4	−14.3	283	0

The righthand column of Table 6-10 indicates the probability of each sales level. Thus, there is a .1435 probability that sales could have been 1 million units if 900,000 units were produced, and thus that there would be 100,000 unsatisfied customers. The expected number of unsatisfied customers, for this output is, then, 100,000 × .1435, or 14. On the other hand, fewer than 900,000 units may be sold. The probability that inventory increases by 100,000 (sales of 800,000) is .1675; by 200,000 it is .1790; by 300,000 it is 1630; by 400,000 it is .1120; and by 500,000 it is .1020. The expected inventory build-up is the sum of the five products: inventory increase times the probability of that increase. Expected inventory increase and expected loss of sales for other output levels were computed in the same way.

6. Table 6-16 presents a probability distribution of cash flows for each level of output. For example, if output is 800,000 units, the probability is about .03 that the cash outflow will be $25 million or more and only .005 that there would be a cash inflow of more than $5 million. This information is obtained from matrixes 6-12.1 to 6-12.35. The cash flows are grouped into broad classes for convenience.

A very large number of very simple computations are involved in the preparation of these tables. With a little experience and indoctrination, an intelligent clerk could prepare these tables in 4 to 5 hours without the use of a computer. It is most unlikely that any executive could hope to appreciate the implications of the original forecasts without having these tables prepared.

With this information, Mr. Jones can reasonably hope to reach an output decision. He reasons as follows: If I care about nothing but protecting the firm's cash position, my wisest course is to produce very little—say

Table 6-16
PROBABILITY DISTRIBUTION OF CASH FLOWS

Output (in thousands of units)	Cash flows ($000)									Total
	−35,400 −30,000	−29,999 −25,000	−24,999 −20,000	−19,999 −15,000	−14,999 −10,000	−9,999 −5,000	−4,999 0	+1 +5,000	+5,001 +10,000	
400							.040	.960		1.000
500							.162	.838		1.000
600					.018	.087	.170	.724	.001	1.000
700				.053	.082	.085	.193	.581	.006	1.000
800			.031	.060	.127	.144	.260	.373	.005	1.000
900		.097	.079	.096	.122	.172	.198	.222	.002	1.000
1,000	.102	.106	.128	.112	.152	.148	.132	.104		1.000

500,000 units. I'd be running very great risks of suffering a large cash drain if I decided to produce, say, 1 million units. As Table 6-16 shows, we'd run a chance of one in three of suffering a drain of cash as large as $20 million. (This represents the total of the bottom numbers of the first three columns.)

Further examination of the tables, however, makes it clear to Mr. Jones that his decision will not be very simple. The tables show a basic conflict between considerations of cash flow and of "lost sales." By a very conservative output policy he could certainly minimize the risk of an unfavorable cash position, but he would thereby almost certainly lose a large amount of business. For example, the output that means the lowest "expected" cash drain (actually, it shows that an increase in cash is to be expected), which was to produce 400,000 units, also means that the firm must expect to lose a substantial volume of sales. Specifically, if 400,000 units were produced, the company must "expect" to lose 317,000 units of sales. So great a volume of lost sales not only spells a loss of profit on each sale, but also a serious risk of permanent loss of customers. The latter would represent a serious blow to the company's future earnings prospects and possibly to its very survival.

Viewed in this way, Mr. Jones recognizes that he faces a choice between cash liquidity on the one hand and current sales and a larger number of regular customers on the other. How can he choose between these alternatives?

Mr. Jones reasons along the following lines. There are some risks in the choices open that are too serious to take; these involve both risks of cash drain and of loss of customers. The first step, he decides, is to rule out any output decisions that would involve "inordinate" risks of cash embarrassment and of customer loss; he sets the outside limits as a .05 chance of a cash outflow of $20 million or more and expected loss of 200,000 units of sales. By setting these limits to a decision that he considers acceptable, he rules out decisions of producing over 800,000 units and below 600,000 units.

He recognizes that within these limits he is really asked to exchange added satisfied customers (by producing more) for reduced cash position; by increasing output he increases the risk of facing financial embarrassment. Consequently, he recognizes that, one way or another, he has to establish a "rate of exchange" between cash and satisfied customers because he is pursuing two objectives that are in conflict.

In an attempt to establish such a rate of exchange, he decides to apply "marginal analysis" to the decision. He starts by comparing the levels of output 600,000 and 500,000. At the higher output, the expected cash

Table 6-17

Summary of Cash Flows and Loss of Sales at Different Outputs

Output levels (in thousands of units)	Decline in expected cash flow	Reduction in expected loss of sales	Amount of worsened expected cash flow for each expected sales loss avoided
500–600	$1,000,000	78,000	$13,000
600–700	2,000,000	63,000	$32,000
700–800	3,200,000	44,000	$73,000

position declines by $1 million while the expected loss of sales declines by 78,000 units. That is, for each additional expected sale of a unit, the expected cash flow position is worsened by about $13,000. Table 6-17 summarizes this information for each of the acceptable levels of output.

Mr. Jones now realizes that the output decision depends upon how much it is worth to the company, in terms of a worsened cash flow position, to avoid a possible loss of sales and customers. Moreover, his forecasts have been compressed into a form that highlights the implications of alternative output levels.

At this point, the decision hinges on information not given here. To balance the conflicting effects of cash flow and dissatisfied customers, Mr. Jones has consulted both his sales manager and the controller. The sales manager preferred a very high output so that few, if any, sales would be lost. He pointed to the strenuous efforts necessary in the past to recover lost customers and only reluctantly agreed that other aspects of a production program "really mattered." The controller objected that high production levels threatened the company's cash position and quoted Mr. Brill on the subject of self-financing. Mr. Jones has pressed both to express the consequences of cash flow and lost sales in monetary terms.

The output of 700,000 units is finally selected on the following ground. If 600,000 units are produced, the company has sacrificed an expected cash flow of $13 to avoid an additional expected loss of one unit of sales. Mr. Jones believes that the cost to the company of lost sales is much higher than this. On the other hand, by producing 800,000 units the company risks an adverse cash flow of $73 to avoid the loss of one sale. Since Mr. Jones regards this as far too high a price to pay, 700,000 units was the output level chosen. If the company produces 700,000 units, it is paying about $32 in expected cash flow to avoid the expected loss of an additional sale.

Chapter 7

BUSINESS OBJECTIVES: A POWERFUL DECISION-MAKING TOOL

ALL OF US have many objectives—far more than we can realize. People therefore think hard and long about how to get what they want and in picking what is best for them. Accordingly, our objectives, which may be defined as unfilled wants, lie at the bottom of most thinking and decision making.

Objectives and decision making are related in another way. Whenever we decide, we select among alternatives; we try to select the one that is best. By that, we surely mean the one we expect will fulfill our goals better than the others.

Thus, objectives do and should direct most of our thoughts and actions. To give direction and guidance to decision makers, objectives must be stated fully, clearly, and in some detail. If they are ambiguous, vague, unclear, incomplete, or contradictory, decision makers will rarely achieve much of what they seek. After all, we cannot reach our destination if we do not know where we want to go. It is possible to turn our thoughts about objectives into a powerful decision tool—and thereby increase the number and appropriateness of the alternatives we consider and the validity of our choices.

A decision maker can do far more than simply list what he wants to attain. Objectives can be processed systematically to obtain maximum guidance in devising a basic strategy for his enterprise or for his own career. Although a by-product of rigorously stating objectives, the identification of strategies may represent its most valuable benefit.

An executive must deal explicitly with two aspects of objectives: They are usually stated, unwittingly, on different levels; and they invariably conflict. Unless these two problems are overcome, an executive's decision will frequently backfire.

Statement of Objectives on Different Levels

Certain goals* are ultimate. These are goals which, when one is asked why they are desired, lead to the answer, "I just want them"; they represent purely subjective preferences, things that are desired for their own sake.

Other goals are instrumental; they are desired because they help to achieve ultimate goals, but have no intrinsic value in themselves. For example, we want our boss to view us as highly efficient in order to gain financial and possibly ego rewards. We want to do well at golf to win the admiration of our friends or to build our sagging self-esteem.

Most executive decisions have only an indirect and unclear relationship to the firm's ultimate objectives. For example, a director of advertising would not be helped much by being told that top management's ultimate goal is to maximize profits. A big gap separates decisions about advertising copy, media, frequency, and weight of advertising from maximum profits. The director of advertising needs intervening objectives or instrumental objectives to fill that gap—to inform him. He needs to be told what function advertising is expected to perform in the firm's marketing program. Specifically, is it to win the patronage of retailers by persuading them that they will obtain superior service from the manufacturer or that the advertiser's line will produce a higher profit for retailers than competitive brands? Or, should the director of advertising be instructed by top management that the firm's objectives for advertising are to create increased brand awareness, to inform potential customers of the special product features offered by the brand, and to create a feeling of trust in the brand? Such intervening objectives (goals that have no value other than to contribute to the firm's profitability) will help the director of advertising identify attractive courses of action and to select the best among them. Without such guidance, the director could easily seek other means of increasing the firm's profits that were not consistent with the firm's basic marketing strategy.

Now let us consider a more specific example within the advertising department—the objectives of the person responsible for selecting the

---

* The terms "goals," "objectives," "ends," "prizes," "purposes," "aims," and "benefits" will be used interchangeably. The only distinction made here is between ultimate and instrumental goals.

media in which the firm's advertising will appear. To make those selections, the executive responsible for advertising media must make himself knowledgeable about the desired brand image, numbers of reader-viewers of the desired type, the prestige of media, and the kinds of information to be transmitted to specified numbers of potential customers. The media manager would pursue these goals because they contribute to the firm's profitability, survival, and growth by enhancing both revenues and advertising effectiveness. In short, between decisions about advertising media and ultimate objectives, there are several intervening levels of objectives. (See Figure 7-1.) Such intervening objectives give valuable guidance in selecting among alternatives.

Figure 7-1. Ultimate and intervening objectives.

Ultimate objective

Intervening objectives

Increase profits

Increase sales

Improve brand image

Gain favorable associations for brand from media

Reach desired type of reader-viewer

Select appropriate advertising medium

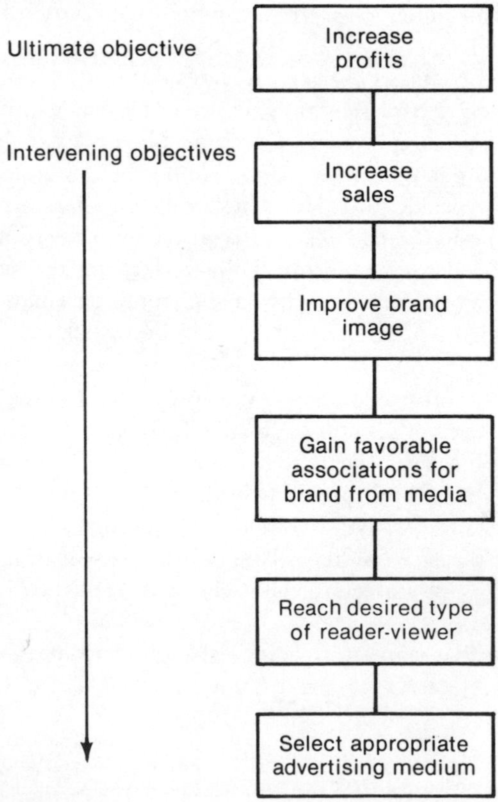

DEVELOPING INTERVENING OBJECTIVES

How might a firm identify its intervening objectives? Once a firm has established its ultimate objectives, do its intervening objectives fall readily into line? Firms can pursue profits, survival, and growth by many diverse means. Individual firms might not choose the same intervening goals even though their ultimate objectives were identical. *A firm's intervening goals basically reflect its strategy.* More specifically, its selection of intervening goals will be based upon an assessment of its capabilities, resources, and opportunities and its bright ideas for their exploitation. It will seek profits, survival, and growth by means that capitalize on the capabilities it possesses rather than by means requiring skills that it lacks. It will seek to lead from its strengths and avoid its weaknesses.

Sometimes a firm will employ several means to attain the same end; occasionally, however, the alternative means are conflicting—they offset one another. Even when they are compatible, that is, not offsetting, they usually compete for limited resources so that a firm cannot pursue all the alternative means without limit and must either select among alternatives or balance their use. Its decisions presumably will reflect management's assessment of its capabilities and opportunities.

Let us make these general remarks more concrete. For the sake of brevity (but at great sacrifice of realism), assume that a firm simply pursues the ultimate objective of short-term profitability. Short-term profitability is defined as the difference between short-term revenues and short-term costs. To maximize short-term profits a firm will seek to attain the greatest difference between short-run revenues and costs. Management must decide how it will achieve high revenues and low costs and whether it wishes to place particular emphasis upon expansion of revenues or contraction of costs.

Some managements would be wise to adopt a policy of tight cost control and limited expenditure because they are particularly skilled at economical operation. Other firms with identical ultimate goals might stress measures to increase revenues while incurring relatively high costs, because their main strengths lie in the area of demand creation. The first firms would want to consider alternative means of limiting their costs. Should they stress mechanization? Removal to a low-cost location? Labor training? Close supervision? Use of low-cost materials? Perhaps they should stress economies of marketing with limited expenditures on advertising, personal selling, customer service, special product features, and so on. Alternatively, they could virtually eliminate all staff service, research and development and reduce the number of very high-calibre executives. These methods of achieving low costs are partly incompatible or internally incon-sistent; for example, in order to achieve low costs in both manufacturing and marketing, a firm presumably will require more rather than fewer high-calibre executives. The path to follow presumably will reflect man-agement's estimate of the things it can do well. If it is inefficient at market-ing it cannot reasonably expect low marketing costs, without suffering a substantial drop in revenues. On the other hand, if the firm possesses considerable expertise in production, it might pursue its goal of low costs by employing its outstanding talents for efficient manufacturing and engineering.

Consider now a firm that pursues high profitability in the short run mainly by stressing high gross revenues. It, too, might employ many different means to achieve this end. It could offer highly attractive product features and appealing product design; it might advertise extensively, win the support of prestigious distributors and retailers, offer special customer services, and the like. If it were to employ *all* these methods of increasing revenues, its costs would be very high. A firm must select among these measures, or at least limit its expenditures for some of them. The firm's decision to emphasize customer service or advertising, for example, pre-sumably would depend upon whether the firm was an effective advertiser or provider of customer service. Similarly, if it was skillful at product design or the development of product features, it would rely heavily upon these methods of expanding revenues and spend relatively little on alterna-tive means that it employed with no particular skill. (See Figure 7-2.)

We have explored how a firm might proceed in logical steps from an initial statement of ultimate objectives to a selection of the instrumental means for pursuing these objectives. In brief, the method consists of defin-ing what the ultimate objective means, in order to help clarify the goals (it is useful to recognize that profits simply represent the difference between total revenues and total costs); identifying alternative means of pursuing the ultimate goal at intervening levels; and selecting among or balancing of these alternatives mainly according to what the firm does relatively well.

Figure 7-2. Alternative means of attaining high gross revenues.

After a firm has established one level of intervening goals in this manner, it can add other levels simply by repeating the process. Each of its intervening goals could be pursued by a variety of means, each representing potential intervening goals. As indicated, management will presumably select among or balance these alternative means on the basis of their cost-effectiveness for the particular firm—given its ability to employ them.

CONSTRUCTING A HIERARCHY OF OBJECTIVES

One can also construct a hierarchy of objectives by starting below the very top. Indeed, it is wise to start a hierarchy with very clear and accepted purposes—like the improvement of engineering designs, more effective advertising appeals, faster delivery from one's suppliers, and the like. With such goals as starting points, one can identify higher-level objectives by asking, "Why do I want that?" Thus, one wants better engineering design for the purpose of reducing manufacturing difficulties and overcoming some product defects; these goals are sought because they would speed production, reduce risk of loss, and permit the use of less skilled personnel; by overcoming product defects the company hopes to achieve greater customer and reseller satisfaction. In turn, these are desired because they contribute to reduced production costs, greater customer loyalty, and wider distribution. (See Figure 7-3.)

This process of developing intervening objectives can be continued until executives at all levels obtain the direction and guidance they need to select among alternatives. That is, when they make any of the myriad decisions that arise, they will know the specific ends they seek and how those ends

Figure 7-3. Network of consequences resulting from improved design.

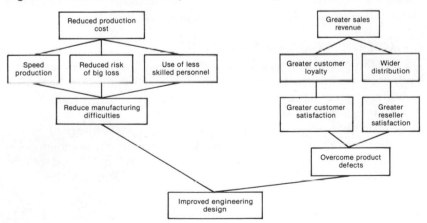

contribute to the attainment of higher-level goals up to and including that of the firm's ultimate objectives. Only when objectives are developed in a series of layers in this manner will most executives receive the guidance that they require to make rational decisions. In the absence of such a developed hierarchy of objectives—that is, ultimate objectives and intervening goals arranged in proper sequence—executives will not know what standards to apply in selecting among alternatives and will therefore probably make many mistaken choices.

A well-developed hierarchy of objectives yields another major benefit: it qualifies each intervening goal by referring specifically to its higher-level purpose. For example, an executive might desire good labor morale to increase productivity and reduce costs in order to enhance profitability. If he recognizes that he pursues good labor morale only to raise profits, an executive will pursue that goal only when and to the extent that it increases productivity and lowers cost, and not for its own sake. Unless he realized his higher-level reason for seeking good labor morale, he might adopt costly measures that *did* improve morale but did *not* increase productivity.

The process outlined here yields more than a hierarchy of objectives; it also develops a detailed business strategy. As indicated, different firms pursuing the same ultimate objectives would select dissimilar intervening goals. Their intervening goals would vary with their ingenuity in perceiving special opportunities, their knowledge of the effectiveness of the means at their disposal for achieving particular ends, and their own special strengths and weaknesses. In other words, the process sketched here produces a combination of intervening goals and strategies all directed toward achieving clearly specified ultimate objectives.

This technique applies equally well to nonbusiness objectives as well as to business objectives. To make that point, for illustrative purposes sample hierarchies have been constructed in Figures 7-4 and 7-5.

Resolving Conflict Among Ultimate Objectives

Up to this point, we have emphasized the need to sort out objectives by level. We now face the fact that organizations and individuals ordinarily pursue multiple objectives which may conflict: that is, to achieve one goal it may be necessary to sacrifice some other goal.

No matter how single-minded they may be, executives invariably desire more than a single prize or benefit from their efforts. For example, individuals will want to get many things out of life, including good health, material comfort, freedom from tension, a family, respect, prestige, security, opportunities for pleasurable activity, mental stimulation, and the like. Business firms pursue success, which is in most cases an amalgam of

Figure 7-4. Personal objectives.

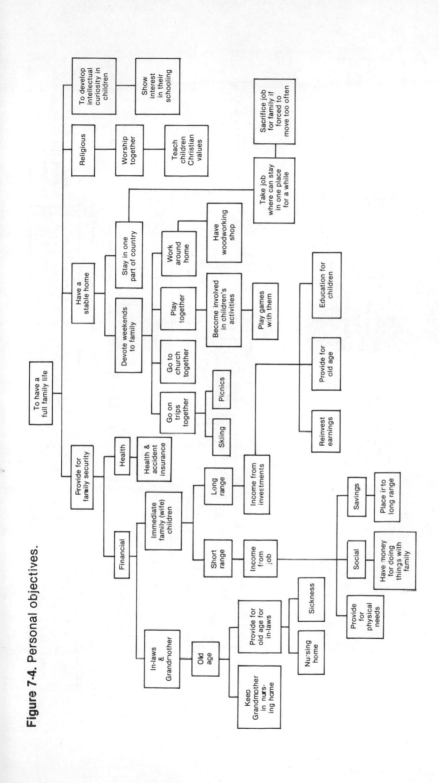

Figure 7-5. Objectives of an MBA program.

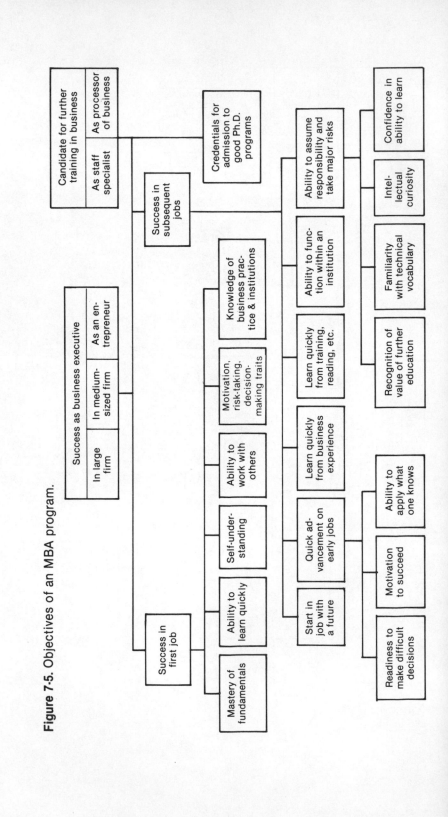

high dividends, high prices for their stock, stable dividends, a broad market for their stock, security of income, and the like. Armies will seek to destroy an enemy, discourage or intimidate potential enemies, acquire territory, minimize casualties, shorten the conflict, foster confidence in the armed forces, and strengthen civilian morale.

When pursuing multiple goals, organizations and individuals must place explicit values on these goals; a mere listing of their goals will not provide the guidance required to make their decisions. Questions of relative importance and incompatibility of goals arise when multiple goals are involved.

What does it mean to say that a firm seeks both long-run profits and growth? Certainly we are not saying that these goals are equally important to the firm's owners. We would expect profits to be more important to the owners than growth. Are we suggesting that they desire growth as a means of attaining profits? Possibly. We could mean that the firm's owners want both long-run profits and growth in and of themselves; or, they seek success, which for them involves both profits and growth. In that event, these goals would be on the same level—that is, one is not desired simply as a means of achieving the other. Yet we cannot assume that they are equally valuable; goals on the same level usually differ greatly in importance. To use an analogy: a housewife may require both roast beef and olives for the dinner she plans to serve her guest; however, the roast ordinarily would be far more important to her than the olives.

When individuals or organizations pursue multiple objectives they face more than questions of *level* (is one goal the means of attaining another?) and *importance* (if faced with a choice, which would one prefer, or for which would one be willing to pay a higher price?). They must also consider the compatibility of specific goals. For example, in some situations if a firm is to grow, that is, increase its total sales, it would be forced to accept lower profits; to act in a publicly responsible manner might likewise be possible only by lowering profits.

Generally speaking, multiple goals on the same level will often come into conflict. That is, a higher level of achievement of one goal will be possible only by accepting less of some other goal. Now that we have defined what we mean by a conflict among objectives,* let us examine why objectives do conflict under most circumstances.

Mainly, *objectives conflict because they require use of common, limited resources—money or time.* In other words, if one seeks pleasurable activity and health, the first may mean staying out until late dancing, say, at the

---

* We will not develop the concept of incompatible goals—goals that actually cancel out and offset each other. For example, one might endanger one's health to achieve certain athletic goals.

expense of needed sleep; moreover, the cost of nightclubs would involve the sacrifice of material comforts in the household (air-conditioning, for example) or the security benefits of a larger bank account, thereby jeopardizing the second. Objectives may also be almost inherently incompatible. A person who sought great career success would usually be forced to devote large amounts of time to travel, work, or study away from his family, whose welfare was another of his goals. The very emphasis on career (even if it did not deprive his family of his time) might diminish his contribution to or enjoyment of his family. Some more intrinsic incompatibilities of goals might be: attainment of material success and the enjoyment of the affection and companionship of many people—in the event that great success puts an individual in a relatively lonely position and makes his personal contacts somewhat strained, at least for others. Whether because they compete for common resources that are limited in supply or because of their intrinsic incompatibility, multiple goals usually conflict.

The potential conflict among goals again raises the question of importance. When goals conflict, which one should the individual or organization favor? One would expect the answer to be, the more important goal—the roast beef rather than the olives. But this answer is a little too quick. If one has already attained a large measure of a certain goal, he may at some point place a low value on more of it and consider other goals more important than he had when his situation was different. Once a man has become rich, he places less value on additional income and more on health, prestige, or time with his family. Or, when the housewife already has more than enough roast beef to serve her company, the olives become more essential to her than more meat.

What we have said is that the importance of individual goals, their rank order, is not constant; it varies with one's circumstances. In particular, it varies, as indicated above, with how much one has already attained of one's various objectives. The importance of goals is also likely to vary over time, for as they mature, individuals' and organizations' goals ordinarily do change. How can one express the relationship between conflicting objectives in a manner that will inform a decision maker who must select among alternative activities?

Several techniques are available to an executive for this purpose: indifference curves, trade-offs, and rating scales. In most cases, rating scales will meet an executive's needs best. They are used in a subsequent example, and their method of construction is discussed along with indifference curves and trade-offs below.

INDIFFERENCE CURVES

The indifference curve technique was developed by economists to over-come a seemingly serious weakness in formal economic theory: the assumption that the psychological satisfaction (usually called "utility") that an individual derives from a product or service can be measured—quantified—with considerable precision. If that were possible, the combination of goods and services that an individual should purchase at prevailing prices could be determined with high accuracy. (Similarly, it was assumed that the disutility of different activities—work, assuming risk, waiting to consume, giving up the use of one's assets,—could be quantified accurately.)

These assumptions have been rejected by most social scientists, but economists have been able to support the chief conclusions of neoclassical theory without assuming that utility and disutility are measurable. They have done this by "indifference analysis," which revolves around the assumption, easily verified, that individuals can determine what combinations of items give them the same amount of satisfaction. They can identify pairs of items they consider equally valuable to them—they are indifferent as to which pairs of items they have—because both pairs give them equal utility.

An indifference curve depicts combinations of two items that yield a particular individual equal satisfaction. An executive might conclude, with the help of a skilled interviewer, that at present he would give up $25 of income to have a half-day of leisure to spend on a golf course. We can express that idea as a trade-off of time for money equal to $25 and a half-day; or, the rate of exchange today between income and leisure (for golf) is $25 to one half-day. Now, we observed that the value one might place on a goal would depend upon the amount one already had achieved of that goal. The same individual who would be willing to forego $25 for a chance to play golf for a half-day might be willing to give up only $10 if he felt pinched for funds to pay his income tax installment; on the other hand, if his income were to rise substantially he might be willing to give up the chance to make $100 in order to play golf. Conversely, if he had been playing lots of golf in recent days, he might not be willing to give up much income at all to be able to play more on the following day. This last relationship simply expresses the principle of diminishing utility, according to which the more one has of something, the less he values added quantities of it.

In Figure 7-6 this relationship between two desired items is described by the use of indifference curves. Rather simple geometry says very clearly

Figure 7-6. Indifference curves depicting data in Table 7-1.

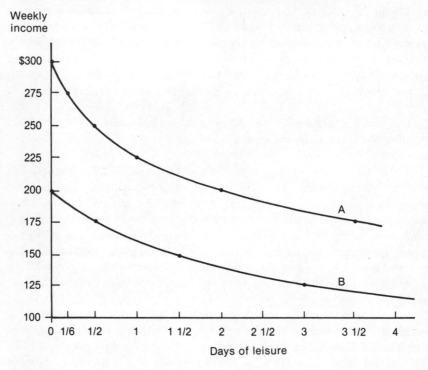

what remains vague when expressed in words. This technique builds upon the demonstrated ability of individuals to specify many combinations of two items—like amounts of beef and olives; income and golf; high dividends and high security prices; interesting work and after-tax income; added leisure and prestige—that they find of equal value. The numbers underlying the curves presented in Figure 7-6 are set forth in Table 7-1.

One can construct lines in two-dimensional space which show the many combinations of two items that are of equal value to some person. Line A in Figure 7-6 is such a line, and is called an "indifference curve." Each axis measures quantities of a particular item—money and leisure in this case—and the line represents the many combinations of money and leisure that (during one period of time) are equally valuable to a specific individual. For example, at a certain point he would have $250 of income (in that week) and a half-day of leisure, which he would devote to playing golf. He is indifferent as between the two, valuing them equally. The other combina-

Table 7-1

HYPOTHETICAL COMBINATIONS OF WEEKLY INCOME AND DAYS OF LEISURE
THAT ARE EQUALLY ATTRACTIVE TO A PARTICULAR PERSON

A		B	
Weekly income	Days of leisure	Weekly income	Days of leisure
$300	0	$200	0
275	1/6 day	175	1/2 day
250	1/2 day	150	1½ days
225	1 day	125	3 days
200	2 days	100	more than
175	3½ days		full-time
			leisure

tions depicted on the diagram are no more or less valuable to him than
these two combinations.

Line B, like line A, shows combinations of income and leisure that are
equally valuable, but this one shows combinations that are on a lower
level—that is, they yield less satisfaction because they involve smaller
quantities of money and leisure. In other words, we learn from this curve
what was not shown by the other—namely, what combinations of income
and leisure were equal in value to this person's $200 of income and no
leisure in that week; the other curve only considered combinations of
money and leisure equal in value to $300, and no leisure.

What must be observed is that the indifference curve is truly a curve,
rather than a straight line, because the trade-off between money and leisure
is not constant; rather, the more money the person has, the greater the
amount of money he would be willing to give up for some extra leisure
time; conversely, the more leisure he possesses, the greater the amount of it
he would give up to increase his income. Expressed in more technical
language, *the rate at which he can substitute money for leisure* (and end up with
the same amount of satisfaction) varies with the amount he already has of
each. This rate of substitution varies; for any particular combination of
items one can determine the "marginal rate of substitution"—which expresses the amount of one that one would be willing to trade for a unit of
the other *at that point*. An important principle explaining the rates of substitution of one item for another is the "principle of the diminishing
marginal rate of substitution," which simply means that the amount of
one item that a person will give up to obtain a unit of another diminishes

as one has less of the former—that is, one gives up less and less of item x for item y as one slides down the indifference curve and has less of item x.

TRADE-OFFS

A trade-off represents an exchange of items that leaves at least one party to the trade no better and no worse off than before. If I can exchange my tennis racket for a sweatsuit and feel neither injured nor benefited by the exchange, then that exchange represents a trade-off. It should be self-evident that an indifference schedule or indifference curve includes many implicit trade-offs. Figure 7-6 and Table 7-1 describe a hypothetical individual who was making $300 and had no leisure; we learned that he would have paid $25 per week for one-sixth of a day of leisure. That would describe a trade-off. What is particularly confusing is that if he were making $225 and already had a day of leisure a week, he would give up $25 of income only if he could gain another full day of leisure. Trade-offs thus are not constant but vary with one's circumstances and especially with the amount of the items already possessed.

During short periods of time, circumstances are fairly constant. Consequently, it is often possible to establish trade-offs between two items—they could be objectives—that would help to make decisions involving conflicting objectives. For example, if one knew that his trade-off between dollars and leisure were $20 these days, he could make many of life's daily decisions much more easily. For example, he could compute the cost to him, in dollar equivalents, of painting his bedroom, mowing his lawn, going downtown to buy something that is available in the neighborhood, and the like.

The use of trade-offs can thus be very helpful, even though one must recognize the unlikelihood that trade-offs are constant, even during fairly short time periods. Still, their use often makes for a far better decision than intuitive snap judgments.

Let us return to the substance of the argument, for we have digressed to discuss modes of communicating some important ideas. We have shown that certain goals that are coordinate—on the same level—can conflict; and, we can resolve that conflict by means of trade-offs. These trade-offs are not constant; it is possible to depict varying trade-offs by means of indifference curves.

Consider now the usual situation where several intermediate goals which are capable of producing the same higher-level goal are in conflict. For example, assume that a sick person wants medical care, rest, and the assistance of others with his work—in order to regain his health. These goals conflict both in time and cost; how does one reconcile such a conflict among goals?

The answer is fairly simple; the sick person would divide his time and money among these three competing intervening goals in a way that would produce the greatest amount of regained health. He would not give up an hour of rest to see his doctor if his health would benefit more from an hour's rest than the doctor's care. Similarly, he would not spend sums for personal assistance if those sums spent for medical care would do more for his health. We express this process as "the allocation of resources"* among alternative uses in a manner that yields maximum benefit—that is, it attains the highest level of goal achievement. In such cases, one is only balancing alternative means of achieving the same goal; the situation does not reflect basic conflict among goals—but alternative means of attaining the same goals.

Conflict sometimes arises among goals that are on different levels and not related to one another as means and ends. For example, intervening goals on the third and fourth level of a hierarchy may compete for scarce financial resources or for a top executive's limited time. The value of each goal depends on its contribution to the individual's ultimate goals. A low-level goal that contributes heavily to a vital ultimate goal, like survival, might be far more important than a higher-level goal for attaining, say, prestige. Let us examine a simple hypothetical illustration.

Assume that Mr. X's hierarchy has three ultimate goals: income, prestige, and family fulfillment. Let us assume that he values them as follows: income 60 percent, prestige 15 percent, family fulfillment 25 percent. This hierarchy, along with his intervening goals (labeled A through H), is shown in Figure 7-7.

Mr. X can, for the same cost in time, add to either H or C; the fact that C is on a higher level than H does *not* make it a more valuable instrumental goal than H. If B was by far the major determinant of income and H had a dominant effect on B, then H has a major influence on income—Mr. X's main ultimate goal. Conversely, if C has relatively little effect on Mr. X's prestige, which he values far less than income, it is not an important goal—though a high-level goal.

Much of the foregoing discussion was expressed in terms of individuals' rather than organizations' goals. The same conclusions hold for both, without exception. For example, Figure 7-8 presents a structure of business

---

* This vital process, which calls for application of the equimarginal principle, is discussed in detail in Chapter 3.

Figure 7-7. A weighted hierarchy of ultimate and intervening goals.

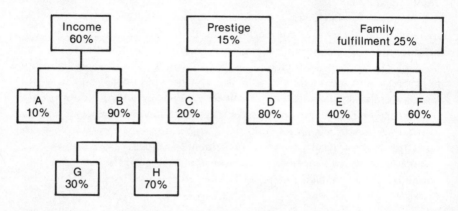

goals in the form of a three-level hierarchy. Potential conflict exists among goals at each level, and perhaps on different levels. The numbers in parenthesis are weights that inform the decision maker of the importance of each goal. They provide a decision maker with the information he requires to make his choices and to reconcile conflicts. Knowing the weights makes some choices among alternatives intuitively obvious. When the choices are more difficult, the decision maker can employ the rating scale technique described below.

Thus, we conclude that if the owners of a business want their executives to reflect their values, they must present them with hierarchies of objectives and assign weights to their top-level objectives. Without such guidance, executives would not know what importance to attach to differ-

Figure 7-8. Business objectives: financial goals with trade-offs.

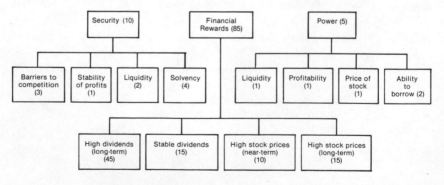

ent goals and usually would be forced to make value judgments that properly should be made for them by the business owners.

RATING SCALES AND THE ASSIGNMENT OF WEIGHTS

We are constantly evaluating things, people, and ideas. Almost always, we seek many attributes in our choice. For example, we pick a jacket from among three of equal cost that seem to please us most. One is more attractive in appearance than the other two, the second fits most comfortably, and the third is least likely to soil. These jackets differ in other respects as well. How should we choose among them? The process used is the same one we would employ in selecting investment projects, employees, vacations, and plant locations.

A choice among alternatives usually involves at least the following steps: (1) itemize the benefits (attributes) that you seek; (2) decide how important each one is to you; (3) describe each alternative in terms of each desired attribute—that is, how much do you like the appearance of the jacket on a scale of 1 to 100? How comfortable does it feel? How likely is it to soil? One's choice can be valid only by accident unless all three elements enter into the selection.

A rating scale is built out of these three ingredients, organized as shown in Table 7-2. Observe that this table indicates the attributes in which we are interested—that is, our objectives; it calls for an indication of the importance of each attribute and, finally, it describes each of the items among which we are choosing with respect to those attributes.

In the table, the column titled *Importance* has been left blank, for it is more complex than others. We seek numerical values to express the value we place on the three attributes we want. On the surface, that task seems simple enough. We may say that we mainly seek something attractive, fit is secondary (partly because it affects a jacket's attractiveness), and resistance

Table 7-2

A RATING SCALE FOR JACKETS

Attribute (1)	Importance (weight) (2)	Description of alternatives		
		(3)	(4)	(5)
Appearance (style)		90	75	80
Fit		75	90	75
Resistance to dirt		55	60	95

to dirt is least important. On that basis and after some reflection and juggling around of the numbers, we might assign weights of 50, 35, and 15 to the three attributes. One serious nonobvious difficulty must be faced in this manner of assigning weights, and there are other difficulties as well.* That is, the importance of an attribute depends on its amount. For example, resistance to dirt may be relatively unimportant and deserve a weight of 15. If, however, the jacket is made so that it will soil almost immediately and therefore look terrible, then resistance to dirt can become a fatal flaw. Similarly, fit may not be vital, unless the garment clearly looks as if it was intended for a different person altogether.

In other words, the importance of attributes may not be linear—the importance of the attribute may vary with its level; also, it may be affected by the other attributes with which it is combined. (This second point will not be developed here, but also poses difficult problems in making evaluations.)

This difficulty is conceptually very crucial. Fortunately, in practice it is far less so. In making our initial selection of alternatives, we are likely to weed out unacceptable alternatives—the jacket that soils too easily and fits poorly get discarded immediately. Those alternatives that are exceptional (that is, they dominate the others) usually are obvious to the decision maker, eliminating the need for sophisticated techniques. A jacket that was just beautiful, fit adequately, and was satisfactory on grounds of resistance to soiling would clearly be selected.

Decision makers unconsciously adjust to the fact that attributes are not linear in importance. Very low levels of an attribute may disqualify an alternative altogether—it is not up to an acceptable threshold. Similarly, if a choice is outstanding in a particular attribute, its weight *may* warrant a substantial increase.

However, we are content in this case to assume that linear weights will do no violence to our results (within the limited range of differences we deal with). The steps that remain after Table 7-2 has been constructed are as follows:

1. Express each valuation (columns 3, 4, and 5) as percentages of the largest value there. In the case of "appearance/style," the numbers would become 100, 83.3, and 88.9 (see Table 7-3). (This step is termed normalization and is required to avoid distortion of the

---

* One often makes judgments about weights *in the abstract* that turn out to need modification after one examines alternatives. Before assigning weights to individual attributes, one would be wise to consider carefully a few realistic alternatives, for that experience is likely to affect one's initial weights rather markedly.

Table 7-3

A RATING SCALE FOR JACKETS

Attribute (1)	Importance (weight) (2)	(3)	Description of alternatives (normalized) (4)	(5)	Weighted description of alternatives (columns 3, 4, and 5 times column 2) (6)	(7)	(8)
Appearance (style)	50	100	83.3	88.9	50.0	41.7	44.5
Fit	35	83.3	100	83.3	29.2	35.0	29.2
Resistance to dirt	15	57.9	63.2	100.0	8.7	9.5	15.0
Point score					87.9	86.2	88.7

weights assigned in column 2. Other methods of normalization are defensible; the one used here seems both simplest and most reasonable.)

2. Multiply these adjusted valuations by the attribute weight.
3. Total the resultant score for each alternative (jacket).

Observe that the final rating shows all three jackets to be essentially equal in value—to the decision maker. He might therefore want to purchase the jacket that pleased him most. One could hardly consider the rating scale a precise technique; differences of a few points cannot usually be considered significant.

Financial Objectives: Differences in Level and How They Conflict*

Most executives say that their primary objective is to make a profit. We intuitively understand what that means: they try to obtain income greater than their costs. While the concept of profit is clear in the abstract, its measurement presents great practical difficulties. Because profit can be measured in different ways, it does not represent a clear objective and consequently may give unclear or mistaken guidance to a decision maker. The ambiguity and vagueness of profits as a goal result from ambiguities in the definition of both costs and income and from difficulties in assigning both to particular periods of time.

Some puzzling questions can be asked about profits as a business objective. For example, should management be more interested in absolute

* Prepared with extensive and valuable assistance from L. Scott Miller.

dollars of profit or the rate of return on the firm's investment? Should it pursue maximum return on sales, net worth, total assets—or some other base? What different financial and nonfinancial objectives do and should businesses actually pursue?

This section discusses the objectives that firms might use to measure financial performance and as standards for evaluating investment projects.* The discussion establishes three conclusions: First, firms should pursue many financial goals on different levels, since some goals are simply the means of attaining the higher-level goals, and should be pursued only to the extent that they contribute to those goals. Second, management's financial goals—as well as nonfinancial goals—often conflict, because projects that promise high returns if measured by one financial goal might yield low returns when measured by another. Executives require guidance to resolve such conflict, especially because the various financial goals are not equally important. Third, a technique exists for stating a firm's objectives that would provide its executives with the guidance they require to make crucial decisions. This technique and its rationale will be sketched here.

Alternative Financial Objectives

Listed below are 16 financial objectives that firms might properly use as indices of financial success. Executives will try to select the projects that rate highest when evaluated by one or more of these indices. This list is not all-inclusive; several items are very similar to one another, and the validity of individual items may be disputed. Since our main purpose is to understand the significance of differences in the level of individual objectives and to learn how to decide in the face of conflicting objectives, these possible shortcomings in the list will not be considered.

Plausible Financial Objectives

1. Maximum long-run stock price.
2. Maximum short-run stock price.
3. Maximum long-run dividends.
4. Maximum short-run dividends.
5. Stable dividends.
6. Stable stock prices.
7. Maximum return on investment.

---

* Those interested in understanding these financial objectives in greater depth should consult one or more textbooks in the field of finance. One excellent source is James C. Van Horne's *Financial Management and Policy* (Englewood Cliffs, N.J.: Prentice-Hall, 1971).

8. Maximum present value of future income.
9. Most favorable financial statements.
10. Maximum net dollar profit.
11. Ability to borrow from institutions at low cost.
12. Financial liquidity.
13. Ability to float stock at attractive prices.
14. Freedom from financial constraints.
15. Maximum short-run earnings per share.
16. Maximum long-run earnings per share.

All the objectives listed above appear desirable and valuable in themselves. However, since some overlap, one might serve in place of several. Although several appear similar, they are actually different. More to the point, some of these financial objectives may conflict. Actions which would increase one of the items on the list will frequently decrease one or more of the others. Some of these objectives are expressed in dollar amounts, while several are ratios; some concern items as they appear on a firm's financial statements, while others represent estimates of future earnings; some are built on traditional accounting information, while others call for estimates of "economic" costs;* some relate to a firm's ability to increase its resources from outside sources, while most reflect a change in the firm's internal resources. Little wonder that they do not all vary together, in the same direction, or by the same degree.

The items listed above should make quite clear that firms do and should seek many goals that are financial in nature. We must now determine whether these are truly different goals or possibly the same goal viewed on different levels. Also, we want to assess their relative importance, though that issue is highly subjective; business owners and top management must reflect their value judgments in the objectives they pursue and in the weights they assign to them.

Sorting Financial Objectives by Level

Many things differ in level. Judged by authority possessed, a colonel is on a higher level than a corporal; a company president is on a higher level than a clerk; and so on. Similarly, judged by generality, a tree is on a

---

* Economic costs represent actual reductions in the value of assets through use, the passage of time, or direct expenditure; accounting costs, on the other hand, represent charges against income made in the course of preparing financial statements. Economic costs are estimated on the basis of existing market values—replacement costs in most cases—while accounting costs are based on historical acquisition costs. Sometimes the economic and accounting costs of a given action differ very greatly, although in most cases the difference is not great.

higher level than a branch, which is on a higher level than a twig; a state is on a higher level than a county or town; clothing is, similarly, on a higher level than shoes or hats. The notion of level is sometimes subtle, mainly because one can arrange the same items according to different criteria. By one criterion, an item will be on a higher level than another item, but the relationship may be reversed if another criterion is used. For example, an executive may be on a higher level than his subordinate in the company but on a lower level in his firm's ranking of golfers.

The basis on which we will assign financial objectives to different levels is their means-ends relationship. This process places anything that is a means for achieving something else subordinate to it and on a lower level. For example, a firm can free itself from financial constraints on its choices by increasing its ability to borrow. On that basis, we place freedom from financial constraints (objective 14) on a higher level than ability to borrow (objective 11). If high present value of future income is desired for maximum long-run stock price, then it is on a lower level than maximum long-run stock price. To arrange financial objectives by level, then, one must understand causal relationships—that is, what items affect what other items.

The importance of individual objectives to firms depends upon whose viewpoint is adopted. Some persons—either owners or executives—may make frequent trades in a firm's stock. They ordinarily would emphasize the firm's near-term stock prices. Top managers are more likely to stress freedom from financial constraints, so that they can carry out the programs they favor; they also emphasize favorable financial statements and high dividends, for those strengthen management's position with the board of directors.

In order to simplify the discussion, we will adopt the view of stockholders who plan to hold their stock for a long time. What are the main financial goals of such persons? Are they all on the same level? Rather than describe the ultimate goals of such owners in specific cases or even in general, we will suggest a plausible set of financial objectives for such persons.

Stockholders planning to hold securities for a long-term capital gain clearly are interested mainly in long-term appreciation in stock values, high dividend disbursements, and stability of both stock prices and dividends. What about the other financial objectives listed above? Are these of no concern to such stockholders?

On the contrary, they desire virtually all the items on the list, though not equally or possibly not even for the same reason. Let us sort out our 16 objectives by constructing a hierarchy, as in Figure 7-9, in which items

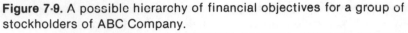

Figure 7-9. A possible hierarchy of financial objectives for a group of stockholders of ABC Company.

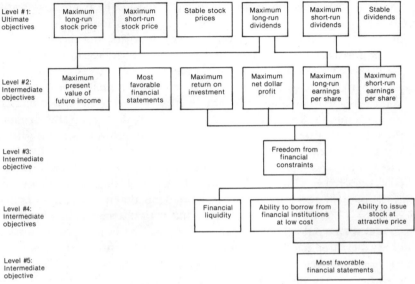

that are placed high are more important, more general, or closer to ultimate objectives than those that are low.*

Summary and Conclusions

Firms err in the formulation of objectives in many ways. Some fail to provide their executives with any explicit statement of objectives or give them statements prepared only for public relations purposes. When top management does set down the firms' objectives, it usually states only the top-level objectives, frequently with omissions. In addition, top manage-

---

* Note that this hierarchy of objectives would be changed if we adopted a different group's viewpoint. Top management, family owners, stockholders who are also suppliers, all might have quite different objectives from those of long-term stockholders. For example, top management may have the ultimate objectives of financial security (the desire to retain high salaries, bonuses, stock options, and pensions), the prestige of running a large firm, and the satisfaction of planning and implementing new projects. Speculators in a company's stock may be interested only in the short-term price of the common stock. A different hierarchy would be required for each of these groups. These differences are developed by G. Donaldson, "Financial Goals: Management vs. Stockholders," *Harvard Business Review*, May–June 1963, pp. 16–29.

ment typically fails to indicate the extent to which individual goals should be pursued, placing emphasis upon such goals as market share and sales increases without specifying that these are desired only as means toward attaining the higher-level goals of profits and growth. Sometimes top management specifies objectives solely as numerical targets, and these typically are set at unreasonably high levels and are therefore ignored or resented. In general, the statements of objectives available to executives contain large gaps so that executives often must guess at what top management thinks. Beyond these shortcomings, most statements of objectives do not specify trade-offs among ultimate objectives; inasmuch as these typically conflict, decision makers again face an "objectives gap" and must guess at the values of top management.

The remedy for almost all errors in statements of objectives is a hierarchy of objectives. Usually, it is wise to develop such a hierarchy by starting both in the middle and from the top down. In the course of developing a hierarchy, an executive is likely to discover some objectives that otherwise would be overlooked, recognize the importance of distinguishing between long- and short-run objectives, and, most important, order his objectives by level so that he will not become locked in to a low-level objective and pursue it far beyond the point where it contributes to a higher-level objective.

Measures of Payoff and Objectives: A Dialog

Paul and Tony are senior executives in a medium-sized firm which is a leader in the production and sale of major items of hospital equipment.

This company evaluates capital projects by means of "discounted cash flow" (DCF), a technique of investment evaluation developed by Joel Dean. This technique starts with a forecast of the cash inflows and outflows over the life of an investment project. By trial and error, vastly simplified by the use of a computer, the analyst finds a discount rate that would make the present value of all the cash flows equal to zero. (This discount rate is often described as the "internal rate of return.") The larger the discount rate, thus defined, the more attractive the investment. This technique is illustrated below by an extremely simple numerical example.

Assume that the cash flows associated with a particular investment are those presented in Table 7-4. These data represent management's collective best estimates of the cash flows that would result if this investment were undertaken. The discount rate that makes the cash flows total to zero (with the present value of the outflows just equal to the present value of the inflows) is about 14.5 percent. (The table shows the effects of discounting the cash flows by 14 percent and by 15 percent.)

Table 7-4

DISCOUNTED CASH FLOW ILLUSTRATED

Year	Net cash flow	Present value of $1 at 14%	Present value of $1 at 15%	Present value of net cash flows at 14%	Present value of net cash flows at 15%
0	−11,000	1.0	1.0	−$11,000	−$11,000
1	− 3,000	.877	.870	−$ 2,631	−$ 2,610
2	+10,000	.769	.750	+$ 7,690	+$ 7,500
3	+ 9,000	.675	.658	+$ 6,075	+$ 5,922
Net present value of project				+$ 134	−$ 188

The DCF technique does not produce a measure of return on investment (ROI) in the usual sense of the term. Indeed, this term is misleading, as commonly used, and is ambiguous at best. The reader will understand why this is so if he would try to define "investment" or "investment requirements" and compute their size in the foregoing hypothetical example. The DCF technique processes all flows of cash associated with an investment by adjusting them for the time they occur.

PAUL: Tony, I've got a problem that you could help me think through. Can you spare a half hour to straighten me out?

TONY: Sure, I'm flattered that you think I can help. What seems to be the problem?

PAUL: I suppose you could say it lies in the area of objectives. I must choose the best standard for selecting among alternative investments and, of course, the choice of standard will determine which investments I select. I now cannot accept the standard I've been quite content with for many years.

Let me be more specific. I'm chairman of the capital projects committee, as you know. Like most committees, this one largely reflects the views of its chairman. I therefore act as if the decisions were really mine, even though occasionally my colleagues actively participate in some decisions. I really give each of our capital project decisions a very thorough analysis.

TONY: I would hope so. That committee assignment is probably the most important job around this company. I assumed that over the years you developed a reliable standard for judging capital projects.

PAUL: We did. My problems all started when my son, Ken, who is studying for his MBA, visited me last week and asked lots of questions about my duties here. He was particularly interested in how the capital projects committee operates. What came out of that discussion changed my view of the value of going to school, and even more, of the validity of return on investment as the standard for evaluating projects. You, of course, recognize that we have been using Discounted Cash Flow (DCF) techniques to evaluate projects, which we often call ROI, even though it really isn't the same thing.

TONY: Yes, I know you use DCF and I also know that you call it ROI. What does your son find wrong with DCF? One could always question the estimated inflows and outflows of cash that underly a DCF computation. And to the extent that we use a figure for the cost of capital, we might be too high or too low. But I know of no method of evaluating projects that is free from those two difficulties.

PAUL: Ken's objections were different and probably more fundamental than those two. He considers those difficulties unavoidable. It would save time if I showed you the letter I got from Ken yesterday. I had suggested that he set down his misgivings about what we are doing and give his recommendations for improving our methods. He must have spent a lot of time on his reply because he boiled his thoughts down to just a few terse pages. Why don't you read it while I make a phone call and then we might resume our discussion.

TONY: Fine. I must take care of a few matters first. Then I'll read the letter. I'll be back in about half an hour.

*   *   *

TONY: That really was an excellent statement you got from Ken—better than most of the consulting reports we get around here. I sure hope he changes his mind and decides to join this company, even if it means that some people will think he's getting ahead because of his dad's influence. He really seems to be getting a business training that comes to grips with real-life problems.

His long list of financial objectives that a firm's management should consider was useful, and the notion that they must be sorted out by level and given weights was new to me. I see your problem now. But it isn't really your problem to resolve, you know—only one to raise. Your committee can't determine the objectives that the firm should pursue. That's the prerogative of top management. All you can do is evaluate projects according to their financial consequences.

PAUL: Yes, I realize that. But I now realize that we should consider more than financial matters when we pick our investments. I'd like to suggest some nonfinancial goals that top management might want to endorse. Aren't some objectives "right" for this company?

TONY: I'd guess that there is a more correct set of objectives for this company at this time, but no single right answer for all companies at all times. The goals of the owners and board of directors are understandably different from company to company and from time to time.

PAUL: Does that mean that all standards for judging investments are right? Are no standards clearly wrong?

TONY: I would suppose that many objectives or what you call standards for evaluating projects could be wrong because they are not related to the higher-level objectives set down by top management. These standards would be wrong because they are inconsistent with the firm's higher goals. Let's take ROI, for example. How do they relate to the firm's financial goals of increasing the value of the firm's securities, or improving its ability to borrow, or its liquidity, or showing the level of accounting profits that the firm wishes to report this year for tax purposes?

I guess that I'm asking—as your son did—which of the firm's top-level objectives will you be achieving if you pick the projects with the highest ROI? Have you selected the yardstick of ROI because it does truly measure the achievement of the goals set down by top management?

PAUL: That's the source of my problem. We're picking projects on the basis of ROI and apparently ignoring any other objectives. Our objectives probably include things that may not be directly related to ROI.

TONY: Frankly, I haven't faced up to this issue before, and it seems important to resolve it if we can. Some thoughts come to my mind that may narrow the issues we should discuss. First, I think that the ROI computations permit us to reject projects that don't meet our minimum financial requirements. These are projects that don't promise to produce what we believe we could earn, if only we would wait a while. Second, the key questions that we might raise about other objectives—like the effect of a given project on the value of our securities, our ability to borrow, and the like, could be added to our computations of ROI and considered by the committee at the time it evaluates individual projects. I assumed that this happens most of the time. When a project has important effects that are not reflected in ROI, won't someone stress the omission and see that it does get taken into account?

PAUL: Well, the answer is yes in some cases, but certainly not in most. Maybe that is the key point. ROI may be the most useful yardstick for projects whose nonfinancial effects are trivial. But when other consequences of a project are important, we must take them into account. We often do, as you said, but in a nonquantitative and unsystematic manner. We do it by making an extra input into our deliberations. But it is not at all clear how much weight that input receives. And if we only mention additional considerations without including them explicitly— preferably numerically—in our estimates of the net outcome, what effect do they have?

I remember hearing at least a dozen times in the last two years that particular projects wouldn't yield as high an ROI as some others but that they would produce important benefits in the form of improved employee morale, more favorable brand image, and good public relations.

TONY: The problem we started with has now expanded from how to take account of the firm's full range of objectives—both financial and others—to a related but different subject. The other subject is, how to compute *all* the consequences of our projects, and in particular how to place a value on the intangible effects of projects where they have major nonfinancial effects. What seems clear to me now is that the whole ROI approach deals only with tangible financial effects and ignores other effects. It really takes account only of cash inflows and outflows and not of other things that might be important values to the firm's owners and top management. ROI does nothing to take growth into account, for example, but most of our board of directors speak constantly of growth as one of our main goals.

Let me put my point more systematically. You first raised the question of how our firm should rank individual capital projects and indicated that we use ROI as the method of evaluating each one. Second, you pointed out that by doing this, your committee considers only the financial effects of capital projects, whereas top management often talks of nonfinancial objectives—like growth, survival, public service. Third, we have begun to talk about how, if at all, we do, or could, take intangible effects of projects into account. We should try to keep these issues separate—at least be clear as to which one we're discussing at any time.

And one last point. What I've learned here is that ROI is defective on at least two scores. It only ranks projects by financial return, and therefore ignores our nonfinancial objectives. And it does not take account of intangible effects at all—even if they have important financial implications.

PAUL: You clearly are on the same track that I'm on since I talked to my son.

On this intangible business, I don't think that they should be taken into account unless they ultimately have tangible effects. I think our decision should consider, say, the effects of a project on our brand image or employee morale only if that effect alters our costs or sales in the future. When that happens, we'll either get tangible benefits or incur tangible costs. We'll take those things into account when their effects become tangible.

TONY: It's true that when intangible consequences of a project subsequently reduce our revenues or increase our costs, our books will show higher income or higher costs. But that's very different from evaluating those tangible effects when the decision is made. Clearly, we should take those subsequent tangible effects into account at the time we estimate the return on a project.

PAUL: You're perfectly right. Even though we get a higher level of sales due to improved brand image, that benefit won't be associated with the project that brought it about unless our original estimates included them.

Around here we have been very hard-nosed in our insistence on including only clear, direct, and tangible effects of projects. We tend to be impatient with talk about indirect effects and intangibles. If anyone said that his project would improve our brand image and as a result would increase sales by 2 percent per year, and that that would add $120,000 to net profit before taxes, and if he included those figures in his estimated return on investment—he'd be hooted out of here.

TONY: I'm not surprised, but we should be asking how such effects could be taken into account properly. Strangely enough, we don't hoot at people who recommend that we spend very large sums on advertising in order to improve our brand image—though I realize that such proposals do not come before your capital projects committee. We have a glaring inconsistency here. Either a better brand image is or isn't a valuable benefit to this firm. If it is, then any project that improves our brand image should include it as a benefit.

PAUL: Your reference to advertising suggests something to me. Why don't we place a value on the improvement in our brand image due to some project by estimating how much it would cost to achieve the same result by means of advertising. Or we might even estimate how much we would be willing to pay for such an improvement in brand image, regardless of the means by which it was attained.

TONY: Those are interesting ideas and even seem practical, but we couldn't accurately estimate the cost to achieve the same improvement in brand image by advertising or even get much agreement on the value

of a given degree of improvement in brand image. I suppose our advertising director would have some idea of the worth, or at least the cost, of
any particular improvement in brand image, but he would certainly
refuse to make such estimates.

It's now becoming clear that we've been discussing three questions
that we should keep very separate: First is the measurement or forecasting problem, especially of intangibles—like assessing a project's effect on
brand image and then how that will affect sales. As you agree, we face
the same problem in deciding whether and how much to advertise. The
second is the conceptual problem of what effects should be included in
the evaluation of a project. We seem to agree that nonfinancial effects
could constitute central considerations in many capital projects. If so,
we must deal with them, but how? Third, how do we take account of
trade-offs among such objectives as long-run and short-run profits,
growth, survival, and the like.

PAUL: I see the problem of tangibles as one of measurement or forecasting
rather than a conceptual issue. If I really knew that the improvement in
brand image brought about by a proposal would yield a 2 percent increase in sales in 18 months, I'd include that benefit without hesitation.
I'd treat it like any other increase in sales resulting from a major outlay.
To be specific, we just voted to hire four new sales specialists to call on
hospitals and schools and estimated the sales that would result. We
certainly don't know what sales those four specialists will produce, but
we authorized the project on the basis of our estimates. Judged by our
past track record, our estimates are likely to be far off the mark on that
one. Still, we make our decisions on the basis of such estimates. My
problem with brand image, employee morale, distributor goodwill, and
such things is that I even have trouble defining them and almost certainly can't measure them. How in the world can I hope to estimate
them and their effect on other things?

TONY: I don't minimize the estimation problem. It's easy to go far
wrong, but you have at least indicated what should be estimated and
have even suggested an interesting way of placing a value on it. You say
that in dealing with intangibles, we should be concerned with their
ultimate tangible effects. That seems right to me and also quite helpful,
even though such estimates could prove to be far off the mark.

PAUL: You're giving me more credit than I deserve, but I'll accept it
gladly. My thoughts on intangibles are much better sorted out now, but
the nonfinancial objectives issue remains pretty clouded in my mind
still.

TONY: Come to think of it, we've ignored a whole class of intangibles—

and that may be where much of our difficulty arises. For example, one of our firm's ultimate goals is to be recognized as a good member of the community. If that's so, then a project that makes a social contribution should be credited with producing something that top management values, even if it does not give rise to a subsequent tangible benefit. In other words, it represents a benefit in and of itself without increasing revenues or reducing costs. As such, it should be treated as equivalent to some amount of money income and should perhaps figure in the return on investment when that project is compared with others.

PAUL: Hold on there. That's going much too far, even conceptually. Are you prepared to argue that in computing a return on investment we should place a value on service to the community? How would you estimate its value in the first place? That line of thinking would make all calculations of return on investment hopelessly confusing—no one would know what they meant.

TONY: You obviously believe that my suggestion would destroy the purity of what otherwise would be quite accurate and unambiguous estimates of return on investment. Face it, our estimates are necessarily based on guesswork, because no one knows what will happen in the future. And they usually are wide of the mark. You seem to feel that if we include as a "return" on a project a sum of money to express the value to the owners of the business of performing a valuable service to the community, then we're mixing apples and pears. You now seem to be saying that our evaluation of projects should be based on traditional financial considerations. Your son apparently has not altered your thinking after all.

PAUL: Maybe I did revert to my former line of thinking. But still, how can you add together such different things as dollars of sales and sums to represent the value of such things as doing community service in a DCF computation.

TONY: It does *seem* wrong, but we were discussing whether it *is* or is not. You started this conversation because you were dissatisfied with what you've been doing. What I'm saying is that if service to the community is truly a goal of our top management, then it should be valued concretely in the projects that produce those benefits. Unless it is given a numerical value, then it probably will not affect the committee's selection among projects.

PAUL: I'm impressed by the logic and consistency of your argument, but the conclusion is so uncongenial that I resist it. Let me see, what you're now saying is that when we compute ROI, we should include allowances for intangible costs and benefits that never become tangibles just as if they were cash flows. The reason you give for doing this is that they reflect a project's effects on the extent to which we attain our goals. If they bring us closer to our goals, whatever those goals may be, they should be credited with that contribution in the form of some addition to "return" or "benefits" or to "revenues." That means that if a project injures certain prized goals, we should place a negative value on that injury and treat it as if it were a money cost of equivalent size.

TONY: You've stated the case very well.

PAUL: I still reject it and know that none of my colleagues would accept it. But I do see the logic of your position, and I recognize that by following your suggestion, we would build into our evaluation of capital projects a proper consideration of their nonfinancial as well as their financial effects. And that would resolve the dilemma that I raised with you at the start. It would also take account of the problem of handling different classes of intangibles. But DCF would no longer be descriptive of cash flows and would become more of a cost-benefit technique.

TONY: That's right. I agree that we're not ready to make such a great change. Still, I'm glad that you raised these issues and am convinced that you should get your committee to face them.

PAUL: What I now see clearly is that the use of ROI as a standard for evaluating projects is really a shortcut. When you use it, you assume that the project under consideration has only trivial, nonfinancial, or intangible consequences—or the same effects—and they can therefore be ignored. Maybe most decisions meet those conditions.

TONY: I don't really know whether they do. Don't forget that a firm pursues a variety of financial goals—not only what we measure by ROI. As I said earlier, our financial goals include high prices for the company's stock, liquidity, stable dividends, the ability to borrow at low rates, an attractive financial statement, and the like. By using any single standard to appraise the effects of projects, we assume that it reflects the effects of projects on all of those financial goals. But we both know that such is not the case at all. Projects with identical ROIs can have completely different effects on security values, for example.

PAUL: That's right, and that's why Ken was exactly right. He argued for the use of a rating system that includes all our objectives and assigns a weight to each of them. He said that it would be necessary to estimate the effect of each project on the attainment of all our objectives and then derive a total point score for each project. The scheme he describes is similar to the one that our purchasing people use to rate different sources of supply and that consumer rating organizations use to rank different brands of a product in order of quality.

TONY: I agree that Ken is completely right, and I look forward to hearing that our capital projects committee has adopted that procedure.

Business Objectives: A Dialog

The Binder Company has produced specialized agricultural equipment and supplies for almost a century under family management, growing and prospering along with the industry. Since about 1968, some professional managers have been added to top management and a substantial minority of the firm's stock has found its way into the hands of private investors living in the general area of Omaha, where the firm's plant and home office are located. The company's sales in 1978 were $24 million, and profits were about 8 percent after taxes.

In 1978, Mr. Tiller, the new chief executive officer and the first outsider to hold that post, started to "professionalize management," as he called it. He was determined to use the many techniques, approaches, and concepts that he had been taught at a leading graduate school of business, that had been applied by the large corporation for which he had worked earlier, and that were discussed in the various executive development programs he had attended. Toward this end, he took two bright MBAs (who had been with the company between two and three years) from their regular duties, designated them as assistants to the president, and assigned them to special projects. He had them work together on the same project in the belief that he would get greater productivity and creativity in that way.

During the late spring of 1977, he gave them an assignment in the following words:

I want you two to set down the objectives of this company. Don't tell me what you think our objectives should be just yet, though I'm interested in that also. First, I want to know what goals we are actually pursuing—whether consciously or unconsciously. In particular, I want to know whether all members of top management have the same picture of our firm's objectives; if not, I want to know the chief differences among them.

Moreover, I want you to arrange these goals in a hierarchy; I'm not content with a simple listing of our objectives. I'm sure that our ultimate goals include: profits, security, and appreciation in capital values. But I want to know what subgoals must be achieved on many levels further down if we are to achieve these goals.

You should hold informal chats with members of top management to find out what goals they think they are pursuing. See whether they think top management and the firm's owners seek the same objectives. Then, determine what goals they believe our firm should pursue.

When you have done all this, report back with two things: A description of the actual goals of this company, and your critique of those goals.

My own objectives are to see that all of our executives hold a common view of the company's direction. In that way, I'll increase the probability that executives on all levels will decide things in the way that top management would want them to do and won't be working at cross purposes with one another.

The assistants to the president, Mr. Wood and Mr. Lind, discussed the assignment briefly with Mr. Tiller and then retired to the plush office that they shared to continue the discussion there. The following is a summary of that discussion and others that followed during the next few days.

WOOD: I don't know how you feel about this assignment, but I don't look forward to it with particular pleasure. I can foresee that our time will be largely wasted. I've tackled this issue of objectives before and always conclude that the only way to improve matters is by changing executives' basic outlook and approach.

LIND: Are you suggesting that someone must be brainwashed or psychoanalyzed before he can think through and apply a well-formulated set of objectives—like the ones we're working on?

WOOD: Maybe so. You and Tiller are kidding yourselves if you think that formulating a well-constructed hierarchy of objectives will get executives around here to change their decision making much. And if the hierarchy of objectives won't have that effect, who needs them?

LIND: We certainly don't want to prepare a mere piece of window-dressing, but I don't understand your pessimism. I regard objectives as perhaps the most important and mishandled phase of decision making.

WOOD: There's no dispute between us on that point. I contend that you can't make much progress with objectives on a simple intellectual-logical level. You've got to break down the bad habits, defenses, and fears that caused non-goal-directed behavior in the first place. The idea that executives should be clear about their objectives in making a decision is about as obvious as you can get. But when they don't do it, you must suspect that big forces are getting in their way.

LIND: You're exaggerating now. To deal usefully with objectives does involve really complicated ideas—hierarchies, conflicting objectives, and choices among different financial goals, like high dividends, or present value of future earnings. I wouldn't call those issues simple.

WOOD: Yes, I grant that some aspects of objectives are complicated. My point is very different. I've observed that many people completely ignore the issue of objectives when faced with questions to which objectives are central; others lose sight of their objectives even after making them explicit. Some don't state their goals to themselves or others and seem to go chasing off in several directions.

LIND: Yes, I know. The interesting thing is that they do it time and again, even after their error has been called to their attention.

WOOD: That suggests that their problem is not the genuine difficulty of refining one's objectives, of sorting them out on different levels and reconciling conflicts. It appears that many executives are not willing to allow their objectives to dominate their decisions.

LIND: I agree. What you say is true of me. I'm often embarrassed to find that even after I've worked over a problem carefully, a question from Tiller, and even from you, asking what our objectives are will show that I've drifted a long way from my original goal.

WOOD: We're dealing with something that obviously is essential but also constantly ignored. When that's the case, you are naive to think you'll change matters much by issuing a statement that represents company's objectives. That's why I'm afraid this assignment will prove to be a waste of time.

LIND: I might buy that, but let's sort out our own objectives. We like our jobs and the paychecks they bring us. So we'd like to be perceived by Tiller as doing a good job on this assignment—whether or not we think it would affect the day-to-day decisions that are made around here. After all, this firm is still quite profitable, despite its unclear and conflicting objectives.

WOOD: Sure, we'll carry out the assignment. But my objective isn't just to please the boss and get ahead. My goal is to please him in ways that strengthen the company. In the long run, that would make him most pleased with me and do the most for my advancement.

LIND: What would that mean in this specific case? That we go back to Tiller now and tell him how pessimistic we are—and why—and maybe suggest a massive program that would get them to keep their objectives clearly in mind when they make their decisions? I think he could do some obvious things that would help matters. For example, Tiller could insist that every proposal made to him should start with a statement of objectives. He could ask for a statement of objectives in every discussion held with him—so that everyone would get the habit of thinking in terms of goals.

WOOD: Don't you think that requirements like that would breed resentment, if profound emotional forces actually do make us push objectives into the background? I'm not convinced that nothing useful could be done on this issue, but I'm sure that nothing will be accomplished by our developing a rigorous statement of objectives.

LIND: Remember that our assignment is *not* to prepare a statement of objectives but to describe what our executives believe them to be. That seems like a reasonable enough assignment to me at least. I agree that little would be achieved if we simply prepared a great statement of objectives and didn't attack the strong forces that seem to keep most people from identifying their goals. Also, I agree with Tiller that the starting place to improve matters is with the perceived or implicit objectives of top-level executives.

*   *   *

LIND: How are we ever going to learn what objectives our senior executives are currently pursuing? Even our closest friends might not want to admit to us and in confidence that self-interest often takes precedence over the welfare of the corporation. We can't take answers to direct questions about objectives at face value.

WOOD: True, but we have to at least go through the motions of asking them the question fairly directly. To determine a person's objectives, I draw my inferences from their actual behavior as much as possible. I place very little stock in a neatly typed set of objectives that a manager shows me for his department. If we are going to learn the objectives that are actually motivating our executives, I believe we should interview the two or three most senior executives in each of our main divisions and infer their goals from what they do rather than what they say.

LIND: Good thinking. It seems that our assignment is larger than Tiller thought. He seemed to think we would interview the senior vice-presidents about our highest-level objectives and then report back. That would be worth doing in itself, but I can guess what we'd learn. Jim Jones will be concerned almost totally with earnings per share; Art Lewis's main goal is increased value of our common stock, and Jim Holden wants us to have high and stable dividends. In other words, our top executives' views about the firm's ultimate objectives do differ. However, almost always all make decisions that add most to dollars of profit. By that I mean, in any concrete decision situation, differences in their stated objectives don't lead to a different decision.

WOOD: In other words, we should deal with lower-level objectives to find situations where either unclear objectives or differences in objectives would result in different decisions. But I think the problem remains whether we simply want to get answers to direct questions about objectives or ask about their actions and infer their objectives from those answers. Maybe we should ask them about hypothetical situations and ask the executives how they would decide. We could even phrase questions to get estimates of their trade-offs among different objectives.

LIND: That sounds great, but could you give me a concrete example? I certainly would favor discussions of real-life examples rather than general discussions of objectives. Frankly, I'd most want to ask them questions about decisions they actually made—but that might make them defensive. Well, anyhow, could you give me a sample question that would get an executive to reveal his objectives and the trade-offs he would make among them?

WOOD: Don't expect a wonderful example right off the top of my head; but let me illustrate what I have in mind. I might present them with three choices, projects A, B, and C. For each of them, I'd set down best estimates for the various relevant outcomes. Say I was dealing with very high-level objectives. I might offer the executives, one at a time and independently, the following choice. (I'd present them with a neatly prepared table.) Project A would have the effect of increasing our common stock price by 2 points, would add, say $100,000 to net profits before taxes over the next two years; it would reduce our current asset ratio from 3.6 to 3.2 and would have an effect on the firm's long-run profits, that is, would raise the future level of profits about $20,000. They would be shown expected results on the same indicators for the two other projects.

The executive would then be asked to state his preference. After he had done so, the numbers would be changed in ways to determine what would be required to alter his preference. In that way, we'd learn his trade-offs. For example, if he picked project B over the others, he would be asked to indicate what increase in dollars per share, net profits before taxes, current ratio and level of future profits would be required to make project A and C preferable to B. Let me be clear: he would be asked, leaving everything else the same, what increase in common stock prices would be needed to make project A equally attractive with project B.

LIND: That's very clever, but let me suggest another example. Suppose you were interviewing the credit manager. You could ask him how he'd decide if our sales manager asks him to approve a sizable amount of credit for a new customer that the sales department has been trying to land for months. The customer would have to be described fully so he would know what kind of credit risk was involved. We could try different descriptions of the customer to see where the credit department would draw the line.

WOOD: Those credit guys are always trying to get their bad debts down to zero. Maybe we should set them a target *above* some ratio of bad debts to sales rather than below a target. That might permit us to use credit to stimulate sales, rather than to limit them. They represent a beautiful example of people whose objectives seem to be almost upside down.

Your questions would make them indicate the extent to which they were motivated by bad debt considerations relative to those of increasing sales. And it would be concrete. It seems an excellent kind of question.

LIND: Maybe there is an even better way to proceed. We might ask the credit people—and others—to tell us in detail about the toughest cases they actually decided during the last few months or so. After we heard that story, we might then be able to ask more general questions about their objectives.

WOOD: Yes, that would be very useful. We could do that as well as offer hypothetical choices. It is not likely that one kind of question is right and best in all cases. We should try different kinds of questions; different lines of questioning should add depth to each executive's view of his objectives.

I hope you don't expect to get answers to these different kinds of questions that can be summarized numerically and neatly. We will almost certainly end up with qualitative summaries of each executive's views.

LIND: I agree thoroughly, but I can't see any way out of that dilemma that would not result in less valid conclusions.

*   *   *

LIND: I've spent the weekend studying interview techniques and I think I have that problem under control. I had an interesting discussion with Ron last night during dinner about our project. [Ron Giles is V.P. Personnel]. Ron is convinced that our senior executives are pursuing dissimilar objectives which he believes are also contradictory. Moreover, he maintains that at least one of those objectives is illegitimate.

WOOD: What goals does he consider illegitimate?

LIND: It's the desire to boost the short-run value of our common stock by making acquisitions. Ron thinks the firm should concentrate on long-run profits for distribution to stockholders. He emphasizes long-run profits over all other goals. Ron thinks that all this concern with getting high stock prices, acquisitions, multiples, and so on diverts our best brains from tending to the main problems that our business faces. You must admit that our senior people are not *mainly* thinking about new customer needs, segments, technological developments—or even about our new competitors. They're out beating the bushes for acquisition prospects, negotiating with them, going over their books, quizzing their executives.

WOOD: So Ron is worried about the diversion of our best brains from their regular duties? I can see that as a real issue. Does he see threats to our long-run profitability resulting from this preoccupation with stock prices and acquisitions?

LIND: Yes, he sees overemphasis on making a showing in the short run. Some things we have been doing help make current profits higher but are storing up some future problems, or so he claims. He didn't give any examples.

WOOD: It would be very helpful to me if we would sort out the different objectives we've been talking about. Let's construct a hierarchy of objectives out of items like high security prices, short-run profits, long-run profits, growth, dividends for stockholders, public responsibility, concern with legitimate interests of consumers and labor, and such things. These are ultimate or very high-level objectives and are common to all the firm's divisions.

LIND: That sounds like it's worth doing. The list you gave doesn't include all important high-level goals, but maybe that isn't important at this point. The items that I especially want to get cleared up are: stock prices, long-run profits, short-run profits, and growth.

Most people say that a firm's true ultimate objective is long-run profits. But shouldn't we ask why the firm's owners would want long-run profits? It's clear to me that profits are not usually an ultimate objective.

WOOD: We want high long-run profits because they give the owners of the business the two things they want most: high long-run dividends and high prices for their stock. Those are the two ways that owners get their financial rewards from a business. And those who just own stock must be owners of a business solely for financial rewards, it seems to me. So if one writes these goals in the form of a hierarchy, at the very top would be: high long-run dividends and high security prices. I'd like to add another box called "other" to indicate that we may be overlooking something. On the next lower level I would put high long-run profits. This is the way I would draw it:

LIND: That looks right to me. Now let's see where growth and short-run profits fit into the picture. I for one would not want growth for its own sake but only because it usually adds to long-run profits. When growth does not contribute to profits or impairs it, I would not desire it at all. Do you agree?

WOOD: Yes. So in our hierarchy "growth" would be put on a level below "long-run profits" to signify that it is a potential method of increasing long-run profits and, moreover, is to be desired only if and to the extent that it enhances long-run profits. On this matter of short-run profits, I have mixed thoughts. I was forever hearing at school about the conflict between short-run and long-run profits. The problem arose when a firm could take actions that would yield profits soon but would also impair long-run assets like good will, brand image, and labor morale. That seems a real choice, don't you agree? And doesn't that mean that these are on the same level on our hierarchy?

LIND: Yes, it does. Then we must add short-run profits to long-run profits on our second line. I have deep misgivings about that because I see short-run profits as mainly a means of increasing long-run profits—though they can also increase short-run security prices and even short-run dividends. Here I go making things more complicated rather than sorting them out.

WOOD: Let me add to the confusion by building on what you said. The owners of the business surely are concerned with their dividends and their stock prices in both the short run and in the long run. They may have special needs for cash, they may find themselves forced to liquidate their securities—so that near term stock prices and dividends are of real concern to them. But they are mainly concerned with longer-run dividends and security prices, it seems to me. So I'd want to redraw our hierarchy to put long-run and short-run dividends and security prices on the top level. Then we could put short- and long-run profits on the lower level. Interestingly, we would put on the third level: short-run profits again, as a way of enhancing long run profits, and growth—and probably some other things as well. How does that strike you? Here is how it would look on the hierarchy [Figure 7-10].

LIND: That's very helpful. But could we take another look at the way short-run profits can affect long-run profits?

WOOD: Sure. Short-run profits can contribute to long-run profits in the following ways, among others: One, they can provide the firm with resources, which through reinvestment, can increase efficiency. By that I mean they often take the form of cash that permits the firm to mechanize, for example. Two, by showing greater short-run profitability, the firm can borrow from banks more easily, float public security issues more easily and on better terms. And three, short-run profitability is doubtless good for executive morale and is likely to build *esprit*. And it should help attract high-quality executives to the firm.

Figure 7-10. A three-level goal hierarchy.

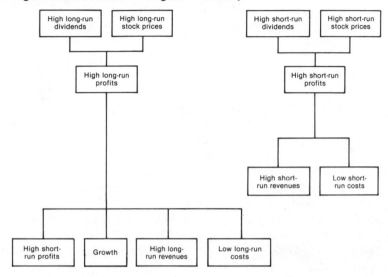

I have deep trouble with this distinction between short- and long-run profits. In one sense, there should be no problem at all. What an executive must do is simply express profits, whenever they would be obtained, in terms of their "current values." He would simply apply the proper discount rate or cost of capital figure to make profits earned at different times comparable. So he really need not make a choice; he need only make a simple calculation.

LIND: That was a very important statement, if it is true. I can't find any fault with your reasoning. It would seem to be a simple matter of looking up the numbers on a table to tell whether you would be better off if you did something that gave you $400,000 extra profit this year or an extra $175,000 each year three and four years hence.

WOOD: That's right. However, I still feel that short- and long-run profits are different in a way that *cannot* be handled by translating everything into current values. Do you share any of that feeling?

LIND: Yes, I do, and maybe I can shed some light on the point. When I think of long-run profits, I don't think of profits in particular years—like in years four, five, and six from now. I think of a general enduring state. By that I mean that year in and year out the firm's profits will average around, say, $1.2 million rather than, say, $2 million. So long-run profits are really related to the enduring ability of a firm to make profits.

WOOD: That means that if we say that an executive makes a decision that will raise long-run profits by $50,000, we mean that over the next 10 to

20 years, perhaps, they can be expected to average, say, $50,000 more annually than in the absence of that decision.

LIND: Exactly. That is just what I mean. Theoretically, one could discount higher income in perpetuity to get a current value figure. However, I don't think that process adequately measures the effect of an enduring change in profits.

One of my difficulties with the whole concept of an enduring increase in profits is that nothing really endures forever. We are saying, though, that some things look enduring and though we know they will not be *eternal*, we cannot tell how long they will last.

We've made some progress with fairly sticky ideas; let's see what all our discussion adds up to by examining a simple illustration. Let's return to the hypothetical example where a firm is choosing between two projects: one would raise profits this year by $60,000; the other would raise profits by $100,000, which would be obtained in three equal amounts over the next three years.

Here we would seem to have a clear conflict between short- and long-run profits—as most management specialists look at the matter. We say, however, that the problem represents a simple exercise in discounting future profits to compute their present value.

WOOD: That's right. As you present the illustration, in neither case has there been a change in the enduring level of profits. So both projects are equal with respect to long-run profits in that sense. Consequently, the executive would be justified in basing his choice on a comparison of the present values of the profits in both cases.

LIND: Exactly. This discussion has helped to clarify something that has troubled me for a long time. We're saying that a firm's main goal is to achieve the highest possible enduring level of profits. That would give its owners the most of what they want. Short-run profits are to be valued primarily if they help to raise that long-run level of profits in the ways we already mentioned.

It follows that an executive must never select short-run profits in preference to long-run (enduring) profits. Short-run profits can legitimately be favored over profits several years in the future—partly because they may actually help to raise future profits greatly. And, of course, they may be required for survival. However, the goal is to create a firm that continuously makes high levels of profit. Short-run profits can never be preferred to that.

WOOD: Every generalization has exceptions. Some business owners would rather make a fairly quick killing rather than wait to obtain the benefits of increased enduring profits. Basically, I would agree with

your statement, which does sort out many important issues. Why don't
you sum them up?

LIND: I'll be glad to. We have distinguished three time periods: first, the
now and the very soon, and we've called this the short run. Second,
there is the few years out, which we might call the future; and finally,
you've spoken of an enduring level lasting over a long period. This last is
the long run and is—or should be—the chief concern of a firm's owners
and top management. We are concerned with the other two periods
simply as a means of increasing long-run profits.

WOOD: That statement shows we need to add another item to our hierarchy. Maybe we should call it "future profits" and consider it a means of
affecting long-run (enduring) profits. As you said, short-run and future
profits may conflict, but any such conflict should be resolved by translating them both into current values. One would select among short-run
and future profits mainly according to their effect on the firm's enduring
level of profits.

LIND: I'll buy that statement. Now, let's tidy up our hierarchy and call it
quits for the day. This kind of abstract thinking wears me out. What is
finally dawning on me is that we should be thinking of enduring levels of
dividends and enduring levels of stock prices rather than future levels.
Let me see, if we do that, then our hierarchy would look like this [Figure
7-11]. What do you think of it?

Figure 7-11. Revised and extended hierarchy of objectives.

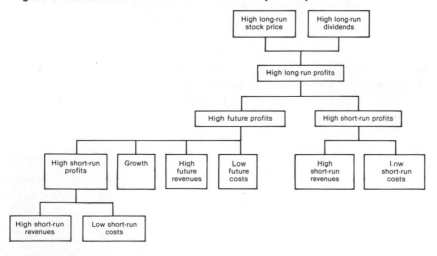

Chapter 8

COMPUTING THE COSTS
OF EXECUTIVE DECISIONS

CONTRARY TO COMMON BELIEF, there is no such thing as *the* cost of any item. To accountants, costs are to be computed in particular ways. Accounting costs, which are mainly "standard costs," meet particular business needs. The needs of an executive making decisions are different from those of accountants. In a word, decision makers need to know how a particular decision affects their firm's costs. More specifically, they need to know how the firm's total costs would be different from its costs if they did not make that decision.

As explained in the following chapter, many different kinds of costs can be computed; it is difficult to understand the differences among them and the purpose for which each is best suited. However, by adopting the viewpoint of a decision maker, we drastically simplify the task of cost estimation. We are interested in one very simple concept of cost: "decision cost," which simply means the cost resulting from specific decisions. This chapter discusses the steps involved in estimating those costs.

One unpleasant fact of life should be recognized at the outset: executives' estimates of costs will never be exact. But it is not necessary that they know their decision costs precisely. They must do the best they can under the circumstances. They must settle for estimates that are "good enough," for it would be foolhardy to pursue the unbusinesslike goal of complete precision.

Steps in Estimating Decision Costs

A valid estimate of costs for each alternative course of action under consideration requires that the decision maker take the following steps:

1. Spell out in detail the course of action that is contemplated.
2. Describe the circumstances under which the action will be taken.
3. Specify the aspects of the business that would be affected by the action and the extent to which they would be affected.
4. Assign monetary values to each sacrifice.
5. Estimate the impact of the action on prospective future opportunities.

Each of these steps is discussed below and illustrated by a simple nonbusiness example—the costs of driving from New York City to Philadelphia and back on the same day.

STEP 1: SPELL OUT THE COURSE OF ACTION

Costs inhere not in a product or service, but in decisions that relate to their production. This view of costs conflicts so sharply with the prevailing view that many people cannot bring themselves to accept it. Every day we face the question "How much does that cost?" And in most cases we are able to answer that question as if a specific cost did inhere in the product. However, in many situations the cost of a given product or service will vary according to the decision to be made with respect to it. A cost that is assigned to a product—rather than to a decision that pertains to it—is invalid for many purposes, as the following illustration should make clear. The starting point in estimating a cost is a detailed and explicit description of the decision under consideration. Ordinarily, to describe a decision requires answers to questions concerning who would do how much of what, in what places, with the help of whom, and on what scale. No executive can estimate accurately the cost of a blurred and vague program of action.

If an executive were considering a trip by car from New York to Philadelphia, he probably would not assume that such a trip had a clearly known cost—equivalent to the cost of a particular brand of men's shirts at a specific department store. The cost of such a trip would depend on whether it was made in a Volkswagen or a Cadillac; whether premium or regular gas was used; whether the executive drove the car himself or used a chauffeur; whether the trip was made over a toll road or a nontoll highway. Also, the cost would be affected by the routes chosen, which in turn would determine number of miles traveled and the speed at which the executive could drive. Obviously, each of these alternatives could produce quite different costs. To estimate the cost of such a trip would require a specific and detailed description of each way the trip might be made. The same principle holds true for decisions about the production of men's suits, dog food, air trips, haircuts—you name it. Those who object strongly to the notion that one must measure the cost of a decision, rather than the cost of a product or service, will describe this step as defining the product or service whose cost is being estimated. However, when the product is defined to such an extent, it is in fact defined for the *decision*.

STEP 2: DESCRIBE THE CIRCUMSTANCES UNDER WHICH THE ACTION WILL BE TAKEN

Even if an executive knows precisely what he wants to produce, he cannot estimate its cost unless he specifies the circumstances under which it will be produced. These relate to time, supply of labor and materials, and other factors to be taken into account in estimating a business decision. If one goes to a winter resort during the peak season, his costs will be higher than if he goes off-peak; if one has electrical or plumbing work done when persons plying these trades are very busy, he will pay far more than during periods when such men are looking for work. If a manufacturer uses raw materials that are in excess supply, his costs will be far lower than if those raw materials are difficult to find.

One of the factors to be considered in most decisions is the amount of idle resources suitable for use in production that will be available at the time the decision is carried out. When a firm possesses idle resources, the cost of these resources will be relatively low; when an action makes demands upon already fully utilized resources, its costs will be relatively high. Other circumstances which might influence the sacrifices that flow from a particular decision are state of employee and executive morale; the receptivity of management, resellers, and salesmen to the project under consideration; and special opportunities that will affect the ability to sell the item at a small sales cost.

Accordingly, the decision maker should describe the relevant state of affairs likely to prevail when the selected course of action will be taken. An action rarely takes place at a "normal" or average time.

The importance of this second step in cost computation can be illustrated by carrying forward our hypothetical estimate of the cost of driving from New York to Philadelphia for a day. We already saw that costs would vary with the car used, the route, and the speed of travel. How would the general circumstances prevailing affect the costs of the trip?

In the first place, if one's car were not available for use, because another member of the family had a stronger claim on it, then one's costs might include rental charges. If the car were not functioning properly, one's cost estimate should include an item to cover expected repairs, towing charges, and so on. Another factor that would affect the cost would be whether it must be made during a period of peak travel, when there would be a great deal of stop-and-go driving, or during a period when traffic is light. Again, if one had an opportunity to go with someone else who had reason to drive to Philadelphia on a convenient day, that circumstance would have a major effect on the cost of the trip.

Business examples of the effects of special circumstances on costs are easy to find. A firm that wished to introduce a new product would expect to incur sizable selling costs. However, if its salesmen were already making regular calls on customers for the new product, selling costs for that new product might be very low. The important factor when computing costs for a decision is to isolate the *added* costs the decision will create. Two firms can incur substantially different costs to implement an identical decision. In a decision to manufacture a new product, raw materials will be an important part of the total cost. If, for company A, the raw materials are waste products from its regular production activities, the cost will be low. If company B must purchase these materials from an outside supplier, the cost could be quite high. Such special circumstances often exist and have a significant effect on the cost of a decision.

STEP 3: SPECIFY THE EFFECTS OF THE ACTION ON THE BUSINESS

Business decisions and actions often are complex, involving many things done by many people at different times and places. The effects of these complex actions usually are numerous, dispersed in space, and often delayed. It is therefore very difficult to estimate precisely what consequences will follow from given decision actions. Some errors in estimating costs are almost inevitable for these reasons. The most important part of step 3 is to identify what the effects are and when they are likely to occur. *An error in estimating the magnitude of an effect usually is far less serious than mistakes due to wholly overlooked consequences.*

Some consequences of business actions are overlooked because executives do not look hard enough and in the right places for all the effects of their actions, and they don't look where they should because they sometimes do not know where to look; that, in turn, results from incomplete understanding of the full implications of their actions. That incomplete understanding is partly due to the fact that less attention has been devoted to such problems by business specialists than the importance of the subject would warrant. Even more, it results from the strong influence of traditional accounting procedures upon attitudes toward costing. The first point is fairly self-explanatory; the second is less obvious and will be discussed first.

Traditional accounting procedures as a reason for overlooking consequences of action. Cost computations by business enterprises have become highly ritualized; most business executives have become accustomed to thinking about costs in the terms employed by accountants—even when they do not apply. The effect of these traditions upon the appropriateness of cost computations, and in particular the danger that executives will ignore completely some essential elements of costs is suggested by the following points.

First, the accountant stresses the tangible and measurable effects of decisions and generally omits those effects that involve highly subjective judgments. Consequently, even business decisions that are intended to produce intangible benefits—like improved brand image, better employee morale, and the like—are treated, for purposes of cost computation, as if they involved only tangible factors. The most important costs are sometimes omitted altogether as a result. Second, accountants base their estimates upon historical costs; the use of some assets possessing substantial resale value that have already been fully charged off is treated consequently as if it involved no cost, when that is not the case at all.

Why should a decision maker be concerned with intangibles unless they do affect his firm's tangible assets or liabilities? A decision may cause some changes that do not immediately affect the firm's tangible fiscal position. Subsequently, these changes will alter a firm's sales, cost prices, ability to borrow, labor productivity, ability to attract executives and employees, degree of government regulation, and so on, and any of these factors can directly affect the firm's profits. The tendency to ignore intangibles when they occur leads executives to overlook the subsequent tangible sacrifices that result from those very intangible effects.

In summary, traditional approaches to cost computation create prejudices in the ways that executives view and compute the costs of their decisions. Those traditions lead executives to be concerned with the kinds of items measured in the cost accounting system and to neglect intangibles and items that have already been charged off as costs of past periods, or perhaps are not included in formal accounting records at all.

Consequences overlooked because of lack of understanding. Businessmen do their jobs as well as any other group—and perhaps better. However, they often receive poor support from specialists in the field of business, especially in the areas that affect business decision making. One cannot find any significant body of writings on the subject of what businessmen must not overlook when computing costs for particular types of decisions. If an executive is contemplating a merger or acquisition, a major price adjustment, the introduction of a new item or some other major action, he will not find any published guidance on what things to consider in computing costs. Businessmen at present seem to rely on crude rules of thumb or routine procedures that provide an answer, but not a valid one. A few illustrations might help.

For purposes of price decisions, most businesses employ some form of "standard costing." This form of cost computation is highly ritualized in each firm—different company accountants will produce essentially the same results by using it. As a rule, these procedures do not call for the inclusion of intangibles. A firm that is contemplating the acquisition of another enterprise will ordinarily project its earnings, taking account of possible economies due to the combination of the two businesses. These projections of earnings and consideration of economies will also ignore major intangibles. Both of these procedures for estimating costs and benefits give the appearance of dealing with all the elements in the problem, but they do not do so. By virtue of the fact that they are routine—involve the same steps irrespective of the particular situation—they tend to include items that do not apply and omit others that definitely do apply.

Some illustrations. The following illustrations are not intended to suggest that we know more than the executive does about the effects of his decisions. However, a few simple illustrations may dramatize the importance of considering every possible effect of a proposed course óf action.

In computing the costs of an auto trip from New York to Philadelphia, we must ask what are all of the sacrifices of such a trip by the person making it. We can readily take account of his payments for gas and oil and tolls, and even try to make an estimate of the costs of "wear and tear." (We will not include some element for depreciation, insurance, and such items, which would not be affected by the decision to make the trip. These expenses relate to owning a car, and not to driving it on a particular trip. Our traveler will incur these expenses, whether he takes his car to Philadelphia or not.) In computing these costs, we would be reflecting traditional accounting approaches. What are the other effects that might pass overlooked? For example, if the trip were exhausting to the driver, his efficiency in his work the following day might be impaired and might even reduce his income somewhat. Or, by using his car to make the trip, he might hasten the time at which he would be forced to take it in for a lubrication or general checkup, causing him to devote time to his car at an inconvenient time. Or, he might be forced to move his car from a good parking space which he would not be able to get back after he returned from Philadelphia, imposing a major burden on him to find another.

Consider another example. A woman is displeased with the appearance of her living room and decides to replace her most worn piece of furniture—an old, but comfortable sofa. The new sofa arrives and is as lovely as the woman thought, but now everything else in the room seems dowdy. The original appearance of the room, although unsatisfactory, was more bearable than the present one. What follows is a series of unexpected purchases to make the room seem "of a piece" and expenditures far greater than were anticipated.

Or, to take another case, a family is dissatisfied with its home and decides to move to a larger house in a more prosperous neighborhood. The breadwinner stretches almost to the breaking point to finance the purchase of the home. When the family moves into the new quarters and becomes acquainted with the neighbors, it finds that its usual ways of doing things are not highly regarded. All members of the family feel impelled to buy more fashionable and expensive clothes; it becomes necessary to send children to expensive camps, to contribute to local charities, and so on, on a level not necessary at the previous location. The cost of that move will have been badly underestimated. If the family cannot afford to keep up with the Joneses then the costs would take the form of intangible discomforts and embarrassments.

Determining the sacrifices that result from the contemplated actions. The effects of any action by a firm upon its costs are essentially technological. That is to say, the forces acting on existing production arrangements impose certain sacrifices upon any firm that provides particular products and services. Beyond the effect of technology, any action to provide some product or service ordinarily requires efforts and outlays that are special to that particular decision and firm. Consequently, to forecast the sacrifices that will result from a specific action, one requires a thorough knowledge of the particular firm's situation and the technology of its operations. The decision maker must possess specialized knowledge and experience, for frequently even an experienced executive cannot forecast accurately all the sacrifices that will flow from a contemplated action. Usually, specialists must be consulted or made responsible for determining some of the results that will follow from courses of action under consideration. Firms frequently have special departments, such as production engineering, whose duty is to supply the detailed technological information on which cost estimates are based. Another useful source of information about the sacrifices involved in an action are the cost records of similar decisions in the past. Unfortunately, both these sources will ordinarily be guilty of important omissions and may include some items that do not belong. The decision maker must be sufficiently familiar with his operation to recognize these discrepancies.

An executive cannot expect to compute the costs of a decision from a great distance and on the basis of very general knowledge. To determine what sacrifices would result from a contemplated action requires detailed and searching analysis, with careful attention to intangibles and to delayed consequences; it requires, in particular, a conscious effort to avoid the traditional approach to cost estimation and a readiness to consider any and all possible adverse effects that might flow from a decision.

Step 4: Assign Monetary Values to Each Sacrifice

This step should identify the *magnitude* of the sacrifices expected to result from the particular decision. An itemization of the sacrifices will not suffice for purposes of decision. They must be stated in a common denominator, preferably the same units that are used to tally the benefits that will flow from the decision. Of course, the common denominator usually employed is money.

To compare and evaluate each sacrifice the decision maker generally must assign a monetary value to each of them, which many businessmen refer to as "computing the costs." But such a phrase can be misleading. Assigning monetary values to the costs identified in steps 1 through 3 may indeed be called "computing the costs." However, decision makers often reach this step too soon and find themselves manipulating figures toward very uncertain ends. To them, the whole problem of cost identification in decision making is embodied in cost computation. At this point, the reader should be able to place cost computation in its proper context.

The computation of the dollar value of cost components of a decision alternative is never easy, even after those alternatives have been correctly identified. The chief difficulty in computing any particular component of cost is the degree of uncertainty attached to it. Some costs are very certain, and they present few problems. For example, if our traveler from New York to Philadelphia has decided to drive his car, the cost of gasoline may be computed quite easily. The traveler may have historical gas mileage records for his car, and he certainly has a good idea of how many miles he will drive. The price of gasoline per gallon is also readily learned. With these factors, the traveler can make a very accurate estimate of fuel costs. The same is true of his expected toll costs. An office of the AAA will readily supply the tolls for any route he decides to take. The tolls are prescribed by law, and are not at all uncertain.

Unfortunately, many other costs do not lend themselves to such precise estimation. The key word, again, is uncertainty. For example, a breakdown on the road would probably result in substantial expenditures for towing and repairs. But what is the likelihood of such a breakdown and, if it occurs, what will be the extent of the damage? Certainly a flat tire and a cracked piston will entail different repair costs. What dollar amount should the traveler include as an expected cost for such an uncertain event?

Another uncertain aspect of the proposed trip relates to sacrificed income. While driving to Philadelphia, the traveler cannot use his time profitably in New York. What is the likelihood that a lucrative job will have to be rejected due to the trip commitment? What dollar cost should the traveler attach to such an uncertain event? The list of uncertain sacrifices is usually substantial, and the problem of assigning them dollar cost figures will be solved with imprecise estimates at best.

Decision makers often react differently to the difficulty of assigning dollar values to intangible sacrifices. Some, recognizing the uncertainty of the situation, completely reject the items from consideration. In their view, it is a waste of time to attempt to make an estimate if it will admittedly be imprecise. Others more correctly recognize the assignment of dollar values as a task calling for special effort on their part. Certain techniques are available that help the decision maker to improve the accuracy of his estimates and thus help him make better decisions. Techniques such as utility value analysis, the assignment of probabilities, and the computation of opportunity costs are all valuable aids to the decision maker, as he attempts to assign reasonable dollar values to uncertain sacrifices.

This book will not delve into the specifics of cost computing techniques. The important thing to remember is that as one moves through the steps in assigning dollar costs to identified sacrifices, one should be assured that there is an increasingly rich body of knowledge available to help him. Dollar costs must be assigned in the most accurate manner possible if one is to evaluate decision alternatives on a rational basis. The decision maker must consequently make his dollar estimates of costs as best he can under the circumstances.

STEP 5: ESTIMATE IMPACT OF THE DECISION ON FUTURE DECISIONS

Sometimes a firm will carry out a decision and then return to the condition it occupied before. However, many decisions alter a firm's condition for a very long time and thereby affect what it might do in the future and the costs it would incur in the future. For example, a firm's decision to add a new item to its product line might involve low costs because the firm possessed idle capacity. Once devoted to this use, the firm may have no excess facilities should future needs arise. The first decision thus effectively raised the cost of many potential future decisions to the extent that it could not be reversed. Many decisions involve "commitments" to customers, resellers, labor, and the like, that make them irreversible. Consequently their full effects may not be clear for a considerable period—if ever. This point may be expressed as a form of "opportunity cost"—as indeed can all cost factors. Some business decisions apply idle resources to a particular use with the result that the firm will be forced to expand its facilities earlier than it would otherwise have been required to do so. The decision maker should attach a cost to this effect. Although this kind of cost might properly be considered one of the intangibles that should be identified in step 3, it is sufficiently different and important to warrant separate attention.

Step 5, then, directs the decision maker to adopt a long and broad view of the alternatives under consideration. Presumably, he will have already identified the immediate sacrifices attached to the proposed courses of action, and will have assigned dollar values to them. In step 5, the decision maker calls on his judgment and understanding of the business to determine the likely effects of an action on other departments, as well as how it might affect future decisions. Returning once again to our proposed trip to Philadelphia, let us consider the impact of such a trip on the future. Perhaps the traveler is allowed only one day of travel per week. If he takes the trip on Monday, he will have to react negatively to out-of-town calls for the rest of the week. Or, perhaps he is simply trying to hold his travel to some minimum. If he makes the trip, how can he refuse other out-of-town clients, when they hear he has visited someone in Philadelphia? How will he be able to avoid another trip to Philadelphia, the next time his client there asks him to come down? All these factors must enter into the decision to drive to Philadelphia. Although they may be the most uncertain and intangible of our possible costs, these too must be assigned some numerical dollar value.

Conclusion

It is generally difficult to compute the costs of a specific decision alternative. Perhaps that is why executives who can do it, and do it well, are prized so highly in the business world. Some successful decision makers do not consciously follow the program we have described for making decisions. They may claim to do it by "feel" or by "long experience." Nevertheless, their minds must somehow consider the factors listed in this chapter. Consistently good decisions are not made by "shooting from the hip." They come from the application of sound cost analysis, based on the best and most relevant cost estimates available. The procedure outlined here is not a substitute for experience or good judgment. It simply provides an orderly way to apply these priceless decision-making raw materials.

Incremental Costs: A Dialog*

Joe and Max are good friends and partners in their own small manufacturing business. Since they each have a personal ownership interest in their business, they have a very keen concern for the profitability of that business. They work together very closely and discuss most decisions that are not routine.

MAX: Sit down and join me in a cup of coffee, Joe.

JOE: Thanks, Max. Boy, wasn't it a great weekend? I sure hated to come back to work. Jane and I were still barbecuing steaks at ten last night.

MAX: Well, I can't blame you. I see you already had Spellman in for a talk this morning. Was he late again?

JOE: Yes, he was. Funny guy, Spellman. Does good work once he gets here, but he just can't seem to pull himself out of bed on Monday mornings. How many Mondays in a row have I had to talk to that guy? Know what his problem was this time? He told me he didn't want to be late, so he rushed out of the house, slammed the door, caught his tie in there, and damn near strangled himself!

MAX: (Laughing) His stories get wilder every week, but at least he keeps you laughing, right Joe? Speaking of crazy people, Spellman's not the only one in the world. Look at this order in from Foremost this morning.

JOE: Foremost? They're that new West Coast firm, aren't they? What are they doing ordering from us?

MAX: Well, according to this order, their truck will be making a delivery in our area late this week and they'll have an empty backhaul. They wrote that they're interested in picking up a thousand of our units. But, guess what they want to pay per unit?

JOE: Well, I don't know—they sure would save substantial shipping costs if they did that.

MAX: These people want to drive their truck in here on Friday afternoon, and pick up a thousand units. That means we'd have to get them on the production schedule by tomorrow at the latest. But they say they won't pay more than $10 per unit. So why bother? Our price is $15 per unit. Our costs run at $13, so there's nothing in this order for us! Our price has been $15 per unit ever since we went into business—almost two years ago. If anything, we should be thinking about a price increase! And these people think they can just roll in here with their truck and get a thousand units for $10. We can sure do without that kind of business!

* Prepared by Ronald R. Bern, in collaboration with the author.

JOE: You know, Max, we've batted this question of costs and price around before.

MAX: That's right—and I can feel what's coming!

JOE: Well, you're right, too. I'm thinking about incremental costs again. This is just the kind of order that definitely requires an incremental approach. What do you say we take a few minutes and reason this one through, together? If you don't agree with me when we finish, you can chuck the order. That's what you had in mind for it, anyway, didn't you?

MAX: Damn right I was going to chuck it. But—it's Monday morning, and I'd like another cup of coffee, anyway. So, fire away, Joe. I'll listen one more time. But, I'm warning you—if I don't agree with something, you'll hear about it!

JOE: Max, I *want* you to yell when something doesn't look right to you. If I can't convince you, then maybe I'm wrong. If we do something to hurt our profits, that hurts me as much as it does you. But if we do something to improve our profits, we both gain. So, let's take one more look.

MAX: Fine, I'm ready. Talk to me!

JOE: Okay. Let's go back to the decision we made 18 months ago, when we decided to come into this business.

MAX: Good grief! Do we have to start with a history lesson? I thought you wanted to talk about this Foremost order.

JOE: Max, I'm trying to make a point. Now, just follow this along. Eighteen months ago we were faced with a particular decision, and that decision was whether or not we should go into business for ourselves. That was no easy decision, as you will remember, and we had a lot of things to consider. I still smile when I think of the nights we spent in your basement, hashing this whole thing through, with our wives upstairs making coffee and thinking we were a couple of damn fools. Our problem then was to add up all the possible costs we would incur as a result of going into business and to compare them with the benefits the business had to offer. Agreed, so far?

MAX: Keep talking.

JOE: And if we saw more benefits than costs, we would take the business. If not, it was back to the Product Improvement Group at good old GM for both of us. Well, Max, what were some of the things we counted as costs, for that decision?

MAX: Seems to me we considered *all* costs. You were so darned particular you even included toilet paper for the men's john!

JOE: (Laughing) That's right Max. That's right— I included everything and if I could have thought of something else besides the toilet paper, I would have thrown that in, too. Because we knew if we couldn't cover these costs, at our expected level of operation, it was pretty silly to go into business at all. Now, what were some of those costs?

MAX: Well, I still have the list, you know. Of course I've had to adjust it from time to time, to reflect changes, but I still use it as a reference for cost analysis. Let's see, there was rent on the building—payments on the new machines—the cost of our office equipment—labor, in the plant and here in the office—salary for the salesmen—and, of course, that red hot advertising program you worked up. Then there were the raw materials, general overhead expenses, and, as I recall, we even tacked on a factor for the heavier burden the business would be on our time. That included the static we'd get from our wives, if we were down here all the time, instead of at home.

JOE: Well, I'm glad we didn't miss that one!

MAX: So am I! But, Joe, when we finished juggling these figures around, we came up with an average cost of $13 per unit—and from there we decided on a selling price of $15. Now, I've kept track of our costs, and we hit them right on the button. Our cost today *is* $13 per unit, and that's why we have to maintain a $15 price.

JOE: Now Max, don't get excited. You promised to hear *me* out, remember? Let's not jump to any conclusions. We're just getting started. You're right— for *that* decision, we did come up with a $13 per unit cost. Now, on the basis of those cost figures, what decision did we make?

MAX: Well, damn it, we're sitting here today, aren't we? Of course, we decided to take the plunge and go into business. And it's worked out pretty well, too, but that's no reason for us to start playing Santa Claus all of a sudden! We have a price of $15, and that price just nicely covers our costs. Now, that's the way this game is played. If your price is higher than your costs, you make a profit. That's how people make a living! This Foremost outfit is looking for charity. We may be getting big, Joe, but we're not the federal government, yet!

JOE: (Laughing) All right. All right, so we're not the federal government. Now let's establish what we've done so far. We had a decision to make—whether or not to go into business. To make the right decision, we had to know every cost related to that decision. We had to be sure we could cover all of those costs, and still turn a profit. Well, we decided that it was possible. We set our price accordingly, and here we sit—a couple of hot shot capitalists.

MAX: Hear, hear!

JOE: And now it's Monday morning, and in flops that order from the West Coast. I say it represents a brand new decision, and the question is, how do we handle it?

MAX: Well, you know what I think!

JOE: Max, I say when you opened the mail this morning, and pulled our that order from Foremost, we had a new decision on our hands. And that decision is whether or not it will be profitable for us to fill this particular order, at the price they request—$10 per unit. You say that's not much of a decision. It seems to me that before we can decide, we have to draw up a *new* list of costs—a list that applies to this particular order. And that list shouldn't include costs that we will incur even if we turn down the order. It should include only costs that are added because we accept this particular 1,000 unit order. If those costs come to more than $10 per unit, I'll personally throw that order out the window!

MAX: Okay, Joe. I think I see what you're driving at. You're saying that, for an item to qualify as a cost for *this* decision, it must be one that we would not otherwise have incurred. Right?

JOE: You've got the idea.

MAX: All right. The first cost is raw materials. My records show this cost running at a steady $3.50 per unit.

JOE: That's good. Let's write that one down. Every one of those 1,000 units will definitely include the full amount of raw materials. Now, what about the labor?

MAX: Well, for a normal run, labor is running at $1.75 per unit. But the men are scheduled right to the straight-time limit, now. Those extra units will have to go at an overtime rate of $2 per unit.

JOE: That's fine. If we're going to have to pay overtime, let's recognize it now. I'm entering labor at $2 per unit.

MAX: Better be careful Joe. You're getting so generous with these costs, you'll defeat your own case.

JOE: Just to show you how generous I really am, I'm also going to throw in the costs for packaging and power. What are they running per unit?

MAX: Well, I'm figuring power at 25 cents per unit, and packaging, since we started using the shock-proof boxes a year ago, has been running at 50 cents. It's been a good investment, though. Our breakage returns are way down.

JOE: Okay, that's another 75 cents for power and packaging. Add that to the $5.50 we have for labor and materials, and that gives us $6.25, so far. Can you think of anything else, Max?

MAX: Well, yes. I've been doing some figuring on our sales cost. Of course, the salesmen get their commission (of 25 cents per unit) but in addition to that, they are running almost 40 cents per unit in straight road expenses, so . . .

JOE: Wait a minute, Max. Why do you want to include those costs? Are we going to pay any commissions on this 1,000 units? When the order came in by mail, from a company one of our men doesn't even contact?

MAX: Well, no—no, we can't pay a commission for something like that.

JOE: And what about those road expenses. Are we paying salesmen to contact people on the West Coast? How can this order possibly affect those expenses?

MAX: I guess you're right, Joe. So, scratch the sales expenses, for this order, at least. You know, I'm starting to get the hang of this.

JOE: Good. Now, I can think of at least one other item we should include. The order will require billing and supervisory time. Does another 25 cents per unit sound reasonable for that?

MAX: Sure, I'll buy that. Where does that put us, $6.50?

JOE: Right, $6.50 it is. Now, can you think of anything else?

MAX: Well, I guess you won't accept rent on the building, or machine payments, right?

JOE: No, Max. Those costs stay the same, regardless of whether we fill this order. Don't you agree?

MAX: I guess so. Frankly, I'm stumped. I can't think of anything else.

JOE: Max, you must be getting soft in your old age. There's one thing I was sure you'd hit me with. You did the last time we covered this ground. But you've completely forgotten it this morning.

MAX: What's that?

JOE: Shouldn't we worry about the money we could lose if we took an order for less than our regular price, and then got an order for full price that we couldn't fill because of it?

MAX: You know damn well that's always bothered me! To me, making a sale today at below cost, when tomorrow you might get an order at full price, just doesn't make sense. I'd throw this Foremost order out, for that reason alone. But how can you place a dollar cost on a thing like that?

JOE: Max, the chance of not being able to fill a full-price order worries me, too. Why shouldn't it? If selling this order for $10 means missing a chance to sell one at $15, that's just not good business—even if our costs were only 50 cents a piece. Now, let's try to place a dollar cost on that risk.

MAX: You're the magician, so proceed.

JOE: This situation seems made to order for probability analysis, Max. Now, hold on, Max—don't fall out of your chair, or spill your coffee. There's nothing mysterious about probabilities. Let me show you what I mean. Here we sit with essentially two choices. On the one hand, we have this order from the West Coast, offering to buy 1,000 units for $10 each. On the other hand, we *may* get an order for those same 1,000 units, but offering to pay our full price of $15 each. If we fill one order, we won't be able to fill the other, right?

MAX: Okay so far.

JOE: Now, if we were equally sure of each of these two possible orders, we'd choose the one for $15 every time. After all, we're not stupid. But the thing is, Max, we know that those two orders don't have the same chance of coming in. We've got the $10 order for sure, right now. You're holding it in your hand. Now, what are the chances of getting an order for 1,000 more units this week, at full price?

MAX: Who can tell? I just don't know. Most of our orders do come in a month or so in advance, so we can schedule them. But sometimes we get a rush deal. You know that's true. You just can't tell when. That's the problem.

JOE: I know that, Max, and I wasn't asking you to predict positively whether we were going to get such an order this week. If we knew that, we wouldn't have a problem, would we? So all we can do is make a good educated guess. There's nobody else in the world who could make a better guess about the possibility of getting such an order than the two of us. There isn't anyone who knows our business better than we do, so let's have a shot at it.

MAX: I sure agree with that. We won't find the answer written in any book, will we?

JOE: Nope. It's up to us. So let's get our guesses down on paper. You write yours on this piece of paper, and I'll write mine over here. Let's guess in terms of the number of chances in ten of our getting a $15 order this week.

(They both pause to think, and then write. Joe finishes first, then Max.)

MAX: Okay, Joe, what do you have?

JOE: Two chances in ten.

MAX: I guess three in ten.

JOE: Okay, let's compromise and accept your guess—three chances in ten. Now, we know that, if we take the order for $10, and then miss a chance to fill one for $15, we will have lost the opportunity to make a sale that would bring in $5 more than the price we accepted. We'd collect $10 for each unit we would sell, and could have gotten an additional $5 for every one we sold. But we just agreed that there is only a three-in-ten chance of getting the full price order. That means we have only a three-in-ten chance of losing the $5, right? So, the dollar cost we place on our fear of losing that extra income is equal to the size of the potential loss, multiplied by the probability of its occurrence. In our case, we multiply the $5 potential loss by a probability of 0.3, to get an expected loss of $1.50. That is the cost figure we use for the Foremost order, so let's add it to the list!

MAX: Wait a minute. How'd you get that cost knocked down to $1.50 per unit?

JOE: Okay, Max. Let's go over this probability thing one more time. I think we both agree that poorly defined misgivings don't provide a very good basis for making good business decisions. So if the alternative we have under consideration (in this case, an order for $10 per unit) doesn't seem to be the best one we could possibly have, it's our job to get busy and find a better one. Now, in the decision we're working on, we *have* found one better alternative—selling the 1,000 units at full price. If a full-price order were certain to come in, our decision to sell at $10 would mean a sacrifice of the $5 we would gain per unit if we could get an order for $15. However, since there's only a three-in-ten chance that we'll incur such a loss, we adjust the $5 by its probability of occurrence. And that's how we came up with $1.50 as our expected loss—for this decision. If we were sure that a full-price order would come through, then the expected loss would be the full five dollars.

MAX: Okay, I follow you, now—we adjust the face amount of the loss to reflect the uncertainty of its occurrence, and consider the result as one of the costs for this decision.

JOE: Exactly. Now, let's get back to the cost of filling this Foremost order.

MAX: Oh, yes. I was hoping you had forgotten about that. I have a feeling you're setting me up for the kill, but, lay on, Macduff!

JOE: All right, but Max, remember my offer to accept any cost you can show resulting from this particular order. You're welcome to dig in and come up with anything you think applies. What's our cost total, so far?

MAX: We were up to $6.50 per unit. By adding the $1.50 expected loss, to cover the risk of losing extra income from a full-price order, we come to a total of $8 per unit.

JOE: An incremental cost of $8 per unit. That's what I have, too. Now, Max, can you think of any costs we might have missed?

MAX: Frankly, Joe, I can't. I think we've pretty much covered the waterfront.

JOE: I believe you're right. So, let's wrap this up. When we left the office last Friday evening, this West Coast order didn't exist, as far as we knew, at least. It came into existence when you opened the mail this morning, and at that time, it created a separate decision for us to make. We have considered every incremental cost associated with filling the order, and have come up with a cost of $8 per unit. Foremost is offering to pay us $10. Do we take the order, or don't we?

MAX: Okay, Joe, we'll take it. But don't think I've gone soft. I'm learning about your incremental cost idea, and from now on, I'm going to be looking for the kind of costs that *do* apply to an order like this.

JOE: Max, that's fine. It's the only way we'll be able to make the incremental approach work. In fact, let's follow this order all the way through—until the time the Foremost truck drives away—to see just how much we do spend to fill it. You know, if we keep good records of these sorts of costs, we should be able to make even better decisions in the future.

* * *

JOE: Did you know, Max, it has already been over a month since we took that order for 1,000 units at a price of $10 per unit. Shouldn't we check back and see what actually happened? We could learn whether we were wise to take the order or lost money on it, as you feared we would.

MAX: Good idea. How do we do it? I realize that we got $10,000 that we would not have received but we still face the problem of getting an accurate measure of our costs. It still seems to me that the best measure is the figure we use all the time of $13 a unit, which is our standard cost. If that figure is wrong then maybe we should fire our accountant and get someone who can give us an accurate figure on cost.

JOE: You seem to have regressed back to where you started a month ago, Max. Look, we're now in a position to find out what we actually spent as a result of the decision to take that order. We can look at what we actually spent as a result of accepting the order. In that way, and only in that way, it seems to me, can we tell whether we did right. I dug out our calculation—the one we made last month that led us to accept the order. Let's see where, if at all, we went wrong? By doing this we should be able to decide how to react to other orders below our standard cost if they were to be offered under similar circumstances.

MAX: I agree. So, let me look at the figures again. I want to see, in particular, what we know now that we didn't know then. Let's see. We know that we didn't have to give up any other order at regular prices so that the $1.50 that you called a future opportunity cost doesn't apply.

JOE: It certainly is true that we did not have to give up any order to take this one. But, I'm not sure that we should not always include that kind of an item in future calculations on such prospective orders. What we collected was an insurance premium against a hazard that didn't turn up, it later turned out.

MAX: That's an interesting point and I'm frankly confused by it. However, I would agree with you. We should include that kind of an insurance premium in the future—so we should include it as a cost of the order—even if we didn't have to pay it.

JOE: Agreed. As I look back on the last month and ask myself what we spent extra as a result of accepting that order from out West, I see nothing that is not on our list. They came in to pick up the order about 15 minutes early on a Friday, as I remember it. Our shipping department was ready for them and loaded the truck without any difficulty. The merchandise was in inventory and we were able to maintain our inventories at the desired level during the last month. They paid cash on delivery, so we had no billing or credit costs. I can't see any extra or unexpected costs.

MAX: Did we have any overtime charges to the shipping department as a result of this order? That's an example of an item that would be covered by our G&A—which we did not include here.

JOE: Right. I'm not 100 percent sure, but I'm almost certain that we have had no overtime labor costs of any kind for several months now. But, on the billing, collection, and other costs associated with this order, there were no extras. In fact, I can't think of a dollar we spent extra to take the order—other than the cost of replacing what we sold in inventory. That is where almost all of the dollars are involved. Did we underestimate the costs of the goods?

MAX: That would be very difficult to pin down, but we could check with the purchasing department and see how well our estimates held up.

JOE: True, but that needn't be done in this case because we didn't disagree about the production costs—and especially about the cost of raw materials, components, and supplies. So whatever happened to production costs, it would seem that our decision was well reasoned. And, as it happens, I think our costs to replace the merchandise we sold were lower, if anything, than what we estimated—because we have been improving the productivity of the plant, as you know.

MAX: The real issue we should be discussing is whether we were right in concluding that we would incur no General and Administrative Costs. That really was the issue in this case. The biggest item in G&A is our two salaries and the insurance on our lives.

JOE: That's right, and we didn't increase those costs as a result of taking the order. What we did do was spend time discussing whether we should accept the order that could have been spent doing something else for the firm that might have been profitable.

MAX: Good point—I wish I had thought of that, but we were going to discuss the order to decide whether or not we took it—so whatever time we spent, and it was less than ten minutes as I recall, was not really a consequence of accepting the order, but rather the result of receiving the inquiry.

JOE: That's very good thinking, Max. You're doing a great job of separating out the costs that result from a particular decision—in this case, those resulting from accepting a special order. I would say that we should do that kind of thinking on all of our decisions.

MAX: That approach to computing costs may seem to be valid for off-price orders, but I'm certainly not prepared to apply it to all of our decisions. It seems to me that we must judge each decision separately—taking account of the particular circumstances existing at the time.

JOE: I certainly agree on the importance of the existing circumstances, so I'm prepared to let the issue rest here. Really, Max, I'm pleased that you were open-minded enough to listen to my viewpoint and that we took the order and that it seems to have worked out as predicted. It would have been nice if this case had proved my point for all time, but I can afford to be patient.

Chapter 9

COST DETERMINANTS, COST CONCEPTS, AND COST MEASUREMENT

T HIS CHAPTER discusses three related and vital subjects: the factors that determine the level of decision costs in specific situations; the main concepts that assist in the computation of decision costs (some drawn from accounting and others from economic theory); and problems in assigning specific numerical values to costs in concrete decision situations.

Determinants of Decision Costs

What factors explain the amount it costs to carry out decisions? Why does the decision to produce an item sometimes involve much higher costs than it would have only a few days earlier? Why do some firms in an industry incur substantially higher costs than others to make similar products? Why does it cost the same firm more to add output of a given product in one of its plants than in another?

Many factors influence the costs to carry out a decision. The more important of these will be sketched here. Attention will be concentrated on the basic economic forces that underlie costs and that may be unfamiliar to many executives.

Six basic factors determine the costs that a firm incurs as a result of carrying out a decision:

- The prices paid for the factors of production: wages, salaries, interest, rent. (Of course, one could look behind these prices to see the factors that determine them, like union strength, activities of the monetary authorities, the existence of rent control.)

- The productivity of the factors of production and of management.
- Commitments of the firm to its factors of production.
- Legal and institutional arrangements, like minimum wage legislation, fringe benefits, union contracts, special premiums for overtime and Sunday work.
- Available productive capacity: short-run costs.
- The scale of the organization's operations: long-run costs.

The first four factors listed are quite straightforward and can be dealt with expeditiously. The last two will require a review of traditional cost theory, albeit a sketchy one.

The Prices and Productivity of the Factors of Production

The cost of making anything reflects both what must be paid to those who produce it plus the efficiency with which they produce. Low pay to labor that is very unproductive results in high cost. So costs reflect both prices paid and productivity. In large organizations, most individual employees have relatively little influence over their productivity, which depends mainly on the tools they are given to work with, the manner in which production is arranged, and the caliber of supervision provided by the employer.

Commitments of the Firm to Its Factors of Production

Employers sometimes feel a moral commitment to provide employment to employees with a long history of loyal service; sometimes they have a contract which requires them to provide employees with some minimum number of weeks of work; employers usually regard particular employees as so essential to their long-term welfare that they would not lay them off even temporarily when they have no immediate need for their services. Whatever the basis for the commitment, employers are usually committed to some employees to provide them with income, whether or not there is work for them to do. To use such employees to carry out a decision does not, then, impose added costs on a firm—if otherwise they would not do anything of value for the firm.

Legal and Institutional Arrangements

Considerable legislation bears on payments to factors of production. Most of this legislation affects payments to employees, but some relates to land use, payments of rent, special payments for work on holidays or Sundays, and the like. To estimate accurately the costs of specific decisions, a decision maker should be familiar with such legislation and know how it will affect the costs of the decision at issue. Legislation also requires licenses to operate in certain occupations and often has the effect of limiting entry into a field and thus raising charges. Prices paid for factors of production and their productivity are affected in many ways too numerous to mention both by statute and by conventional arrangements.

Available Productive Capacity

The cost of decisions carried out when an organization possesses idle resources will usually be far lower than when the same decision is carried out with a shortage of resources. With excess capacity, a firm can increase its output with little or no extra cost by making fuller use of resources that are not fully utilized. Conversely, when a firm is suffering from bottlenecks or a general shortage of facilities, it must make substantial outlays for added resources to increase output; and, ordinarily it must use them unproductively. Accordingly, the amount of productive capacity available at the time a decision is carried out represents an important influence on a firm's decision costs.

Let us now adopt the distinction made by economic theorists between short-run and long-run costs. Short-run costs are at issue when a firm wants to carry out a decision that will use facilities already in its possession. We are concerned with long-run costs when, in order to carry out the decision, management has the time to obtain all additional resources it desires or to discard excessive resources in its possession. How then do economists explain cost conditions when a firm uses facilities it already possesses to carry out a decision?

Short-run costs: producing with existing facilities. Most decisions made by an executive are carried out by using an already existing organization. That is, they use skilled employees and facilities already in place. These facilities could be huge, costly power plants or an enormous communications network or mere desks and pens. We speak of such decisions as involving the use of "fixed" factors of production. That means that during the period that the decision would be carried out, the amount of particular factors of production—skilled personnel, specialized equipment, and space—are limited in amount; a substantial period of time would be required to expand their supply significantly. From the standpoint of the decision in question, therefore, their supply is fixed.

Economic theory helps explain the costs that typically are incurred as an existing organization expands output. That is, cost theory explains what costs are incurred when an executive decides to produce extra units of something with fixed factors of production. A decision to produce an extra unit means producing 107 units instead of 106—that is, the single 107th unit; 11 instead of 10; 294 instead of 293. Figure 9-1 presents a highly

Figure 9-1. Costs to produce additional single units.

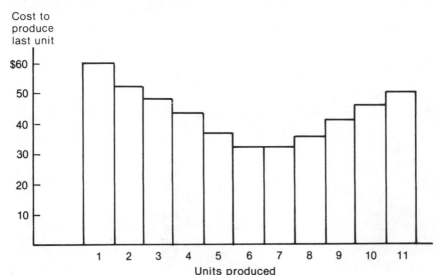

simplified view of the costs of decisions to produce individual extra units of a hypothetical item, when the firm is already engaged in producing that item.

Figure 9-1 and Table 9-1 (column 2) show that the decision cost to make a single unit with an existing organization is relatively high.* (The decision here is to make one unit instead of none.) Although not shown on the diagram, the cost to produce no units at all is vastly higher. What we mean by the cost of zero output in this case is really the cost of maintaining the organization in a state of readiness to produce. These costs, sometimes termed "fixed costs," pay for the so-called fixed factors of production. This statement is not strictly accurate; fixed costs include some items not required to keep the organization ready to produce. Once the organization is in a state of readiness, the cost to produce one unit is not very large, but it is larger than the cost of making the second unit; that in turn is higher than the cost of the third, and so on. (We describe these as "decision costs.") As Figure 9-1 depicts, the decision to produce added units would ordinarily require progressively smaller additions to cost—up to some level of output. At this point, an output of six units in this case, the cost of additional units would level off and, after a while, would increase. Let us examine

---

* Figure 9-1 does not exactly depict the cost data presented in Table 9-1. However, the relationships and general patterns are similar and conform to those discussed in the text.

Table 9-1

Computation of Different Costs: A Hypothetical Example

Units (1)	Decision cost* (2)	Total incremental cost (3)	Average incremental cost (4)	Fixed cost (5)	Total cost (6)	Average total cost† (7)
1	$ 64	$ 64	$64	$300	$ 364	$364
2	58	122	61	300	422	211
3	52	174	58	300	474	158
4	48	222	55.5	300	522	130.5
5	47	269	53.8	300	569	113.8
6	46 ⎤ Min.	315	52.5	300	615	102.5
7	46 ⎦	361	51.6	300	661	94.4
8	48	409	51.1 Min.	300	709	88.6
9	52	461	51.2	300	761	84.6
10	59	520	52	300	820	82
11	69	589	53.5	300	889	80.8 ⎤ Min.
12	81	670	55.8	300	970	80.8 ⎦
13	95	765	58.9	300	1,065	81.9
14	110	875	62.5	300	1,175	83.9

* Most volatile.
† Least volatile after first few units.

why costs typically conform to that general pattern when output is produced by an already existing organization.

Several fundamental forces influence the costs that an organization incurs as it adds to output, when utilizing a fixed quantity of plant, equipment, and skilled employees. The most important of these is "specialization." As an organization produces larger quantities of an item in any time
period, management can subdivide tasks more and more finely. As individuals perform the same task with great frequency, their skill increases;
when the tasks that are repeated are quite narrow, the increase in proficiency can reach remarkable levels and lower costs correspondingly.
Laymen tend to grossly underestimate the productivity gains from labor
specialization and to exaggerate the gains from mechanization.

Beyond some point, which we call the point of diminishing returns, the
decision to produce added units would result in higher unit costs. (In
Figure 9-1, this point is reached with unit 6.) Cost would increase at that
point because the organization does not possess sufficient fixed factors to
produce additional units with maximum efficiency. To be more specific,
the organization would require more plant, equipment, and/or skilled employees to produce this added unit at the lowest unit cost, that is, with

maximum efficiency. The "law of variable proportions" explains that if an organization has fixed quantities of particular factors of production, then at some level of output it will be using all its resources with maximum efficiency. (That is, it will be using all of its factors of production in ideal proportions.) However, as output expands beyond or falls below that output level, production becomes less efficient and costs rise because the proportions in which resources are being used depart more and more from the ideal.

The costs of producing added output have been depicted and expressed in Figure 9-1 and Table 9-1 (column 2) as the cost of single extra units—technically termed "marginal units." Costs of output can be described in terms of averages, when more than one is involved. So if an executive decided to produce, say, 10 units of something, he could total the costs to make each of the 10 units and then divide the total by 10. If he was already producing 6 units, he could total the cost of making units 7 through 16 and divide the total by 10 to compute the average cost of the decision to produce an extra 10 units when already making 6 units. Cost data can be processed in many different ways.

Figure 9-2 shows the average costs of an idealized firm. (The average cost is figured from zero units in each case.) (Table 9-1, column 4, indicates the average of the decision costs shown in Figure 9-1.) The shape of the average decision cost curve reflects the statements already made: the organization would incur substantial costs to maintain fixed factors of production in a state of readiness so that it could produce on command, the added costs to produce extra units would reflect the influence of specialization,

Figure 9-2. Typical pattern of average costs.

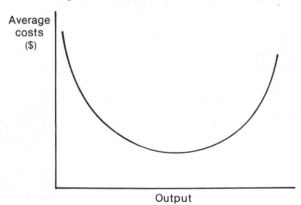

and costs per unit would fall as output approached the point at which productive factors were used in ideal proportions and would rise as output exceeded that point.

We have ignored fixed costs up to this point. They are assumed to be $300 no matter how many units are produced, up to 14 units. (We have little interest in what happens with larger outputs because decision costs are already very high.) The average costs at different levels of output reflect these three factors plus the "averaging" of fixed costs over a larger number of units. Accordingly, average costs are shown in Figure 9-2 to fall to a minimun at some point (which is termed "economic capacity") and to rise thereafter. The decline up to that point results partly from spreading the fixed costs over more and more units. (Table 9-1, columns 4 and 7, makes this clear by presenting average incremental costs and average total costs. Observe that average incremental costs vary between $64 and $51.1 for the same outputs; average total costs fall from $364 to $80.8.)

"Economic capacity" was defined as the output at which average total costs are at a minimum. (Observe that this output is different from the issue of diminishing returns.) An organization usually is capable of producing far more than its output at economic capacity—but only by incurring higher average (total) costs than the minimum. The reader should avoid the trap of assuming that an organization must operate at economic capacity in order to prosper, or that minimum cost operation is a worthy end in itself. Executives should decide what and how much to produce after considering the benefits to be obtained (price/revenue considerations) as well as costs. Maximum profits often are obtained at some output other than at economic capacity.

The Scale of the Organization's Operations

What has been sketched above is the determination of costs in the short run when an organization possesses fixed amounts of the factors of production. Now we shall investigate how the costs of a firm's output decisions are affected by changes in the quantity of fixed factors it possesses. In effect, we ask what typically happens to the cost of making an item if one makes it in small, medium-sized, and large factories. In more technical jargon, we shall explore the effect on costs of changes in scale operations; we shall discuss the economies of scale. We shall present only the bare bones of long-run cost theory and try to relate it closely to the computation of decision costs.

Long-run costs. Given enough time to do so, an organization can add to or discard some of its fixed factors of production. That means it could operate on any of many scales, varying from tiny to huge. Some executives must make a determination on this matter. Presumably they do so by estimating costs to produce the output they expect to need with different scales of operation—that is, they explore what they would gain or lose if they were to build a larger organization. In effect, they estimate costs at different levels of output with organizations of different size. More technically stated, they construct a planning curve, which indicates the minimum cost of producing different outputs with organizations constructed on different scales. Figure 9-3 presents just such a planning curve.

Observe that seven individual cost curves, similar to the average cost curve presented in Figure 9-2, have been drawn in Figure 9-3. Each represents an estimate of the average costs to make the product in different quantities if an organization of different size is created. As drawn, the larger the scale of the organization (the more space, equipment, supervisory staff) the *higher* the unit costs if small amounts are produced and the lower the unit costs if large amounts are made. (Line 7 is an exception to this general pattern and depicts a condition in which the costs of production rise with increased scale of operations because of the sheer complexity of managing a huge enterprise.) To create a large organization—to purchase large quantities of fixed factors—thus poses risk: if demand is small, costs will be very high; low unit costs will be incurred if demand is large.

In some activities, notably mining and agriculture, the long-run cost curve may begin to rise after a modest scale of operations is reached. In these fields, increases in scale of operations ordinarily mean the use of lower quality natural resources—poor land, or thinner seams of coal, copper, lead.

We have come a long distance from the kinds of problems that were discussed in the preceding chapter, which were decisions to be carried out

Figure 9-3. Planning curve.

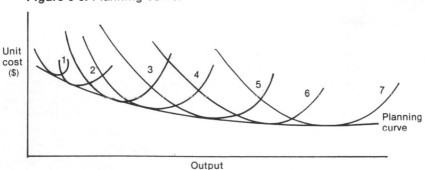

with existing fixed factors. The costs of a decision reflect the particular scale of organization in existence when the decision is carried out.

Let us pause briefly to look more closely at decisions regarding investment in additional plant capacity. How should an executive make such a decision? Recognize that a firm would already possess facilities; these ordinarily could be sold, but for substantially less than they are worth to the firm owning them. Consequently, the executive is not in the position postulated by the planning curve. He does not start from scratch but rather builds onto what he already possesses. Ordinarily, he will not end up with the very latest technology, but with a combination of different technologies; he'll not have a plant of the latest design but a hybrid of some kind—perhaps a modern new plant, but one much smaller than it would have been if the firm had sold its existing plant. The firm will usually continue to use the facilities it possessed at the time the capacity expansion took place.

In other words, firms that expand capacity do not, in fact, move along their planning curve. Decisions to expand capacity typically are very complex, involving estimates of sales levels into the future and estimates of costs over the same period—assuming no expansion occurs and assuming also different amounts of added capacity. By trial and error, an executive would work his way toward the best decision to make under the circumstances.

Key Concepts Related to Decision Costing

The preceding discussion of the computation of decision costs described six steps involved in such computations and the main factors which determine the magnitude of decision costs in specific situations. In this section, we shall explore the concepts that help a decision maker estimate accurately decision costs for concrete decisions.

Specifically, we will start by sketching the main cost notions employed by accountants, and especially those notions employed by specialists in cost computations. It happens that most of these notions are derived directly from economists' writings on costs; we have met some of them already. These notions are generally of a lower level of generality than the profoundly important and somewhat complicated concepts discussed in the following section: incrementalism and opportunity costs.

ACCOUNTING COST CONCEPTS

Executives get almost all their cost data from accountants. They should therefore become fully acquainted with the terminology of accountants and the way they think about costs and the way they view their job responsibilities. Executives must learn how to approach accountants for information and how to interpret what they receive from them.

Fixed and variable costs. The simplest cost notions employed by accountants are those of fixed and variable costs. Fixed costs are expenditures that are unaffected by changes in a firm's output. We described them earlier as outlays required to maintain the enterprise in a condition of readiness to produce; they are the costs of the "fixed factors of production." To be very specific, fixed costs represent an unvarying sum which a firm spends regardless of its output. On the hypothetical example developed earlier (Table 9-1), that sum is assumed to be $300 and it remains the same whether zero units or 14 are produced. (It is possible that if the firm were to produce some larger number of units, it could do so only by incurring additional costs for fixed factors. But, given the size of its incremental costs, it is clear that management would be unwise to produce any more than 14 units from that one plant. (From a minimum of $46, decision costs have increased to $110.)

It is possible to depict fixed costs as a total, unvarying at different levels of output. This is done in Figure 9-4 by the line labeled TFC. Figure 9-5 describes fixed costs as an average—that is, fixed costs per unit; that quantity is designated by the curve AFC. This line drops sharply as the total is divided over two and three units, cutting the per-unit fixed cost in half and then by two-thirds. Very quickly it falls to modest levels: at six units, fixed costs are $50 per unit; at 10 units they become $30.

Variable (or incremental) costs do vary with changes in output, though not necessarily in direct proportion to output. Typically, to increase output, some increase in costs is required to cover the cost of added raw materials, labor, and power. Table 9-1, column 3, and Figure 9-4 indicate total variable cost as output expands. This quantity is designated by the curve TVC in Figure 9-4. The AVC line in Figure 9-5 represents average variable costs—the total divided by output. For example, in Table 9-1, we see that with an output of six units, total incremental (variable) costs are $315; the average incremental cost is $52.50.

One can add fixed and variable costs to obtain total cost (TC). Table 9-1 shows a total of fixed and variable costs (column 6). It presents this total in the form of an average also—that is, an average of fixed and variable costs combined (column 7). That averaged sum is labeled AC in Figure 9-5.

Total, average, and marginal costs. We have already described fixed and variable costs, and a combination of the two, both as a total sum and as an average. These are simply different ways of describing the same phenomenon. Marginal costs are a relatively unfamiliar notion, but they are also derived from the same basic cost information—total costs. They represent

Figure 9-4. Fixed and variable costs expressed as totals.

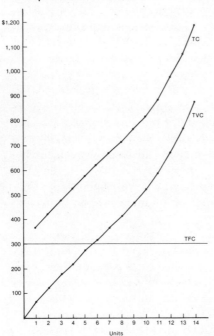

Figure 9-5. Fixed and variable costs expressed as averages, plus marginal costs.

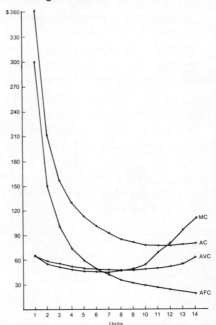

the addition to total costs that results from adding a specific extra unit of output; that is, they represent the added cost to produce the sixth unit if one is already producing five units. The word "marginal" is synonymous with the "last unit." What is the "last" in any specific case depends, of course, upon your output at the time.

Table 9-1 or Figure 9-5 provides the data we require for illustrative purposes. In column 6 in Table 9-1 we find total costs for different numbers of units: it costs a total of $364 to produce a single unit, $761 to produce nine units, and so on. If we ask how much extra it costs to produce, say, the seventh unit, it would be the difference between the total cost to produce six and the total cost to produce seven—or $46. (This is the same sum that is presented in column 2 as the decision cost of the seventh unit.) This is shown by the curve MC in Figure 9-5.

Incremental costs. Decision costs and incremental costs are synonymous for most purposes. Technically, incremental costs represent the added costs to produce some increment of output; if one is considering more units of the same product that the enterprise is making, then incremental costs are simply the combined marginal costs of the individual units in question. For example, if one is computing the costs of adding three units to an output of eight units, then the resultant figure is an incremental cost which is equal to the marginal cost of the ninth, tenth, and eleventh units. Accordingly, the incremental cost of those units, given the data assumed in Table 9-1, would be $180—$52 plus $59 plus $69. The concept of incremental costs is discussed more fully later in this chapter.

Standard costs. The concept of standard costs is purely an accounting creation: It represents a measure of costs that can be used as a standard; the figure shows what costs would be if the firm operated at relatively high efficiency and at a fairly typical level of capacity. Standard costs often are the basis for price decisions; they are used quite as much to determine whether and in what respect production arrangements are defective.

Standard costs usually are constructed by a combination of time and motion studies and analyses of the materials and components that enter into a product—including allowances for wastage, scrap, defective materials, and the like. Data are collected routinely which permit comparisons of actual costs with standard costs to obtain "variances"—differences. When these differences are in the direction of actual costs higher than standard costs, the presumption is made that production arrangements need change. At least, management attempts to ascertain the cause of the variance; if a defect is found, efforts will be made to correct it; sometimes its cause is uncovered and nothing can be done about it. Variances represent signals that difficulties exist; they start a process which may culminate in the elimination of some defect.

Full costs. Full costs are often contrasted with incremental costs. The latter do *not* include allocations of cost, by formula, for overhead and common costs. Full costs are often termed "fully allocated costs" and are constructed so that each item of output is charged for some portion of common costs. The objective of full-costing is to assign all of a firm's costs to its current output. Incremental costs only include variable costs and exclude so-called fixed or overhead costs.

Economic Concepts Relevant to Decision Costs

A small handful of economic concepts are crucial for the proper computation of decision costs. Specifically, "incrementalism" and "opportunity costs" are vital notions that must be mastered (and not simply understood) by those who wish to estimate decision costs accurately. Each will be discussed in turn.

INCREMENTAL COSTS

The concept of incremental costs represents perhaps the single most important economic idea applicable to decision making. Assume an executive makes a decision to add a new item to the firm's product line. What is the cost of that decision? It is the difference between the total costs the firm would incur if it did not add that item and the total costs if it did add that item to its line. Table 9-2 presents a hypothetical example which illustrates what is involved in computing incremental costs in a lifelike (though highly simplified) situation.

Recognize at the outset that decision costs are essentially incremental costs. We say "essentially" because in some instances we should use short-

Table 9-2

COMPUTATION OF INCREMENTAL COSTS

	Total cost without new item	Total cost with new item	Cost attributable to new item
Sales	$10,000,000	$11,150,000	$1,150,000
Less: Cost of goods sold	7,600,000	8,550,000	950,000
Production costs	6,500,000	7,150,000	650,000
Raw materials	2,000,000	2,200,000	200,000
Purchases	2,200,000	2,450,000	250,000
Direct labor	1,200,000	1,350,000	150,000
Supervision	300,000	320,000	20,000
Fringe benefits	200,000	220,000	20,000
Power	150,000	155,000	5,000
Depreciation	200,000	200,000	—
Property taxes	200,000	200,000	—
Interest charges	50,000	55,000	5,000
Sales costs	1,100,000	1,400,000	300,000
Salaries and commissions	600,000	750,000	150,000
Advertising	200,000	300,000	100,000
Customer service	100,000	110,000	10,000
Marketing administration and research	200,000	210,000	10,000
Gross margin	2,400,000	2,600,000	200,000
Less:			
General and administrative	1,100,000	1,150,000	50,000
Research and development	200,000	200,000	—
Public relations	100,000	100,000	—
Top management salaries	700,000	700,000	—
Miscellaneous	100,000	150,000	50,000
Net profit	$ 1,300,000	$ 1,450,000	$ 150,000

run incremental costs; in other cases, long-run incremental costs would be the proper figure. However, that is a refinement we can afford to pass over here. In addition, opportunity costs are included in decision costs, but more will be said about this later.

Certain decisions involve negative costs; the computation of decision costs is made in such cases in the same manner as when positive incremental costs are involved. For example, if management is considering dropping an item from its line, it would compute its total costs if it were to retain the item and its total costs if it dropped it. The difference would be negative; this figure would then be compared with the change in total revenue that would result from dropping the item to determine the profitability of the decision.

It requires very little space to explain the concept of incremental costs. The concept is not difficult to understand. However, many executives find the concept difficult to accept; consequently, they often do not apply it when it is appropriate. Since the concept is so crucial to effective decision making, we should understand the strong resistance to the idea.

In specific cases, a situation arises in which an item is added to a firm's product line without being "charged" with any of the company's overhead costs. (See the earlier discussion of full costs.) The reason that is done is that no increase in the firm's overhead costs is anticipated as a result of adding the new item. Given what we have said here, the overhead costs of the decision to add the item to the line is zero. However, some executives might protest that "it is unfair" that other items should cover the overhead on that item; it should carry its fair share of the overhead. Let us state as a cardinal rule that questions related to decision costs have nothing whatsoever to do with fairness. Costs either do or do not increase as a result of a decision; that is the only issue that must be decided if one is to estimate decision costs accurately.

A moment's reflection should win acceptance for the conclusion that the cost of a decision is what results from carrying out that decision—nothing more or less. Only the sacrifices incurred by a firm as a result of a decision should be charged against that decision. The issue is a factual one—how did your costs actually change as a result of that decision. To get an answer, it is necessary to see what happened as a direct consequence of the decision. One need not answer any philosphical questions like "how much should be allocated against this product or that."

Opportunity Costs

The concept of opportunity costs is one of the most central of all economic ideas. It is also one of the most troublesome to understand and apply. One source of the difficulty is the name given to the concept. It does not help most people who hear it for the first time. Also, opportunity costs have several quite different applications so that it seems more like several quite different ideas rather than a single idea.

Our goal in discussing opportunity costs is to have the reader end up with a series of questions he should ask whenever computing costs. These questions should be asked for nonbusiness as well as business decisions. By answering them, a decision maker can determine how much, if anything, should be added to costs to take opportunity costs into account.

The concept of opportunity costs rests on the inescapable fact that to do certain things one must forgo the opportunity to do other things. It affirms the agony of choice that is stressed by the existentialists.

Executives sometimes can do everything they wish to do; much more often, however, their limited resources prevent them from doing some things. Their choice in any situation thus may force them to sacrifice something of value—what they could gain by exploiting some alternative. Limited resources* thus are the source of opportunity costs; executives incur no opportunity costs when they possess unlimited resources (and can do everything they would like to do).

Accordingly, opportunity costs arise only when executives must forgo opportunities they would like to exploit. The cost in such situations does not involve an actual outlay of funds or a reduction in the value of assets but rather the giving up of what one could have obtained.

The concept of opportunity costs serves an executive in two main ways. First, it helps to identify cost-creating actions and decisions that might otherwise be ignored. More specifically, it directs attention to certain costs that are not usually recognized and are not recorded in the regular books of account. Second, it guides an executive to the proper measurement of costs that are not accurately reported in the regular accounting records. Accordingly, the opportunity cost concept is valuable mainly because accounting records either omit certain costs or measure them inaccurately *for decision-making purposes.*

Costs not usually recorded in regular books of account. One does not find, and would not expect to find, in a firm's accounting records valuation of things that the firm did not do—its forgone opportunities—and an accounting department would not be in a position to obtain such information. Forgone opportunities can only be valued by the executives who make the decision

---

* A particular form of limited resources—bottlenecks, which represent an imbalance of resources—deserves particular attention. Bottlenecks exist when one resource—the scarcest—prevents full utilization of the others. (Bottlenecks thus give the appearance of both surpluses and shortages of resources.)

that gave rise to the opportunity cost in the first place. Let us make this point clear.

Ms. Jones is selecting media in which to place her firm's advertising during the forthcoming year. She has identified three highly attractive magazines; after making a careful assessment of the three, she selects magazine A; she estimates that by placing her advertising there, she will obtain, say, a 15 percent return on her investment in advertising. Magazine C is next best in her opinion and would yield a 13 percent return. In that instance, the opportunity cost of the decision to invest advertising monies in magazine A is what would have been earned by advertising instead in magazine C. This estimate of a 13 percent return would have been made by Ms. Jones and possibly not even reported to her supervisor; certainly no record would have been made of it for the accounting department.

If Ms. Jones had placed her advertising in magazine C, then her opportunity cost would have been the 15 percent return she could have obtained by advertising in magazine A. In that case, even though she showed a 13 percent return on the books, the true outcome was a 2 percent "opportunity loss" or "decision loss." By making a poor decision, she would have lost 2 percent for the firm. Thus one cannot evaluate a decision simply by examining its outcome; one must consider the alternative actions that might have been taken instead.

To apply the opportunity cost concept in this manner an executive must turn up the most attractive feasible alternatives and select the most attractive among them. The concept of opportunity costs does not explain how to search for attractive alternatives and doesn't help one decide when one has searched long enough for attractive alternatives. It does, however, require an executive to be explicit about the alternatives that were considered and to place a value on them. The decision rule offered by the concept is embarrassingly obvious: Pick the best of your alternatives.

Apart from forgone opportunities, certain other costs sometimes are not recorded in an organization's regular books of account. These are the costs for the use of the owner/proprietor's time, for the initial capital the owner has invested in his enterprise, and for the use of undistributed profits, which are one form of owner's capital. Often, the owners of a business or professionals conducting a private practice are paid no salary; they take their pay solely in the form of profits. But as the concept of opportunity costs instructs, these people usually give up the opportunity to take gainful employment with others in order to serve their own enterprise; what they could have earned then represents a cost of working for themselves. Similarly, if they invest funds in their enterprise that could have been invested elsewhere to produce a return, they would also incur a cost. To ignore these costs is to exaggerate the profitability of projects; if their costs were computed accurately, they might not be undertaken.

The cost of using undistributed profits is an important special case of the same class of opportunity cost. When a firm makes profits beyond what it distributes in dividends, it gains resources that it can devote to various undertakings. These resources could also be distributed to the owners of the enterprise. Consequently, their retention in the firm imposes an opportunity cost. In specific cases, it is usually very difficult to estimate the size of this cost. Many firms employ a "cut-off" rate of interest to deal with this issue. That is, they set a minimum rate of return that a project must yield to justify an investment. This rate of return is an estimate of the investment opportunities that the management has good reason to expect to uncover. The cut-off rate of interest thus represents a tool developed to take account of the opportunity cost of capital.

Let us now consider some simple applications of the concept. When a lawyer, accountant, architect, or professor paints his home or finishes an attic, he usually greatly exaggerates his savings. He usually ignores the benefits he would have realized from the things he would have done if he had not done the painting. These might include such things as professional reading, the cultivation of clients, reflective thinking, some writing, or even resting. The concept of opportunity costs thus enjoins executives to be particularly alert for the hidden costs of resource uses that are not associated with either money outlays or accounting costs. (Also, they should consider the benefits to be obtained from the use of resources that do not appear directly in accounting income.)

Costs incorrectly measured by accounting records. The most illuminating and neglected application of the opportunity cost concept concerns the amount to charge for the use of a resource. The concept stresses that the true cost may not be what the organization has paid, or is currently paying, for the resource. Rather, the true cost to the organization—what it actually gave up—is what it would have gained from putting that resource to its next best use. Thus, if a firm has raw materials in inventory for which it paid, say, $10,000 but which has no resale or salvage value, then the use of those raw materials to make a product would impose no cost—if there were no other use for them. Conversely, their true cost would be more than $10,000 if more than that sum would be necessary to replace them and if they were needed by the organization to conduct its business. This last application of the opportunity cost concept has become widely recognized as nations have become afflicted with persistent inflation. It is usually described as using replacement rather than acquisition cost.

The irrelevance of acquisition cost or even of current payments by the organization for certain resources goes unrecognized in many, perhaps most, organizations. For example, it is almost universal practice for a firm to charge against a project the sums paid to employees and executives who are engaged on that project, rather than what they would produce for the organization if not assigned to that project. Most valued employees and executives have a backlog of vital projects—projects whose completion would produce far more value for the organization than their salary and fringe benefits. Consequently, to charge a project for their time on the basis of their salary (and fringe benefits) would greatly understate the true cost of their services. This practice frequently results in decisions to accept projects that will reduce a firm's profits.

This application of the opportunity cost concept is far-reaching and sometimes counter-intuitive. It instructs organizations to value resources they already possess or command by what they produce rather than by what they are paid. This instruction is difficult to follow, but is crucial, especially in decisions involving heavy use of senior executive time, the services of highly skilled technicians, scarce machinery, and components and raw materials in inventory.

The valuation of future opportunities. There is still another application of the opportunity cost concept. It properly belongs under the heading of costs not included in a firm's system of accounts; but it is treated last because it is complicated and can be understood best once the other applications of the concept have been studied. It is the valuation of future opportunities.

To take an action now may, because it consumes limited resources, foreclose opportunities that would arise in the future. For example, a construction firm may be offered a low-profit contract to help build a school. Accepting such a contract would prevent the firm from accepting any other project for about eight months. Specifically, it would be unable to accept a high-profit contract if it were to be offered two weeks later.

This dilemma is fairly common. Also, in most cases, the decision maker possesses considerable information about his future opportunities—jobs hanging fire, job prospects, or jobs likely to come through. So when offered the low-profit contract on the school, the construction executive would know what kinds of jobs were hanging fire. His task is to place a value on them. He is in the position of placing a value on his "birds in the bush" which he would then compare with the value of the "bird in hand"—the school project.

The valuation of future opportunities is complicated and consequently is discussed in an appendix to this chapter. However, one should not accept a scrawny bird in the hand when many plump birds are in the bush and are likely to emerge very soon; this conclusion can be drawn from the opportunity cost concept and can even be quantified. Since most organizations possess limited resources, they should give explicit attention to the future alternatives they may give up by making particular commitments in the present.

In summary, the important concept of opportunity cost holds that any action forecloses other actions when one has limited resources. A wise decision maker will search out alternatives conscientiously. He will also (1) pick the best of those alternatives known to him; (2) include as costs the value of resources used to carry out a decision, even though no payments or accounting charges were made for them; (3) value resources already possessed or employed by what they could produce for the organization in alternative activities rather than by what they cost originally or are paid currently; and (4) identify and place a value on future opportunities whenever they are about to commit sizable amounts of resources.

Problems in Assigning Numerical Values to Costs

Perhaps the greatest difficulty faced in computing decision costs is in determining whether or not an item should be considered part of decision costs. This problem is quite simple conceptually—the answer should depend upon whether or not the cost resulted from the decision. Once it has been determined that an item should be included in decision cost, the decision maker must estimate the amount of the cost. It is with that issue that we deal in this section. In particular, we will discuss problems resulting from lack of relevant cost information, uncertainty about future conditions, and the problem (or, rather, the nonproblem) of common costs.

Lack of Information and Uncertainty About the Future

These two factors are interconnected; because of a lack of information, decision makers are uncertain about things that might be known. However, the future is unpredictable mainly because we do not understand fully the forces that affect the phenomena with which our decisions deal. No matter how much information we have, we will still face some uncertainty for that reason alone. Beyond this, our information always deals with the past or near-present, and not with the future in which our decisions will be carried out.

A decision maker will rarely find already available precisely the information he requires to help with a particular decision. Most companies possess considerable "programmed" accounting information—data collected routinely to meet their usual needs for cost data. However, they do not have "special purpose" information to assist with the many sudden and unexpected decisions that management must make. Decision makers are faced with the choice of guessing at costs—building guesses upon the most relevant information available—or collecting information afresh to meet their particular needs. Very often, they will elect the first alternative and guess at quantities on the basis of meager clues.

If they were to collect information specially for each decision at hand, decision makers could draw upon a variety of resources in the average large firm; they are not limited to the accounting information that firms collect routinely. They can call on time-and-motion specialists and request special cost analyses and even estimate costs by statistical means. Large firms employ specialists in the analysis of business processes and their associated costs.

Moreover, it is a rare firm that produces exactly the same things in the same way under the same circumstances for any length of time. Thus, each decision is likely to be unique to some degree and information about past decisions or experience cannot apply fully to the decision at hand.

Uncertainty stems from many sources: unpredictable variations in levels of sales, unforeseeable changes in conditions of production, labor difficulties, interruptions in supplies, changes in product specifications, defects in component parts, and the like. These uncertainties foreclose complete certainty in cost estimates.

Common Costs

Accountants have great difficulty estimating costs when they involve expenditures which are to help the production/distribution of many products rather than only one. Individual decisions by executives of multiproduct firms usually pertain to a single item but estimates of their costs involve a disentangling of the costs for many items.

Virtually no business decisions require an accurate allocation of common costs. Most allocations of common costs are not required for purposes of business decision, though many businessmen apparently do not recognize this fact. Accordingly, the decision maker should keep clearly in mind the specific decision for which the cost computation is intended.

Several quite different classes of common cost situations should be distinguished: Production or distribution requires overhead costs that are common to many items; raw materials and processing costs are common to several items (usually called "joint costs"); and alternative products may be produced with the same facilities. The lines separating these three are not always clear-cut.

Some business activities are really costs of conducting a business rather than costs directly related to the specific products offered by that business.* General and administrative expenses and real estate and many other taxes would seem to be unrelated to individual products—but nevertheless are necessary or unavoidable—for the production and offering of all of them. Similarly, some of the overhead costs of a factory or warehouse, for example, the factory manager's salary, may be incurred on behalf of *all* items made or stored therein. How, if at all, are we to take account of these types of costs in decision making? What kinds of business decisions require or appear to require an allocation of overhead costs to individual items? Following are sample decision situations in which some executives require a consideration of overheads in computing decision costs.

Should we make or buy? A firm is offered a chance to buy a component that it now makes for itself at a price below its computed cost to provide it. Included in its computed costs are factory overhead and general and administrative costs. If these were excluded from its costs, the firm would continue to produce the item for itself. What should it do? Is the answer the same in the short run as it would be for the long run?

Should we add a particular new item to our line? Decisions of this type arise quite frequently in firms when the price that is obtainable for the new item, based on prices currently prevailing, is moderately below the firm's full costs plus its ordinary profit margin. Again, the costs include factory overhead and general and administrative costs. How should the decision maker compute costs for this decision?

Should we drop a particular item from our line? Here we face a reverse situation. The product does not yield sufficient revenue to cover factory and general overhead along with its direct costs. It does produce revenue beyond its direct costs, however. Should it be continued in the line because the costs of the decision are smaller than the revenue loss that would be occasioned by a decision to drop the item?

Should we add a particular feature to our product? A proposal might be put forward to add a feature whose incremental costs would be quite low. However, with the usual overheads included, the price of the item could not be increased enough to cover those costs.

Will we accept a particular price for a special order? Some large orders ₴re received contingent upon a very substantial reduction in price. The price would be attractive if only incremental costs were considered, but the addition of all overheads would suggest that the order could only be filled at a loss. What should the executive decide?

Let us be clear about what is involved in seeking an answer to these

---

* Thus, if they relate to any business decision, it is whether to remain in business; they were earlier described as costs incurred to be in a state of readiness to produce.

questions. *Accountants in the process of income measurement* for a particular period usually find it necessary to make somewhat arbitrary allocations of factory overhead costs to individual products. This allocation enables them to estimate the "full cost" of each product which is then used for purposes of inventory measurement. (This full cost does not include elements of general and administrative expenses.)

An example may clarify the process. Suppose a firm which is involved in producing two products incurs a cost of $1,000 for electricity consumed for lighting its factory for a month. At the end of the month the cost accountant wants to determine the cost of the various goods produced by the firm. To do so he usually must include the cost of the electricity consumed as part of the unit cost of each product produced. How can he do this? Any method used will be somewhat arbitrary. One approach would be first to allocate the electricity costs to the different departments in the factory on, say, the basis of the proportion of floor space occupied by each department or the number of lighting fixtures in the department. Having ascertained the departmental cost, this sum must then be charged to the individual items produced by the department in this month. Again, the basis for doing this will be somewhat arbitrary; for instance, the charge might be split between the various products on the basis of the proportion of total labor hours consumed in producing each product. Thus, if the cost of electricity for a department making two items is $100, and the number of labor hours on product A is 1,000 and product B 3,000, then the charge to products A and B for electricity would be $25 and $75, respectively. The foregoing is a highly simplified illustration which indicates the arbitrary nature of the underlying process.*

Let us now return to the key question, namely, is it necessary to use any such allocations when estimating costs for decision purposes? It is extremely unlikely that business decisions will require such cost allocations. Overhead costs usually continue unaffected by the decision. Conceptually, the process involved in estimating the costs (including overhead costs) of a decision is very simple and might be represented as shown in Table 9-3.† This approach calls for an itemized list of all the items of expenditure which might be affected by the decision (column 1); a statement of what these would be if the action contemplated in the decision was not taken

---

* In real-life situations, computations such as this will not occur each month, since standard percentages will be used, but the basic process is the same.

† The type of approach suggested here has been discussed at length in the accounting literature under the heading of *relevant costing*. See, for instance, Charles T. Horngren, "Choosing Accounting Practices for Reporting to Management," *NAA Bulletin*, September 1962, pp. 10–12.

Table 9-3

Estimating Decision Costs

Cost item (1)	Total costs if decision is not implemented (2)	Total costs if decision is implemented (3)	Cost of decision (3) − (2) (4)	Decision costs with full costing (5)
Raw materials	$10,000	$11,000	$1,000	$1,000
Direct labor	4,000	4,400	400	400
Factory salaries	3,000	3,000	—	100
Indirect labor	2,100	2,400	300	350
Maintenance expenses	1,500	1,550	50	80
Administrative expenses	10,000	10,000	—	—

(column 2); and an estimate of what these would be if the action was taken (column 3). The cost of the decision (column 4) is the difference between column 3 and column 2. This procedure can be elaborated somewhat to take account of opportunity costs, but the basic procedure is conceptually very simple and seems logically unassailable. However, the key problem, namely, identifying and estimating the entries to be made in column 3, still remains in any particular situation.

These estimation problems suggest many of the arguments that have been advanced in favor of using a full cost (including allocations, such as those shown in Table 9-3, column 5) approach to estimate costs for decision purposes rather than the incremental approach. Let us examine these arguments closely, for they highlight some of the dangers in an unsophisticated application of incrementalism. A key argument revolves around the problem of estimating the long-run cost impact of a decision versus its short-run impact. In the short run, the costs affected by the decision may be few and their magnitude small because of temporary spare capacity, a particularly favorable market situation, or the like. However, over the long term, the spare capacity may disappear and many of the fixed costs may change, as for instance when it becomes necessary to build new facilities.* The concept of "creeping overheads"† captures this phenomenon of over-

---

* Joel Dean, *Managerial Economics* (Englewood Cliffs, N.J.: Prentice-Hall, 1951), pp. 122–123, refers to this problem as follows: "Additions to existing costs that are often unforeseen at the time of the introduction of the new products are likely to occur, so that the businessmen's rule-of-thumb of loading on the new products [their] full share of common overhead cost is often the most appropriate method after all."

† See Alfred Oxenfeldt and Myron Watkins, *Make or Buy: Factors in Executive Decision* (Consultant Report to Industry, published by McGraw-Hill, New York, 1956), pp. 44–50.

head costs which increase, almost imperceptibly at first but significantly over time, as a result of the decision.

The estimation of the long-run opportunity costs of a decision may be difficult. For instance, acceptance of an order by a construction firm with spare capacity may use up the firm's spare capacity and push forward, possibly by years, the time when it must acquire added facilities. It could be advantageous or the opposite to expand capacity earlier rather than later. Rarely is it a matter of indifference. Accordingly, this eventuality should influence the decision.

Proponents of full costing argue that since mistaken estimates of incremental costs are inevitable because we do not know enough to take all contingencies into account, the safest thing to do is to use a simple rule of thumb. They would allocate a proportion of common overheads to the decision, even when these overheads apparently would be unaffected by the decision. More explicitly, the usual overhead items in column 3 in Table 9-3 would be assigned by full-costers to each of the products before arriving at the cost of a product for such decisions as whether to add or drop an item from the line (see column 5). Thus, some authorities maintain that allocation is desirable even for decision making. John A. Becket, in discussing the problem of determining whether to continue offering an item, puts it in these words:

> In the area of pricing, allocation and proration have a definite and valuable use—that of making products bear the amount of indirect cost which management feels is necessary to warrant continuation of the product in the *long run*. There are better ways of measuring short-run relative importance of products, but for the long pull, allocation and proration are valuable tools of appraisal.*

The arguments that one must estimate common overheads for purposes of making a decision thus revolve around the notion that full costs reasonably approximate the long-run cost of the decision.

To summarize: First, the allocations involved in full costing are rarely relevant for decision making since common overhead costs do not usually change as a result of a decision. Second, a decision maker must concentrate on the *changes*, if any, in the common overheads that result from the decision; he should be suspicious of any formula for allocating overheads. Third, a decision maker must take account of the long-run effects of his decision; creeping overheads should be considered as well as long-run opportunity costs in estimating decisions costs.

*"A Study of the Principles of Allocating Costs," *The Accounting Review*, July 1951, p. 333.

How Firms Compute Costs: A Dialog

Bill Warner is a young assistant to the vice president of marketing, John Cichner. Warner has been given a special assignment, which calls for him to reappraise their firm's pricing policies. The following conversation takes place two weeks after Bill undertook the assignment.

BILL: John, I'm having a lot more trouble than I expected with the assignment you gave me to reappraise our pricing policy.

JOHN: I guess I'm not surprised. Pricing is really a tough problem, because it's necessary to weigh so many factors—how customers will react to each feasible price, how your competitors, distributors, suppliers, and even your own colleagues will react to them, to mention only a few.

BILL: I haven't even gotten around to any of those problems yet; I'm having great trouble in getting bread-and-butter information about our costs.

JOHN: That's surprising. I thought we had a good cost system in each of our seven plants. What kinds of facts do you want about costs anyway?

BILL: Mainly, I want to know how our production costs are affected by changes in output. You see, I'm exploring the hypothesis that at lower prices, we'd generate enough extra volume to achieve substantial production economies and would end up in a more profitable position.

JOHN: I would question that hypothesis inasmuch as we don't have really heavy fixed costs; consequently, I wouldn't expect increased output to affect unit costs very much.

BILL: You may well be right, but we might alter our whole method of manufacture—in the direction of greater mechanization, for example, if sales increased substantially.

JOHN: True, but you'd have to go to the engineers to find out whether production methods would change if output increased substantially and to get an estimate of the effect of the change on unit costs; you couldn't find that out by examining our present costs.

BILL: Right. Actually, I want to know how changes in production volume affect costs in our existing plants using our prevailing methods; I'm trying to construct what an economist would call a short-run cost curve for each plant. They gave me their standard production cost figures for each of our departments and their monthly variances for the last year.

JOHN: Even though I don't know exactly how those figures are put together these days, I'm sure they don't give you the information that you need. When I was well informed about such matters, our costs were estimated periodically for a standard level of output—it was 75 percent of capacity, as I recall. Those figures don't indicate the effect of changes in output.

BILL: That's right. When I discussed the subject with our accountants, they admitted that they don't know precisely what happens to unit costs as output gets closer to or exceeds production capacity. What's more, they have an unclear definition of capacity, though they know what they mean in units, all right. Apparently, someone has set an output figure for each plant which they describe as the rated capacity.

JOHN: Do you think that our cost information is not what it should be?

BILL: I doubt that it is worse than in most other corporations. But, it certainly doesn't indicate the effect of changes in volume on unit cost with any precision.

JOHN: Well, that's not a simple matter. In the first place, I doubt that the effect of changes in output is the same in each of our seven plants. After all, our two new plants don't even use the same technology as the old five. Those are pretty much the same, I'd guess. Also, what is the most efficient level of operation almost certainly varies from department to department—so the best level for the plant is some kind of average for the various departments.

BILL: Those are only part of the problem. Even in our five old plants, each pays substantially different wage scales; productivity levels also differ from place to place, according to some people I talked to.

JOHN: By the way, didn't anyone refer to flexible budgets, which contain estimates of how each department's costs would be affected by variations in output?

BILL: Yes, they did, and I looked them up and learned that they are very rough estimates that no one seems to take seriously because of the casual way they're made.

JOHN: So you're implying that we need a separate cost curve for each of our seven plants. But even if you had that, you'd face some knotty problems in constructing a cost curve for the corporation as a whole.

BILL: Sure I would. Still, many corporations face exactly the same kind of problem: they operate many plants, these plants have different wage rates, levels of productivity, transportation costs, and the like. And, presumably, their managements want to know how changes in volume affect costs.

JOHN: Our problem clearly is very general, but I wonder whether it is ever solved. I doubt that any large corporation has a cost curve for all its plants combined. Such a curve wouldn't help with any operating decisions that I can think of. Besides, I expect that most have only very limited knowledge about the effects of volume changes on costs in any single plant and for each of the products they make.

BILL: You'd know much more about that than I do. Your opinion sure is surprising in view of all the attention that economists attach to this issue. It's difficult for me to believe that most manufacturing companies do not have an accurate measure of their unit costs at different levels of output.

JOHN: I'm sure that if you asked your friends in other corporations, they'd say that they did have such information—even as we'd say the same if we were asked. But I doubt that many have accurate cost information of that type, given the great difficulty of getting it. And, I might mention, we seem to get along pretty well without it.

BILL: The more important question is how much better we might do with it.

JOHN: Touché. In any event, I suggest that you push along and see whether you can construct a cost curve for each plant—or for all plants combined—without enormous cost and difficulty. That information should at least help us to decide which plants to utilize most fully.

BILL: I agree that we could use that information for more than setting price. That brings me back to the reason I'm here. I'd like your views on how such a cost analysis might best be made. I don't want to go to the accountants until I'm sure about what I want. At one time you were fairly close to the accounting department, weren't you?

JOHN: Sort of, but that was a long time back. I can't give you a quick answer, but maybe we can work one out together. Let's get our goal clear straightaway. As I understand it, you want to know how unit costs of production would be affected by variations in output in each of our seven plants. At this point, you are interested only in production costs, is that right?

BILL: Yes, that's right. But I had assumed that I wanted to construct a production cost curve for the entire corporation, rather than one for each plant.

JOHN: Let's concentrate on cost curves for each individual plant, and then see whether we need to combine them. Why couldn't you do the job by simple correlation?

BILL: I take it you mean that we should plot unit costs and volume for, say, each year and see how they correlate—maybe even compute regression equations.

JOHN: Yes, except that you might use data for each month, or quarter year—or maybe even for individual weeks or days.

BILL: The shorter the time period, the more observations we'd have and the better our basis for reaching a conclusion. But I thought the accounting department only has standard costs based on a detailed analysis dating back several years.

JOHN: If we're limited to annual data, we'll have few observations for any plant and really couldn't hope to construct an average cost curve.

BILL: You said it. And if you knock out those years when we had such extraordinary events as strikes, fires, or production difficulties, we have information for very few years that we could use.

JOHN: More than that, you find that for each plant, annual output has not varied much over the last 10 or 15 years. Consequently, by this method we could only get a small section of a full cost curve.

BILL: While you are adding difficulties, note that the data would be distorted by changes in wage rates and in technology—because over the last 10 to 15 years we have been introducing some new machines and have learned some new production tricks that have raised output. That really means that we'd be using data from different universes, in a strict analytical sense.

JOHN: When you put all of those difficulties together you can understand why I doubt that any company has an accurate picture of its cost at different levels of output.

BILL: My guess is that, if it is done at all, it is done by an accountant or production engineer, sitting in an armchair, estimating the effects of changes in volume on the utilization of labor, power, raw materials, and the like. I very much doubt that it is done by statistical means. And, I wonder whether they check out the validity of their estimated cost curves.

JOHN: That is all very well for them, I suppose. But, now that you have brought the matter up, I want to try to construct a cost curve for our plants by statistical means. How might we go about it?

BILL: Before I try to answer that question, I want to know what cost data we should get for a short time period like a week or month, so that we might be able to measure the effects of substantial variations in output.

JOHN: Good point. Even though output may not have varied much from year to year, I'll bet that there have been major output variations from month to month—especially on the high side. We both know that output has exceeded capacity from time to time. Why not see what data we have?

BILL: Good idea. Let's make a date for Thursday lunch and continue our chat after lunch. That should give me a chance to inform myself on what cost data we have—and what we might get collected especially for us—as well as do some more thinking.

JOHN: Fine, that's a date.

* * *

BILL: As I was saying at lunch, this problem gets more and more complicated the closer you get to the nuts and bolts.

JOHN: That's always the case when you try to measure something precisely. I hope that you're not aiming for greater accuracy than you need for your purposes.

BILL: That's a possibility. Still, we certainly don't have the data we need to understand how costs are affected by changes in volume.

JOHN: When you need data for a specific purpose, you must put it together for yourself. It's rare that you can get what you need by simply asking. But since we don't have to construct cost curves frequently, I'm not worried about spending a little money to get what we need. In the course of exploring costs along the line we have been discussing, we'll undoubtedly learn a great deal of value—even though we may not end up with reliable cost curves.

BILL: That's true. Perhaps I've been a penny-pincher. If we're prepared to adjust the data and have some special tabulations made expressly for this purpose, I'm certain that we can put together some useful data. However, we may find that output will not vary much from week to week, so that we may be forced to wait a considerable period to obtain cost data describing widely different levels of output in all seven plants.

JOHN: That's true, but if, as you said, we have no useful cost records for periods shorter than a year, we have no choice but to make special cost tabulations. To avoid unnecessary expenses, I suggest that we make our mistakes on just one plant before we start collecting cost data on all seven.

BILL: I agree. I'll start with our local plant so that I can be on hand and see what kinds of difficulties arise and maybe help to overcome them; in that way, I'll be able to tell the other six plants how to make their cost studies.

JOHN: That makes good sense. You surely recognize how lucky we are because we produce essentially a single product; or, you might say that we can easily translate our output into standard units of output. Let's see, what are you going to ask the accounting department to do for you?

BILL: That raises a question right there; should we try to get the information we want from the accounting department or from the production control department? Or, perhaps, there is some better place to go for cost information?

JOHN: I should think the answer would depend on the kind of information we want and the degree of cooperation we can get from each. I'm sure that either could do the job, once we told them what we wanted. Have the people you've approached so far been helpful? Do they know their stuff?

BILL: I may not be a good judge, but I must say that I haven't been impressed with most of the people I've talked to.

JOHN: What's the problem? Possibly you need more rank to get the attention you need from the people who have our cost data?

BILL: I'm not sure. Most of the people I've talked to about costs seem to be high-grade clerks, even though they're called accountants. They apparently are responsible for a few accounting items and don't seem to know anything about other items. I've met several people who understand what I'm after and who recognize the relevance of that information for business decisions. But these people don't know the specific details of our cost situation. They clearly know the proper procedures, the tax regulations and some general theory, but they don't seem to know the specific problems we must overcome to get an accurate measure of costs at different levels of output. When I get specific, they always send me to one of these clerk-types I've been talking to you about.

JOHN: I guess I should have warned you about that; we're like most other large firms in that respect. We're so big that our accounting function has been subdivided into small pieces. The most useful people are the factory accountants—they really know what things cost. They are in personal contact with what is going on in the factory; they can see when the accounting costs do and don't realistically reflect what is actually occurring on the factory floor. You might say that these men know and manage information about physical quantities and processes as well as about money. By that I mean they know about man hours worked, quantities of goods moving into and out of inventory, physical output, hours devoted to repair and goods in process. They are able to relate physical activities to their financial counterparts; and that is really what costs are. A cost doesn't have much meaning unless it is attached to some physical product or process.

BILL: They sound like the people I should turn to.

JOHN: Possibly so. Maybe you have learned a valuable lesson that we should teach more of our executives. Many decisions have an important cost side so that an executive must be able to estimate the costs of his decisions. However, he usually depends upon others for cost information. Unfortunately, most executives seem to believe that the information they need is readily available in some document in the accounting department and that it is very accurate.

BILL: I will admit that I had that impression. Certainly, I thought that some one individual was very well informed about our costs and could tell me what effect a change in output would have on unit costs. Now I know that it isn't so, but I'm still surprised. It seems that you have to find the right person to ask for the cost information you want. Even then you may not get what you want and you have to tell them how to put it together to meet your needs.

JOHN: That's quite right. But those clerical types you referred to before have an enormous amount of cost information; and, given time and direction, they can put together accurate cost estimates on almost anything you might choose to know. But it's not available in a fully processed state just for the asking. I think of our cost information as a collection of semi-processed goods in inventory. These can be pulled out of inventory, combined with other items, and processed into almost anything you might need. And most of our factory accountants can make highly informed cost forecasts based on their extensive knowledge of the past. In other words, if you tell a good accountant that you want him to depart from his usual accounting procedures and make an estimate of future costs, he can often be extremely helpful.

BILL: It seems very clear now that we'll have to tell the accounting people what we want to know and may even have to tell them how to get it from their own data.

JOHN: Remember, you may want to ask that some data be collected especially for this project. We may want some production engineers to do some time and motion studies. It may even be necessary to get back to some original invoices on goods purchased, figures on scrappage, and all kinds of things that influence costs.

BILL: I certainly hope not, because I'm a babe in the woods with regard to such things.

JOHN: I'm sure you can do it with the help of the many people we have around here working on costs. It won't be easy for you, but I doubt that anyone in the company could do it better. Let's be specific about what we want to ask for.

BILL: Good idea. First, I want historical cost information for short periods of time. In particular, I want data for many periods, each so short that no wage-rate or productivity changes would be likely to occur during the entire time span covered by the individual periods. In other words,

I'd like to have cost records for enough periods of time so that I might employ statistical procedures and still be confident that those data describe situations in which wage-rates and productivity levels were stable. The only thing I want to vary during the period I study is the level of output.

JOHN: I can see that this requirement is very important. What would worry me a little is that any short period—one in which wage rates and productivity were constant—might also be one in which the level of output was fairly constant. I just don't know what we'll find on that score.

BILL: I'd expect that we'd find substantial variations in output from week to week if we covered a period like four to five months. Wage rates and productivity would probably be stable for periods of that duration.

JOHN: We'll only know after we look into the matter. We can certainly hope so. What else would you want to ask the accountants?

BILL: I'd certainly concentrate on the measurement of variable costs. I would be especially careful to take account of any allocated costs; they are usually the ones that cause the errors.

JOHN: What's the reasoning behind that statement? Would you elaborate on that point a little?

BILL: Sure. I'm suggesting that we're most interested in, and can measure most accurately, the costs incurred for direct labor, materials, power, supplies, and even factory supervision on a weekly basis—and maybe even day by day. But, when we deal with R & D, general and administrative costs, insurance, taxes, warehousing, the operation of the purchasing department and the like, we get into fairly deep water when we try to assign them to particular weeks and to particular activities. It doesn't seem to make much sense to think in terms of a week's operations for certain activities.

JOHN: That explanation helps, but it doesn't really seem to go far enough. I'm not sure that we have the same idea of what we want to measure. Are you trying to measure fully allocated costs or incremental costs?

BILL: You are opening Pandora's box when you raise that question. I mainly want to measure the cost of a decision to expand output from, say, X to Y, but I also want to know what our costs are at any particular level of output.

JOHN: That means that you're interested in incremental costs, as I use the term. You seem to be calling it the "cost of a decision to expand output." If that is the case, I'm not sure that we need to be much concerned with allocations of cost for R & D, G & A, insurance, taxes, and the rest. Those do not seem to vary with changes in output; or at least, they are not affected by small changes in output.

BILL: Yes, I am aware of that; however, you realize that supervisory labor does vary with output changes over fairly small ranges—or so I've been told. And I wouldn't assume away possible changes in storage, wastage, and insurance costs without studying the matter directly. Let's not make more assumptions in our study than are absolutely necessary. We should let the facts inform us rather than assume the facts.

JOHN: Right again. Why don't you proceed along the lines you outlined? Talk to the accountants and to the production control people; maybe talk to them together after you have seen them individually. Then decide which of them you will rely on to gather the data for you. You may want to ask me to put together a special task force. In that way, we might raise the level of thinking in both groups. At some point, set down on paper the procedure you plan to use to gather the data and indicate how you would interpret it once it has been collected. Then let's discuss the matter before we actually start the process.

BILL: Great. I'll get back to you on paper next with a description of the proposed plan for gathering the data. When you have reacted to it, please call me.

*   *   *

To: John
From: Bill
Subject: Proposed procedure for the collection of cost data for the
           construction of cost curves

After holding informative discussions with the Accounting and Control Departments, I propose that we use the following method for developing production cost curves:

1. Costs are to be gathered for each one of the different departments of the production process of the plant.
2. Specific weeks are going to be designated for the collection of cost data, based on the production schedules. The director of production planning is to make the choice of weeks to insure that they are representative.
3. Select two weeks with fairly similar output schedules; otherwise collect data only if output is going to be substantially different from other levels for which costs were studied.
4. Take representative samples of data on the different weekly levels of output for which data costs are desired.
5. Special forms are to be prepared in order to facilitate the collection of data.

6. According to 3 and 4, arrange for MTM studies with our industrial engineers, to update our estimates of costs for different levels of output if that is considered necessary.

*   *   *

BILL: Did you get a chance to review the proposal I submitted to you?

JOHN: Yes, I did. In fact, I've been brooding about it a great deal and may have come to an unexpected conclusion.

BILL: Oh, what's that?

JOHN: Well, I'm beginning to doubt the value of this enterprise. I just wonder whether it's worth all the effort.

BILL: Actually, I'm delighted to hear you say that because this phase of my pricing assignment is taking much more time than I think it's worth. After all, I'm pretty sure that a low price strategy, based on the expectation of a sharp drop in costs, probably is not in the cards. And even if it yielded substantial cost savings, I'm afraid that at least Lyons, among our competitors, would follow us down and we would not gain much.

JOHN: I agree, but the problem is even bigger than that. If you're really thinking about a sharp decline in costs, then that will come about as a result of a change in the production method, rather than a change in volume. I think the economists speak of that as a change in production function rather than simply a change in scale or level of output.

BILL: That's right, my projected study wouldn't get at that at all.

JOHN: That's why I've been moving toward the conclusion that we'd be undertaking sizable burdens with this study and would still have little hope of getting commensurate benefit. This problem is interesting and challenging in itself, but it isn't likely to help much with our pricing problems.

BILL: I agree. Still, do you think we should drop our effort to determine our average cost curve altogether? Shouldn't we have such information around here for a variety of purposes, quite apart from pricing applications?

JOHN: I'm not suggesting that we give up that objective; I'm only suggesting that we go about it in a very different way. I'm somewhat surprised at where I come out in this. To put it very simply, I don't think that the data that you'd collect would be even as reliable as the estimates that an intelligent and well-informed person could make just sitting in his armchair.

BILL: That's a strange conclusion from such a confirmed empiricist. How do you figure you can estimate costs perched in an armchair? How much confidence would you place in numbers arrived at in that way?

JOHN: That's what is so interesting. I thought long and hard about the value of what we'd get if we went down the route sketched in your proposal. Frankly, I could think of several things that would make me hesitate to accept the results of a study made that way.

BILL: Oh? I'd be interested in what they are.

JOHN: I probably wouldn't accept the representativeness of any data that you collected. There are so many things that can happen to production in any week that you would be attributing changes in costs to the effects of volume that really come from breakdowns in machines, some slow-down due to worker dissatisfaction, unexpected resignations of workers and the like. I don't know all things that make every day and week seem exceptional to a factory manager, but I know there are many such.

BILL: When you get down to the specific details, lots of things can keep your results from being just what you wanted. Are there other things, more important than the risk of getting unrepresentative data, that persuade you to give up the information gathering that I proposed?

JOHN: I don't know. I just think that any production run or runs will be exceptional in some respect. If we want to get fairly reliable data, we'd be forced to conduct the study in many, many weeks in the hopes of getting such factors to cancel out. I'd have more confidence in the reasoned judgment of someone who was very familiar with the production processes—like the factory accountants—as to what kinds of costs would be increased and which would not rise as you expand output.

BILL: I can see the merit in that, if you have high confidence in your accountants. They should have a lot of experience and data on which to draw, as well as a basic understanding of what's involved in a change in output.

JOHN: Exactly. You see, when it comes to estimating costs with a very big increase in output—on the assumption that by feasible price reductions we could really spur a big increase in sales—we'd be forced to depend on the estimates of engineers, who will not even have had any direct experience with the new production arrangements. So why should we be so finicky and empirical when it comes to the effect on costs of modest changes in volume—something with which we've had lots of experience.

BILL: The more you think about it, the clearer it becomes that we have no thoroughly reliable cost information for decision-making purposes. Any cost computation involves some assumptions and guesswork, whether we collect data evolving from actual production or estimates from knowledgeable people. It is not as if by gathering facts we can avoid questionable assumptions—like the representativeness of the information, the kinds of conditions that will exist when the decision is carried out, and the like.

JOHN: You just summed up my thoughts exactly. I doubt that the method that you outlined in your memo would be more accurate than the opinions we could collect from our most informed people about what happens to costs when we expand output.

BILL: I really can't disagree with you; and what's more, I'm relieved to drop that project. But where do we go from here? How are we going to collect these informed opinions you've talked about? And aren't you going to want to get at least one really solid benchmark—some solid data for a level of output near average for the last year or so?

JOHN: I guess it would be a good idea to get a solid figure to start with—from which to estimate the effect of changes in volume. I had thought that our standard costs studies would serve our needs very well. Aren't they reliable enough for that purpose?

BILL: I really can't say for all our plants and each individual department. And I get the distinct impression that they haven't been kept very current. I'd want to check their accuracy, if I were building estimates on to them. So I guess that I would opt for making a re-estimate of our standard costs at one plant at least. And on the basis of those estimates I suppose we should poll the factory accountants in each of our plants on how they'd expect costs to vary with specific changes in volume.

JOHN: That sounds reasonable. The results we get in this way should be quite adequate for our purposes, even though they will not be exact. But as we seem to have established, we really don't know how to get exact data.

BILL: There was a time when I would have been positively shocked by that conclusion. I used to think of large firms as the height of precision—solid facts, everything computerized, cutting costs by pennies and mills, great attention to detail, and all of that sort of thing.

JOHN: We'd be foolish to spend our resources to learn things precisely for their own sake. We want information about the effect of volume on costs for a specific purpose. Great precision would serve no important purpose—certainly it would not justify great expenditure.

BILL: How can we know how precise we should be in any specific case? I might agree that we rely on the factory accountants' estimates, but how will we know how accurate those estimates are, unless we do make a really definitive study?

JOHN: You are asking some tough, but fair, questions that I should think about. Still, for now, I'd want to get the estimates of our factory accountants. I'm sure that we'll learn a good bit by comparing their answers. If we find differences of opinion, we might learn something really interesting—something that would never turn up by collecting lots of numbers.

BILL: That's right. Well, I'll try to draft a statement that will get us the information we want. I'll try to get it to you by tomorrow afternoon.

JOHN: Swell, I'll call you after I've had a chance to read it. Let me make two points before you leave. Just imagine what troubles you would have had if we, like most firms, produced many—instead of one—product. And, recognize that executives are rarely in the position of solving a math problem, where you have all the facts you need to arrive at a solution. Business is much more like a guessing game.

APPENDIX

The Valuation of Opportunity Costs

Opportunity costs must be quantified if they are to influence concrete decisions; but sometimes it is very difficult to place values on forgone opportunities. To make clear what difficulties must be faced and how they might sometimes be overcome, hypothetical examples will be discussed.

Consider a consulting firm that is built around a core of professional persons. The first decision problem we will consider arises at a time when the firm has just completed a major assignment and must now choose between the only two alternative new assignments open to it. The revenues and costs from the assignments are shown in Figure 9-6 (for simplicity, we will assume that all costs involve current cash expenditures).

What are the relevant opportunity costs in this case? Clearly, the opportunity cost of assignment R must include the $4,300 of profit forgone on assignment S; subtracting this from the net profit obtainable on assignment R leaves a "decision loss" of $400. By the same reasoning, one might conclude that the opportunity cost of assignment S is $3,900 (the profit obtainable on assignment R). If this were subtracted from the net profit of $4,300 on assignment S, it would leave a "decision profit" of $400. That is, one might complete the profit calculations in Figure 9-6 as follows:

	Assignment R	Assignment S
Net profit (excluding opportunity costs and fixed costs)	$3,900	$4,300
Opportunity cost	4,300	3,900
Decision profit (loss)	$ 400	($ 400)

Figure 9-6. Revenues and costs for two alternative assignments.

	Assignment R	Assignment S
1. Revenues: Consulting fees	$20,000	$25,000
2. Salaries of consultants	10,000	12,500
3. Secretarial salaries	3,000	3,500
4. Supplies	2,000	4,000
5. Traveling and entertainment	1,000	500
6. Miscellaneous	100	200
7. Total costs	$16,100	$20,700
8. Net profit (excluding opportunity costs and fixed costs)	3,900	4,300

Looking carefully at these new figures, however, we find that something strange has happened. Instead of the original difference between the two alternatives of $400 profit (line 8 in Figure 9-6) there now seems to be a difference of $800, namely, the difference between $400 loss on assignment R and $400 profit on assignment S. This confusion arises from the incorrect use of opportunity cost figures. Once we include oppportunity costs (as we used them in this illustration) in the evaluation of a particular alternative, it is no longer legitimate to make the usual types of cost comparisons, because we have in fact already incorporated one of these cost comparisons into the evaluation of each alternative. What the inclusion of opportunity costs does enable us to do, however, is to reject any alternative that shows a loss compared with other opportunities.

The difficulty of taking account of the cost of forgone alternatives is multiplied when more than two alternatives arise. It is therefore helpful to have a standard procedure that will simplify comparisons of alternatives while taking opportunity costs into account. Such a procedure is used by operations researchers in their derivation of opportunity costs. This procedure requires us to compute an opportunity cost by taking the *alternative with the highest profit* and subtracting that profit from *all* the alternatives; when we do this, each of the other alternatives results in a loss and the best alternative breaks even (zero profit or loss). If this procedure were applied to our example, alternative A would show a $400 loss and alternative B a zero profit:

	Assignment R	*Assignment S*
Net profit (excluding opportunity costs and fixed costs)	$3,900	$4,300
Maximum profit	4,300	4,300
Loss	$ 400	$ 0

As outlined here, the computation of opportunity costs may seem trivial, and the question may be raised, "Why bother with opportunity costs at all? Couldn't we just compare alternatives and choose the one offering the highest profit?" The answer is no, for many applications of the opportunity-cost concept are anything but trivial.

Let us examine a decision for which the computation of opportunity costs is far more difficult. Our consulting firm now has one assignment that it can accept or reject as it sees fit. It will yield a contribution of profit of $15,000. The firm also has several *potential* assignments in prospect. We assume that it could accept only one project—either the one it has been offered or one of the four in prospect. Several jobs have been "hanging fire" for some time. One in particular (A) had been virtually promised six weeks before, but the go-ahead has not yet come. Although the job was not canceled, its status is most uncertain (the president feels there is one chance in ten that it will materialize.) The job would mean a substantial amount of work and a large contribution to the company's profits ($40,000). It would also require the services of the most able person in the consulting group. Three other projects vary from being good to reasonable prospects; they are shown below with their respective probabilities.

Assignment	*Contribution to profits*	*Probability of event**
A	$40,000	.10
B	20,000	.40
C	15,000	.60
D	10,000	.70

The problem that the firm faces, then, is: should it accept the assignment that is already in hand or reject it in the hope of securing one of the other projects?

* These probabilities do not add to 1 because the assignments are independent events. Also, the fact that the probabilities in this case total far more than 1 does *not* mean that the firm will certainly have at least one of these assignments offered to it.

Table 9-4

CALCULATION OF EXPECTED PROFITS FROM FOUR INDEPENDENT EVENTS

Event (1)	Probability of event (2)	Subtotals (3)	Profit if event occurs (4)	Expected profit (2) × (3) (5)
1 ABCD	(.1)(.4)(.6)(.7) = .0168		$40,000	
2 ABC$\overline{D}$	(.1)(.4)(.6)(.3) = .0072		40,000	
3 AB$\overline{C}$D	(.1)(.4)(.4)(.7) = .0112		40,000	
4 AB$\overline{CD}$	(.1)(.4)(.4)(.3) = .0048		40,000	
5 A$\overline{B}$CD	(.1)(.6)(.6)(.7) = .0252		40,000	
6 A$\overline{B}$C$\overline{D}$	(.1)(.6)(.6)(.3) = .0108		40,000	
7 A$\overline{B}\overline{C}$D	(.1)(.6)(.4)(.7) = .0168		40,000	
8 A$\overline{B}\overline{C}\overline{D}$	(.1)(.6)(.4)(.3) = .0072	.10	40,000	$ 4,000
9 $\overline{A}$BCD	(.9)(.4)(.6)(.7) = .1512		20,000	
10 $\overline{A}$BC$\overline{D}$	(.9)(.4)(.6)(.3) = .0648		20,000	
11 $\overline{A}$B$\overline{C}$D	(.9)(.4)(.4)(.7) = .1008		20,000	
12 $\overline{A}$B$\overline{CD}$	(.9)(.4)(.4)(.3) = .0432	.36	20,000	7,200
13 $\overline{AB}$CD	(.9)(.6)(.6)(.7) = .2268		15,000	
14 $\overline{AB}$C$\overline{D}$	(.9)(.6)(.6)(.3) = .0972	.324	15,000	4,860
15 $\overline{AB}\overline{C}$D	(.9)(.6)(.4)(.7) = .1512	.1512	10,000	1,512
16 $\overline{ABCD}$	(.9)(.6)(.4)(.3) = .0648	.0648	0	0
	1.0000	1.0000		$17,572

Observe that the profit to be obtained from alternatives A or B is higher. (The problem may seem strange for discussion under the heading of costs, since we have not shown any cost computations. However, cost calculations underlie the profit figures shown above, and our concern here is solely with opportunity costs.)

To solve this problem, we must identify all different possible configurations of outcomes. These are shown in Table 9-4, column 1. (The notation used is as follows: A means that assignment A materializes while $\overline{A}$ means it does not materialize; similarly, B means that assignment B materializes while $\overline{B}$ means it does not.)

There are 16 possible outcomes (configurations of opportunities) which the firm could experience. These are collectively exhaustive—that is, they include all the possible outcomes which the firm might experience—and mutually exclusive. Since the assignments are assumed to be independent, the joint probabilities of each event are obtained by multiplying the probabilities of the underlying assignments. For instance, the probability of event 4 is the product of the probability of getting assignments A and B (.1 × .4) and of the probability of *not* getting assignments C and D (.4 × .3), or .0048.

Column 4—the profit that would materialize if the event occurs—is obtained by following a simple rule: if we receive two or more assignments, then we will always pick the one offering the highest profit. Thus, for event 13, we have put in the profit obtainable from assignment C as the profit figure, although we would also have the option of accepting assignment D.

The last column (5) representing expected profits is obtained by multiplying each profit figure by its probability (that is, column 4 by column 3) and summing. We are now in a position to decide whether to accept or reject the assignment in hand, which is worth $15,000. The expected value of postponing the decision is shown to be $17,572. The opportunity loss resulting from the acceptance of the assignment would therefore be $2,572 ($15,000 less $17,572). Assuming, then, that the survival of the firm would not be endangered if none of the four prospective assignments materialized, the prudent decision would be to postpone acceptance of the assignment in hand. If the firm's survival did depend on immediate procurement of one of the five assignments, these figures would require adjustment by means of a utility analysis.

This illustration highlights some of the problems that arise in computing opportunity costs when all relevant alternatives, both present and future, are known. When the alternatives cannot be completely enumerated, the decision maker must guess their magnitude and likelihood before employing the procedure described here.

Chapter 10

THE LIFE CYCLE
OF A COST

I N EXPLAINING the determination of price, economists distinguish between
market price, short-run normal price, and long-run normal price. These
are differentiated by the extent to which sellers can adjust their production
arrangements to changes in demand; in turn, their ability to adjust depends upon the amount of time that has passed since the demand change.
In an analysis of market price, the economist is concerned with a period of
time so short that the quantity of goods offered for sale by the industry (or
firm) cannot be increased by additional production. Holders of the existing
stock of goods can make them available for sale or withhold them from the
market for possible future sale.

In the short run, additional quantities of goods can be produced but only
by using existing productive facilities. Certain factors of production are in
fixed supply and hence cannot be increased or decreased; ordinarily these
are thought to be a stock of plant and equipment, but it might be the
quantity of skilled labor or marketing facilities that are not subject to
increase or decrease in the short run. When additional time is available for
adjustment of the size of the firm, more and more changes can be made—
we have a series of short runs, in other words. Finally, there is a period of
time sufficient to adjust fully the quantity of all the factors of production;
this is the long run.

This chapter was written in collaboration with my colleague Professor Carl L. Nelson.

The individual firm is faced with a series of decisions over time that parallel the economist's analysis. To maximize his profit, a seller must compare his expected costs with his expected revenue and make decisions on the basis of this comparison. He needs to know his cost, therefore, but *the costs that are relevant to his decision depend on the stage in the history of his enterprise* at which the decision is made.

A man who is considering entering the men's clothing business would be vitally interested in knowing what his costs would be. The amount would differ markedly from the cost figure he would need when deciding how many suits to produce after he has started the business and has purchased plant and equipment. This cost, moreover, would be quite different from the cost he would consider in how to dispose of a stock of suits already manufactured. In other words, there is no such thing as "the" cost of a suit of clothes. One can only speak of the cost to a producer of suits of clothes when he is in a particular stage in the life of his business.

The importance of time as a determinant of cost can be conceptualized most clearly as the "life cycle of a cost." This notion suggests that the cost of any product—say a suit of clothes—undergoes substantial change from the time at which someone initially contemplates its production, during the time when some facilities have been acquired to produce it, when facilities are already in place for its production, when the product or brand is losing popular favor and is being superseded by another product, and when suits have already been produced and are ready for market. To illustrate, let us examine the cost estimates of Mr. Kelly from the time he contemplates entry into the men's suit industry until he leaves the business some 25 years later. This detailed illustration requires the application of key cost concepts to several related decision problems.

For the sake of simplicity and clarity, we will assume that the costs of inputs—labor, materials, equipment, space, power, and the like—remain constant throughout the entire period, that the suits manufactured are the same in quality and style, and that technology is not altered. These unrealistic simplifying assumptions permit us to isolate the effects of time upon costs without invalidating the conclusions that are drawn.

Estimated Cost Before the Business Is Established

If Mr. Kelly simply wanted to produce a single suit of clothes, he would surely not establish a factory and business organization; he presumably would hire a skilled tailor and would make the product essentially by hand, using crude tools such as scissors and needles. Mr. Kelly's interest in the cost of a suit of clothes relates to the question of establishing a business to produce men's suits over a substantial period of time. Consequently, he wants to know how much it will cost *per suit* if he were to establish a business that would make many suits. Moreover, he wants to know how much it would cost him, rather than how much it costs others who are making suits at present. Further, he is interested in the unit cost over the life of the business, rather than how much he will have to pay out during the first year of operation. His interest in these aspects of costs stems from his facing the decision of whether or not to enter the suit manufacturing business.

Mr. Kelly would be forced to acquire many "fixed" factors of production to enter the men's suit industry. Among the more important of these would be plant (space), and cutting, sewing, pressing, and other equipment. In addition, he would be forced to assemble a labor force and some executives. He probably would need to purchase the services of an advertising agency, a law firm, a public accounting firm, a marketing research firm, and so on. All these items involve costs.

If he could not recover all of these costs, plus an amount to compensate him for his own efforts and capital investment (that is, opportunity costs). Mr. Kelly would be unwise to enter the men's suit industry. In other words, the costs associated with the decision to enter upon the production of men's suits includes the payments to lawyers, accountants, market researchers, advertising agency executives, and so on, as well as to cutters, pressers, sewing machine operators, and for raw materials, power, salesmen's commissions, and the like. In addition, during the period when the plant is being built and people are being hired, it would be necessary for Mr. Kelly to devote considerable time to organize the business and supervise the acquisition of facilities and manpower, and thus he would forgo income he could earn from other endeavors. The prospective suit company should be able to compensate him for these opportunity costs as well as his cash payments to others, or Mr. Kelly should not enter the business.

In this early period in the history of the business, costs are particularly difficult to estimate. Mr. Kelly, despite his previous experience, will find it difficult to estimate costs before he has actually started the production of suits. In addition, he will make large payments for goods and services the benefit from which will be received over a time period uncertain in duration. Mistaken estimates of cost are more likely to occur at this stage than at any other of the business life cycle.

On the basis of his experience, Mr. Kelly has decided that he would like to operate a business which will sell approximately 40,000 suits per year. To operate a business of this size will require the purchase of land, a building, and of machinery and equipment. He has seen an eminently satisfactory plant that could be purchased for $75,000, of which $8,000 can be considered the value of land. The cost of the machinery and equipment that would be needed is estimated to be $125,000. Thus, $200,000 would have to be spent before a single suit could be produced.

Mr. Kelly estimates that it will take three months from the time he decides to enter the business until operations can be started. While he is ordering the equipment and having it installed he will be hiring people and putting the organization together. He will be devoting time that could be used to earning an income in some other activity. Mr. Kelly estimates that he could earn $2,000 per month if he were not involved in organizational activities. He has an opportunity cost of $6,000 for this period. (After the firm begins to operate, Mr. Kelly will pay himself a salary of $24,000 annually.)

Next, Mr. Kelly realizes that there will be certain special introductory costs. For instance, he must do introductory advertising in trade journals. He estimates that an adequate campaign will cost $5,000. The production, distribution, and general administration processes will need to be debugged; these costs are estimated at $15,000. This aggregate cost of $20,000 will not be repeated, although some advertising will be necessary in future years. Less than 100 percent efficiency in operations is to be expected during the entire life of the business. The amounts he is concerned with here are the introductory costs—amounts that will not have to be spent in subsequent years.

Mr. Kelly will thus have total costs of $226,000 at the inception of the enterprise which will not recur during its life. These are perhaps the most difficult of all costs to evaluate in making a decision to enter a business. Mr. Kelly might conceivably use any one of the following types of reasoning:

• If I produce only one suit of clothes and then decide to quit and walk away from the business, the suit cost me $226,000 (in addition to other types of costs to be considered later).

• If I operate for one year and am able to sell only 20,000 suits and as a result sell the land, building, and equipment for the best price that I can get for it and that turns out to be $150,000, my first year of operation will cost me $76,000 for plant, equipment, and other initial expenses. But there is another related cost that should be considered; I will have $226,000 invested for one year and I can get a 15 percent return if I invest that money in another business. That means an additional cost of $33,900. My total costs arising from these outlays is therefore $109,900, and that makes an average cost for indirect items of about $5.50 per suit on an output of 20,000 suits.

• I wouldn't go into business if I thought I would get out at the end of the year. The machinery and equipment ought to last for 20 years. The building, although it was built sometime ago, ought to last for another 20 years. I'm 40 years old and am probably good for another 20 years. If I plan on a 20-year life of the business, I'll have a worthless building and machinery, but I'll have a piece of land that I ought to be able to sell for at least its present value of $8,000. If I have costs of $226,000 today and will recover $8,000 in 20 years, somebody ought to be able to reduce it to an annual basis, but I can't. (Mr. Kelly's nephew, who is a recent Columbia Business School graduate, happened by at this moment and, after a few minutes of calculation, told his uncle that the annual cost related to these initial outlays, including a return of 15 percent on his investment, would be about $36,000. What Kelly's nephew did was to determine the annual payment one would receive for 20 years if he bought an annuity today for $226,000 and received an interest income of 15 percent on his money.* He ignored the $8,000 resale value of the land on the grounds that it was too small to have any significant effect on the result. The $36,000 figure represents the average annual cost of the initial investment over the expected 20-year life of the firm—or less than $1 per suit if output is 40,000.)

Mr. Kelly knows that the 20-year figure is a very "soft" one because technological change might make his equipment obsolete and changes in the industry might occur that would prevent him from selling about 40,000 suits per year for 20 years, but he knows of no better figures to use. He is pleased to note that these most troublesome costs amount to only 90c per suit and rejoices that he is not in the petroleum refining, meat packing, hydroelectric power, or some other business where these capital costs are of far greater importance.

Mr. Kelly next turns his attention to those costs that will require annual outlays but that will not vary significantly with the level of output. On the basis of his experience, he feels more comfortable making these estimates. His estimates (assuming 40,000 suits are sold each year) are:

General overhead—nonproduction employees, property taxes, insurance	$100,000
Advertising and other marketing costs, not including compensation to salesmen, who will be paid on a commission basis	100,000
Research and development on styles and production and marketing research studies	15,000
	$215,000

* At a discount rate.

He realizes that he will need to invest funds in addition to those used to finance the plant and equipment and start-up costs. He will be forced to hold inventories of cloth and of manufactured suits; moreover, he will not be able to make his sales on a cash basis. All of this will require an investment of $300,000 which could have been invested at 15 percent in other businesses. (We will assume that he could not borrow these funds.) He will forgo the $45,000 return from these investments and hence he will not enter the clothing business unless he can recover the $45,000 in the sales price. In addition to this opportunity cost, there is the compensation for his own services which, at the rate of $2,000 per month, is $24,000 per year. The total of these annual costs is therefore $284,000.

Lastly, Mr. Kelly takes a look at those costs which would vary with the

Table 10-1

ESTIMATED COST OF PRODUCTION OF MEN'S SUITS (CALCULATIONS MADE BEFORE ENTERING THE BUSINESS)

		Per year	*Per suit*
Initial costs			
Land	$ 8,000		
Building	67,000		
Equipment	125,000		
Kelly's time	6,000		
Introductory advertising	5,000		
First year inefficiencies	15,000		
	$226,000		
Pro-rated over 20-year period plus a 15% return on the investment necessary by Kelly		$ 36,000	$ .90
Annual costs			
General overhead		$100,000	
Marketing costs		100,000	
Research and development		15,000	
Return on investment in working capital		45,000	
Kelly's time		24,000	
		$284,000	$ 7.10
Product costs			
Production labor			10.00
Materials			28.00
Power			.05
Salesmen's commission			2.20
			$48.25

number of suits to be produced and sold. His direct production labor he estimates to be $10.00 per suit, his material costs, $28.00, and the cost of power to operate the machines, $.05. He plans to pay his salesmen $2.20 for every suit sold.

Mr. Kelly concludes that he must receive at least $48.25 per suit to justify his entry into the business (see Table 10-1). Since comparable suits are sold in the range of $50 to $60, Mr. Kelly decides to start his business. The most significant assumption underlying his decision is that he can and will sell 40,000 suits per year.

Cost After Plant and Equipment Have Been Purchased

Mr. Kelly, carrying out his decision to enter the business, purchased the plant for $75,000 and purchased the equipment for $160,000. (He had made some errors in estimating the equipment costs as $125,000.) His introductory advertising cost him $6,000, and the time required to actually start operations was five months rather than three.

In addition, an increase in men's suits imports had weakened the market. Considerably shaken by his bad luck to date, Mr. Kelly called in a consultant to recheck his cost estimates. Perhaps he ought to get out while he could? He thought he could get about $180,000 if he sold the plant as it stood—before a wheel had turned.

The consultant rechecked all the annual costs and the product costs and could find little fault with the estimates. Looking at the initial costs, the consultant pointed out that Mr. Kelly had the choice of pocketing $180,000 from the sale of the plant and equipment or operating the business. He couldn't get back the $235,000 he had spent, so that neither the $235,000 nor the initial estimate of $200,000 was of any relevance. The question that Mr. Kelly had to decide was whether he could recover more than $180,000 by using the plant to make men's suits; consequently, $180,000 can be considered the correct cost of plant and equipment to Mr. Kelly *at that point*.

Kelly's five months of work in organizing the business and the introductory advertising costs were also irretrievable. Finally, the consultant concluded that the figure of $15,000 for the cost of initial inefficiencies was probably too low by $8,000. The net result was to make the initial costs $203,000 ($180,000 + 15,000 + 8,000) rather than $226,000, now that certain outlays had been made. This lowered the annual cost associated with these initial outlays from $36,000 to under $33,000 or about $.83 per suit. Inasmuch as the total cost per suit would be below $50.00, Mr. Kelly gratefully paid the consultant's fees of $3,000 and decided to start operations.

Costs for a Spring Marketing Plan

Mr. Kelly found out that estimates could be too pessimistic as well as too optimistic. The first year's operations went very well; the inefficiencies were less than were expected. He set a price of $52.00 and the dealers and consumers liked his product. Although at first he was able to sell only 30,000 suits per year, the sales gradually climbed so that he was selling 45,000. By careful scheduling he found that he could produce the added number without running into expensive overtime.

In October of the fifth year of operations, he began to plan for the output to be sold the following Easter. Industry forecasts were gloomy. A forecasted low level of economic activity indicated that sales of men's suits would hit a catastrophic low. It appeared that price cutting would be widespread. Perhaps he should drop out of the market for six months? What would it cost him to produce suits for the spring market?

Taking a look at his plant and equipment costs, Mr. Kelly concluded that if he stopped operations for six months, he would not lengthen the life of either the building or the equipment. He couldn't use it for anything else except that a neighboring manufacturer would probably pay him $2,000 to use the building for storage space. Thus he would give up the $2,000 rent if he produced for the spring season; this sum would represent his plant and equipment cost to produce for the spring market.

Looking at the annual costs, Mr. Kelly realized he would save little here if he temporarily suspended operations. He had worked hard to build up a successful operation and he was not going to discharge anyone except those performing routine tasks. The only reductions he could see possible were:

General overhead	$10,000
Marketing costs	5,000
	$15,000

He could not see any alternative use of his time; he was needed to keep the organization together, whether he suspended operations or not. The $300,000 working capital would be freed for six months, but the best use for this short period of time would yield only 5 percent per year, or $7,500. He concluded, therefore, that the overhead costs of operating rather than not operating (other than the product costs) were only:

Rent on space	$ 2,000
General overhead	10,000
Marketing costs	5,000
Return on investment in working capital	7,500
Annual costs	$24,500

On the other hand, he concluded that he had better increase his sales-men's commissions to $2.60 per suit. He thought he might be able to sell 10,000 suits at a lower price and therefore the per-suit cost would be:

Annual costs	$ 2.45
Production labor	10.00
Materials	28.00
Power	.05
Sales commissions	2.60
	$43.10

He set a price of $45.00 and ordered the materials.

Costs When the Materials Are Already Purchased

Orders came in slowly, but Mr. Kelly kept production going. By January, only 5,000 suits had been ordered and 5,000 had been produced. He could see no more orders on the horizon. He refused to consider an additional price cut for fear that it would damage his reputation. If he did cut his prices, he would have to extend it to the retailers who had already ordered at the $45.00 price. But what was he to do with the materials for the unsold and unmanufactured suits? He could not hold them over until the following year—the risk of style change was too great. Shopping around, he found he could sell the lot for $100,000 ($20.00 per suit) and had about concluded to get out from under when he received an inquiry from a discount chain that was interested in 5,000 private-label suits—but only if the price was right.

The opportunity to rent storage space was gone. Too short a period of time remained to permit any reduction in outlays for general overhead or marketing. Eliminating production during the remainder of the season would free $200,000 working capital for two months and thus enable him to earn about $1,667 at a 5 percent interest rate. Thus, the production of the 5,000 suits would result in additional costs of only:

Return on investment of working capital ($1,667 divided by 5,000)	$ .33
Production labor	10.00
Materials	20.00
Power	.05
	$30.38

After some fast bargaining, Mr. Kelly closed the deal at a price of $32.

Costs After the Product Has Been Made

Mr. Kelly recovered from the shocks of the unsuccessful season, and business returned to and even surpassed previous levels. Sales climbed above 50,000 suits, and it was necessary to run the plant overtime at certain periods of the year. Mr. Kelly eliminated almost all seasonal fluctuations in production because he was able to get advance orders from retailers. Since the dealers did not want to hold large stocks, the suits were held by Mr. Kelly. His finished-goods warehouse was frequently filled to capacity.

The fall season in the eighth year started out propitiously. For the first time, Mr. Kelly had to call his salesmen off the road—orders had outrun production even with a 48-hour week, the maximum that he was able to operate the plant. Orders were received for 30,000 suits and 30,000 suits had been made. Toward the end of the season, 5,000 suits were on hand when suddenly Mr. Kelly was deluged with telephone calls and telegrams canceling orders. Mr. Kelly consulted his attorney and was assured that firm contracts existed and the dealers could be sued for the loss resulting from the cancellations. However, Mr. Kelly realized that a lawsuit was a good way to lose a customer, and he needed the customers. He was left with 5,000 suits—too late in the season to attempt to sell them.

One possibility was to hold them over until the following season, but it was already obvious that changes in lapels and widths of trouser legs would make them unsalable next year. He couldn't endanger the Kelly reputation for good styling by trying to sell out-of-style merchandise. They just couldn't be sold with a Kelly label.

Another possibility was to sell them to a private-label dealer next year. But again there was a chance that they couldn't be sold. Although Mr. Kelly stayed away from selling his suits except under his own label, he realized that buyers were style-conscious regardless of what label they bought.

The only real choices were to give them away to charity or to dump them fast. He knew there were "tax gimmicks" on donations to charitable organizations, but he considered them dishonest. The only cost he would incur by selling the suits to a distress merchandiser was the cost of removing the Kelly labels and sewing in another label. This would cost about 25¢ per suit. He was very happy when he received an offer for the 5,000 suits at $10 apiece.

Costs After the Firm Has Begun to Lose Ground

After 25 years of successful operation, the Kelly firm began to decline. Mr. Kelly had taken in a partner five years earlier, but he had run the business too long to share authority and the partner had departed. The firm lacked the aggressiveness that it had formerly possessed—it manufactured a good quality suit, but its styling and merchandising had slipped.

Its plant was old—it had outlived its estimated life by five years—and Mr. Kelly knew that he would not replace it. The only value in the plant and equipment was the land; it was now worth $100,000 and probably would continue to be worth this amount or more. The Kelly label was well regarded and could be sold for $250,000—either this year or next year.

In making his decision as to whether to continue in operation one more year, Mr. Kelly included his product costs, his annual costs (these would decrease considerably as a result of eliminating research activities and a large part of his marketing expenditures, but these gains would be offset to some extent by higher repair and maintenance costs), and costs to allow for the fact that he would receive the $350,000 from the sale of the land and the label a year from now rather than now. Here was another opportunity cost—say, 15 percent of $350,000.

Conclusions

We saw that the items included in costs varied from one stage of the Kelly firm's life cycle to another. The size of the differences varied and would vary from one firm to another. In some cases, these differences would be substantial.

The greatest uncertainty about costs occurs during the early stages of the firm's existence. The very survival of the firm is in question at such time, and certainly the level of its output cannot be estimated accurately. The firm is likely to suffer a substantial disparity between facilities and skilled manpower available and the amount needed during its infancy. Conversely, during the firm's maturity it meets few surprises and generally enjoys a good balance of facilities with output.

Ordinarily, the variable costs of a product are not much affected over the life of an enterprise because of changes in the life cycle of the enterprise. What large changes take place result mainly from changes in the states of nature. Price levels might change, labor rates change, technology might improve, and so on. The main influence of the life cycle on variable costs results from changes in *scale* and level of operations.

The foregoing illustration provided practice in thinking realistically about the computation of costs. It suggested that the cost of a suit of clothes—produced by the same firm, of identical quality with an unchanging technology, with a labor force of equal productivity—did not fluctuate sharply. Nevertheless, it did vary with circumstances related to the life cycle of the firm. One must therefore avoid the trap of thinking that there is such a thing as a cost of a product that is independent of the circumstances under which it is produced. It is most useful to think that cost results from a decision to produce an item under particular circumstances and does not inhere in the item itself.

Chapter 11

DECISION BENEFITS AND DECISION ANALYSIS

Costs relevant to decisions were shown to be quite different from those that firms use for other purposes; further, most cost estimates apparently are made without regard to purpose. The same situation prevails for benefits also. Accordingly, in this chapter we consider the difference between apparent benefits and decision benefits and discuss the estimation of decision benefits. Before we do either, we shall discuss "benefits analysis" and develop a brief list of the main benefits that firms can obtain from each of the main parties to the business process.

Benefits Analysis

One can usefully view executives as generators of (net) benefits for their organization. As such, they constantly search the environment for methods of achieving benefits for their organization, for their goal is to make their firm better off than it would have been without their services. If that were not done, they would not "earn their salary" and their tenure would be uncertain at best. In other words, the firm should be closer to achieving its objectives because of every executive's efforts than it would have been without their services.

This view of executives' decision-making responsibilities has important implications: it suggests that executives should do the following:

* Identify the benefits that they might obtain for their organizations. Specifically, they will want to list all the significant benefits they

might gain for their organizations. Mainly they would be instrumental objectives—that is, means of achieving higher-level objectives.
*   Identify the means available to them by which they might gain those benefits. That is, they will want to be familiar with all variables under their control which they could use to further their firm's objectives.
*   Understand how the means available to them work and in particular how they might be used to attain the benefits sought.
*   Develop programs of action that use the means available to achieve benefits that they might achieve.

This view of executives' functions may appear to complicate the obvious. It is difficult to believe that executives do not know "the object of the game" of business. Indeed, every executive is keenly aware that he is expected to contribute to his organization's profitability. However, most employees are not usually told what instrumental objectives (benefits) to pursue in order to further their firm's profitability; they generally are left free to devise their own strategy for doing so.

As we stressed in our discussion of business objectives (Chapter 7), several alternative paths ordinarily are available for pursuing a particular objective; management makes strategic choices among these alternatives. The point urged here is that in the absence of detailed hierarchies of objectives, most executives get little guidance as to the instrumental objectives (benefits) they might pursue. They may not even know some important instrumental objectives, for many are not at all obvious.

Similarly, the varied means that executives might employ in pursuit of their firms' objectives are not always apparent. Especially if they examine each instrumental goal possibly worthy of attainment to determine what they might do to achieve it, executives may discover that they possess the power to do things they had either overlooked or undervalued. A few illustrations might establish this important conclusion.

Let us start with what appears an obvious example. One tool available to every executive is the possibility of asking employees what they might contribute to achieving their bosses' goals. The idea that one might ask employees to propose the tasks they will perform is still a relatively unutilized instrument available to all executives. And, as the experience of many firms (not all) with "Management by Objectives" can attest, the power of this instrument sometimes is great.

Let us take a more concrete example: every executive seeks high output from his subordinates measured both quantitatively and qualitatively. That instrumental objective is fairly obvious—even though some executives mainly seek maximum output from themselves rather than from their entire organization. If we ask what the executive might do to increase his subordinates' output, we see that the subject is complex. It surely is not easy to list all feasible means at an executive's disposal. Further, we recognize that many of the means he might employ are subtle and intangible—such as flattery, challenges, criticism, warm friendly feedback, silent disapproval, special assignments, job enrichment, a reduction in personal conversation, and the like. It is high vanity to assume that one's repertoire of behavior includes *all* actions that might be employed to elicit better performance from associates.

We can be more concrete still: a sales manager recognizes that he gets little and delayed information from his salesmen about what is happening in the marketplace. He does not know what dissatisfactions are expressed by potential customers to whom distributors offer his products. With what product features are they most pleased? What do customers ask for that is not currently offered? Some sales managers even overlook the possible benefit they could give to top management by providing such information. They would not be able to identify many feasible measures they might employ to obtain that benefit. Surely, the first step is to determine whether distributors are in a position to gather such information, even if they desired to do so. If so, then the next step is to devise means for encouraging distributors to collect the desired information. Then, special means must be employed to insure that the firm's own salesmen will obtain and report accurately what distributors could tell them. What we are stressing is the nonobviousness of both the instrumental objectives and the means for pursuing them. As a rough rule, executives can serve their organizations in many more ways than they recognize and have many more means available for furthering their organization's objectives than they recognize. In the hypothetical case under consideration, the sales manager—preferably with the active cooperation of the market research director—could devise a program of action which meshed the activities required of the firm's salesmen and the incentives offered to them with the inducements offered to distributors that were designed to elicit their support.

To design such programs of action calls for a combination of knowledge, experience, and imagination. Sales managers often have occasion to seek the cooperation of their distributors and can learn from colleagues, predecessors, and their opposite numbers in other firms what inducements might be offered to distributors. Their own experience will generally suggest what works best with their particular distributors at the present time. (The effectiveness of such inducements varies, particularly with executives' experience with similar inducements in the recent past.) Invariably, the opportunity exists to devise new and better ways of gaining distributor support. However, an executive should not always try to invent a "better way," especially if he already knows something that is likely to work.

Underlying programs of action is knowledge or belief as to how the means available to an executive work to provide the sought-after benefits. Specifically, how will distributors respond to the statement that if they provide better information about customers' responses to the products offered the manufacturer will improve his products and thus enable the distributors to sell more? How will they respond to a visit from the manufacturing firm's vice-president backed up with a dinner invitation to the distributor and his wife?

What we are discussing may be interpreted as "functional relationships" between controllable variables and a firm's objectives. That sounds like a very stuffy way of describing the answer to the question, How much cooperation would you get from distributors if an important executive called on them and showed them considerable personal attention? Still, that is just what is involved. We are discussing the connection between what an executive does and the benefits it produces. Knowledge of such functional relationships—plus awareness of the many different benefits that an executive might attain for his organization and the large number of instruments available to him for pursuing them—is perhaps the main contribution of a business executive. He knows what is needed and what can be done to get it.

The foregoing description of benefits analysis presents a fairly simple noncontroversial view of an executive's responsibilities. That view opens up large areas of an executive's responsibilities that may be relatively unexplored. By exploring them, executives may alter their behavior profoundly, to their own and their employers' advantage.

A Classification of Decision Benefits

The instrumental benefits sought by most organizations are surely numbered in the hundreds. We will not attempt to prepare an exhaustive list but will only list the main benefits. We will suggest a method of classifying decision benefits that may help executives identify benefits that are currently overlooked.

Benefits, like costs, originate in many sources. In business decisions, the main sources are colleagues, ultimate customers, rivals, resellers, suppliers, and government. Apart from the varied sources of business decision benefits, they can be distinguished by their tangibility, level in the hierarchy of objectives, and the promptness with which they can be obtained. Table 11-1 identifies numerous benefit types, with illustrative examples. The examples were selected to establish that some potential in-

Table 11-1

A Classification of Benefits from Business Decisions

Source	Benefit	High level		Low level	
		Near term	Long term	Near term	Long term
Ultimate customer	Tangible	Increased sales; higher prices	Increased usage; more users	Customers hold larger inventories	Increased sales on credit
	Intangible	Stronger brand preference; habitual brand selection	Loyalty to brand; loyalty to company	Strong word-of-mouth support	Increased brand awareness
Rivals	Tangible	Form trade association; win higher tariff protection	Improved information available on industry		
	Intangible	Reduced defamation of rivals; reduced deception of consumers	Better market discipline; increased customer confidence in industry		
Resellers	Tangible	More resellers carry brand; better resellers carry brand	Invest more of own money in support of brand		
	Intangible	Provide more market information; submit helpful marketing suggestions	Greater reseller loyalty; improved sales skills of resellers		
Suppliers	Tangible	Charge low price	Hold large inventories	Provide premium quality	Give preference when supplies are short
	Intangible	Provide information about rivals		Friendly relations with firm and its executives	Try to help rather than take advantage
Government	Tangible	Warn rather than punish	Withdraw regulation		
	Intangible	Provide helpful information			
Colleagues	Tangible	Help to make programs work			
	Intangible				

strumental benefits are nonobvious; these examples may suggest others that may be overlooked at present.

Colleagues as a Source of Decision Benefits

In many ways, the distinction between individuals and organizations within and outside a firm is artificial; it makes a difference in degree into one of kind. Large organizations, and many smallish ones too, behave like loose aggregations of independent—if not vigorously competing—organizations. Executives often feel more antagonistic to executives in other divisions of their own firm than they do toward the management of rival firms. Often they have good reason for such sentiments. Colleagues can be the main competitors for advancement, for allocations of funds, and for the personal favor of the top executives and members of the board of directors. Also, colleagues sometimes are responsible for an executive's apparent past failures.

Colleagues can provide benefits, even as they can cause difficulties. If they perform their functions effectively in joint programs, if they make constructive suggestions, if they desist from hostile criticisms and sabotage, they are providing benefits, for the opposite behaviors surely impose costs. Let us be more specific about the nature and importance of colleague-based benefits by considering real-life examples.

The marketing vice-president of ABC Corporation has put pressure on his director of product planning to revive sales of the firm's line of refrigerators by introducing a potentially attractive product feature that has been under development for many months. The product planner must persuade the research engineers to settle on a particular version of the product feature—that is, make their designs final—and he must arrange for manufacturing to turn out models including this feature. He must also arrange for advertising to develop materials for distributors, retailers, and ultimate customers, including tags or booklets to be attached to individual refrigerators which describe and "sell" the new feature, and so on. The product planner, on behalf of the entire firm, must enlist the cooperation of several divisions of the business. In the course of attempting to do so, he may alienate them so that in the future, he will find them less cooperative. Or, he may seek their help in ways that increase the likelihood of greater cooperation in the future. He certainly recognizes that the success of the new feature depends upon each division's doing its part and in maintaining some synchronization of their activities. In addition, he knows that the means he uses to get the help of these divisions will have some effect on his ability to obtain their help in the future. His present assignment could increase the amiability of his relationships with the other divisions or the reverse. In deciding to add this new product feature, the decision maker should be alert to the potentially heavy costs and major benefits that may result from the decision's effects on colleagues.

Consider another example: A sales manager has the opportunity to win a large order if he can promise early delivery and a small (as he sees it) product modification. By getting this order, the sales division will attain sales beyond the amount planned for the period; the sales manager therefore has almost committed the company to accept the order. The effect of taking this order, as viewed by an objective observer, would be to almost tear apart the management of the company. Manufacturing already is in turmoil because of the sudden death of the number two executive (who is number one in work contribution); it has already been exceeding its planned costs because of similar promises of early delivery and product modifications. The feelings on the part of both sales and production executives are already hostile; one finds evidence of minor sabotage and near-slander on the part of both. An accurate forecast of the costs and benefits of the decision to accept that order would show it to be a "big loser." However, for the sales manager, it would be a big gainer. In this case, the negative benefits that matter most relate to colleagues rather than to the ultimate customer or rivals.

A final example: The sales department has turned up an order that does not seem particularly attractive. It turns out, however, that this order would relieve a severe cash flow problem for the firm resulting from an unexpected build-up in inventories. The finance department makes it clear that it would greatly appreciate the acceptance of this order and would return the favor in the future. Such exchanges of favors represent an important ingredient of intrafirm relationships.

SUPPLIERS AS A SOURCE OF DECISION BENEFITS

Suppliers take many forms: they are raw material producers, producers of components or subassemblies, providers of funds, suppliers of labor, and providers of professional services—legal, market research, advertising, and so on. Many decisions imply benefits—and costs—vis-à-vis suppliers. Some decisions involve orders for suppliers that will strengthen the relationship with them and thereby win favors that will reduce costs or raise profit margins in the future. Some involve impositions on suppliers or the exercise of pressure which could have a lasting negative effect.

Similarly, decisions not infrequently call for demands on the labor force that are very welcome. It could mean more work at a time when income has been low; it could call for overtime work when labor was already restive because of heavy demands for overtime. Similarly, a decision might involve a request for short-term loans from commercial banks; at certain times, such requests may lead to future favors while at others they may obligate the firm's management to give future business to the bank in exchange for present service.

The foregoing examples offer fairly obvious examples of the varied benefits and anti-benefits (costs) that flow from business decisions vis-à-vis suppliers of various sorts. Clearly, executives must recognize their presence, devise decisions that will obtain many such benefits, and reckon them in their cost-benefit analysis.

How Benefit Computations Are Handled Currently

Every decision has a cost and a benefit side which figure equally in the decision made. However, the effort devoted to the measurement of costs and to benefits is highly unequal. Whereas cost estimates ordinarily involve enormously detailed computations, estimates of benefits (generally they represent forecasts of sales in units or sales revenue) are global and relatively crude. And despite the real difficulties faced in computing decision costs, the cost estimates made in most business decisions are more carefully and accurately made than are benefit estimates.

The reasons for these differences are partly historical and institutional. Cost control offered enormous benefits when production was overlaid by tradition and conducted in a nonbusinesslike manner. Also, the tax collector inspired business to keep cost records.

Estimates of sales prices and related matters are more difficult than cost estimates, a fact that should ordinarily lead to increased effort devoted to the more difficult task. But the reverse situation obtains at present. Cost computing specialists are numerous; almost no one would admit to being a benefit specialist.

In one sense, an executive is the firm's expert on the benefits his activity provides. But not infrequently executives emphatically repudiate responsibility for estimating benefits. An advertising executive will often come forward with a budgetary request; when asked what sales effects (or other communication benefits) he expects, he will often say he doesn't know—and that no one knows.

Many executives imply that they know what their firm should do even though they admit that they cannot forecast the effects of their actions. Perhaps they could resolve this apparent contradiction by saying that they do not know just how much benefit will be gained by what they propose but they know that it is more than it will cost.

Decision Benefits and Their Measurement

In Chapter 8, we met the concept of decision cost and stressed that costs are to be computed for specific purposes. The same conclusion holds for benefits. Most firms could compute the sales revenues obtained from each product they sell; however, that is different from computing the revenue resulting from a particular decision related to that product. And our interest is in decisions—which necessarily relate to the future—rather than in the history of an item during the past year or quarter, which reflects many decisions.

For example, an executive might learn that Model X 632 produced sales last year of $110,000. (He might also learn that the costs assigned to that model were $100,000.) He could *not*, however, infer from those facts that the benefits of keeping that item in the line—that is, of a decision to continue to offer it—are $110,000 of gross benefits or $10,000 of net benefits. As we shall see, benefits are rarely what they seem. A common sense view of measuring benefits can get a decision maker into lots of trouble.

Let us examine a very simple example, involving a firm that only sells expensive fur coats. The shop owner operates only a month each year, expecting to sell all that could be sold in that time. He sells all his coats at the same price, though they vary in size. His problem is what price to charge for the 20 coats he has purchased. His best estimates are shown in Table 11-2. The table indicates the revenue and the added revenue for different price decisions. Specifically, if he reduced his price from $2,000 to $1,900, he would give up one extra coat to get an extra $700; if instead of $1,900 he charged $1,850, he would give up one coat for an extra $1,200. Similarly, if he charged $1,750 instead of $1,800, he would get an extra $6,200 for four extra coats.

This numerical example helps to clarify some essential ideas. The key idea is that a decision maker can look at different facts to determine the benefits resulting from his decision. He could ask, "How many will I sell at, say, a price of $1,800?" The answer would be 16 coats. Or, he could ask, "How many *extra* will I sell if I were to charge $1,800 rather than $1,850?" The answer would be two coats. He could ask similar questions about total revenue, namely, "How many dollars of revenue would I get at a price of $1,800?" or, "How many *extra* dollars would I get if I charged $1,800 instead of $1,850?" In both pairs of questions, one deals with the expected outcome of his decision; the other asks about the change in outcome resulting from doing something different—that is, charging a differ-

Table 11-2
REVENUES AT FIVE DIFFERENT PRICES

Price	Sales* (units)	Total revenue	Extra revenue	Extra revenue per unit
$2,000	12	$24,000	—	—
1,900	13	24,700	$ 700	$ 700
1,850	14	25,900	1,200	1,200
1,800	16	28,800	2,900	1,450
1,750	20	35,000	6,200	1,550

* We are assuming that he has his coats on consignment and can return any coats he cannot sell without penalty.

ent price. To answer the second question, one needs to know both what action is planned and what would be done otherwise.

This example was termed very simple, even though the idea of extra revenue is elusive to many, because our fur seller deals only in one product. What he does about his prices on fur coats does not affect the sale of any other items that he sells; or, in this example, it does not affect his sales of fur coats at other times. In most real-life situations, a firm's decisions related to one of its offerings—whether it be a change in its price, quality, promotion, or availability—usually does affect its sales of other things and at other times. To estimate those effects in specific decisions is extremely complicated.

The phenomenon that creates such estimation difficulties is known as interrelated demand. The term is self-explanatory and directs attention to the fact that the demand for one product and changes in its terms will sometimes affect the demand for other products. These interrelationships take several forms and we must sort them out. Demand interrelationship generally refers to competitive products. The term directs attention to the connection, for example, between the prices for wheat and corn; or to the relationship between the demand for steel, glass, and cement; or to the interrelated demand for aluminum and copper. These sets of items are substitutable in important uses, and a substantial price change for one of them will affect the demand for the others in the set. (That fact explains why, in forecasting the sales of any one of them, one must make specific assumptions about the price of the other; and, in constructing demand schedules one must specify the price of the other.)

We are *not* here interested in such interrelationships among primary demands or in the issue of competitive products, though this phenomenon is important in other connections. Our interest is in the interrelationships among *the demands for different items sold by the same firm.* For example, we are interested in how a firm's introduction of a new model of auto or desk chair or spectacle frame or refrigerator affects its own sales of other models and items that it offers for sale. Another facet of the same question is how a firm's decisions on a particular model of auto, desk, chair, or spectacle frame affect its own *future* sales of the same item. The plain fact is that what a seller does about the design, price, promotion, product features, availability, assortments of one of its offerings usually affects its sales of other things and of the sales of the same things in the future.

What kinds of decisions create the most difficult problems of estimation of demand due to demand interrelationships? Problems stemming from the identification of items that will be affected will be distinguished from those related to future effects on demand.

Demand Interrelationships for Items Offered by a Single Seller

Three types of relationships exist among products offered for sale by an individual seller: (1) substitution, (2) complementarity, and (3) neutrality, or complete independence.

If items offered by a firm are direct substitutes, then the sale of one of those items will foreclose the sale of any other. One sale replaces the other; to sell one item, the seller must give up the sale of another. Under such circumstances, the seller wants to ensure that the sale he makes is as valuable to him as the sale he forecloses.

Not all sales of substitute items represent pure, or one-for-one, substitution. By promoting the sale of a particular substitute item, a seller may induce customers to buy something that they will consume in greater quantities than the replaced item. For example, if shoppers were to be shifted to chicken from, say, ham, they might eat more and spend more for chicken than for ham. Another departure from pure substitution is quantitatively important; in this case the seller hopes to attract added customers by altering one of his offerings. So, he now sells to people who would not have bought another of his offerings because they did not deal with him before. In other words, when a seller alters an offering or adds an item to his line, he may give up the sale of other things to some customers, but he also may increase that customer's consumption of the item and attract other customers.

Complementarity among items is one form of demand interrelationship. It exists when the sale of one item increases the probability that the customer will purchase another item from that vendor. For example, sell a woman a handbag and you increase the probability of selling her a pair of gloves in your own shop on the same shopping trip. Attract a customer into your store by a phonograph record promotion and you increase the likelihood that he'll buy some other item offered by your store. (The average customer is likely to buy something in addition to records, but it is impossible to predict what items they will be.)

Neutrality or complete independence describes a condition of no demand interrelationship. It exists when whatever is done to one of the items in a line of offerings has no effect on the demand for any of the other offerings. For firms with broad lines of products, such a condition is quite uncommon.

Decision Benefits vs. Apparent Benefits

We are now ready to take a big step: we can explore why decision benefits often differ from what they appear to be. We are about to see that the powerful concept of incrementalism applies to demand as well as to costs and that the business world is full of traps into which decision makers can easily fall. The benefits that result from decisions rarely are what they seem.

To compute decision benefits, an executive should apply the same reasoning as in computing the cost of a decision; he should compare total benefits if the decision is made with total benefits if the decision is not made. The difference between them is what can be attributed to the decision. So far, so good—even though estimates of both quantities are likely to be inaccurate. Errors in estimating decision benefits result from using measurements that seem eminently reasonable, but are not. (The same cause underlies most errors in computing decision costs.)

Let us examine a realistic example. If an executive estimates the benefits resulting from the addition of a new item to the product line, he would estimate its average price and unit sales over its life. But that quite reasonable-seeming measurement would ignore important influences of that decision on the firm's total revenue. Specifically, the new item is likely to affect the sale of other items in the line in the near future. That effect might be to increase the sale of the firm's other items but it is more usual for a new product introduction to reduce its sales of other items; a new-item introduction often increases the sales of some of the firm's other offerings while reducing the sale of other items. Whatever the effect of the new item on the firm's sales of other items, it must be reckoned in its decision benefits. A decision maker can make a wise decision only if he knows all the effects of his decisions on benefits.

Let us then explain specifically two methods of estimating decision benefits. The first method requires the decision maker to make separate estimates of benefits for different time periods over the life of the decision; the decision maker would estimate total benefits with and without that decision in the different time periods. The difference represents decision benefits. The second method requires the decision maker to estimate separately for each time period: (1) the sales of the newly introduced item; (2) the increased sales of other items already in the line due to the decision to introduce the new item; and (3) the reduction in sales of other items due to the introduction of the new item. By totaling the first two and subtracting the third, one arrives at decision benefits. (See Table 11-3.)

The item most difficult to estimate and understand thoroughly is "reduced sales of old items." Let us consider further the example of the firm contemplating the introduction of a new item in its line. Assume it to be an improved and more costly version of its main product; the company will retain the old version which it will offer at a reduced price. Moreover, the firm has substantial unfilled orders for the old version of the product.

Table 11-3

Estimating Decision Benefits

	Time period					
	1	2	3	4	5	6
Method 1						
1. Total sales (no decision)	___	___	___	___	___	___
2. Total sales (with decision)	___	___	___	___	___	___
3. Difference = decision benefits	___	___	___	___	___	___
Method 2						
1. Sales of new item	___	___	___	___	___	___
2. Added sales of old items	___	___	___	___	___	___
3. Reduced sales of old items	___	___	___	___	___	___
4. 1 + 2 − 3 = decision benefits	___	___	___	___	___	___

If the decision maker were to look only at the estimated sales of the new version, the project might appear to be exceptionally profitable. But how much would be lost in the form of a reduced price for sales on its older version, or in the loss of orders for the old version when the new one is introduced? It could turn out that the new product would actually reduce total revenues rather than increase them—though such a result is unlikely. However, by considering those two sources of reduced sales, the profitability of the new item could be totally negated.

Consider another highly common error made in estimating decision benefits. A product planner has been reviewing his product line and finds that certain items, mainly the "promotional" items, have not been yielding enough revenue to justify their cost; those items show either very low profit or actual losses. However, by following the second method of estimating decision costs, one would soon recognize that if the firm dropped its promotional items, its sales of other items would drop substantially. In effect, part of the revenue on other items should be attributed to the promotional items—but that is not shown on the firm's books.

We meet here again the phenomenon of interdependence: decisions about one thing affect not only that thing but other things as well. These interdependences are extremely difficult to uncover, and they pass unrecognized, sometimes forever.

The difficulty of computing decision benefits reaches an extreme in the commonplace case of a supermarket's weekend promotion. What effects must a merchandise manager estimate when he is considering a recommendation that his chain of supermarkets run a special on three cuts of beef during the weekend, starting four weeks ahead? The proposed reduction in gross profit margin would be different on each of the cuts of beef, ranging from 30 percent to 15 percent, in the store's profit margin on beef. The reduction in price to consumers would be substantially larger because the meat packer would charge the supermarket a lower price on a substantially larger volume. How would the merchandise manager estimate the effects of that special promotion on beef on the revenues of his chain? Obviously the merchandise manager must somehow end up with a quantitative result, though he need not settle on a specific number.

It is proposed that the merchandise manager should estimate three sets of quantities: first, the actual sales of the three promoted cuts of beef for approximately a three-week period following the promotion, week by week. Second, he should identify the other items the chain sells whose sale would be affected by the change in beef prices; he should separate those items whose sales would be increased from those whose sales would be reduced. For each of these items, he should make separate sales estimates for several weeks following the promotion also. (He should assume no gain or loss of customers in making these estimates.) Third, he should estimate the number of customers who would be attracted to the store by the beef promotion and estimate their purchases of beef and other things; and he should also estimate the proportion of those customers who would be persuaded by their experience with that promotion to become regular patrons of his chain.

No merchandise manager can make such difficult estimates with any confidence; most do not even try. But when they approve of a promotion, they are implicitly estimating that the benefits of the promotion justify the reduced margins from the sale of the three promoted cuts of beef. One cannot criticize the merchandise manager for failing to make detailed numerical estimates unless one can provide him with a reliable method for making them.

Chapter 12

THE DETERMINANTS OF DECISION BENEFITS

THE BENEFIT SIDE of cost-benefit analysis is far less developed than the cost side. Whereas businesses have many persons actively measuring costs, they have no specialists in measuring benefits. Nevertheless, the benefits of any decision clearly are no less important than its costs.

Most business decisions involve low-level instrumental benefits such as: increased customer awareness of a brand, stronger customer brand preferences, increased product usage, the gaining of distributors to handle one's product, increased sales support from resellers and the like. As these examples illustrate, many decision benefits take an intangible form; subsequently, they may affect revenues.

Nonfinancial benefits are ultimate objectives for some executives: power, prestige, and public service are examples (discussed in Chapter 7). This chapter, which discusses only financial benefits, concentrates primarily on the goal of high total revenue, that is, the determinants and measurement of the revenue aspects of executive decisions.

One important financial benefit sought by business firms is a higher price for their securities. Although we will say little about this benefit or its determinants, the discussion of the determinants of revenue does relate to profitability, which bears directly on the price of securities.

The total revenue of a firm mainly reflects the demand for its own output—that is, the price it receives times the number of units it sells. But the demand for any firm's output is related to and usually strongly affected by the demand for the output of its entire industry. Despite some differences in their individual experience, all members of an industry are "in the same boat." They are buffeted by the very forces that affect their rivals, though not necessarily to the same degree. Accordingly, we explain the total revenue obtained by any firm in two steps: first, total industry demand—"primary demand," and second, the demand for a particular firm's output—"secondary demand."

Determinants of Primary Demand

In discussing forecasting, we identified the forces that affect sales of a product and the level of general business conditions. Our purpose here is different from environmental forecasting. We want to explain changes in total demand as a first step toward explaining the demand for one firm's output.

DIFFERENCE BETWEEN DEMAND AND SALES

In layman's language, a forecast of demand means an estimate of sales; in technical economic parlance, demand means the desire of all potential buyers for a product/service combined with an ability and willingness to pay for it. One might abbreviate that statement to read, "people's readiness to buy"—a notion that describes attitudes, intentions, intensity of desire, rather than the specific action of buying.

Certain things can be done to increase the purchases (sales) of an offering without increasing customer willingness to buy or the intensity of customer desire. For example, if the offering is more readily available to customers, that is, it can be bought with less effort because it is sold in more stores, sales would increase without an accompanying increase in demand. Similarly, if price is reduced and more is purchased, we would say that demand remained unchanged but more was bought because of a lower price.

This troublesome notion becomes much more clear if one describes demand, or readiness to buy, by a "demand schedule" or "demand curve." Table 12-1 expresses the quantities of widgets that would be purchased on a given day at different prices—without any change in readiness to buy. As stated earlier, differences in amounts purchased will result from changes in price, *not* in the intensity of buyers' desire for the product or in their ability or willingness to buy.

Observe that unit sales are shown to be greater when prices are low than when they are high. That relationship represents the "law of demand." To describe an increase in demand, over what is represented in Table 12-1 (column 3) we would show larger unit sales at the indicated prices. We might construct another demand schedule showing unit sales at some given

Table 12-1

UNIT SALES OF WIDGETS AT DIFFERENT PRICES WITH DEMAND
UNCHANGED

Price (1)	Unit sales (2)	Increased demand (unit sales) (3)
$92	1,200,000	1,325,000
91	1,300,000	1,500,000
90	1,450,000	1,700,000
89	1,625,000	1,850,000
88	1,810,000	2,000,000
87	2,000,000	2,175,000

price—say, $89—with different numbers of stores offering widgets for sale (Table 12-2). As the number of retailers carrying widgets increases, widget sales ordinarily would increase, though not in direct proportion.

The foregoing examples illustrate changes in sales without a shift in readiness to buy on the part of potential customers. These cases should be distinguished from changes in demand, when the number of units bought changes because of greater customer desire for the item or greater ability to afford it. For example, a shift in tastes or lifestyles might lead people to value a product more than before; or the desire for the item might be heightened by increased advertising by sellers; or demand might increase because of a rise in personal incomes.

The figures in both Tables 12-1 and 12-2 represent demand schedules. They indicate the effect of changes in price and number of retailers, respectively, on unit sales. Both these demand schedules hold constant all other factors that affect the demand for widgets—like the prices of substitute products, expected changes in technology, import regulations, and many other factors.

Table 12-2

WIDGET SALES AT $89 PRICE WITH DIFFERENT NUMBERS OF RETAILERS

Number of retailers	Sales	Number of retailers	Sales
100	1,625,000	130	1,790,000
110	1,700,000	140	1,820,000
120	1,750,000	150	1,840,000

Dimensions of Primary Demand

Demand for any offering has several dimensions: price elasticity, income elasticity, and volatility over time. Price elasticity denotes the responsiveness of customers to changes in price—that is, are their purchases affected much or little by a change in the item's price (all else remaining unchanged)? Income elasticity of demand denotes the responsiveness of an item's sales to changes in the level of national income—do sales go up (down) much when people are "better off"? The volatility of demand refers to the magnitude of changes in sales of an item at a given level of price and income over time. Let us clarify the first two of these concepts.

Price elasticity of demand. The responsiveness of sales to changes in price can be expressed in different ways: for example, one might say that a $10 drop in price results in added sales of 2,000 units, or a 1 percent drop in price results in a 1.4 percent increase in unit sales. Price elasticity expresses the relationship between percentage changes in price and percentage changes in unit sales. Stated symbolically:

$$\text{Price elasticity} = \frac{\% \text{ change in unit sales}}{\% \text{ change in price}} = \frac{1.4}{1.0} = 1.4$$

The convention for describing the responsiveness of sales to changes in price (all else remaining unchanged) is very illuminating, once you get used to it. For example, you learn quickly that a price elasticity of 1.0 is a situation in which total expenditures (receipts by sellers) remain the same whether or not prices are changed. That is, the effect of the price change on revenue is just offset by an opposite change in unit sales.

Not very much is known about the factors that determine the price elasticity of demand. Two of the propositions propounded on this issue are (1) where nearly substitute products exist, price elasticity is usually high, and (2) if the product is a necessity, price changes will have relatively little effect on sales.

A Sample Demand Curve and Schedule

The sales of any product are influenced by many factors, which determine the demand for that product. Among the most important determinants of demand for any item are buyers' tastes, their lifestyles, income, inventories of the product and the condition of their inventory, expected improvements in the product, expected price changes, and the relative prices of substitute products.

Recognize that demand has a vital time dimension in real-life situations; this dimension is largely ignored in theoretical analyses. An executive must

Table 12-3

Demand Schedule for Widgets

Price	Number of units	Total revenue	Marginal revenue	
$150	1	$150	—	
125	2	250	$100	
115	3	345	95	
105	4	420	75	
95	5	475	55	
87	6	522	47	
80	7	560	38	← Unit
70	8	560	0	← elasticity
60	9	540	−20	
50	10	500	−40	
40	11	440	−60	

be concerned with such issues as: What will be the initial impact of the proposed action on sales? After customers get used to it how will they react? If I do something that discourages purchases over the next week or two, will I nevertheless get that business in subsequent weeks? The initial response of customers to changes of all kinds is temporary and they may revert to their usual purchase patterns before long.

We ordinarily try to isolate the effect of individual determinants of demand—and particularly to isolate the effect of price changes on sales—by holding other factors constant. The result represents a schedule showing sales of widgets by all sellers combined at different levels of price.

Table 12-3 and Figure 12-1 present a hypothetical demand curve for widgets, shown both graphically and in tabular form. The demand curve describes conditions at one instant in time, when all else remains unchanged. The price elasticity of the assumed demand curve varies at different prices, which implies that the responsiveness of unit sales to price changes depends on whether price is high, medium, or low.

Determinants of Primary Demand Summarized

We have examined the bare bones of the conceptual apparatus developed by economists to explain the demand for an entire product, as distinct from the demand for the output of individual firms that produce it. This apparatus is closely related to the discussion of cost determinants in Chapter 8, both in level of generality and the medium in which the models are expressed.

Figure 12-1. Demand curve for widgets.

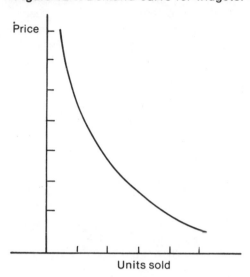

The specific factors that influence the unit sales of any product will vary somewhat, depending upon the durability of the product, the kinds of customers who buy it, and the number of firms that sell it. But sales of all products and services are affected by price, personal incomes, the availability of substitutes, people's tastes, and their expectations of future price and quality changes.

One should distinguish between shifts in sales and changes in demand and recognize that the responsiveness of individual products sales to changes in price, income, availability, and so on differs greatly—that is, the various elasticities of demand are quite dissimilar for individual products.

Determinants of Secondary Demand

The demand (schedule) for the output of a single firm expresses the relationship between that firm's prices and its own unit sales. Many forces influence a firm's demand, the most important being environmental factors; efforts by the individual firm itself; the activities of others, particularly resellers and government; and the behavior of rivals.

ENVIRONMENTAL INFLUENCES ON INDIVIDUAL FIRM DEMAND

Perhaps the single most important determinant of a firm's demand is the demand for the total product—primary demand. A close second is the number and behavior of firms that are trying to serve that demand—that is, with how many other firms must the firm in question share total primary demand? Also, general business conditions and specific geographic market developments affect the demand for an individual firm's output. These environmental influences must be taken into account when forecasting the sales of any sizable firm.

THE EFFORTS OF THE INDIVIDUAL FIRM ITSELF

Every management considers the possibility of increasing the demand for its firm's output; whether they try to do so or not depends upon cost-benefit analyses (however intuitive or elegant) of the tools available to them. An overwhelming majority of industrial and commercial firms do try to increase the demand for their output. To understand that process, we will discuss the "marketing mix." We will also distinguish devices which increase a firm's sales without altering its demand schedule from those that affect both sales and demand. More important, we want to distinguish a firm's efforts which are directed at the ultimate customers for its wares from those efforts directed at its resellers.

A firm's actions to increase its demand can be subdivided for analysis into the following categories: the number of product and geographic markets in which it operates, the magnitude of its outlays to expand demand, and its marketing skills. Clearly, by adding products and entering new geographic markets, a firm can expand its sales; those actions need not, of course, add to its profits. Similarly, firms that spend heavily on varied promotional efforts are likely to increase sales more than those who spend little; again, those expenditures need not increase profits; the greater a firm's marketing skill, the more means it will find to expand the demand for its wares and the more profitably it will do so.

It is essential to consider separately the influences on a firm's demand on the ultimate customers and resellers. The demands of both customers and resellers interact in strange ways to determine the demand for the output of individual firms.

Distinction between ultimate customer and middleman demand. Producers of most things sell to two classes of customer. First are the buyers whom they contact directly and to whom they actually transfer their output. These ordinarily are middlemen, or resellers, and include mainly distributors, wholesalers, and retailers; some of their customers are "original equipment manufacturers" (OEM) who assemble components and resell the finished product. Second are the ultimate buyers—those to whom the resellers sell; these ordinarily are members of households. Most producers view the ultimate customer as the chief determinant of demand and accordingly as the chief target for their marketing efforts. However, since middlemen can block them from the market, producers must make considerable efforts to win the favor of resellers. The marketing budget of any large manufacturer usually includes funds designed to increase the demand of both ultimate customers and resellers. Often the sums directed at ultimate customers are greater than the others, even though the producers sell only to resellers.

The marketing mix. The large bundle of activities that sellers can combine in order to attract patronage is called the marketing mix. The word "mix" suggests a blending together of elements and the likelihood that the elements may re-enforce one another rather than operate independently. The elements out of which marketing specialists fashion a mix vary but mainly include the following: price, advertising, personal selling, customer service, product design, product quality, credit accommodation, assortment, availability, and packaging. Because of their large number, and their qualitative as well as quantitative dimension, marketing mix elements can be composed in an infinite variety of ways. There is great scope for imagination and creativity; the opportunity for grievous error is also great.

Individual firms within the same industry probably differ far more in marketing skills than in any other regard. As a result, some firms win a far larger than proportional share of total demand, and they usually help to increase primary demand also.

Some elements in the marketing mix increase sales without increasing demand and others increase both. In the first category are price changes. In addition, activities which make the product more accessible by widening distribution, by offering the product through mail-order, or by easier credit accommodation also increase sales without apparently affecting desire. Other elements in the marketing mix clearly can alter customers' desires: advertising, personal selling, distribution of samples, attractive displays of merchandise, packaging refinements, and the like are demand increasing—when they are effective.

Marketing executives may not be much concerned with whether their activities are demand increasing as long as they do increase sales. It does matter that in one case the seller must alter individuals' desires and attitudes—a very difficult task—while in the other they need only make it easier for customers to satisfy their already existing desires for the product.

THE ACTIVITIES OF RESELLERS

Resellers are demand creators for their suppliers as well as their customers. They also set prices for their suppliers' wares. Beyond these functions, resellers perform a variety of logistical functions that make them a vital part of a nation's economy. Our concern here is solely with resellers' activities as determinants of demand for the output of individual producers.

Resellers as creators of secondary demand. Some items are almost entirely presold; the manufacturer does such an effective job of creating desire for his output that resellers need merely make it available, and without further urging, customers will ask for it or take it off the shelf. No product is presold to *all* buyers; some buyers of any brand of any product must be considered reluctant buyers. They require urging. At least, they need to be reminded of the product's existence, attracted by the package, or informed (if only by its presence) that the product exists. While these are low-level demand-creating activities, they are vital to most producers of branded products.

In some cases, the chief responsibility for creating sales rests with resellers; the manufacturers do nothing to attract ultimate customers. An increasingly important example is the retailer-private brand. Supermarkets are increasingly selling their own brands of foods and of cleaning and paper products (among other things) that are produced according to their specifications for them and carry their name. Much of the clothing of the nation remains unbranded and its sale mainly reflects the skills of resellers and their salesmen, window designers, store layout men and advertising departments in creating a preference for the wares of one firm over others.

Much of the sale/demand-creating activities of resellers may be considered "competitive," that is, their efforts may not increase total sales so much as they determine which producer's output will be favored over others. Still, the general level of consumption expenditures in the United States is high partly because merchandise is so readily available, great skill is devoted to creating desires for articles of consumption, and payment arrangements are made so convenient, and the entire culture—possibly for the foregoing reasons—seems to say "don't just stand there, buy something!" Middlemen are largely responsible for making products readily available, attractive—to the point of spurring impulsive buying—obtainable in attractive surroundings, and purchasable on easy payment terms.

The sales of any make of TV set, auto, refrigerator or brand detergent, toothpaste, or gasoline depend on the size and quality of the distribution network that offers it for sale. The same conclusion holds for industrial products. Most of such products are sold through a network of industrial distributors or sales offices owned by the manufacturer, but acting almost as independent demand-creating organizations. In other words, to explain the demand for any individual firm, one must take into account the sales activities of all persons and organizations which help to sell it—whether or not they are in the direct employ of the manufacturer.

Our discussion of demand determinants lacks one vital ingredient which seems to reverse the causal chain. Ultimate customers buy many items on a single shopping trip or when they "place an order"—not a single item. (The weekly main shopping trip to the supermarket is the clearest example.) In such cases, the customer picks a regular store or supplier. When a household customer decides to shop for something, he will go to his regular store—whether it is a department store, supermarket, drug store or clothing store. Similarly, a firm that requires an unusual item ordinarily will inquire of its favorite supplier to see if it handles the item. Thus, we find that resellers create a demand for their services—almost apart from the items they offer for sale. Instead of a demand for Brand R of TV sets, we find that many customers will demand Retailer M's assortment of TV sets—for a retailer usually carries more than one manufacturer's brand. These customers ordinarily will not even consider brands that Retailer M does not stock. Similarly, firms that buy industrial supplies will generally accept a brand that their regular industrial distributor carries. The first step in the two-step demand process is the demand for the vendor and then the demand for one of the items he carries.

The upshot of the foregoing discussion is that in explaining the demand for any firm's output, one must determine whether most customers "buy the manufacturer" or "buy the reseller." Is their main trust and loyalty in one or the other? Must it be for both before they make a purchase? Must we explain two separate demands or only one? And which is prior and determining? After all, if a customer's demand is to buy from a particular retailer, he will not even see most brands that are being offered.

This issue is extremely complex, partly because individual buyers vary in their loyalty and commitment to particular resellers. And even when a buyer is very loyal to a particular reseller, a manufacturer can make a strong direct sales appeal via advertising that would persuade most of them to search out his brand, even from a different vendor. Of course, to do that, the manufacturer usually must incur a heavy cost.

It seems clear that most customers buy sets of products rather than one and they do so from a favored seller. Even if they mainly buy one item at a time, they basically have bought a particular vendor rather than the brand of a particular manufacturer. The fact that most customers have favorite stores and suppliers is a condition which cannot be ignored in explaining or forecasting demand; that fact explains why manufacturers' efforts to spur the demand for their output sometimes have little effect on customers. It also explains why manufacturers attach such great significance to having their brand carried by many and the most popular retailers and industrial distributors.

Having discussed resellers' effects on ultimate customer demand, we now turn to an explanation of the demand by resellers themselves for the wares of manufacturers. The demand of ultimate consumers for Company A's widgets and the demand of firms that resell Company A's widgets need not vary in the same way: the chief difference consists of changes in resellers' inventories. Two economic concepts help to explain reseller demand: The concept of "derived demand," and the "acceleration principle."

Derived demand. The concept of derived demand distinguishes items that are desired for their own sake from those that are desired for resale or to produce other things. The latter class of items is demanded essentially when and to the degree that the other things are demanded. The most common derived demands are for the factors of production like labor, management, supervision, land, cash, space, materials, components and subassemblies. The demand for these factors is derived from the demand for the items they help to make. Similarly, the demand by resellers for, say, widgets is derived from ultimate consumers' demands for widgets.

The concept of derived demand goes much too far in explaining resellers' demand solely by ultimate customer demand; other factors affect reseller demand. In the first place, middlemen are creators of demand as well as passive reflectors of demand; their sales reflect the amount and skill of their marketing efforts; so, similarly, if they buy large quantities of an item that sells poorly, they will strenuously try to increase its sale. Also, as indicated, resellers decide whether a product is even to be exposed to ultimate customers, so a demand by ultimate customers may exist that is not registered by resellers. Furthermore, resellers do not really know the demand for, say, widgets, they forecast it. Their forecasts may be erroneous. Many manufacturers try to persuade resellers to make optimistic forecasts for their widgets so that resellers will accumulate large inventories. Once they have done so, manufacturers feel assured that resellers will somehow sell the item. For these reasons, it would be a serious mistake to view resellers as merely passive transmitters to manufacturers of the demands they receive from their customers. They are both influenced by their suppliers and can influence the demands of their customers. Consequently, they are independent and often powerful determinants of the demand for the output of individual firms.

The acceleration principle. The acceleration principle explains a special kind of connection between final demands and certain derived demands. In particular, this principle is employed to explain why the purchases of equipment and inventories of goods fluctuate more violently than does the demand for the finished product. In other words, the application of this principle suggests that if ultimate customers were to increase their purchases of widgets by 10 percent, then resellers might increase their purchases by 11 percent—part of their increased purchases would go to increase the size of their inventories. In that way, they would continue to hold the same percentage of the higher volume of sales in inventory to protect against unexpectedly high purchases. (Many resellers try to hold a fixed proportion of sales as inventory; their inventories therefore rise with sales.)

Similarly, the demand for widgets would affect manufacturers' demand for equipment to make them, for equipment is a derived demand, as explained. In the event of a 10 percent increase in demand for widgets, once they were operating near full capacity, widget producers would need to expand their capacity. On the assumption that their equipment lasted ten years, so that 10 percent was usually replaced each year, the need to expand capacity by 10 percent would result in a doubled demand for capital equipment.

Thus, derived demands for inventory holdings by resellers and for capital equipment fluctuate more violently than ultimate customers' demands for the same product. The converse holds for declines in final customer demand also: derived demands for inventories and capital equipment fall more than final customer demands for those items.

THE ACTIVITIES OF GOVERNMENT

We have seen that resellers exert a strong influence on the demand for the output of firms whose products they distribute. Let us now explore the influence of government on demand.

Government is itself an important customer for products in almost every nation; that fact is assured by the huge size of military establishments. In its regulatory role, government also affects the demand for many items, especially in its regulation of imports, its efforts to spur exports, and its measures to stabilize the general economy. Mainly, government regulation revolves around prices and rates—in public utility regulation, regulation of transportation agencies, its charges for postal services, and the like. Overwhelmingly, the effects of government fall upon primary demand; its actions affect all sellers equally.

In its procurement activities, however, government must select among vendors from time to time. On occasion, selections are not impartial. Still, government must be considered a minor influence on secondary demand, except for the items it buys for its own use.

THE BEHAVIOR OF RIVALS

A single firm's demand is special in that it depends less on buyers' responses to price changes than it does on the reactions of competitors. To take an example, if one firm reduces its prices modestly while no rivals alter price, its sales are likely to rise substantially because it will attract some customers from most of its rivals. Conversely, if all other firms immediately reduce price by the same amount, the first firm would not increase its sales much; other firms' customers would have no added incentive to patronize it.

Thus, to describe the sales of a single firm at different prices—that is, its demand curve—one must forecast the responses of rivals. That is not always easy to do. Consequently, in most real-life situations, a seller must be vitally concerned with the timing, magnitude, and form of rivals' responses to his own actions. As is explained in Chapter 14, markets differ greatly in the interdependence of rivals. In certain markets—like monopolies, those dominated by a single firm, stable price leadership arrangements, and purely competitive markets—rivals' responses are easily forecast. The overwhelming proportion of industrial and commercial markets, however, have relatively few sellers; and rivals strongly influence one another. Unfortunately, the behavior of individual sellers is difficult to predict.

The main determinant of Firm A's demand, thus, is the behavior of its rivals. If they set low prices, Firm A's price will be depressed; if they engage in severe price cutting, his prices can be pushed below his costs (even his incremental costs). Thus, the level of demand usually depends directly on the behavior of rivals. No matter how high primary demand may be for a product, a major rival can "ruin" demand for an individual firm.

The influence of rivals' responses on the demand for a single firm's output has been explored in some detail. One way of expressing this influence is to describe its effect on the shape of an individual firm's demand curve. When we adopt this approach, we say that the nature of the market in which a firm operates—its competitiveness, in layman's language—determines the shape of an individual firm's demand curves. We will elaborate that proposition with respect to a few of the market situations that are discussed later in this chapter.

Demand in purely competitive markets. If a firm is only one of many thousands and makes something that buyers value no more and no less than what the other firms sell, then its demand curve will have the following characteristics:

1. It can sell all that it is able to offer at the prevailing price. Since it is tiny, even if it dumped all of its holdings at once, the change in total supply that would result would be imperceptible. Conversely, if it withheld its output, no perceptible drop in supply would take place. Conse-

quently, its actions would not affect price. By saying that it can "dump" all of its holdings on the market without reducing price, we are saying that it can sell all it has available at the prevailing price.

2. If the firm tried to charge more than the prevailing price, it would get no customers at all. Customers have ready access to many other suppliers at the prevailing price. They have no reason to pay any one firm more for its output than it would pay the other, since they value the output of all firms equally.

The kind of demand situation described can be represented by a demand curve for each seller in the market that is a horizontal line at the level of the prevailing price (see Figure 12-2). Under such conditions, the price is determined for the individual firm, which must adjust to it—and presumably it will alter its output according to the prevailing and expected price. The firm would have no incentive to make efforts to increase demand for its output since it can already sell all that it wishes at the prevailing price and would not be able to command a higher price. Clearly, it would have no incentive to lower prices in order to increase its sales since it can already sell all it wishes to at the prevailing price.

Demand in oligopolistic markets. Let us consider another competitive situation—one that is far more common than pure competition. We are

Figure 12-2. Demand curve for firms in a purely competitive market.

referring to markets where only a few firms operate, each of which is such an important supplier that its actions do affect the prevailing price. Also, its actions affect the sales by the other firms in the market. As explained earlier, the demand for each firm's output reflects the responses of its rivals to whatever actions it takes. In the situation we are assuming, each firm's efforts to increase its share of the total business threatens the others with a loss of business for at least part of any increase in that firm's business

Figure 12-3. Individual firm demand in price leadership market.

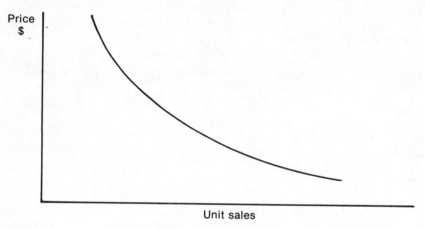

Figure 12-4. Individual firm demand in kinky demand situation.

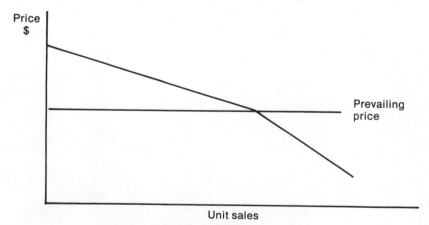

would come from the other firms. Accordingly, they presumably would protect themselves to the extent they could.

It is possible to depict graphically the demand for individual firms in oligopolistic markets. But we now recognize that to do so requires assumptions about the responses of their rivals to their price changes. We will depict two situations: one in which each seller's price is followed equally and immediately by the others; we will term this a "price-leadership" situation (see Figure 12-3); the second is more complex and assumes that rivals will only follow price *reductions* immediately and fully but will not *raise* price when their rivals do so (see Figure 12-4).

To represent graphically the demand for individual firms in oligopolistic markets we must distinguish between situations in which rivals sell identical products from those in which their offerings are significantly different, in the view of customers. For the sake of simplicity, we will assume the offerings of all sellers to be perceived as identical by customers; we can now reason that no seller can obtain a price higher than the lowest price at which the item is offered.

We have only scratched the surface of demand theory to sharpen our earlier discussion of the difference between primary and secondary demand. In so doing, we have seen one type of model—one that is widely discussed in the business press and one that underlies much of the thinking which forms present public policy toward competition.

The Contribution of Demand Theory to Benefits Analysis

Demand theory can be applied to the identification and measurement of decision benefits in several ways. First, it suggests the more important determinants of primary demand—which is a major determinant of secondary demand, and in turn a chief determinant of financial benefits. Second, we can extend demand theory to acknowledge the existence of many different elasticities of demand—not only one. That is, we can, and should, speak of the promotional elasticity of demand, the personal sales elasticity of demand, the customer service, product redesign, credit elasticities. In each case we would be describing (forecasting) the change in unit sales—as a percentage of its current level—that would be associated with a one percent change in expenditure. (It is assumed that the expenditure will take the most effective form that management can devise.)

In certain situations executives would be wise to concentrate their efforts on obtaining higher prices whereas in others their emphasis should be on increasing unit sales. These goals usually conflict because expansions in sales may be possible only with price reductions; and, if one seller devises measures that increase his sales significantly, he typically will force some of his competitors to counter by reducing price. On the other hand, his successful efforts to increase his price should not injure them, hence should not provoke retaliation.

We must distinguish between measures that a firm can take that would increase customers' readiness to buy—their desire for the offering—from inducing them to purchase it by lowering its price. In the second case, one is lowering the barrier to purchase, without increasing the intensity of customers' wants for it. The first path toward increased sales is the more difficult of the two and should usually be pursued only after trying the second.

Summary and Conclusions

This chapter has primarily discussed determinants of demand for the output of individual firms, whether they represent goods or services. It does not attempt to explain the many types of intangible benefits that are sought by businesses and thus is limited to determinants of firms' financial benefits. More specifically, it mainly discusses the factors which determine the number of units of output that a firm will be able to sell at different prices.

A firm's sales can be explained by factors common to all sellers in its industry as well as by factors that affect it in particular. To a considerable extent, a firm's sales reflect its own activities and most particularly its marketing skills. The concept of marketing mix illuminates the decisions that management must make in allocating its resources among the alternative means it might employ to increase sales. It was suggested that most firms differ far more in marketing than in production capabilities.

Actions firms take to increase demand—readiness to buy—were distinguished from those simply aimed at increasing sales. The first is usually far more difficult to accomplish than the second. In addition, the demands by ultimate customers for a product were distinguished from the demands by middlemen for the same product. The concepts of derived demand and the acceleration principle help to account for the difference between demands by middlemen and ultimate customers for the same product, but beyond these, middlemen are a highly complex barrier between a producer and his market.

The characteristics of demand for an individual firm depend heavily upon its industrial environment and especially on the nature of competition it faces. In purely competitive markets, individual firms can sell all they choose at the prevailing price while, at the opposite extreme, monopolists' demand curve is the same as the demand for the entire industry and conforms to the law of demand. Demand conditions in oligopolistic markets are highly complex and depend primarily upon the manner in which rivals respond to one another's actions market.

The Computation of Benefits: A Dialog

Dave Guest and Jim Kisch are brand managers for the Harmon Stove Company. Both have been employed by the company for over five years since their graduation from college. Both are extremely ambitious and have pursued the study of business techniques very aggressively. This conversation, like many others between them, expresses their strong belief that "there must be a better way."

DAVE: We have to do something to improve the quality of our reports. This report, for example, is full of cost information, but the benefits data are nothing but vague prayerful assertions.

JIM: I know the problem, but it seems unavoidable. You can get accountants, purchasing agents, and engineers to provide lots of data on costs; but when a report writer gets around to estimating the benefits of an action, he is largely on his own. Usually he ends up by providing thinly disguised guesses.

DAVE: Does it have to be that way? Can't we develop specialists in estimating benefits just the way we have them in estimating costs? After all, their estimates needn't be precise and fully reliable—certainly our cost estimates aren't accurate much of the time.

JIM: It's probably much easier to estimate costs than benefits in the great majority of situations. But aren't most of our executives supposed to be specialists in estimating benefits? I thought that our director of advertising was our chief expert on the benefits we get when we advertise, and that our sales manager was an expert in estimating the effects on sales of using more or different kinds of salesmen.

DAVE: You're right in a way, but there is a major difference between estimates of costs and estimates of benefits. Advertising and sales managers and others just don't regard themselves as expert estimaters of benefits. Most of them even deny that anyone can be an expert in such matters. Some managers have been outraged when I asked them to estimate the effects of expenditures in their specialized area.

JIM: But we do get some numbers on benefits. We get statements like "We should obtain an increase of at least 10 percent in unit sales, with a probable increase of over 15 percent." Sometimes we get more cautious statements like "Our best conservative estimate suggests that the sales increase obtained if this program is executed as herein described will be in the neighborhood of 15 percent." From that point on, the report is written and the computations made as if a 15 percent increase in sales is an absolute certainty.

DAVE: I know what you mean. The report I'm complaining about was Bill's proposal to redesign our line of stoves—to improve their performance capabilities as well as their attractiveness.

JIM: Well, it's about time we did something like that, given the mediocrity of our sales performance and the length of time since our last redesign.

DAVE: I agree. I wasn't complaining about the proposal but about the fact that there was nothing you could get your teeth into on the subject of sales or price increases that we could hope to get.

JIM: A product redesign would help us with our distributors and key retail accounts who've been hollering for some improvement in our stoves for quite some time now.

DAVE: Sure, but that's not the point. You should see the enormous detail that Bill presented on costs—a model of thoroughness and detail; it was so well presented that it took me a while to realize that the really key numbers were just pulled out of thin air.

JIM: The cost section probably was prepared for Bill by one of the young eager beavers in the accounting department. I sure hope that Bill looked over his shoulder, though, or we'll find all kinds of cost allocations in his figures that really don't belong.

DAVE: I don't know who prepared the cost data, but whoever it was sure did intimidate everyone. No one would dare to question the numbers, unless he spent many hours finding out how each one was put together. But the estimate of the sales effect of the redesign consisted of a single figure, simply labeled as "our sales department's best estimate."

JIM: It could be that a great deal of market research went into arriving at that figure, even though that fact was not noted in the report. On the other hand, it could simply be that the number was arrived at very casually by several guys who have no particular competence for making such estimates.

DAVE: I didn't want to embarrass Bill by asking how that estimate was arrived at, because after all, he's one of my closest friends—I'd ask him questions like that in private. But no one else asked, either. It seems that all of us have come to expect and accept such loose estimates of benefits. As long as that continues, our estimates will continue to be loose—and lead us to make some foolish decisions.

JIM: As a minimum, you'd think we would get a list or range of outcomes, perhaps with probabilities assigned to different outcomes. And you'd think we'd be told what factors would account for the different outcomes.

DAVE: That is the very minimum that we should tolerate, but we almost never get up to that minimum. Still, I sympathize with anyone who tries to estimate the effect of a redesign of our line on prices and unit sales. Apart from separate estimates of sales and prices—which should be made for at least two years ahead, since the effects are not all immediate by any means—a lot of important intangibles have to be considered, like the reactions of our distributors and the largest retailers who sell our line.

JIM: That's right; those intangibles may be the chief benefits we derive, but they should be translated into some monetary equivalent.

DAVE: That's true and very important. If we don't do that, we end up by either ignoring them or by assigning such a high but unspecified value to them that we go ahead with the redesign no matter how small the monetary returns.

JIM: This whole issue of quantifying intangible benefits—or costs, for that matter—is thorny. You have to link intangible benefits to some subsequent tangible gain. For example, if we redesign our line of stoves, it's not just to win the appreciation and love of our distributors for its own sake; we want to please them so that we can get more from them in one way or another.

DAVE: That's right; we want to induce better distributors to carry our line and get rid of some of our weak-sister distributors. And we want to be able to get our stoves into some large metropolitan retailers who now stick their nose up in the air when our salesmen call on them.

JIM: Right. We must ask ourselves how many and what kinds of distributors we expect to attract by the product redesign and what effect they will have on our sales and net profits. By estimating those effects, we can change our intangible benefits into tangibles. The biggest mistake we could make is to assume that because distributors would be pleased we will automatically benefit. Sometimes you do things that make our distributors very happy but they don't do anything to increase our business.

DAVE: Yes, but by pleasing our distributors we accumulate goodwill that permits us to displease them in the future. What I'm saying is that goodwill also can get translated into a tangible benefit in the future—it could enable us to do something to our advantage that displeases them. For example, we might persuade them to have their salesmen put some of our point-of-sale signs in retail stores, or even take lower margins on a few models during a special sales promotion.

JIM: I have no difficulty with that point—in that event the things we might do that displease them presumably would yield us some measurable benefit. That is what we'd want to estimate and include as our tangible benefit.

DAVE: I think that approach makes excellent sense, even though it still requires lots of soul-searching. But at least it tells you what to search your soul for.

JIM: The thing that makes the job manageable for me is that I don't try to come up with a single figure. Instead, I list a series of outcomes that seem reasonable to me and then assign each of them a probability.

DAVE: That isn't very easy, but it sure is easier to identify a variety of outcomes than try to forecast the single true outcome.

JIM: Yes, it is easier, and for an obvious reason. No one knows the true outcome—and may not even know it after the event. So, why even try to do domething that is manifestly impossible. On the other hand, reasonable people can think of the outcomes that might come to pass—and estimate their likelihood.

DAVE: You make the process sound simpler than it really is. But I buy the logic of it. So we come back to my original question about developing experts in estimating benefits. Are there principles and concepts that we might teach our executives that would make them better specialists in estimating benefits?

JIM: Yes, there are. The basic idea is that benefits almost always come from six main sources: from your colleagues, from ultimate customers, resellers, rivals, suppliers, and government. And the benefits divide into tangible and intangible benefits. So you might say we have 12 broad categories of benefits to begin.

DAVE: That sounds like a good beginning. It suggests where to look for benefits and what forms they are likely to have. We could go one step further and try to identify the key benefits we might get from the different sources that you listed, and classify them according to whether they are tangible or intangible.

JIM: That should be very worthwhile. If you like, I'll take a crack at putting something together along those lines in the next few days.

DAVE: Great, why don't you give it a try? Maybe between us we can create a form that permits executives to gather together all the benefit information relevant to key decisions. It would be something like the balance sheets and P & L statements that accountants use—almost any accountant can organize his data without reinventing the wheel, which is what we seem to do every time we set down benefits in a report.

JIM: Good idea. I'll try to organize my thoughts in a structure that might be used as a standard form, of sorts.

DAVE: Fine, why don't you call me when you've made a start that seems promising and we'll talk about it some more. Maybe we can meet the beginning of next week.

JIM: Okay. I'll be calling you in a few days or so to set up a date.

*   *   *

DAVE: So this is the form you put together [see Chapter 3, Table 3-2]. It looks very interesting and useful. Are you satisfied with it?

JIM: Well, I think I could extend the lists of possible benefits; also, it would be useful to provide more room for the report writer to comment about each item.

DAVE: I wouldn't worry about either of those shortcomings at this point. After all, you left room to add benefits that were not listed; and the comments should probably be presented as footnotes anyhow. If you do that, the writer can use all the space he wants.

JIM: True. I guess that another weakness in the form is that it calls for putting one figure in for each item; I wonder whether it shouldn't call for estimates for, say, four successive six-month periods.

DAVE: Good idea; and, maybe beyond those four, you could include a total, which would represent the amount to be obtained over the indefinite future. That amount might be expressed as present value.

JIM: That should be easy to work out and sounds very worth doing. We would then have five columns: one entitled, "Total, present value"; another called "1st six months"; and three others entitled "2nd six months," 3rd six months," and "4th six months." But there's another difficulty that I haven't mentioned, maybe because it's so hard to handle—that is the problem of uncertainty.

DAVE: That really is a tough one, but we don't deal with uncertainty in our cost estimates either. So I won't feel too badly if we simply added an instruction to "express estimates as a range where necessary." This instruction still wouldn't get the estimator to set down the different outcomes that he foresees and the probabilities that he attaches to each one, but it would sometimes get us more than a single figure. If he wanted to give lots of information about different possible outcomes, he could do so in the footnotes.

JIM: Well, the only way we can test and improve this form is by applying it to a concrete proposal. How about some of the major sales promotions we've been working on? Why don't we take the most recent one—the proposal we drew up to run our last Thanksgiving promotion? You know, the one based on the claim that ours is the only stove that will cook turkey with the slow and even heat needed for maximum tenderness.

DAVE: Yes, I remember it well. The creative people got a great idea that we could turn one of our weaknesses into a strength and associate our relatively unchanging stove design with the old kitchen stove that so many people get sentimental about.

JIM: That promotion should help to test this form, but I wouldn't take any one test as definitive.

DAVE: I understand that; still, it makes sense to see how your form might work when applied to that kind of decision, and then maybe we could apply it to the redesign of our stoves. We needn't review the sales promotion decision in detail, only enough to test the basic logic of the form.

JIM: Okay. Let's start. Clearly the campaign was intended to generate added sales—more sales than we would have gotten if we hadn't run the promotion. So we'd expect our main benefit to be in the section entitled "ultimate customer." That's where I would enter the benefit of selling more of our products at retail, even though our firm does not even sell directly to most retailers and never sells to ultimate customers.

DAVE: That makes sense. As I recall, we identified three things involved in that promotion that were expected to boost sales: quality claims that were set forth in the advertising—these were new claims for us; second, we advertised more than we usually do; and, third, we offered a temporary price reduction to our distributors and large retail accounts that we asked them to pass along to their customers.

JIM: That's right. I think we estimated the combined effect of those three factors to be something like an increase in sales of 1,000 stoves during the six weeks of our promotion.

DAVE: That's what I remember too. And we translated that increase in sales into a profits figure by taking the incremental costs on the stoves, which were only about 45 percent of our price, and multiplying that number of dollars by 1,000. That gave us a figure of about $70,000, as I recall.

JIM: That's about right. As I remember that whole calculation—the extra sales and the incremental costs—it was done very cavalierly. We seemed to feel that our calculations were almost academic. At least that's the way I felt. I was sure that we were going ahead with the promotion no matter what we estimated its effects to be—because we almost always have run such a promotion in the past.

DAVE: That's how I felt also—and that's part of our trouble. Another trouble is that we don't usually follow up on our estimates to see how they turned out, in order to profit by our mistakes.

JIM: That sounds a lot easier than it is. Take that particular Thanksgiving promotion, for example. I happened to review our sales records very carefully for the second half of 1978 in another connection. Frankly, I still can't tell you whether that promotion hurt or helped our sales.

DAVE: How come?

JIM: Just to explain one difficulty: you know that our stove sales are quite seasonal, partly reflecting variations in residential construction—both homes and apartments; partly our stove sales are influenced by gift giving, mainly at Christmas but also in connection with June weddings. And we have run a special promotion about twice a year and these have affected sales, like the one we are discussing. Now, how can I tell you how one particular promotion affected sales in any week or month?

DAVE: I still don't see the problem. Sure, lots of things affect sales. We all know that.

JIM: Well, in the first place, our sales before Thanksgiving were far above last year's and the previous months' sales in some areas while they fell behind in some others. That creates some problems in interpretation right there. And in those areas where sales were up sharply in October and the beginning of November—the time of the promotion—they were up as much in August and September over the preceding year. So were they up because of the sale or because of other reasons?

DAVE: I see that the problems of identifying the causes of sales changes from sales records really are fierce. I guess that no one really appreciates the difficulties until he gets his hands dirty working with the data; and very few of us senior executives do that. But, Jim, it seems that we've changed the subject from *estimating* benefits to *reviewing* the benefits of an action taken in the past.

JIM: True, but those issues are very closely related in my mind. You can't hope to estimate things accurately if you can't even measure them after the fact. I admitted that I didn't knock myself out to make very accurate estimates on that sales promotion, but what could we have done if we had wanted to make the best possible estimates? You couldn't even do really useful market research on this problem, as I see it.

DAVE: You might test the believability and power of the new claim, for example, but I agree that market research would not have produced a reliable estimate.

JIM: Well, then, how does one get reliable estimates? How can we develop the specialists in benefits-estimating you were talking about before?

DAVE: To be an expert estimater of the benefits to be obtained from that

Thanksgiving promotion, you should mainly have had lots of experience with similar promotions; and you should have made special efforts to appraise the impact of each one. I'm not ruling out some formal market research in addition. But we should have at least one man in our shop who knows more about promotions than anyone else—not only should he be able to dream them up, he should know more than anyone else how past promotions worked and have pretty good theories as to why some were particularly successful and others failed.

JIM: You really aren't telling me *how* to estimate the effect of a promotion on sales but *who* should be asked to make the estimate. And I'm not sure that the person who is best at dreaming up promotions would also be the guy most skilled at estimating their effects. He'd be too personally and emotionally involved with his brainchildren.

DAVE: Touchée on both points. I am only saying that we badly need good estimates of benefits and that these should be made by persons who regard such estimating to be a central part of their job and who equip themselves to make estimates of benefits as well as it is possible to do—taking account of the costs of estimating, of course. Although we may, in the end, simply rely on their intuitions rather than employ formal forecasting techniques, we might get very valuable inputs for our decisions nonetheless. Right now we get neither the fruits of well-fed intuitions nor the results of careful formal forecasting procedures.

JIM: I agree with your conclusions, and I hope you'll do some missionary work with our colleagues. But let's not give up trying to develop a form that might help executives to organize and set down their forecasts of benefits. We've indicated the difficulties of estimating the sales effects of our promotions and some ways of overcoming them slightly. What about some of the other benefits we anticipated from that promotion? Take this category of "colleagues," for example.

DAVE: I can think of something that goes in that cell, related to that Thanksgiving promotion. Especially this year, it seemed very important to boost our sales because we were facing some layoffs in the plant. We were all asked to devise measures that might avoid the layoffs. So, you might see this promotion as a measure adopted partly to help our colleagues in manufacturing and even in the finance department, which has been hurting a little for some cash flow.

JIM: Fine, we have here another interesting intangible. How do we go about placing a numerical value on it?

DAVE: You can't expect to place numerical values on anything in just a few minutes; you generally must spend some time deliberating and in making some calculations. Still, many executives are impatient with any forecast that requires considerable effort and tend to call it academic or pseudo-scientific. If I were going to place a money value on it, I'd expect to take a fair amount of time to arrive at an answer.

JIM: I understand, but how would you reason about it? What things would you devote your time to measuring or estimating.

DAVE: Well, I'd want to know the tangible effects of laying off the number of men whose jobs would be saved by a sales promotion. For example, in this case, as a result of selling 1,000 more stoves, how many men would be kept on our payroll who otherwise would be dismissed—assuming that those added sales weren't simply stoves that we would have sold anyhow, say, at Christmas?

JIM: Okay, so you'd estimate how many of those 1,000 extra stoves we estimated would be sold during the promotion would be truly extra sales rather than sales moved forward in time by the sale. Say we figured that 700 were really extra sales. Then, I take it we'd ask the manufacturing department what that means in terms of jobs saved? But that doesn't give us a figure of dollar benefits yet.

DAVE: No, but that is the starting point. We then must ask the appropriate people in the manufacturing department what is involved in the way of costs of rehiring that number of men, should we need to replace them; and how they feel these dismissals would affect the performance of the men we kept on the payroll. I understand that when workers see signs that they may lose their jobs because of a lack of orders, they tend to slow down and stretch out their jobs.

JIM: I've heard that said, but I've also seen some men work extra hard so that they'll be kept on while someone else is let go. But I guess our agreement with the union dictates that men be laid off in the order of seniority.

DAVE: I think we may have some choice in the matter. But in any event, those are the kinds of questions I'd ask; I'd take the estimates of experts and try to express them in dollar equivalents. My main problem would be to insure that I was not overlooking any item that was fairly important; some important benefit or injury might occur that you could have recognized but you didn't think of it.

JIM: I'm happy about this example of the layoff because it raises an important point that gives me trouble—and I left no room for it in the form. I'm sure that you would be much happier if we didn't have to fire anyone; it may sound unbusinesslike, but I would be willing to give something—I'd expect the stockholders to make some financial sacrifice—to see that the men who turn out our goods are spared the miseries of unemployment. I'm talking about an intangible benefit in the form of "feeling better" or avoiding the pain or shame of laying men off because we have not been able to find customers for our output—call it what you will.

DAVE: That's a really tricky point you are raising there. I certainly share your feelings about men who are laid off. And I agree that our stock-holders' profits are not sacred—and certainly not more important than our workers' lives. For most men, the loss of a job is terribly upsetting; it affects everyone in their family; it really changes their style of living dramatically and even undermines their self-respect. So of course I agree with you. You're talking about an intangible benefit that does not become tangible. To avoid that outcome is an end in itself—you might call it an ultimate goal. That being the case, we cannot value it by looking at the tangibles that would follow later.

JIM: What does that mean, in practice? Do we make a poll of the board of directors or of top management and ask how much profit they would be willing to give up to keep from laying off the men needed to produce 700 extra stores?

DAVE: I have no pat answer to that question. Logically, the value should be placed on this benefit by the owners of the business, I'd think. So in effect, you'd have to find out how much it was worth to them—in profits or dividends or stock market values for their shares, or whatever—to spare their workers so much pain. Of course, they might not share our view of how painful it is to lose a job.

JIM: I see your reasoning and I understand the process you describe well enough to employ it, should the occasion arise. There's no need to go further except to underline what you said before—that it would take considerable work to make such estimates.

DAVE: Right, but no more than we spend in estimating some fairly unimportant item of cost in some of our decisions. We have lots of men working on our cost information, don't forget. If we want to get valid estimates of benefits, we must be prepared to pay some price for them.

JIM: That's fair enough. Let me see where that leaves us. I think it's pretty clear that some parts of the form I put together would apply and others would not in the case of the Thanksgiving promotion. As far as I can see, no government benefits are involved. Are there some supplier ben-efits, do you think?

DAVE: I'd suppose there were some, but I don't know—and none of us bothered to ask when we were making our estimates. If by selling more stoves we helped out some of our suppliers who were hurting, I'm sure that our actions would give us brownie points with them in the future. But, that's another intangible that's difficult to place a value on—like being given preference if supplies were short, or letting us in on some information about some new developments that we might want to know about—things they wouldn't tell us if they had no special affection for us.

JIM: Maybe we've carried this illustration far enough for our purposes. Several useful things have come out of this discussion. First, we saw that having a form like the one I developed did direct our attention to benefits that were passed over when we made our actual estimates. Second, I get the impression that the benefits listed on the form really do cover the key things that businessmen must estimate. So, it may show that the task of devising a form for revenue-creating decisions may not be so horrendous. Certainly we shouldn't give up the effort. Finally, I have the impression that this form will actually make the job of estimating benefits seem less frightening. It breaks down the task into little pieces. Also, it makes it more respectable to do some research or to ask some questions of others. As you put it, you begin to make the job equivalent to estimating costs.

DAVE: One point comes through most sharply to me. What this or some other form would do is change our image of what a good report includes and of the amount of time and skill that should be devoted to estimating benefits. In that way it ties directly into the main point I made last week when we brought up this whole business—that it is necessary for executives to change their view of the importance of being able to estimate benefits. It is a key part of their job and they have been neglecting it all too long, if you ask me.

Chapter 13

BENEFITS VIS-À-VIS VARIOUS PARTIES TO THE BUSINESS PROCESS

T HE PHRASE "parties to the business process" designates persons and institutions who figure prominently in most major business decisions. With some notable exceptions, major decisions affect most and sometimes all of these parties, namely, colleagues, ultimate customers, resellers, suppliers, government, and rivals.*

Something will be said here about all six parties to the business process; a few will be treated at considerable length—those about which economic writings offer useful guidance to executives; others will be touched on very lightly. Economics contributes most to an understanding of the behavior of ultimate customers, rivals, and suppliers; marketing, a subfield of economics, illuminates the role of resellers.

Our purpose here is not to indicate all that is known of potential value to executives about each of the parties to the business process. Rather, we seek to establish that most business decisions affect the persons and institutions listed above and that costs and benefits take numerous forms, are subtle, often intangible, and frequently are not obvious. More important, the following discussion will concentrate on the potential benefits, on various levels, to be obtained from each party to the business process (the opposite of benefits or the reduction of benefits represents costs), and the concepts that help to understand the effects of typical business decisions on

---

* Decisions to change a process or procedure in order to reduce the cost of achieving a given result represent an important exception to that generalization. Even these decisions often have implications for competitors, suppliers, and colleagues.

each party to the process, with particular emphasis on those concepts that are unfamiliar or counter-intuitive.

A Model of the Business Process

Let us examine a very simple structural model of the business process that positions the different parties to be discussed. Figure 13-1 depicts economic activity as a vertical structure that starts with suppliers of labor, raw materials, components, professional services, and funds. The basic materials and components are assembled and transformed by manufacturers, refiners, and processors in order to produce finished goods, which are sold to middlemen, also termed resellers (wholesalers, distributors, brokers, and retailers of various kinds), which sell to ultimate customers. This model includes all parties to the business process. Observe that colleagues are to be found within the decision-making firm—here assumed to be the manufacturer. The governmental presence has been depicted as pervading the business process. Government maintains law and order and enforces contracts and laws regarding monopoly, restraint of trade, implied performance warranties, and the like.

Figure 13-1. Parties to the business process from a manufacturer's viewpoint.

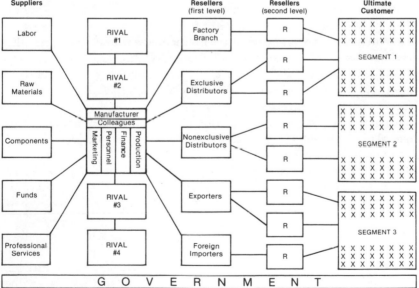

Individual industries differ in their vertical structures; some develop special institutions that are neither depicted nor implied by Figure 13-1. For example, in the industry that produces recordings (phonograph records, tapes, cassettes) one finds several special institutions (see Figure 13-2). The pool of talent which composes and performs music may be considered a supplier to the industry, but it certainly is an unusual type of supplier. In distribution, the industry has developed a variety of forms that are unusual, including rack-jobbers, "one-stops," and jukebox operators. Most unusual is the radio station and even more particularly the disk jockey. These two give exposure to music and largely create tastes. In addition, part of the industry structure consists of concert appearances and those persons who arrange concert tours for musical talent. These expose performers to the musical public and also help to mold demand for particular records and tapes.

Let us now discuss the parties to the business process individually, presenting in each case a list of the most important benefits that a producer may obtain from the source. We will then sketch the main concepts that help to explain the benefits and costs that will result from typical business decisions.

Costs and Benefits Vis-à-vis Colleagues

An executive's relationships with other members of his own firm resemble those between his firm and its suppliers and resellers: they combine elements of dependency, mutuality of interest, and conflict of interest. Although colleagues benefit mutually from the prosperity and growth of their enterprise, they may compete with each other for advancement, they may have personal animosities and jealousies, they may wish to avoid special demands upon their time and resources, and they may even resent reasonable requests from others within the firm and treat them as "favors." Nevertheless, the success of most organizations—and businesses more than most—depends upon cooperation among colleagues, frequently beyond the call of duty. Moreover, the success of most executives and of particular programs depends upon their obtaining the help of colleagues in different divisions. Often the individuals on whom they depend are not even known to the executive responsible for the program.

How Colleagues Might Be Affected

Decisions faced by executives often affect their colleagues, mainly as unintended consequences. For example, they may provide work for another division at a time when it otherwise might be compelled to furlough some workers; on the other hand, they might impose demands on another

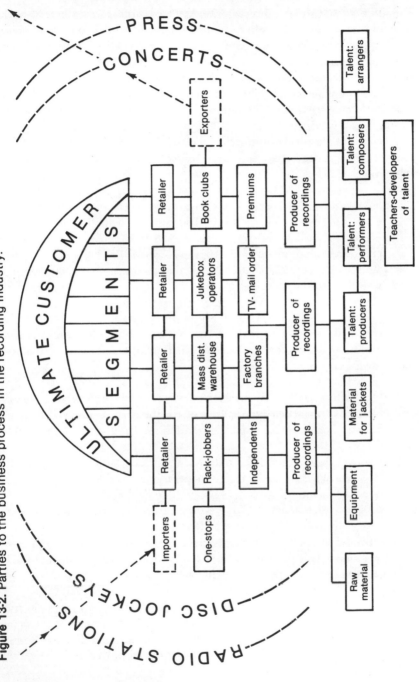

Figure 13-2. Parties to the business process in the recording industry.

division that was already overextended. They could add to or reduce the costs of another division, help to bring it closer to attaining its own objectives or pull it farther away. Such consequences, whether or not they were intended, represent costs and benefits of decisions that must be taken into account. A decision that helps colleagues achieve their objectives is, all other things equal, far preferable to one that would injure them; a decision that wins future cooperation from colleagues is to be favored over one that would create hostility.

To consider the effects of individual decisions on colleagues an executive must answer at least two sets of questions. The first set includes the following:

- Upon which of my colleagues does the success of this decision depend? That is, which of my colleagues will help to implement the decision?
- What level of competence do they possess to perform their function?
- Will they cooperate and do what is reasonably within their power to make the decision succeed?

The answers to these questions are required simply to forecast the actions that will occur as a result of the decision. The following questions must also be asked in order to evaluate the full costs and benefits of almost every decision:

- What effect will this decision have on the performance of my colleagues—on their contribution to the firm's profitability and growth? That is, will it help them to achieve the goals that were set for them?
- How will the contemplated decision affect their future performance in situations where I need their cooperation? Will I get more or less assistance in the future as a result of this decision? And, what favors will colleagues demand of me in the future because of this decision?

Let us now list in fairly general terms the kinds of benefits (and costs) that a decision maker may obtain vis-à-vis his colleagues in connection with a major decision. This list is selective as well as general.

- Colleagues achieve their own objectives more fully—the decision helps them to realize their targets.
- They produce greater profits for the firm—possibly because their costs (per unit) have fallen as a result of the decision.

- They are able to avoid a costly or painful action—like firing some workers or having a furlough.
- They obtain experience as a result of the decision that makes them more effective in the future.
- They become less fearful of us because of their experience on this project.
- They learn what we can do to help them and what they might do to help us.
- We may earn return favors.
- We learn more about what they can and cannot do.
- We gain allies in future potential conflicts.

Colleagues are essentially people with whom one is ordinarily in close contact. An almost endless list of rules has been developed on "how to win friends and influence people" which reflect the wisdom and cynicism of the ages. Before presenting a selective list of such rules, it is useful to discuss several models and concepts that can help executives take account of colleagues in their decisions.

The transactions model.* The basic notion involved in the transactions model is that few relationships endure that are not mutually beneficial. Parties to an enduring relationship must give and receive in roughly equal amounts. If one party must give without getting, he/she has no incentive to maintain the relationship. An oblique way of summarizing this idea is to say, "There is no such thing as a free lunch." If you get something from someone, you must be prepared to give something that person values roughly as much as what he has given to you.

Accordingly, if you seek cooperation from colleagues, you must also offer it. When you receive a favor, you must at least give clear credit and appreciation and also be prepared to reciprocate. In computing the costs of a decision, for example, you should estimate the value of future obligations it requires you to assume.

Communication with colleagues. The word "communication" has been extended to mean just about every aspect of interpersonal relations and thus it communicates very little. The following points related to communications among colleagues deserve emphasis:

- We are always communicating something to others, even when we are silent. Our nonverbal communications often are given far more weight by others than the words we say.

---

* Not to be confused with "transactional analysis" (TA).

- People around us notice us no matter what we do and will invariably form a judgment about us; rarely will this judgment be neutral.
- If we do not disclose something personal about ourselves to others, they will usually mistrust us and will withhold all but trivial information from us. (This notion is an application of the transaction model.)
- People want to know what we think about them, and their evaluations of us tend to match what they believe we think of them. This tendency explains the great power of praise and flattery.
- Almost every individual needs appreciation; to ignore him is to pronounce him worthless; to dislike or criticize him is to set his worth very low. He can forgive neither.
- We all make mistakes; executives inevitably make many; the biggest mistake we can make is to claim infallibility. Defensiveness wastes loads of energy and time and undermines one's credibility.
- The ability to sell—that is, win accepance for—one's ideas is almost as vital to success as the ability to conceive ideas.
- Praise is costless and sometimes far more valuable than gold. One rarely finds examples of damage from excessive approval or commendation. Excessive criticism leave scars that take a long time to heal—and often never do.
- The reactions of others to our ideas often depends on their reaction to us rather than to our proposals. We must not expect to win simply because we are correct. (And how often can we really be sure of what is correct?)
- Everybody is "out for No. 1"—including us. We must cover our flanks and not trust fully those who would gain from our defeats.
- Loyalty of friends and associates cannot be considered permanent. We must therefore avoid the temptation to be *completely* frank and revealing when we feel warm and friendly toward a colleague.
- Most people tend to resent the success of others. They are particularly resentful of claims for credit for some accomplishment that seem excessive.

Benefits Vis-à-vis Ultimate Customers

OBJECTIVES: ULTIMATE AND INSTRUMENTAL

Chapter 12 discussed the determinants of primary and secondary demand, and much of that discussion is relevant here. Stated very simply, the major point is that business executives seek one ultimate goal from ultimate customers above all others—high revenues, or strong demand. This goal can be subdivided into customer willingness to pay a high price, customer readiness to consume large quantities, and stability of purchase over time. (Other instrumental goals will be indicated, but these three are the most important.)

Businesses also seek the ultimate goal of low cost to serve their ultimate customers. Accordingly, they would like to induce their customers to buy in quantities that are convenient and inexpensive for the seller to supply. Similarly, they want their customers to buy when it is most convenient and inexpensive to sell to them, and they want customers to perform services that otherwise would impose costs on the seller—like delivery, assembly, packaging, performing minor repairs, and installing items that require installation. All these benefits would reduce costs to the seller, and reduce money costs to the buyer also. (The buyers' total costs, including time, energy, frustration, and so on, might be greatly increased.)

Some business objectives are more or less sequential—that is, they are attained in a particular order so that one must be realized before the next can be achieved. One such sequential set of objectives is the so-called hierarchy of effects. It suggests that the following stages occur sequentially in a consumer purchase: awareness, knowledge, liking, preference, conviction, and then purchase. Alternative sequential models are: attention, interest, desire, and action; also awareness, interest, evaluation, trial, and adoption. All three of these hierarchies suggest that customers must be attracted, interested, informed, and motivated before they will make a purchase.

Economists discuss demand determinants at length, but mainly on a general and abstract level, and they say little about customers; they stress above all else the effect of personal income and price on demand. An executive making decisions affecting ultimate customers must be concerned with many more factors than these.

Executives have two main interests with regard to their ultimate customers: to forecast demand conditions so that they might produce what customers want in the quantities that are wanted; and to expand demand—that is, persuade customers to buy more and pay higher prices and be loyal and reliable patrons. Figure 13-3 presents the more important benefits a firm might obtain from ultimate customers. They are shown in hierarchical form to emphasize means-ends relationships. The chart also relates these benefits to the firm's ultimate objectives. Table 13-1 lists a number of benefits obtainable from ultimate customers. These are classified according to whether they take an attitudinal or behavioral form.

Most firms can employ varied measures to pursue these benefits—price, product quality, design, advertising, personal selling, customer service, credit accommodation, product assortment, accessibility to the product,

Figure 13-3. Subobjectives related to ultimate customers.

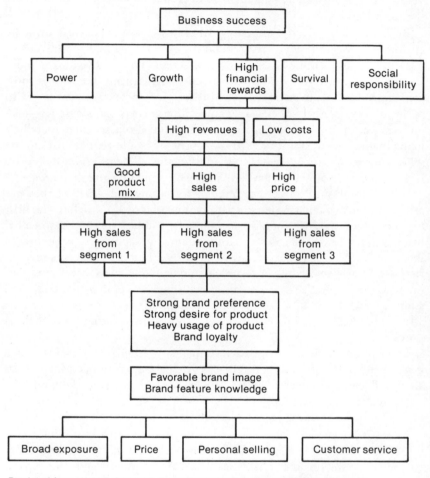

Reprinted from Alfred R. Oxenfeldt, *Pricing Strategies* (New York: AMACOM, 1975), p. 86.

speedy delivery, and the like. Some important concepts relate to sellers' use of these means for influencing customer behavior.

CONCEPTUAL BASIS OF ACTIONS TO AFFECT THE ULTIMATE CUSTOMER

Concepts related to marketing mix elements. Measures that sellers might employ to stimulate demand for their offering are termed marketing mix elements. The effect of each marketing mix element on ultimate customers

Table 13-1

SELECTED SUBOBJECTIVES RELATED TO ULTIMATE CUSTOMERS

Attitudinal Subobjectives
1. Attitude toward product that is wanted in ultimate customers.
   a. That product is essential.
   b. That the purchaser is expected to use it.
   c. That its use gives a person a desired social position.
   d. Favorable belief about the benefits to be derived from the product.
   e. Favorable belief about the kinds of people who use the product.
   f. Belief that the product is within the purchaser's means.
2. Attitudes toward the company that makes the product.
   a. Its preeminence in technology.
   b. Its concern for its customers.
   c. Its capacity to endure and its willingness to honor its guarantees.
3. Attitudes toward the brand.
   a. Belief in its high quality.
   b. Belief in its repair or replacement in the event of defect or failure.
   c. Belief in its social position—actually in the kinds of people who buy it.

Facilitating Purchase Subobjectives
1. The product is readily available.
2. Payment arrangements are convenient.
3. Packaging is convenient and delivery can be arranged.

Behavioral Subobjectives
1. High level of usage.
2. Large-quantity purchase at each transaction.
3. Purchase at time convenient for the seller.
4. Customer performance of service that reduces the seller's costs.
5. Favorable word-of-mouth support.
6. Large customer inventories of the product.
7. Customer purchase by cash or credit, whichever is advantageous for seller.
8. Quick customer response to special inducements.

Miscellaneous Subobjectives
1. Attract potential customer's attention to the product, the brand, special product features, or particular promotions.
2. Increase number of potential customers that consider patronizing you—win and keep a place on their list of acceptable suppliers.
3. Obtain valid market information about what customers want and how they would respond to different actions that the seller might take.

Reprinted from Alfred R. Oxenfeldt, *Pricing Strategies* (New York: AMACOM, 1975), p. 87.

usually differs when taken alone rather than taken in combination with others. The concepts of synergy, redundancy, cancellation, and neutrality describe the different effects of actions in combination.

"Synergy" is sometimes defined as a condition in which two plus two equals five. Synergy thus means that in particular combinations each of two or more activities gains in effectiveness—they achieve the user's goals more fully in combination than when taken separately. Or, the whole is greater than the sum of the parts.

"Redundancy" represents the opposite situation: it may be defined as two plus two equals three. In a redundancy situation, each of the activities is partly wasted because it does what the other activity has already done. For example, a combined price cut and advertising appeal could work as follows: each alone would affect 500 persons and induce them to make a purchase. It might happen that 200 of those convinced by the price cut would also be convinced to buy by the advertising alone. Either one would have been sufficient to induce a purchase. Consequently, the combined effect of the price reduction and the increased advertising was 800, rather than 1,000 (500 + 500). Recognize that the seller would *not* sell 1,000 units if he were to reduce price and increase advertising separately—though taken separately either action would produce sales of 500 extra units.

"Cancellation" might be defined as two plus two equals one. In such combinations, each activity actually reduces the effect of the other. Cancellation occurs most commonly when actions are incompatible or when either action alone is believable, but taken together they create strong mistrust.

"Neutrality" exists when two plus two equals four—the actions have the same affect in combination as when taken separately.

The chief implication of these concepts is that executives should search out synergistic combinations of actions, rather than think in terms of single ingredient actions. And they must be alert to the highly common phenomena of redundancy and cancellation. To sharpen such alertness, they must collect and analyze information about sales determinants to take full account of such interrelationships. Generally speaking, a skilled executive is aware of the "programs"—combinations of actions that provide maximum synergy; they always look for "add-ons"—things that now become effective because of added actions that are to be taken. Above all, they become experts in a new mathematics in which two plus two almost never equals four.

Misperception. A vital concept that explains the effects of sellers' actions on potential customers is "misperception." Different individuals do not see any given situation in the same way. Some don't see things that are there; a few even see things that do not exist. For example, a firm might reduce its price without many of its potential customers perceiving the change; some people may actually mistake the price reduction for a price increase. Sellers accordingly must make special efforts to communicate clearly to potential customers about the benefits contained in their offering. They cannot assume that because something is true—that is, their prices are lower or the service they offer is better—potential customers will perceive that reality correctly. Indeed, they must always question the validity of their own perceptions.

As indicated earlier, one form of misperception is nonperception. The most common example of nonperception in business occurs when a firm does something to influence the behavior of workers or potential customers, but the target of the action does not even know that an action was taken. What people do not perceive will not influence them. Accordingly, to forecast the effects of any decision, one must estimate the number of persons who will perceive it.

Beyond perception, an action intended to alter behavior must pass two added barriers to achieve its intended effects: first, it must be interpreted favorably; and, second, it must be evaluated in the manner desired. Let us examine these two potential barriers to effective action.

From perception to purchase. Most actions can be interpreted in various—and sometimes in contradictory—ways. For example, a price reduction can be interpreted as a genuine improvement in the terms on which one can buy an item, or it may be interpreted as evidence that the item is in excessive supply, is not selling well, or even is defective in some way. One interpretation would increase the probability of purchase; the others would discourage purchase.

Even if individuals perceive and interpret favorably some action taken by a seller, they may not make a purchase. Underlying a decision to buy is an evaluation by customers of their entire situation and the conclusion that, under the circumstances and with the future developments they anticipate, they would be wise to make a purchase. Many individuals who know that prices have been reduced for some item and interpret the reduction as a real bargain nevertheless conclude that they either cannot afford to make a purchase or that they do not need a new one or they need something else more. So despite valid perception and favorable interpretation the potential customer's evaluation may result in a decision not to purchase.

Market segmentation. People, markets, organizations, firms, schools, teachers, employees—indeed, just about everything—are diverse. Even peas in a pod are quite dissimilar. We err seriously if we view all people as being like the average. Perhaps the most common mistake in all walks of life is to assume that the results of some research showing that most people do a certain something imply that everyone does that same something. Very successful businesses can be built on serving people who differ greatly from the average.

If possible, an executive should treat everyone like the unique individual that he/she is. In some spheres of business that often is impossible. For example, most firms try to sell to masses of customers rather than to small numbers, each of whom is known to the producer. So the seller can neither treat them as all like the average or as unique individuals. Rather, the seller must adopt an intermediate position and try to distinguish the most important subgroups or types. A "type" is composed of individuals possessing certain characteristics in common but dissimilar in other respects. For example, one might distinguish among users of toothpaste those who mainly seek to forestall cavities, those who seek pleasant breath, and those who seek whiteness of teeth. Or, one can classify buyers of phonograph records according to whether or not they enjoy shopping in stores where contemporary music is being played at high volume, whether they want to hear music before they make a purchase, whether they buy singles or albums, and the like.

Mainly the practice of dividing a group into its subtypes has been developed by political analysts and later by marketing specialists. As carried out by the latter group, the process is termed market segmentation. However, the fundamental idea is no more complicated than simple classification, with a particular end in view. Segmentation (classification) is most useful for personnel and purchasing specialists and is indispensable to those specializing in financial matters, for they must classify securities, different forms of financial assets, different degrees of credit worthiness, and the like. Unfortunately, this relatively simple and obvious idea is frequently ignored or misapplied.

Inertia. In many respects, modern business is highly volatile; certainly, almost everything about a business changes more rapidly by far than it did, say, 50 years ago. On the other hand, one observes considerable inertia over substantial periods of time. Firms enjoy good reputations for quality of product long after their output is mediocre or worse. Goodwill and customer loyalty are established facts of business life and represent terms that describe the resistance of individuals to change.

"Inertia" means that even though a firm may offer a substantially better value than it did before, many persons who would benefit from buying it will not do so. They will be slow to perceive the change and slow to alter their purchasing habits. As a result of inertial forces, which are largely psychological in nature, the costs of change are very substantial and it occurs slowly.

Costs and Benefits Vis-à-vis Resellers

Few producers sell directly to the ultimate users of their products; consumers buy goods from retailers rather than from manufacturers. Similarly, basic raw materials and the major components that enter into industrial products (such as machinery, complex components, buildings) are purchased by original equipment manufacturers (termed OEM) rather than the actual users of these products and sometimes through sales agents, factory representatives ("reps"), and brokers. Those who buy a product for resale "as is" or for resale after further processing or assembly are omnipresent rather than exceptional. It is they whom producers must persuade to buy in the first instance. Accordingly, their responses are key determinants of the attractiveness of most major business decisions.

Resellers partly respond to and reflect the reactions of ultimate customers. That is, their demand for products is largely derived from the demands of ultimate customers. Beyond this, resellers determine what things will be offered to consumers. They also influence the interpretation that customers put on the claims made by manufacturers and the value they see in rival brands. When resellers offer competing brands, as they usually do, they frequently exert a dominant influence on consumers' brand choices.

Resellers are different from ultimate customers in some vital respects, even though they are ignored in traditional economic analyses. Price theory, for example, analyzes the wholly atypical situation in which producers sell to ultimate customers. The plain fact is that resellers are almost universally present and differ markedly from ultimate customers in important respects. For that reason, they deserve special attention. And in forecasting their responses, one cannot apply to them the economic propositions developed to explain buyer behavior. To understand why this is so, let us first describe the typical relationship between manufacturers and their resellers.

Nature of Manufacturer-Reseller Relationship

The overwhelming proportion of resellers are independent businesses that sell the products of many different suppliers; their overriding goal is profits. The same statements apply to most manufacturers. However, resellers and manufacturers are not unrestrained antagonists in their dealings with one another. They do not simply struggle to win the best possible terms from the other. Indeed, they are more friend than foe because most actions which help one usually benefit the other. For example, both share a common interest in large sales. When resellers sell little, they buy little from their sources; conversely, large sales by middlemen result in large sales by their suppliers. And such large sales are possible only because they can obtain adequate supplies of attractive merchandise. Resellers patronize suppliers in fairly direct proportion to their own sales.

A special feature of the manufacturer-reseller relationship is that both expect it to continue for a long period of time. Accordingly, each one views any action by the other in terms of its impact on his long-run profitability, security, and growth. Not infrequently, manufacturers and resellers incur costs and forgo profits to maintain and strengthen their relationship with one another.

Although their interests coincide to a considerable degree, an underlying conflict of economic interest does exist between manufacturers and resellers. Even while seeking to maintain an enduring and mutually advantageous relationship and evoke the support of the other, each party wishes to obtain as much as possible for himself. Manufacturer-reseller relationships involve implied threats on both the producer and reseller side. In addition to the threat to replace the other, the possibility exists that one will perform the other's function—that is, will integrate vertically.

DIFFERENCES BETWEEN RESELLERS AND ULTIMATE CUSTOMERS

In explaining the forces determining price, economic theorists assume that the seller will seek high prices and buyers will seek low ones. On the other hand, manufacturers must be concerned that their reseller-customers obtain a satisfactory margin of profit on their merchandise for otherwise the resellers will not carry their line. In the ordinary theory of price, sellers seek the price that yields maximum profits and are not concerned with the welfare of their customers.

Another difference: whereas ultimate customers welcome a reduction in the price they pay, resellers may oppose price reductions. Resellers, unlike most ultimate customers, often hold sizable inventories. A reduction in price charged by the manufacturer imposes an inventory loss on the reseller. If the reseller continues to set price by adding the same percentage to his invoice cost, then his unit profit declines when the price he pays is reduced. (With a 40 percent markup on price, a reduction in a manufacturers price from \$20 to \$16 would mean a reduction in the reseller's price from \$33.33 to \$26.67.) Whereas his unit profit had been \$13.33, it would be \$10.67 after the reduction in price to him.

The manufacturer might argue that the retailer could sell more units at the lower price, but that contention probably would be debated. Many businessmen apparently underrate the stimulative effect of price reductions on sales—that is, they underestimate the price elasticity of demand.

These reasons help to explain why many resellers react violently against price reductions, so much so that many manufacturers refund some of the inventory loss to their resellers to soften their wrath. Not all resellers respond in the manner described; however, that response is quite usual and manufacturers must consider it a real threat.

Other differences between resellers and ultimate customers explain why executives should use different theoretical concepts in forecasting resellers' responses to their actions. Resellers often cooperate with manufacturers in order to increase sales to the ultimate customer. For example, manufacturers and resellers sometimes agree to lower their profit margins in order to reduce the price to the ultimate customer and thus increase sales markedly. Resellers sometimes join together in associations for their protection against injury from manufacturers, whereas that is almost unknown among ultimate customers. (Panels of distributors and of retailers are increasingly common and these panels often defend the economic interests of the resellers.) The responses of resellers to actions by manufacturers require many decisions: mainly, whether or not to carry the item, whether or not to give it strong sales support, and how much to buy; for the most part, the ultimate customers' responses are limited to the last of these. Resellers pose one threat that is rarely met among ultimate customers—that of vertical integration; large resellers may decide to produce an item for themselves or they may have them produced for them under a private label.

The "pass-through" problem is another difference between ultimate customers and resellers that requires discussion. A supplier usually wants his resellers to transmit to their customers the stimuli that he gives to the resellers—specifically, price reductions, or product information. We speak of this benefit as "the pass-through" of the supplier's actions.

Finally, suppliers often make demands on their reseller-customers—something they almost never do with ultimate customers. For example, they may run a large national promotion backed up by heavy national advertising at a time that is most inconvenient for their resellers. To participate in such promotions, a reseller may be forced to acquire and pay for added merchandise, rearrange his showrooms, contribute to advertising, alter his margins, indoctrinate his salesmen, and so on—things that might be easier for him at some time than at others. Such demands are always a potential source of resentment from resellers who might feel that "they are being pushed around."

BENEFITS THAT SUPPLIERS CAN OBTAIN FROM RESELLERS

What effects of their decisions on resellers should manufacturers be concerned with mainly? That is, what are the specific benefits and costs that manufacturers can anticipate from resellers? By far the most important benefits that guide manufacturers' actions vis-à-vis resellers are as follows:

- Their best resellers will continue to carry the brand.
- Good resellers will add the brand to their offerings.

Figure 13-4. Benefits a manufacturer might obtain from resellers.

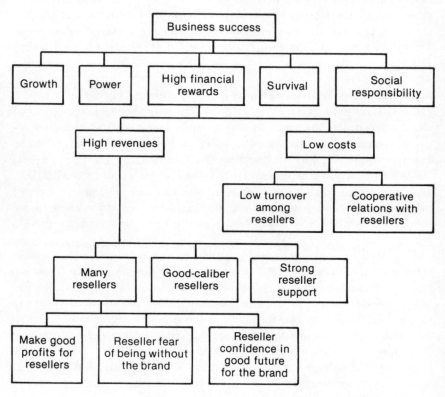

Reprinted from Alfred R. Oxenfeldt, *Pricing Strategies* (New York: AMACOM, 1975), p. 149.

- Resellers will give them a larger "position" among their offerings—that is, buy a larger proportion of their requirements from them.
- Resellers will increase the sales support they give the brand.
- Resellers will carry larger inventories and a larger number of models, colors, and styles.

Figure 13-4 depicts graphically the highest-level benefits that manufacturers might obtain from resellers. Some lower-level objectives and benefits are:

1. Secure broad exposure of product to potential customers.
2. Obtain strong sales support from resellers.

- Have them invest their own funds in advertising, perhaps through co-op advertising plan.
- Obtain disproportionate amount of space in resellers' display space.
- Obtain disproportionate space in catalogs, stores, or shelves.
- Have resellers develop a specialized sales force to sell your product.
- Have reseller salesmen give disproportionate time to your product.

3. Induce resellers to drop rival lines, especially those that are strongest competitors.
4. Induce resellers to hold in stock more items in your line.
5. Have resellers carry larger inventories of each item in your line.
6. Have resellers offer good service on your product, especially in the event it does not function well.
7. Obtain fast and reliable market research information from resellers.
8. Obtain useful suggestions from resellers.
9. Have resellers provide a pool of manpower suitable for employment, especially for such positions as regional salesmen and managers of factory branches.
10. Have resellers carry out and transmit your policies to customers.
11. Have resellers contribute to cost reduction.
    - Induce resellers to place orders at convenient time—generally early in season.
    - Induce resellers to pay bills without frequent urging.
    - Have resellers perform repairs and minor adjustments without involving factory.
    - Have resellers accept delivery at convenient times and in amounts that are economical for the factory.
    - Induce resellers to process orders and return in an efficient way for the factory.

Supplier Actions for Gaining Reseller-Related Benefits

We will try to relate the main benefits that suppliers might seek from resellers to the actions that might achieve them. In particular, we ask what suppliers do to hold and gain strong resellers and to get added sales support from resellers.

Actions that affect the number and quality of resellers carrying the brand. Resellers vary greatly in their worth to a supplier. Some have strong specialized sales forces and can command a substantial share of the market for almost any item they carry; they are financially reliable, carry large and broad inventories, and will undertake substantial promotional activity on their own behalf. Others seem barely able to make sales when customers place orders, are always in arrears in paying their bills, buy on a hand-to-mouth basis, and do not promote. Presumably they are retained because the supplier cannot find anyone better to carry the line, or because they produce some extra business without reducing the willingness of others to carry the line.

For their part, resellers constantly search for products and brands that will yield a profit. Ordinarily they seek brands that have wide customer acceptance, partly because the supplier promotes it actively. In particular, they seek such lines if they yield an attractive profit margin, which occurs only if the brand is protected, in some way, from intensive price competition. In other words, when suppliers do things that reduce the profitability of their line to resellers, the latter will have a smaller incentive to carry the brand. And the supplier will become more vulnerable to a competitor who is actively seeking better resellers. Conversely, as a supplier's line becomes easier to sell and less subject to cutthroat price competition, it attracts the strongest resellers to its line.

The decisions by suppliers that usually affect the attractiveness of a line to resellers are as follows: price decisions; the number of other resellers permitted to sell the brand; decisions about advertising effort—amount, content, audience; product design; willingness to sell to price cutters; provision of credit; quantity discount schedules; and willingness to "hold inventories" for resellers.

Actions that gain sales support from resellers. Just as resellers evaluate lines on grounds of their long-term profitability, they allocate their resources—their salesmen's time, inventory space and funds to hold inventory, their advertising outlays—to obtain the greatest profit. Resellers frequently change abruptly the items they push. Major promotions by suppliers usually are intended to induce their resellers to make greater efforts to favor their brand over others. Again, the supplier's motive, the "real" effects of his actions and the effects that resellers anticipate, surely diverge in many instances.

Decisions by suppliers can produce a substantial change in the sales support that resellers give to their brand. The factors that determine how much effort a reseller makes to sell a particular brand can be divided into emotional and substantive factors. The first of these consists of the reseller's affection and respect for the supplier's firm and its personnel, the number of favors he has received, and his feelings of loyalty to the organization and brand. Most resellers do have emotional favorites among their suppliers. (Some resellers feel and act like members of the supplier's organization; this feeling occurs mainly when the reseller is exclusive with one brand of a product line.) Such emotional factors account for most of the stability one finds in the lines that resellers carry and the sales support they accord individual brands.

Most of what resellers do for a brand can be explained by substantive and profit considerations. Supplier decisions that affect his resellers' profits from sales of his line concern price changes, special discounts, promotions, changes in credit terms, willingness to deliver merchandise to the reseller's customers, changes in product features, willingness to give a large reseller some models of the product with unique product features, and the like. These decisions ordinarily have profit implications for resellers. In addition, the amount of service that a supplier provides his resellers—training of salesmen, provision of point-of-sales signs and advertising mats, the keeping of their inventory records, and the like—also affects resellers' profits but mainly seems to create feelings of friendship and obligation.

How to Estimate the Costs and Benefits Vis-à-vis Resellers from Specific Decisions

To forecast the consequences of alternative actions that suppliers are considering as they affect resellers, it is suggested that suppliers ask the following questions about their resellers' responses to their intended actions in the sequence outlined.

- To what extent will resellers pass-through the action that we contemplate? The answer will take the form of a frequency distribution, for not all resellers will respond in the same manner. Most suppliers would be wise to employ a fairly detailed classification of resellers in making these estimates. Among the more important distinctions they might make are between exclusive and nonexclusive, large and small, profitable and unprofitable, those meeting quota and those persistently below quota, and urban and rural resellers.
- On the basis of the estimated pass-through, what will be the responses of ultimate customers to the action contemplated? The answer might be set down in the form of estimated percentage changes in sales to customers of the different types of reseller.
- Given the estimated response of ultimate customers, how would this action affect the gross profit of each class of reseller? Here the supplier should try to identify the resellers which would obtain a big increase in gross profit and those that might sustain a sizable reduction.
- What costs, both tangible and intangible, must each class of reseller incur to carry out his part in the contemplated action? Under what

circumstances and for what kinds of reseller will the cost be very high? When will costs be very low?

- When one considers both revenues and costs, which resellers will be most injured by the contemplated action? Which will gain most? Which least?
- Which resellers are likely to misperceive the consequences of the intended action? Will they misperceive it in our favor or to our disadvantage?
- With the foregoing analysis as a basis, how many and what kinds of resellers will drop my line? How many and what caliber of reseller will be willing to take it on?
- How many and what kinds of resellers will give me more sales support? How many and what kinds will reduce their sales support? How great a change is to be expected in both cases?
- How many and what kinds of resellers will add to their inventories as a consequence of the intended action? Which will probably reduce their inventory holdings?

The difficulty of answering these questions should not be underestimated; most suppliers will be forced to take shortcuts in developing their estimates.

Suppliers and Cost-Benefit Analysis

A firm transforms inputs into outputs. Its inputs represent everything it purchases and its outputs everything it sells. Supplies of raw materials, components, subassemblies, supplies, labor, management, funds, capital equipment, professional services—all compose its inputs. The prices that a firm pays for these inputs plus their productivity determine its costs. (The caliber of the firm's management, far more than the inherent productivity of its workforce—which reflects its training, skill, and motivation— accounts for the firm's productivity.) Thus, suppliers figure in major decisions mainly in cost computations.

Some firms have relatively simple cost elements. Especially is this true of resellers; by far their largest cost is the price they pay for merchandise. Suppliers of services—such as legal, medical, accounting, or consulting— have mainly personnel and space costs. Manufacturers ordinarily have highly complex cost conditions with no single item accounting for much more than 25 percent of the total.

As a general proposition, most executive decisions *reflect* their organizations' payments to suppliers—that is, their firm's costs—rather than affect those payments. Decisions affecting production arrangements represent an important exception. Decisions about plant location, the adoption of a new technology, and the number and nature of warehouses are intended mainly to achieve cost-benefits. Moreover, some of them—especially decisions related to the location of factories, warehouses, or service centers—also affect the quality and speed of service that a firm can offer its customers. Thus those decisions may yield important revenue benefits as well as cost savings.

BENEFITS SOUGHT FROM SUPPLIERS

As implied, executives mainly seek low costs from suppliers, whether they result from low price paid to them, high productivity, or a combination of the two. Rather than low cost as such, their goal might better be described as costs lower than their rivals'. Many executives and purchasing agents say that they are not nearly as concerned with the price they pay for something as whether they may be paying more for it than their competitors are paying.

In addition to low prices and high productivity, businessmen seek the following benefits from suppliers:

- Continuity of supply—including such factors as no interruptions in deliveries, no strikes, and advance warning of possible shortages of supply.
- Reliability and uniformity of quality.
- Information about technological developments and also about the activities of competitors.
- Preferential treatment—such as priority in the allocation of supplies when shortages occur, first right of refusal to buy closeouts, and the chance to inspect and use a new item that has been developed by the supplier.
- Exclusivity—the privilege of using some distinctive component that is not available to any or many other customers.

NATURE OF THE RELATIONSHIP WITH SUPPLIERS

A firm's relationship with major suppliers resembles its relationship with resellers: their economic interests run parallel and they often are highly personal. A relationship based on mutuality of interest combined with a genuine conflict of interest is better explained by psychologists, sociologists, and personnel specialists than by economic theorists. Such elements as friendship, loyalty, obligation, affection, resentment, personal slight, make up these relationships—along with strictly business considerations.

One often hears the adage "Business is business." But what is business? The adage suggests that business is a self-seeking process in which everyone pursues personal gain without regard to the welfare of others. That statement certainly is not wholly true; nor is it wholly groundless. Business is conducted by people; and in their capacity as income earners—employees, supervisors, executors, lenders—people do not lose their human needs and inclinations. Put very directly, friendship, loyalty, love, anger, resentment, frustration, and personal slight figure heavily in business relationships. Even as suppliers' salesmen seek to win the friendship and loyalty of their customers' purchasing agents, those purchasing agents try to establish personal ties with the supplying firm's personnel—salesmen, executives, service personnel. On both sides, the effort is to transform a commercial relationship into one that is partly personal. And beyond the seeking of a personal relationship to gain commercial advantage, business relationships inevitably are genuinely personal in part—even if they take place only over the telephone. In vital commercial relationships, like those between major customers and major suppliers, the personal element of the relationship rarely is trivial.

The conclusion that one reaches is that if "business is business," then business must be defined to include vital personal and emotional elements ranging from love to hate. More important, business rarely can be kept entirely on a commercial basis; inevitably it becomes personal at least in part. The extent of the noncommercial ingredient of business does vary greatly, depending upon the nature of the individuals involved; some go to great lengths to keep their business relationships solely on a business plane.

Cooperative programs involving mutual sacrifice by several parties are frequently undertaken in business. A manufacturer may solicit his major suppliers' participation in a special promotion. To offer the product substantially below regular price, each supplier—and the manufacturer himself—might accept far less than his usual margin. If the promotion is successful, all will profit by a substantial increase in sales volume. No one supplier alone could make such a promotion successful; an organized effort calling for a lower margin for those accounting for a significant part of costs is required to achieve a substantial reduction in sales price. (Usually resellers are persuaded to accept a lower margin also.) Such cooperative promotions usually are organized by a producer to revive flagging demand.

To obtain preferential treatment, a firm ordinarily must extend it too. We would again invoke the transaction model to explain preferential treatment by suppliers. Preference is not always earned in kind; a buyer may give personal warmth and friendship and in exchange get more speedy delivery of merchandise or better credit terms.

Reciprocity consists of tacit or explicit understandings that one firm's purchases from another firm are contingent upon that firm's purchasing some item from it. One implication of reciprocity is that a sales department should examine the purchases by its firm to see whether suppliers could be turned into customers by using reciprocity as an argument. Behind the argument is the implied threat that the supplier will lose his business to another who would reciprocate.

In dealing with suppliers, a firm represents a customer/buyer. In that role, it might exert pressure to obtain favored terms in the forms already described. The extent of a buyer's bargaining power depends upon several factors, the more important being the number of attractive alternatives available to him, the extent of excess capacity in the supplying industry, the proportion of the supplier's sales accounted for by the buyers, and the extent to which suppliers exhibit market discipline. Beyond these, the buyer's buying power, skill, and aggressiveness influence the terms of sale. Buyers vary in their willingness to "push a supplier to the wall" and exact the best possible terms.

Costs and Benefits Vis-à-vis Government

Government pervades our economic life, but it figures far more prominently in the decisions of some firms than others. Some firms operate under "consent decrees" and direct government surveillance that make them especially vulnerable to governmental prosecution. Some industries are heavily regulated, and these are particularly concerned with the possible effects of their decisions on government.

Executives' decisions must take into account the many layers of government, for "ignorance of the law is no excuse." Businessmen must inform themselves of the many laws—county, city, state, and federal—that impinge on their operations. Not only must they conform to existing law, but they try to avoid further restrictions on their actions. They emphatically will avoid actions that might cause an investigation, let alone a prosecution of their firm under existing legislation.

One may regard "the public" as a separate party to the business process, for government cannot be considered synonymous with the public. Government institutions are composed of individuals with personal interests and goals that could be opposed to those of the public generally. (Government employees are, of course, a part of the public.) Especially in their employment (salaries, pensions, working conditions), the interests of government agencies are often opposed to those of the public at large. In addition, their personal political persuasions may run counter to those of a majority of the electorate.

We shall not consider the public as a separate party to the business process, though it sometimes is a major consideration in a business decision. Plant location decisions, decisions related to any issue that captures the popular imagination at the time—like pollution, energy conservation, investment in nations which deny personal freedoms to their citizens—are examples. On rare occasions, public sentiment becomes so aroused that some people take action, like picketing, or boycotting, against a firm whose actions are considered objectionable.

To return to the government as a party to the business process, what kinds of costs and benefits are likely to be at issue when government is an important factor in a business decision?

NATURE OF THE BENEFITS TO BE OBTAINED FROM GOVERNMENT

What "goodies" can government dispense? The number is large. In the first place, the various levels of government are customers for goods and services. They are particularly attractive customers because they frequently pay more than private industry for their purchases; it appears that most governmental officials do not make strenuous efforts to buy at the lowest possible price. Correspondingly, some firms that sell to government apparently agree—overtly or tacitly—to adhere rigidly to their list prices in their sales to governmental units.*

Apart from government as a regular customer, governmental units can dispense the following favors to business that figure prominently in executive decisions:

- Variances—exceptions to local ordinances about land use and similar restrictions that permit firms to enjoy exceptions from existing regulations.
- Lax administration of regulations related to noise abatement, pollution, traffic congestion, and the like.
- Protective regulation—some industries seek the status of public utilities or something similar, which has the effect of minimizing competition. The transportation industries (airlines, trains, trucks, and buses) are a clear example as are the communications media, especially radio and television.
- Protection against foreign competition, as in restrictions on imports.
- Assistance to enter foreign markets, as in subsidies on exports, or subsidies to the shipping industry.

---

* Several studies show an unusual pattern of identical bids on government contracts for all firms but one. The low bidder usually is a firm that seems to be taking its regular "turn."

The main "goody" that an executive seeks from government is speedy and fair treatment of his requests for a ruling, or, when accused of some violation, that his firm be spared burdensome requests for information and very costly investigations.

Above all, firms seek to avoid formal actions against them by an administrative agency. Such actions ordinarily cause high money costs and large expenditures of time by management, even when the firm is innocent of the charges. When the firm is guilty, the costs are usually far higher, mainly because of the penalties that are imposed, not for the cost of the proceedings.

Government actions against individual firms are rarely even-handed no matter how hard government administrators may try to make them so. Few government agencies have the personnel or funds to investigate or prosecute all suspected offenses; they must operate on the basis of test cases and "making an example" of some offender. In other cases, they may give warnings or extend "friendly advice." Consequently, many firms recognize the importance of winning a sympathetic and understanding attitude from members of regulatory agencies. They may not seek special favors; they mainly want to avoid unwarranted and unfair prosecutions.

Apart from taking specific account of the effects of decisions on government, in the ways suggested above, executives may make some decisions whose very purpose is to obtain benefits, or avoid costs, from government. Some business decisions relate to gathering information about what is going on in agencies whose activities do or could impinge on the industry in question. Ordinarily this goal calls for maintaining a specialist who keeps abreast of personnel changes, administrative actions, and changes in internal policies in the relevant government agencies. To get such information usually involves personal contacts by representatives of the firm with members of government agencies. Such contacts, which can serve a thoroughly legitimate purpose, often create delicate situations for the representatives of both business and government. If handled indelicately by business representatives, the result can be antagonism rather than understanding on the part of government employees. Unfortunately, purity of motive is no insurance against misperception of motive. And purity of motive is not easily sustained in the present regulatory environment.

RECKONING COSTS AND BENEFITS IN PARTICULAR DECISIONS

When a firm's management is contemplating concrete actions, someone who is sensitive to the governmental process should be charged with responsibility for probing potential impacts of major decisions on the government agencies that might be affected. Lawyers are authorities on whether an action is illegal; they are not necessarily the best source on how administrative agencies would respond.

At bottom, someone or some group must forecast the response of government employees to the decision and estimate its effect on the firm. That is, they must attach a dollar value to the probability of some benefit or injury vis-à-vis government agencies. In addition, they should also propose actions that might be taken to minimize the potential injury—as through advance clearance with the affected agencies. (Sometimes major benefits can be obtained by showing full concern with the responsibilities of the government agency which might be affected by the decision.)

Costs and Benefits Vis-à-vis Rivals

A firm's competitors are in many ways the single most important party to major business decisions. Many decisions aim specifically to improve a firm's position relative to its rivals; and a firm's rivals also make decisions having the same aim. Firms adopt counteractions to the aggressive actions of their rivals. The nature and effectiveness of these countermoves largely determine the final consequences of their decisions. It is therefore essential that rivals' actions and their consequences be forecast as part of a decision.

Economists have written a great deal about competition in industry. Moreover, the nature and effects of competition are central issues for every senior executive. Consequently, the whole issue of competition, competitive strategies, and the impact of decisions on rivals is accorded far more attention and space in this book than are the other parties to the business process. Indeed, Chapter 14 is devoted to those subjects.

Summary and Conclusions

Most business decisions affect several parties and often they affect colleagues, ultimate customers, resellers, competitors, suppliers, and government. To make a valid decision, an executive usually must estimate separately the effects of each alternative on all parties to the business process.

Many concepts help to identify the potential effects of business actions and to estimate their size. Interestingly, most of these concepts are drawn from behavioral science rather than formal economic theory. That fact is not surprising since economic activity involves individuals and relationships among individuals. Especially in the case of colleagues, rivals, resellers, and suppliers, the expectation of all parties is that the relationship will be enduring.

A few concepts apply to all parties to the business process and deserve special emphasis. Most important is the notion that individuals perceive, interpret, and evaluate the same phenomenon very differently. In part, one can account for and forecast these differences by taking account of significant differences among individuals. To cope with such differences, businessmen generally would be well advised to segment their ultimate customers and resellers and treat them as if they were separate submarkets. They should often distinguish also among dissimilar subgroups of competitors, colleagues, and suppliers.

Forecasting the Effect of a Price Change: A Dialog

This dialog continues the conversation reported at the end of Chapter 5 on the Bremil Company price program.

TED: As I understand it, Art, you participate in pricing decisions. How do you forecast the effects of a projected price change? I know you don't buy the price elasticity approach, but what do you offer in its place? Are you going to hide behind your advancing years and your very long experience in this business to demand that we rely on your judgment?

ART: That's a fair question, Ted, though asked in an impertinent manner. To be perfectly honest, the reason I reject forecasts of the effects of price changes on the basis of price elasticity is that they lead to conclusions very different from where my judgment takes me. To be sure that I was not wrong, I began to look into what was involved in computing price elasticity of demand and talked to some of our consultants. I even read a few articles and reread my economics text; at one time, I got to be our in-house authority on price elasticity of demand.

TED: Forgive me for saying so, but you still haven't answered my question. How would you estimate the effects of our projected change in price?

ART: I'm not beyond changing the subject to conceal my ignorance, but I wasn't doing that in this case. It is important that you know the background of my answer, because I want you to know how humble I feel about it. I'm quite sure that the price elasticity approach won't work, but I'm not sure of what is the right way to make such a forecast. Still, I won't employ an approach that I consider badly mistaken, even if I don't know a truly correct way to go about it.

TED: I can see the good sense in that position. Still, how would you make a forecast in this particular case? Do you expect some particular result from this price change?

ART: Well, I can name a range of outcomes that seem reasonable to me; what's more, I feel pretty confident that the result will fall within that range. I might mention that Ken's figure is not in that range.

TED: How did you arrive at that range? I'm trying to discover whether you are using a homemade measure of price elasticity of demand or some different methods of estimating the effect of a price change.

ART: Decide for yourself after I describe how I make my forecasts in such cases. I'll try to explain how I would make a forecast in this particular instance, though I cheerfully admit that I have no systematic forecasting method that any intelligent person could apply and arrive at the same results that I get.

Let's start with that statement of yours. You look on this action we plan to take as a price cut like all other changes in price that have occurred in the past. But I consider it a marketing program consisting of a combination of price changes of very different size on individual items in the line, combined with a sizable advertising and personal sales effort. Our plans call for doing several things to exploit the proposed series of individual price changes. In fact, we'll even be advertising quite different "stories" to customers and to our distributors and retailers about this action.

TED: I can see that. We certainly will be changing more than price alone; in fact, I can't think of any situations in which nothing other than price is changed. Beyond that we are changing lots of prices and by different amounts. I don't think there has been an occasion when we changed price since the days of OPA* when we changed every single price by either the same amount or the same proportion.

ART: Right. So you must wonder what in our past experiences is relevant to the proposed price changes. It isn't clear that any of our past actions are really parallel.

To take first one point, for the last eight years or so, we have mainly been raising prices—and changing our products too, I might mention. Now we propose to lower prices. So whether you use statistical or intuitive methods to make your forecasts, you must surely be relying on evidence that is quite old—and almost certainly you know of very few, if any, truly similar situations.

TED: That's right. Any significant decision is unique in some significant respect and this one is very different from what we've done in recent years. That's really the source of the problem; we can't learn much from past examples for most of our decisions.

ART: Maybe that's why we cannot escape reliance on intuition to some degree.

---

* The Office of Price Administration, which administered price controls during World War II.

TED: But say your intuitions don't produce an answer? What if you can't decide whether sales will rise or fall?

ART: That's an interesting question, but such a thing never happened to me. I almost always have a clear idea of what won't happen as well as some reasonable range of outcomes.

TED: Does that range ever change after discussion or reflection?

ART: It does for me.

TED: Let's get back to the specific question of how you would forecast the results of the contemplated price changes—excuse me, I mean of the contemplated marketing program.

ART: You learn fast, Ted. I guess that the very first step I take is to learn exactly what actions we contemplate—in this case, what is to be done to price. For example, is it a set of small adjustments or some major change in both level of price and in individual price relationships? In this case, I'd say it's clearly the latter and the change is to be modest in size rather than major.

TED: I'm surprised to hear you say that. Generally we consider a 10 percent rise in prices quite small and a 10 percent drop tremendous.

ART: There's something to that. But to go on. Next, I'd ask about the other things we'd almost certainly be doing—to advertising, for example. I'd expect the company to do a lot of advertising to let both retailers and consumers know of the change, using separate messages and media for both.

TED: But that advertising would not all be extra. I don't know the specific details in this case, but I wonder whether we'll be spending more on advertising or only using the same number of dollars to say different things.

ART: That's a good point—and on the surface, you'd think that we were not going to spend more on advertising because no increase in advertising appropriation was included as part of this proposal. But my guess is that we'll end up by expending more on advertising. And I have no doubt that the advertising we do in combination with our price reductions would have much more effect than our usual advertising—where we have no very special story to tell.

TED: Your general argument is well taken. We must forecast more than the effect of a change in price alone.

ART: Right, and remember that even the price change is not a simple across-the-board move. You might say that we didn't make such a simple move because we expect the effects of some juggling to be better for us. For example, we'll make a few large price changes—of almost 20 percent—that should help to make this appear a major price change, while we didn't change price at all on two models.

TED: Yes, I noted that. But on those two models, we made a few cosmetic changes, as I recall.

ART: True, but if you look into the matter closely, you'll learn that our cost will actually drop on those two models. We're not reducing the price on those models because they account for a sizable proportion of our total volume—and because they'll be a little more attractive, despite the slight decline in our cost of manufacture.

TED: Are there any other changes to be considered as part of this marketing program?

ART: I'd certainly want to ask some questions to search out changes that don't lie out there on the surface. The places I look to are: advertising, quality changes, personal sales efforts—and there are other considerations as well.

TED: I can see that our salesmen might get new assignments in conjunction with such a price change—they may be kept out of the office more than usual to be sure that the word is spread among distributors and their salesmen.

ART: We might even be giving them a new and more attractive catalog in support of this price program. So you see there are many things beyond price that either do, or might, get changed at such times. Let me tell you about some other things one should think about—these relate mainly to what happens to distributors, their salesmen, our salesmen, retailers—to all people who help to sell our line. This category of considerations is quite large. To take one example, we must forecast whether the distributors will pass the price changes along as we hope—or request.

TED: Yes, I know of some cases when our distributors refused to pass on any price reductions but simply took the opportunity to get a larger margin of profit.

ART: Yes, that can happen. Now we get around to the more difficult part—forecasting the effects of the actions in question, and the timing of those effects. Also, you have to consider the possibility that the program will have different effects in individual markets.

TED: Right, that's what I most want to hear about. How do you forecast the effects?

ART: To begin with, I break the problem down into separate parts.

TED: What are those separate parts?

ART: First of all, I try to face up to the reactions of ultimate customers, because their reactions are crucial in the price problems that I get to face. So I ask, how will ultimate customers react to the price changes that are likely to reach them? Let me make that clear—we want to know what changes will actually reach them—rather than what we hope or try to have reach them.

TED: Would you expect those changes to be the same all over the areas that we deal?

ART: No, I wouldn't. We'll even find differences within small areas, and that makes it terribly complicated to make a forecast. Still, we must recognize such differences. In addition, you have to know whether the customers actually perceive those changes. We often do things—sometimes even large ones—that are not even seen by prospective customers.

TED: That's true. You just cannot assume that because things change, people will see them as different.

ART: That's right. To continue: another phase of the problem that I always think about is the reaction of distributors and retailers.

TED: Hold on, before you move on, how do you forecast potential customers' responses to the changes that actually reach them?

ART: You're a persistent fellow, aren't you. Well, it's a little embarrassing to "tell it like it is," but what I do first is ask, how many—what percentage—of all customers will learn of the change? Then I ask, of those who do perceive the change, how many are likely to interpret it favorably?

TED: That isn't clear. After all, if they do see that our prices have been reduced—and quite heavily on a few models—why shouldn't they interpret that as favorable to purchase?

ART: Some people may think that we were reducing price because many of our customers were passing over our offerings in favor of those of our competitors.

TED: I see that as a possibility, but how do you reach a specific conclusion after you consider the possibility?

ART: Frankly, I don't know the answer. In part, I undoubtedly introspect—ask myself how I'd react to the change. Partly, I draw on whatever information I have at my disposal from the past. As much as possible, I try to keep my forecasts within reasonable bounds. I know that last remark sounds kind of silly, but I shy away from expecting sensational results.

TED: That's a useful thought. Maybe we need to conduct research that tries to get directly at the kinds of issues we are discussing. Like, what different things are perceived by ultimate customers? By what percentage of customers—and how promptly? What different interpretations do different kinds of customers place on different changes? It might even pay to make tests before we take an action to get answers to those kinds of questions—to avoid gross errors.

ART: Right, but for the moment, let's not discuss what *could* be done. Let's talk about what I actually *do*.

TED: Sure, let's go on. Could you carry your description farther? So far, you've described how you try to pin down what actions will actually be taken, and the effects on ultimate customers—how they may perceive and interpret the diverse changes that are to be made.

ART: So far, so good. Another thing I usually do is make separate guesses for different kinds of customers.

TED: How many classes of customers do you think about separately?

ART: I don't always consider the same number of classes. The customer characteristics that are most important determine what classes I think about separately and they vary with the action we are contemplating.

TED: Could you illustrate that point for me?

ART: Sure. If we are planning to change the physical size of our refrigerators—to take a simple example—I think about the physical space available in the kitchens of prospective customers—the proportion of apartment dwellers, the age of homes and apartment houses, the other appliances families keep in their kitchens. I mainly ask what characteristics of customers would make them particularly receptive to the change in the size of the refrigerator and what ones would make them hostile to the change. The customer classes one would consider separately would be very different if we were considering a give-away promotion, a major shift in advertising appeal, or an offering of added service. Although this sounds like a highly complicated process, it gets to be almost automatic after a while—like the many highly complicated judgments we make when we drive a car.

TED: So far you haven't said anything about the responses of rivals and of resellers. How do you take account of rivals and distributors and retailers in thinking through the effects of a price change?

ART: Frankly, I think of four specific firms, and I think of them in considerable detail using as much information as I can find; in particular, I'll often call those salesmen and distributors who have proved to be very knowing about such matters in the past. I try to learn how they have behaved in the past. When I do that I usually find no simple and regular patterns. Still, with the information I obtain, I'm not forced to make my guesses in complete ignorance.

I'm especially interested in information that suggests whether or not a particular firm is hurting for more business; whether it's trying for a big push for rapid growth, whether it has excess capacity, and such things.

TED: It's hard to argue with anything you say, but the process you describe is very complicated.

ART: Yes, and it gets more complicated. Sometimes suppliers or the government become major elements in a forecast of outcomes. Almost never should only one party be considered. It is rare to find a decision that doesn't require close attention to ultimate customers, rivals, and resellers—both distributors and retailers.

TED: But how do you take into account the way these considerations are interrelated? After all, the actions of distributors and retailers determine what the ultimate customers get to perceive and interpret and react to. Similarly, what our competitors do strongly influences the choices available to customers—and thereby largely determine their buying behavior.

ART: That's right. These forces all interact with one another, and I'm sure it would be very difficult to set down that interaction in mathematical form.

TED: But I think I could describe the method you use with some accuracy so that others could use it—at least to some degree.

ART: Fine, let me hear your description of my method.

TED: First, as I've already said, you list the inputs—the actions you expect will be taken. You arrive at that list partly by referring to past marketing programs of a similar nature and, possibly, by checking with some individuals to learn what they plan or expect. So our first step is to set down a list of actions.

ART: I have no quarrel with that, but I wonder whether your list and mine would be the same in this case.

TED: I doubt that they'd be identical, but you can be sure that I'd no longer characterize the proposed marketing program as a 10 percent reduction in price. Frankly, I wouldn't expect our lists to be far apart.

ART: Okay, I can concede that. How would you forecast the effects of those actions?

TED: Well, I'd expect effects other than on immediate sales, including intangible benefits like changes in customers' attitudes toward our brand, maybe improved relations with our distributors and retailers.

ART: Yes, there should be such things. But they should enter into the decision only if and to the extent that they affect sales—or at least profits—subsequently.

TED: Granted. I only want to stress that we should be interested in more than the impact of the change on immediate sales.

ART: Okay. Where do you go from there?

TED: Even though you say that you look first at the ultimate customer, I've concluded that you first ask how much of our action will get through to the ultimate customer. That means your first step involves concern with resellers and not ultimate customers.

ART: You're right, though I thought that I was doing it the other way around. Go ahead with your description.

TED: Well, once having decided what resellers will do—and that means a "mix" of things—not all will do the same thing—you then do something that I see organized in the form of a matrix.

ART: Oh, what would it look like? Could you construct a hypothetical example?

TED: Good idea. First, you identify the key customer segments that you consider central and you ask the following questions about each segment: What proportion of that segment will *perceive* the change? What proportion of that segment will interpret the change (a) favorably, (b) neutrally, (c) unfavorably?

ART: This matrix only gives some inkling of how different kinds of ultimate customers would react to the changes placed before them by resellers. I'd carry through to another stage—which I'd call "evaluation"—how customers would relate the interpreted change to their own situation. That means, do they decide to buy, definitely not to buy, to postpone purchase until they use up what they now have—or what?

TED: Good. That helps a lot. Here's what my matrix would look like. [See Table 13-2.]

ART: I've never used a table like that, but it certainly does carry out my beliefs about what should be done—and possibly I do something remotely like that in a wholly unconscious way.

Table 13-2
MATRIX OF KEY CUSTOMER SEGMENTS

	Segment I	Segment II	Segment III
Size of segment			
Percent perceiving change			
Percent interpreting change			
Favorably			
Unfavorably			
Neither			
Percent evaluating change			
Buying soon			
Buying never			
Considering future purchase			
Buying later			

TED: The question I'd ask is not whether you do this but whether you think that you should do this?

ART: I'd say, yes—it looks very good to me so far. I think that any method to forecast the effects on customers of such things as price changes, sales promotions, major redesigns of the product, and so on should take such things into account. In fact, I think one should do much the same thing in analyzing resellers' reactions.

TED: By doing that we could explain the mix of changes that get through to the ultimate customer. We would find very different types of distributors and retailers, and these differences would be reflected in their perceptions, interpretations, and evaluations.

ART: It seems to me we're making this process vastly complicated, and I have two contradictory reactions. On one hand, I believe that all of the steps we've listed are relevant and necessary. On the other, I resist the notion that the problem is so very complicated. We haven't even discussed the whole process—because we haven't even mentioned what competitors would do—and the job already seems overpowering in its difficulty.

TED: If you make even very simple decisions fully explicit, they appear terribly complicated. But if everything we mention is truly relevant, we should make it explicit, because then we will at least know what we should try to consider. We'd have a full list of the elements that deserve some consideration, and we could then choose those that are really key in the particular situation. So let's go ahead and take account of the actions of competitors.

ART: Okay, but let's handle that on a very sketchy basis because I'm running short on time.

TED: All right. In simplest terms, then, we'd draw up a table for our rivals. Here we would identify specific competitors rather than types, I'd assume, and I suppose you'd ask about their perceptions, interpretations, and evaluations too.

ART: Well, I'm sure they'd perceive our actions, so I'd omit that from my table. But they might well interpret and evaluate them differently. So a fairly similar table would apply to them too.

TED: Good, so now we presumably have developed the basis for forecasting their responses to our actions. Presumably the most important thing to consider is how their business would be affected by what we have done.

ART: Exactly. Let me clarify something here. My first forecast of each rival's response would take into account the probable effect of our action on its sales, costs, and profits. I would also think of how each rival will forecast the effect of our actions on his firm. Also, he will want to forecast the length of time that we'd continue with our new behavior—which presumably would be interpreted from the way we announce and explain our action for the trade press. Then, I'd guess how quickly and how strongly each one might adopt some counteraction.

TED: If one rival were to respond quickly and strongly, then some of the others would be far more likely to respond. And the behavior of all of your competitors would affect the responses of your customers.

ART: That's right. And, depending on their reactions, we might be forced to withdraw our initial action or to modify it. You see, this part of the forecasting process is really sticky and badly afflicted with interdependence. There is no doubt that it all sounds both very subjective and highly complicated.

   I believe that only the main interactions among the different parties affected by our marketing programs can be estimated with any confidence. This seems especially true in the case of predicting our competitors' reactions.

TED: If you are saying that we can only take major factors into account when we make such decisions, I disagree strongly. Most decisions seem to revolve around a large number of relatively minor factors.

ART: Let me make my point clearer. We are in a very competitive and dynamic industry. Most firms in the industry offer something special and have unique capabilities. We cannot simply assume that they will be obliged to match every change we make. When we do take an important marketing move, we try to "fine-tune" our actions so that we either will not provoke our competitors to retaliate or so that they are unable to negate them. As a practical matter, we are not highly proficient "fine-tuners." So we must recognize that our actions will probably induce some of our rivals to make changes to counter them.

TED: Right. And, you might also add that our resellers and final customers will sometimes adapt and react to our marketing programs in wholly unexpected ways.

ART: Exactly. And the chief implication of this for us is that we must always be prepared to alter our marketing programs after we have first introduced them.

TED: I understand your position better now. I can understand that it is extremely difficult to forecast responses of this kind and then take account of how others will be affected in turn.

ART: It certainly is difficult to do and even more difficult to make the process explicit, even when we feel that we can do it reasonably well.

Anyhow, you now know how I forecast the results of marketing programs far better than I did myself only half an hour ago. Now that I have a better understanding of my method, I should get rid of some of its madness.

TED: Let's get one of our bright young executives to set down a description, possibly including a flow diagram of this method we've been discussing.

ART: Good idea. I'd also give him or her the job of making a critique of this method, possibly suggesting improvements. I really think we could all benefit from taking on an assignment of this kind.

TED: If you can bear it, I'd like to wrap up what we've concluded so that I might be able to write a summary of this discussion.

ART: Fine. Then the person who gets the assignment you suggested could begin by reading the summary.

TED: Right. Here's my summary: we start with listing elements in the marketing program. Then, we look at distributors' reactions. Then, we examine retailers' reactions.

At that point, we set down customers' expected responses. Then we ask how rivals would respond to what the distributors and retailers and ultimate customers would do.

Then, after looking at rivals' responses, we'd ask whether we should alter our initial programs.

Then, we'd see whether distributors and retailers would modify their initial behavior.

Then, we get back again to ask about rivals, to see whether they'd be likely to change their behavior.

And, at long last, we would get back to forecasting what customers would do—both in terms of buying actions and intangible benefits.

ART: You added a few steps in that summary that look useful. We went particularly quickly in our discussion of dealing with resellers and competitors—and you can fill those out without any help from me. Just be sure that you do these things. First, recognize a mix of responses on the part of each group affected—which would give rise to a mix of responses on the part of other affected groups. Second, take account of the separate phases of a response. I'm referring to the perception, interpretation, and evaluation phases. Finally, take explicit account of the different types of distributors, retailers, and ultimate customers—and don't think in terms of averages.

TED: I realize that you are in a hurry. What I'll do is write out my summary and conclusions. It might include some things we haven't discussed and omit some items that we agreed upon. It will represent "where I come out" after this discussion with you.

When you get this, will you study it very carefully and let me have a detailed set of comments and criticisms? After I've gotten those, I'll revise the memo and get it back to you. Then we'll be able to decide whether we should have a young executive extend and refine the description and evaluation of the method.

Chapter 14

RIVAL-RELATED DECISIONS

M ANY DECISIONS by business executives are designed to gain an advantage over rivals, to forestall rivals' efforts to gain at their expense, and to influence the competitiveness of their markets in their own favor. Thus, many business decisions seek to produce important benefits vis-à-vis rivals. Inevitably, their decisions also give rise to substantial rival-related costs. Few issues are more important to management than competition. Consequently, skills in managing competitive relationships sometimes determine the very survival of a firm.

To deal successfully with competitors, management must understand market competition thoroughly, as it operates in their particular industry. That means that executives must know far more about competition than the theoretical writings on the subject of competition. Beyond valid models of competition, executives require:

Clear competitive objectives.
Competitive plans and strategies.
Courses of action for pursuing competitive objectives.

We shall discuss these requirements in turn. Our focus will be prescriptive—on what management can do about competition and competitors rather than on what they actually do. Little will be said about what management might do to appeal more effectively to ultimate customers and thus win customers away from rivals. That is the central concern of marketing specialists and need not be reviewed here.

Market Processes and Competitive Problems

Let us start by defining competition. We will then explore the different kinds and degrees of competition that specialists have identified. Competition denotes rivalry among individuals or organizations for scarce prizes. Market competition is defined here as rivalry for the patronage of ultimate customers.* It is a contest among identifiable competitors that takes diverse forms: it varies widely in form and degree. Contestants can initiate varied actions to which their rivals can make widely different responses. Individual market contestants find diverse actions suitable to their purposes depending on their position and power. Market contestants, moreover, are not equally powerful, not equally likely to win, and do not behave in the same way even under similar circumstances.

It is not suggested, however, that markets are chaotic and each one a special case unto itself. From economic theory and elsewhere one can assemble some propositions that provide a good start toward understanding competition. Accordingly, we will sketch the views of specialists on the subject. It will become clear that much must be added to this received wisdom to meet management's needs.

When asked to describe the competitiveness of their industry, experienced executives usually say things like: "it is intensely competitive," "it is absolutely cutthroat," "it is far worse than the average," or "it is not nearly as bad as in other businesses I've been in." Such responses convey little understanding of the things that happen in those industries. Clearly, competition cannot be described adequately by the one dimension of much or little. As a minimum, the following dimensions of an industry should be described: (1) The fairness or "cleanness" of rivalry—do firms defame their rivals, damage competitive products as they sit on the floors and shelves of retail shops, "steal" valued employees, plant harmful rumors, bribe purchasing agents, engage in false advertising, deprecate the quality of rivals' offerings, give short measure, and the like; or do they "play by the rules"? (2) The weapons with which rivals compete—is competition focused on advertising, price, product features, position with retailers, gaining favor with "specifiers"? (3) The main prizes for which rivals vie in their effort to gain market share. (4) The individual firms that are the main source of competitive pressure and their basic competitive goals, strategies, and market behavior. But we have been talking the language of businessmen. What are we told by academic economists?

---

* Economic theorists distinguish between "pure competition"—an extremely rare situation—and conditions of rivalry, where the number of competitors is small enough for each one to be able to identify its rivals and to forecast their responses to its actions. This discussion applies only to markets that depart significantly from pure competition.

How Economists Describe the Competitiveness of Markets

How is the competitiveness of industries actually described at present by economists? (Their classification of industries is the most widely employed.) What are the characteristics that should be considered in a thorough analysis of any industry's competitiveness? What are the most important types of market competition to be found?

Academic economists classify markets and industries primarily by three characteristics: (1) the number of firms operating, (2) the similarity of the firms' offerings, and (3) the ease with which newcomers can enter the market. (They sometimes also stress the number and size of buyers, but only in special situations.) The most common classification of modern markets includes five types: (1) monopoly, with near-impossible entry; (2) homogeneous oligopoly, with difficult entry; (3) heterogeneous oligopoly, with difficult entry; (4) pure competition, with easy entry; and (5) monopolistic competition, with easy entry.

Table 14-1 sets forth these five types and their characteristics, though the meaning and significance of these characteristics requires some discussion.

It is clear what is meant by one seller, but what number constitutes "few" sellers? How large a number of sellers is required before "many" sellers are said to operate in the market? Few sellers operate in a market when sellers recognize their interdependence and know that the efforts they make to gain sales at the expense of their rivals will probably bring retaliatory action. When sellers have no awareness of or concern with possible retaliatory actions, there are said to be many sellers. As a rough rule, if managements can name the individual firms whose actions affect them fairly directly and those firms that are directly affected by their own actions, then they operate in oligopolistic markets. On the other hand, when a seller does not materially affect and is not materially affected by the actions of any seller, we would say that "many sellers" exist.

The characteristic of identical or different offerings is less clear and

Table 14-1

A Classification of Markets: Different Types of Competition

Nature of offering	Number of firms (sellers)		
	One	*Few*	*Many*
Identical	Monopoly	Homogeneous oligopoly (difficult entry)	Pure competition (easy entry)
Different	Monopoly	Heterogeneous oligopoly (difficult entry)	Monopolistic competition (easy entry)

simple then it appears. Observe, first, that the term "offering" is used and not "product," to convey that sellers offer services, location, friendship, trust, and many things beyond a physical product. Second, the terms "identical" and "different" refer to the *perceptions* of most customers and *not* to any objective *reality*. If, as often happens, customers believe one seller's offerings to be superior to another's—whatever the reason—we are dealing with a condition of "different offerings." Third, differences in customer preferences and perceptions can vary from trivial to major.

Ease of entry into a market is almost self-explanatory. It denotes the cost and speed with which a new firm can enter a market and survive in competition with established firms and the risks of such ventures.

Another Classification of Market Competition: Concentration Ratios

A classification of markets and industries in wide use distinguishes markets by their level of concentration—that is, according to how much an industry's total output and sales are concentrated in the largest firms. Industrial concentration is ordinarily measured by the output of the four and eight largest firms. Classified in this way, one can make very fine distinctions among industries and markets, for concentration ratios can be precise to the decimal place. However, do even large differences in concentration ratio indicate differences in the intensity and form of competition? Numerous studies of the consequences of industrial concentration show only slight connection between concentration ratios—however they are measured—and profitability, gross margins, progressiveness, and price stability.* The concept of concentration ratios is the same as the economists' concept of fewness. These ratios tell nothing about firms other than the largest four or eight.

Alternative Classifications of Industries

Many dissimilar types of oligopoly exist, and executives must be able to distinguish one type from another. The following classifications of oligopoly situations have been proposed by economists—all based upon sellers' price behavior: (1) markets where oligopolists follow one another's price reductions promptly but do not follow their price increases (this situation can be represented by a kinky demand curve for individual firms); (2) markets where sellers follow one another's price changes both up and

---

* For a brief but thorough review of the evidence and argument regarding the connection between industry structure (mainly concentration) and economic performance, see John M. Vernon, *Market Structure and Industrial Performance* (Boston: Allyn & Bacon, 1972). For a discussion of the meaning and significance of concentration ratios, see John Blair, *Economic Concentration* (New York: Harcourt Brace Jovanovich, 1972), pp. 7–11.

down—these are price-leadership situations; and (3) markets where most or all sellers collude.

Fritz Machlup advances a classification of oligopoly markets based on the degree of coordination between the actions and policies of competing oligopolists. As he uses the term, "coordination" means much the same as market discipline. He distinguishes varying degrees of coordination in distinguishing one oligopoly market from another.*

Dimensions of Industries Relevant to Competitive Problems

Although the classification systems discussed may be satisfactory for economic theorists, they are far too simple to meet the needs of business executives who must be concerned with specific conditions and actions. To understand the competitive forces operating in an industry and what to do about them, executives must take many factors into account. Below is a list of factors which are sometimes decisive in determining a firm's competitive problems.

1. *Product/service offered.*
   Stage of life-cycle.
   Degree of difference in offerings of individual sellers.
   Complexity of product.
   Degree of risk involved in use of offering.
   Size of "ticket" (money cost).
   Product type: consumer vs. producers goods; durable vs. perishable goods.
   Importance of product to lifestyle or to total costs of the customer.
2. *Nature of ultimate customer/user.*
   Age.
   Socioeconomic status.
   Characteristics of "large users."
   Customer product knowledge.
   Bargaining power of customers.
   Ability of customers to produce items for themselves.
   Location of buyers.
   Number and size of buyers.
   Existence of organizations of buyers.
3. *Conditions of production.*
   Cost conditions: economies of scale.

* See Fritz Machlup, *The Economics of Seller's Competition: Model Analysis of Seller's Conduct* (Baltimore, Md.: Johns Hopkins Press, 1952).

Relative size of fixed cost.

Magnitude of cost differences among rival sellers.

Regional or international differences in costs of rivals.

Sources of cost advantages enjoyed by individual firms.

Degree of vertical integration, and variations from firm to firm.

Profitability of supplying industries.

4. *Distribution arrangements.*

Magnitude of logistical costs.

Relative strength of customer loyalty to reseller and producers.

Bargaining power of distributors/retailers.

Use of exclusivity as a distribution strategy.

Availability of effective distributors.

5. *Competitive conditions.*

Coordination of seller behavior.

Number, size, and location of sellers.

Degree of concentration of sales.

Degree of market segmentation.

Chief tools with which rivals compete (relative importance of different marketing outlays).

Aggressiveness of sellers.

Strength of brand loyalty.

6. *Supply conditions.*

Similarity of access and cost of raw materials to different firms.

Degree of vertical integration in raw materials/components.

Importance of know-how or patents.

Availability of technology to different sellers.

Dependence on supply of capital.

Requirements for unusual technical skills.

7. *Entry conditions.*

Opportunities for customers to integrate backward.

Ease with which other industries might extend operations into this one.

Magnitude of barriers to entry.

Nature and source of barriers to entry.

8. *Demand conditions.*

Growth rate of total sales.

Volatility of sales.

Cyclical pattern of demand.

Availability of nearby substitutes.

Product obsolescence and innovation.

Effect on sales of such things as household formation, residential construction, birth rates, and the like.

A single classification system incorporating all the dimensions listed would include thousands of industry types—far too many to serve any useful purpose. An executive requires a highly selective classification designed to meet his own needs. He must develop it for himself, selecting from the dimensions listed those most germane to his industry and firm. Most executives would be wise to construct several classification systems for the same purpose.

Sample Classification Systems

Tables 14-2 and 14-3 were constructed mainly to help persons responsible for developing market strategies. By placing industries with which they are familiar in the various cells of the tables, they should see the wide diversity of competitive forces operating. One use of such classification systems is to identify other industries that are similar in essential characteristics and from whose experience executives might learn. Recognize that these classifications represent only a few of literally hundreds of promising taxonomies. They are not offered as the best classification systems for all industries and markets.

Executives should be able to identify several industries similar to their own by employing the classification procedure sketched. Having found a few such industries, they should inform themselves about competitive conditions there, with particular attention to the genesis of competitive problems with the maturation of the industry.

The classification systems presented can be viewed in another way: they represent further subdivisions of one of the market types identified by

Table 14-2

A CLASSIFICATION OF MARKETS/INDUSTRIES ESPECIALLY SUITABLE FOR CONSUMER GOODS ITEMS

		Imporance of product to customers					
		High saliency		Moderate saliency		Low saliency	
		Shelf space scarce	Shelf space ample	Shelf space scarce	Shelf space ample	Shelf space scarce	Shelf space ample
Strong brand preferences by customers	Complex products	1)	5)	9)	13)	17)	21)
	Simple products	2)	6)	10)	14)	18)	22)
Weak brand preferences by customers	Complex products	3)	7)	11)	15)	19)	23)
	Simple products	4)	8)	12)	16)	20)	24)

Table 14-3

A CLASSIFICATION OF MARKETS/INDUSTRIES

		Market characteristics							
		Dominated by one firm		Concentrated in a few		Well populated		Crowded	
		Disciplined market	Undisciplined market	Disciplined market	Undisciplined market	Disciplined market	Undisciplined market	Disciplined market	Undisciplined market
Durable goods; infrequently purchased	Great economies of scale	1)	7)	13)	19)	25)	31)	37)	43)
	Minor economies of scale	2)	8)	14)	20)	26)	32)	38)	44)
Partly durables bought with moderate frequency	Great economies of scale	3)	9)	15)	21)	27)	33)	39)	45)
	Minor economies of scale	4)	10)	16)	22)	28)	34)	40)	46)
Nondurables, bought frequently	Great economies of scale	5)	11)	17)	23)	29)	35)	41)	47)
	Minor economies of scale	6)	12)	18)	24)	30)	36)	42)	48)

economic theorists—heterogeneous oligopoly. Both Table 14-2 and 14-3 describe the dimensions of many different kinds of competitive situations.

It does not help much to list the enormous variety of competitive circumstances that prevail in industry and the long list of dimensions to which executives must attend. They vary widely from industry to industry, and it is their particular combination that must be understood, for competitive dimensions interact strongly with one another. By stressing the complexity of competitive situations, we hope to provide an antidote against accepting excessively simple notions about market phenomena.

A simple illustration may establish the complexity of market competition from the standpoint of managers who must cope with it. Consider one firm which is by far the largest in its industry and seeks to expand and entrench its dominance by charging prices relatively close to its costs. In this way, it hopes to gain economies of scale which would make it difficult for small and inefficient rivals to survive and would also deter other firms from entering its markets. A small firm in the same industry may search out a niche to serve; that is, it may cultivate customers with special wants and needs that can best be provided by a small, flexible supplier. The small firm's costs may be moderately high, but it may prosper nonetheless because it meets important needs for which customers are willing to pay. The presence of the dominant firm limits what the small firm might charge and the kinds of products and services it will offer. Because of the operation of such small firms, the dominant firm faces a smaller market for its wares and also is limited in what it charges, lest the small firms become large.

This simple illustration suggests the perils of generalizing about industries, for the competitive position of individual firms ordinarily differs greatly. Also, many economists have claimed that the actions of a firm can be inferred from the structure of its industry and the position of the firm within its industry. No one has demonstrated the validity of this view.*

The lack of valid models of competition handicaps writers about competition far more than managers. On the basis of extensive and intimate market experience, reflection on their own experience, and the exchange of views with other experienced executives, some executives acquire insightful and valid views of competition in their industries. (Skillful interviewing of such executives by market specialists may someday produce a set of market models that are quite valid for many sectors of industry.)

Management's Need for Competitive Objectives

The chief goal of management is taken to be self-evident: to maximize long-run profits, or to maximize the present value of future earnings. These goals give virtually no guidance for the management of a firm's competitive relations. What must the firm do, with respect to its competitors, that will yield maximum profits?

Executives must select strategies by which they may prevail against competitors. These are strategies for the pursuit of particular subobjectives, and most of these subobjectives must be obtained over the opposition of rivals who seek the same goals. If they are to earn high profits, managements must cope with their competitors in a way that will enable them to obtain a large share of these subobjectives.

THE CONNECTION BETWEEN COMPETITION AND PROFITABILITY

What must managements do to prosper in the face of competition? What must they do to gain most and suffer least from competition? It is almost a truism that intensive competition means low profits; conversely, weak competition is profitable for sellers. This simple proposition suggests that a primary competition-related goal of every management is to weaken or de-intensify competition.

Actually, this proposition is too simple. It is not clear that a linear relationship exists between the intensity of competition and the profitability of firms in a market. In unusual circumstances, a firm actually gains from intensified competition—as where a speedy exit of firms from an overcrowded industry is in its interest. Also, some firms that are particu-

---

* F. M. Scherer, *Industrial Market Structure and Economic Performance* (Chicago: Rand McNally, 1970).

larly skilled at managing competition may prosper while their rivals flounder. Still, an intensification of competition ordinarily means a reduction in profits. Accordingly, we ask what management can do to de-intensify competition.

MARKET DISCIPLINE: A VITAL COMPETITIVE OBJECTIVE

Every industry has a "climate" and a "culture" which strongly affect its profitability. Management's market behavior is influenced partly by unwritten rules that establish cultural norms. That climate and culture might be described as some degree of "market discipline." Perhaps more than any other factor, the discipline or lack of it in a market determines the profitability of sellers. Let us explore why this is so.

The market actions of firms are likely to affect one or more of their rivals perceptibly. Indeed, their market actions typically are designed to further their own interest at the expense of rivals. In other words, most of the subobjectives sought by one firm's management are desired by other firms. Accordingly, when one firm achieves an objective, a rival ordinarily loses something it values. Market competition is essentially a zero-sum game.

Since firms are highly interdependent, executives take account of the effects of their actions both on individual rivals and on the climate of their markets. They recognize that their rivals will not usually tolerate a loss of a valued prize to them and that they have options available whereby they may prevent the loss. Also, management recognizes that certain actions will breed mistrust, hostility, and anger that will greatly intensify the competitiveness of their market—possibly for a long time. What, then, do we mean by market discipline?

Market discipline denotes particular attitudes and behavior on the part of sellers in a market. These attitudes and behaviors are best characterized by nonaggressiveness, far-sightedness (that is, having a long-range perspective), trust, willingness to sacrifice, understanding, and cooperativeness. Stated as negatives, sellers do not try to increase their market share very quickly, they do not try to make a killing in the short run by sacrificing longer-run profits, they do not assume that their rivals will cheat or take advantage of them, they will not allow the market to become disrupted in order to avoid a short period of low profits, and they do not seek the destruction of their rivals.

Market discipline varies in degree: some markets have strict market discipline while others have virtually none. Illegal collusion would be an extreme form of market discipline, while cutthroat competition represents the opposite extreme. The level of discipline in a market varies roughly with the number of influential firms that exhibit the characteristics listed.

How do firms behave in disciplined markets? Mainly they refrain from certain behaviors, foremost among which are price cutting (especially secret price cutting), big increases in sales promotion efforts, secret concessions to important customers of rivals in matters other than price, efforts to drive a particular rival out of business, defamation of rivals, and actions that would injure customer trust in the industry as a whole. The positive behaviors associated with market discipline are participation in cooperative industry activities (through trade associations and industry advisory committees), and painstaking investigation of an alleged aggression by a rival to see whether it actually did occur and was aggressive in intent, rather than striking out at a rival on the basis of a rumor. In addition, market discipline is enhanced when firms take punitive action against others that depart blatantly from disciplined conduct without being justified by severe hardship.

Only extreme forms of market discipline are illegal: market discipline emphatically does not require collusion, overt or tacit. It is suggested that management should seek to enhance market discipline in pursuit of profits by far-sighted behavior rather than adopt a short-run viewpoint that works in the direction of market chaos. Collusion is usually a short-sighted and unprofitable policy as well as illegal. On the other hand, the view that management would be wise to "slug it out with competition" and "let the best man win" is also short-sighted and unprofitable. Furthermore, in time, sellers usually are forced to cut corners in ways that damage their customers.

The importance of market discipline as a competitive goal stems from the strong forces operating in the direction of indiscipline. Almost every seller has a strong short-run incentive to engage in secret price cutting if it can keep its price cuts secret. This incentive results from the fact that its regular price is substantially higher than the cost of increased output; the ratio of price to variable cost (designated by P/V) is high. For example, it may be selling units at a price of $100 and could produce extra units at a cost of $76. In extreme cases—airlines, hotels, telephone service, movie theatres—the added costs are trivial relative to price. Under such conditions, a seller can earn sizable profits on added sales even though it offers *some* customers a substantial price cut.

The temptation to cut prices in secret exists especially when sellers possess excess capacity—a very common situation—and when demand has fallen, leaving producers holding swollen inventories. The general temptation to engage in secret price cutting combines with the fact that one or more firms in an industry usually experience severe financial difficulty (possibly because they had a strike, a series of product failures, major cost overruns, or a sudden drop in sales) which creates a high probability of secret price cutting.

Market discipline is fragile also because many buyers try to undermine it in their own self-interest. Sometimes they do this by alleging that they have been offered secret price cuts when that is not the case.

SALES GROWTH: AN ALMOST UNIVERSAL COMPETITIVE OBJECTIVE

Virtually every management wants its firm to grow—almost as an end in itself. If pushed hard, executives say they would forgo growth if it entailed a sacrifice of profits. They make this concession reluctantly because they contend that greater profits are to be obtained mainly through increased sales—growth.

Beyond the desire for growth in absolute size, many managements pursue related and more ambitious goals: increased market share and market dominance. Most managements list increased market share as their primary objective. They generally assume that increased market share results in higher profits in the near future if not immediately. Not infrequently, executives focus far more on gaining market share than on profits.

Given the nearly universal goal of higher market share, the connection between profits and market share deserves examination. Studies of this relationship show that firms with larger market shares have higher profits. However, this relationship should not be confused with the connection between *actions taken to increase market share* and profits. It is suggested that many circumstances represent advantages to a firm, such as low costs of raw materials, valuable locations, or unusually skilled management. These advantages can be used to gain market share even as they also allow the firm to make high profits. On the other hand, if those firms were to adopt measures that increased their market shares further, the effect might well be to lower their profits for an indefinite period.

Still, most managements seek increased market share. This goal cannot be regarded as a necessary or wise competitive objective unless specific account is taken of how actions required to increase market share affect long-run profits. Not infrequently a firm gains in relative size by reducing its profit margins substantially or by actions that injure market discipline—neither of which increases profits.

Recognize that one firm's gains in market share imply losses of market share for its rivals. They will usually resist such losses fiercely and try hard to regain lost market share, especially since they also seek increased market shares. The result of their efforts to redress the damage is likely to accentuate any loss in market discipline occasioned by the aggressor firm's measures.

Much emphasis has recently been placed on the importance of becoming the dominant firm in particular market segments. This line of thinking represents one motivation for market share growth. In part, dominance is sought to gain a cost advantage over rivals via the "experience curve"; another alleged benefit is market leadership. Market dominance need not bring these benefits, however. Industrial history is replete with examples of dominant firms in an industry which are high-cost producers and less profitable than some smaller firms.

Market dominance usually is associated with great market power. This power can be used to contain the growth of and repel threats from rivals. Moreover, dominant firms ordinarily attract the best management and enjoy the greatest favors from suppliers. Thus, market dominance clearly is valuable. However, it is an impractical goal for all but a small handful of firms: there can be only one dominant firm in a market.

Perhaps it would be wise to view market share growth as an appropriate long-run goal while recognizing that in many situations efforts to gain share would be unprofitable. At any time, management must decide whether to try to build market share, simply hold on to what it possesses, or give ground.*

Paths to Increased Market Discipline and Higher Market Shares

Our discussion of competition-related objectives up to this point indicates that a firm's chief financial goal is maximum long-run profits and the maximum price for its equities in the long run, and that these are best pursued by protecting and enhancing market discipline and by increasing sales. But we must ask how a firm can best achieve sales growth and a disciplined market. Four subobjectives or paths suggest themselves: feed off rivals, fend off rivals, cooperate with rivals, and learn from rivals. Each is sketched to suggest measures by which a firm might increase its market share and enhance discipline in its market. Below are some of the actions that firms might take to achieve each of these four subgoals.

1. Feed off rivals.
   - Offer preferential terms to the most valued customers of rivals to lure them away.
   - Offer preferential treatment to strong resellers to lure them away from rivals.

* The emphasis on becoming dominant in particular market segments has resulted in large measure from the efforts of the Boston Consulting Group and especially from the writings of its president, Bruce Henderson. For a brief and incisive factual analysis of this position, see Sidney Schoeffler, "Market Position: Build, Hold, or Harvest?" *Pimsletter #3*, Strategic Planning Institute, 1977.

- Achieve excellence—give both ultimate customers and resellers more of what they value.
- Identify the most vulnerable rivals and concentrate on taking away the customer segments and resellers they now serve and use.
- Attract their most talented executives by offering high compensation or challenging opportunities.

2. Fend off rivals.
   - "Lock up" the executives, valuable customers, and resellers you now control.
     Whenever possible, use long-term contracts with them.
     Acquire a part ownership in reseller organizations when possible.
     Develop strong personal ties.
     Try to limit alternatives available to them.
     Load up customers with heavy inventories of your product.
   - Maintain secrecy about the things you do very efficiently.
   - Do not reveal identity of your most valuable customers, executives, resellers.

3. Cooperate with rivals.
   - Develop close personal contacts between top executives in your firm and theirs.
   - Explain whenever possible that all rivals lose from direct conflict with others of roughly equal strength.
   - Establish industrywide cooperative arrangements for:
     Research and development. ⊚
     Data gathering.
     Dealing with government agencies.
     Public relations.
   - Be quick to offer assistance to a rival in distress to establish the principle of cooperation and to earn the right to reciprocity.
   - Develop institutional arrangements such as trade associations, industry committees, and trade journals.

4. Learn from rivals.
   - Become informed about what the most progressive of them are doing.
     Monitor their product changes, their marketing programs, their personnel policies, and the like.
     Foster personal contacts among your executives and theirs.
     Cultivate close friends among your customers so that they can report on what rivals are offering.
   - Develop skills in doing what they are doing well.
     Acquire resources skilled in copying products and programs.

Hire away some of their employees.
- Study sources that might reveal what your rivals are planning.
Keep records of court cases.

Feed off rivals. If a firm's market share increases, then almost by definition it must divert rivals' customers to itself. (The chief exception is the growing market which permits some firms to increase their market share while their rivals grow in absolute size, even while losing share.) How can a firm take customers away from its rivals? From which firms should it try to take customers? Should it make a special effort to gain more or less equally at the expense of all rivals so as not to provoke retaliation from the injured party?

These issues pose vital strategic problems beyond those already raised. Should a firm's task be to attract ultimate customers away from competing firms by offering better values directly to them, or by leading them to perceive values as better, although they are not, or both? Or should a firm seek increased market share by searching for a rival that is vulnerable to a loss of business and then direct its efforts toward taking business from that firm? The choice is between a customer orientation, which focuses on what a firm offers to its ultimate customers, and a competitor orientation, which focuses on individual competitor's strengths and weaknesses and in particular geographic markets.

Clearly, both strategies for winning customers have a logical foundation. Management must satisfy customers and also prevent competitors from taking away its firm's business. Since the market analyses required to implement each orientation differ substantially, the actions and decisions resulting from each orientation will also differ markedly.

Fend off rivals. Firms tend to lose some customers to rivals while also gaining at their expense; virtually every firm experiences some customer turnover. One path to increased market share is to reduce customer loss while retaining customer gain. But, again, we must ask how customer attrition can be reduced. To answer this question, we must again search for paths, or subobjectives.

Cooperate with rivals. Rival firms share many common interests and would gain from cooperation in varied spheres. Management should be alert to opportunities for mutually beneficial cooperation.

Learn from rivals. Even small and relatively unprogressive firms sometimes produce valuable new approaches to problems, product improvements, and ways of advertising, among other things. Managements must be on the lookout for improvements introduced by rivals and must develop imitative skills.

Competitor-Related Prizes

In discussing fending off, feeding off, cooperating with, and learning from rivals, we referred only to gains and losses of customer patronage. We are now ready to develop the theme sounded earlier that market competition involves rivalry for many subgoals or instrumental objectives (which we will call prizes). Although the idea is very simple, it contributes significantly to an understanding of competition. Factually speaking, *market competition primarily consists of actions and counteractions by firms to win and retain prizes of many kinds.*

Let us illustrate this crucially important proposition. Manufacturers make costly and ingenious efforts to win the services of strong distributors for their products. Moreover, they seek strong sales support from these strong distributors. They desire strong distributors so that they will be able to place their products with strong retailers who will support their offering strongly. Therefore, we can say that strong distributors and retailers are prizes sought by manufacturers. Some manufacturers already possess these prizes, though they have no permanent hold on them; others will try to win these prizes away. The aggressive and defensive efforts made— often involving highly imaginative lures—represent the substance of competition. To be effective in gaining market share and maintaining market discipline, executives must learn a wide repertoire of behaviors for attacking and defending the many prizes for which they contend.

Market share gains and losses that occur in an industry largely reflect the results of struggles among rivals for the individual prizes sought. In other words, customers are won by manufacturers that win the best distributors and retailers, gain the best design engineers, win preferential treatment from suppliers, and so forth.

Our immediate task, then, is to identify and classify the prizes for which most sellers contend. We will distinguish between prizes related to ultimate customers, resellers, suppliers, and specifiers. These classes are not all-inclusive. (Missing are such specialized prizes as the support of disk jockeys for recording producers.)

A Sample Inventory of Prizes*

- Prizes related to ultimate customers.
     Patronage/brand preference.
     Placement on the source list—listed as an acceptable supplier.

* Based on Anthony O. Kelly, *Market Rivalry: An Entrant's Viewpoint* (unpublished doctoral dissertation, Columbia University, Graduate School of Business), Chapter 3, Appendix II.

Invitation to submit bids.

Active support with other potential customers—recommendations, testimonials.

Larger inventories held.

New uses for product.

Valuable information about competitive developments and market conditions and suggestions for product improvements.

Loyalty—special efforts to buy your brand.

- Prizes related to resellers.

Patronage.

Sales support.

Additional salesmen.

Use of specialized salesmen to sell your product.

Better display space.

Strong advertising support.

Your brand favored over rival brands offered.

Wide assortment of your line.

Information about market developments.

Valuable product improvement suggestions.

Deep inventories of each item.

Special services to ultimate customers—packaging, delivery, credit, and repair service.

Ample and effective use of competitive advertising arrangements.

- Prizes related to suppliers of components and raw materials.

Liberal credit arrangement.

Early exposure to new product developments.

An "exclusive" to new items.

Improved and faster delivery—supplier holds inventories locally.

Generous co-op advertising arrangements.

Help or advice in the processing of their materials, when difficult.

Engineering advice in use of their materials.

Help in the development of new products and processes.

Information about activities of competitors.

- Prizes awarded by "specifiers"—those who advise others on what to buy (physicians, architects, book/music/theatre/movie reviewers, interior decorators, disk jockeys).

Endorsements.

Your product's specifications written into contracts.

Prizes take many forms and differ in important respects. Some prizes are possessed in whole or not at all—like the services of an exclusive distributor; others are possessed to a greater or lesser degree—as in the amount of sales support or shelf space obtained from a retail outlet or in the degree of customer brand preference. Some prizes are best expressed by the ranking of the firm relative to its rivals—as in brand awareness, or product feature knowledge. Another distinction relates to the security of a firm's hold on a prize—some prizes are held fleetingly, or insecurely. Finally, some prizes are expansible in amount, as in the establishment of a new distributorship while others are not changeable in quantity, as in market share position. In selecting the prizes to be sought and the amount of resources to devote to that pursuit, these characteristics of prizes deserve consideration.

The prizes listed above are not equally important; their importance will even vary among firms within the same industry and market as well as over time for any single firm. The list nevertheless suggests the many different fronts on which firms compete and therefore the number of domains in which management must prepare to do battle—requiring, among other things that it monitor carefully ongoing developments and acquire resources so that it can sometimes take the offensive and at other times defend what is already possessed. Appeals directly to ultimate customers represent only the tip of the iceberg of market competition.

Thus far, we have suggested that most managements seek sales growth and market discipline; to achieve these goals, they must fend off rivals, gain at their expense, learn from them, and cooperate with them in some spheres. In these activities, managements will seek and defend individual prizes. In other words, firms can adopt aggressive, defensive, and passive postures toward individual prizes.

Ordinarily, firms take actions to gain a particular prize in a specified local market—rather than try to gain that prize everywhere. As a general rule prizes are held by different firms to different degrees in individual local markets—including such prizes as customer brand preference and brand awareness. A firm that is strong with respect to a prize in some localities may be weak with respect to the same prize in nearby localities.

Vulnerability to competitor inroads. Underlying the striving for and the defending of valued prizes is the vital concept of vulnerability to competitive inroads. The term implies that under certain circumstances market rivals can force particular rivals to give up prizes; similarly, they can recognize that they are themselves vulnerable to inroads from rivals.

Several key questions should be asked about this concept. First, can rivals detect such vulnerability when it exists? If so, what are its most common symptoms? Second, are firms ordinarily vulnerable in general to a loss of the prizes they hold or primarily to the loss of specific prizes in particular places? Third, what specific actions can a firm adopt to exploit each form of a rival's vulnerability? Or, do vulnerabilities need no exploitation by others? Fourth, can firms "aim" their marketing actions at specific rivals to exploit their vulnerabilities or do their actions affect all rivals equally? Regrettably, little is known about these issues. Our discussion must therefore be highly speculative and somewhat superficial.

Is a firm's vulnerability to competitive inroads synonymous with having "weaknesses"? Vulnerability and weakness differ significantly; not all weaknesses make a firm vulnerable; and a firm may be vulnerable although not weak.

Because of their weakness, firms will have poor profits and low market share. Vulnerability consists in a high likelihood of *future* losses of prizes. However, it represents a condition that must be exploited by other firms for the loss to take place. Accordingly, vulnerability to competitive inroads consists of characteristics or circumstances of a firm that can be exploited by existing rivals to gain prizes at that firm's expense.

The symptoms of vulnerability to competitive inroads undoubtedly are specific to individual industries and types of firms. They will not usually be the same for large and small firms, for growing and stable firms, for vertically integrated and unintegrated firms, for retail and mining companies, and so on. Also, the exploitation of a rival's vulnerability may be relatively quick, easy, safe, and cheap in some cases and the opposite in others. Vulnerability, then, varies both in degree and kind.

How might management detect potential vulnerabilities of its rivals to its inroads? The following appear to be the places it should look for indicators of a firm's vulnerabilities:

- Customer-related characteristics: customer complaints about quality, price, design, service, availability, lack of trust.
- Reseller-related characteristics: reseller dissatisfaction with the margins earned, demands for more protection against price cutting; complaints about poor deliveries and poor handling of returns.
- Characteristics related to employees and management: poor morale, high labor turnover, absenteeism, criticism of top management.
- Financial characteristics: low cash flow, high interest charges, difficulties in meeting "regular" dividend.
- Supplier-related characteristics: the firm's patronage is not valued; suppliers give them poor service, the firm is most deprived during periods of shortage.
- Cost-related characteristics: costs substantially above average due to outmoded technology, high labor costs, poor raw materials.

How might the concept of vulnerability to competitive inroads be put to use by an operating executive? We will use a fairly obvious example for brevity. The King Manufacturing Company desires the services of the Ace Distributing Company in Atlanta, for its present distributor, the Deuce Corporation, has been performing poorly and is a source of constant grief. King's vice president of distribution, Mr. Williams, has worked on creating a warm relationship with Mr. Jack, the chief executive of Ace; he calls on him whenever he is in the area and has his regional sales manager do the same. Through these contacts, he has learned what Mr. Jack values most and what bothers him most. Mr. Williams is waiting for some indication that Ace might be lured away from the Queen Corporation, its present supplier. That means that he monitors closely developments that might affect Ace Distributing Company.

One day Mr. Williams learned from one of his regional salesmen that Queen Corporation took an action that alienated some of its distributors. Mr. Williams believes that Mr. Jack might be one of those angered by this action. Before calling on him, Mr. Williams has his regional sales manager call on some of the retailers served by Ace to see if Mr. Jack has expressed any resentment of the manufacturer. In addition, he has the regional sales manager call on Ace to see whether it is carrying fewer items or smaller inventories or in other ways showing disenchantment with Queen Corporation.

Armed with whatever information he has acquired, Mr. Williams starts to exploit Queen Corporation's apparent vulnerability—to the loss of the Ace Distributing Company. He now actively "romances" Mr. Jack and composes a deal that would be particularly attractive to him under the current circumstances. The same deal might not have been acceptable before Queen Corporation took its alienating action.

This illustration indicates that vulnerability to competitive inroads often has no tangible external manifestations. Management must often search hard to find them, and, once it finds them, it must develop an action program to capitalize on its rival's vulnerability.

We have discussed the competitive objectives pursued by firms and presented an orientation to marketing activity that is hardly new but is languishing in neglect. It is what we term a competitor orientation.

It would begin the development of marketing plans with questions like: From which of our rivals should we try to take business? Which of our rivals is taking business from us, and who is making a concerted effort to get one of our valued prizes away from us? To which of our rivals are we vulnerable? Which of our rivals are most vulnerable? Where? And to what actions on our part?

We are now in a position to discuss the development of plans, strategies, and action programs which apply this competitor orientation. It is assumed that the marketing planners and strategists will also employ a customer orientation in the development of their plans and strategies.

Competitive Plans and Strategies—Situation Analysis

Planning remains highly diverse, and we shall not discuss the preparation of a marketing plan. However, we will explore that part of management's concerns that relates to competition and individual competitors and suggest methods of dealing with them. Our starting point is the identification of competitive problems and opportunities. Most of a marketing plan will be directed toward remedying the first and exploiting the second.

The development of a plan for almost any activity begins with a situation analysis, which aims to describe significant developments since the last such analysis. Situation analyses are very selective reviews of recent history, emphasizing incipient developments—the earliest beginnings of major changes, and especially changes that management should do something about. A thorough and insightful situation analysis will carry planners far toward the development of suitable strategies and action programs.

We are concerned with a special kind of situation analysis—one that will not only indicate where the firm is headed unless something is done to change direction but will also highlight actionable competitive problems and opportunities. Situation analyses can be conducted in varying depth. What is described here is a very thorough situation analysis that indicates what management might do when it believes it essential to do the best job possible. However, few managements do, can, or would be wise to conduct such thorough competitive situation analyses. The cost is too high. Management must decide which parts of an exhaustive analysis are most essential for its purposes.

Situation analysts should know what kinds of problems and opportunities might exist. If they do not know what they are looking for, they are not likely to discover anything of value. The following are the usual areas studied by situation analysts:

Changes in competitive conditions of the industry.
Changes in the firm's competitive position in its industry.
Competitive conditions in individual local markets.
Individual prize analysis.
Individual rival analysis.
Analysis of individual items in the firm's product line.

These six areas deserve close examination by most firms. Some firms should research other areas in addition. Within these different spheres what should the situation analyst study? The following aspects of the listed subjects suggest themselves as being potentially fruitful.

- Describe the major changes that took place in the sphere by specific other firms as well as your own in behavior, resources expended or acquired, motivation and effectiveness of actions taken.
- Describe in detail the condition, behavior, resources, and motivation of selected key rivals in the particular sphere.
- Identify the best and worst rivals in the particular sphere and those that made the most progress and that lost most ground.
- Describe changes in the firm's ranking in that sphere relative to the rest of the industry and with respect to specific rivals.
- Where relevant, look for "brand switching" between specific rival firms and your own firm.

Changes in the Competitiveness of the Industry

In identifying significant changes in the industry's competitive conditions faced by the firm since the preceding situation analysis, what changes should a situation analyst be sensitive to? (Observe that this section of the situation analysis deals with the industry generally; changes in local markets would be sought in the analysis of individual markets.) What might signal problems and opportunities resulting from changes in competitive conditions in the industry as a whole? The following is a selective list.

- Competitive problems.
    New entrants into the market.
    Evidence that other firms are planning to enter.
    Personnel changes indicating a probable increase in aggressiveness of important rivals.
    Significant innovations in product, marketing, advertising, and the like by important rival firms.
    Increased output or improved offerings by foreigners.
    Expansion of facilities by firms in the industry heralding excess capacity.
    New government regulations prohibiting some present practices.
    Deregulation by government that frees competitive forces.
    Outbreaks of price cutting, defamation of rivals, low-quality product offerings.

- Competitive opportunities.
    - Removal of barriers into certain submarkets, especially foreign markets.
    - Exit of some rivals from the industry.
    - Greater cooperativeness of formerly intransigent rivals.
    - Increased strength and better performance by trade association.
    - Reduced expenditures by rivals on such competitive activities as advertising, sales promotion, personal selling, frequency of product improvements, and the like.
    - Weaknesses—financial, market-related, in distribution—of individual rivals.

The foregoing list includes the more obvious industry developments that might represent threats to a firm or opportunities for it. Management presumably will want to explore the causes of and investigate any such developments and consider their implications for possible action.

Changes in the Firm's Competitive Position in Its Industry

Significant changes in a firm's position within its own industry presumably affect what its management can and should try to accomplish and the means it employs. Moreover, changes in its position in individual markets will ordinarily reflect problems and opportunities that the situation analysis is designed to uncover.

Key dimensions of a firm's position in its industry. What dimensions of a firm's industry position are particularly relevant to competitive problems and opportunities? The following characteristics are likely to be among the most important determinants of a firm's market power and therefore deserve scrutiny in any competitive situation analysis: production costs, market share, customer loyalty, growth rate, profit margins, and marketing costs. Beyond these, a situation analyst should look for changes in the behavior of specific rivals: how they spend their marketing dollars, and how their marketing appeals, promotional activities, and apparent marketing strategies change. Ordinarily, changes in these characteristics are most conveniently described by changes in individual firms' ranking, an improvement or a worsening in position, and by more precise numerical assessment, like percentage of customers listing each firm as their first preference.

Executives must learn significant competitive developments in the industry as a whole as well as those in separate markets. Some of a firm's rivals operate in many local markets and their characteristics reflect their combined experience in all markets. More specifically, their profitability, cash flows, strategies, and production cost position mainly reflect the composite of their experience in all their local markets. It is for that reason that a situation analysis reviews changes in the firm's competitive position in its industry as a whole.

A situation analysis should indicate whether a firm's cost position relative to its rivals has changed and in what way; whether it is gaining or losing market share; to which of its rivals it is losing patronage and from which it is gaining customers; how its allocation of marketing expenditures among different activities compares with those of its rivals currently, compared with the past. In addition, it should describe changes in the relative position of other firms in the industry in the same respects. In other words, it should describe changes in the competitive position of all significant rival firms within the industry.

The analysis should take account of rival firms' experience in other industries in which they are engaged. Rivals' overall profitability and cash flow as well as the pressure on their management to produce immediate revenue will influence their market behavior. What kinds of competition-related changes should the situation analyst search for? What changes are likely to suggest opportunities or problems for management action?

Table 14-4 presents a classification scheme that helps situation analysts describe significant competition changes. It requires them to place their firm and significant rivals into cells of a matrix according to changes in relative costs, distribution strengths, profit margins, and underlying growth trends. Observe that it deals with these attributes *in combination* so that an entry in cell 7, for example, would represent a firm whose profit margins increased and that strengthened its distribution position and grew more rapidly than the average firm but apparently became a higher-cost producer. A firm listed in cell 73, on the other hand, enjoyed relatively lower production costs and stronger distribution but grew less rapidly than the industry generally and showed reduced profit margins. Other classification schemes could be devised to achieve the same purpose. (Executives, incidentally, can also use this classification scheme to identify firms in other industries that occupy similar competitive positions. The experience of such firms, especially of the most successful, might be highly instructive.)

In constructing such a matrix as presented in Table 14-4, a situation analyst should be governed by management's views as to what constitutes problems and opportunities. Such tables should indicate what management considers symptoms of vulnerability to competitive inroads, a subject discussed earlier in this chapter.

Table 14-4

A Classification of Changes in Position of Individual Firms
in Industry, 1978

Changed production cost position	Changed distribution strength	Growth faster than total industry			Growth same as total industry			Growth slower than total industry		
		Profit margins up	Profit margins same	Profit margins down	Profit margins up	Profit margins same	Profit margins down	Profit margins up	Profit margins same	Profit margins down
Lower	Stronger	1)	10)	19)	28)	37)	46)	55)	64)	73)
	Same as before	2)	11)	20)	29)	38)	47)	56)	65)	74)
	Weaker	3)	12)	21)	30)	39)	48)	57)	66)	75)
Same	Stronger	4)	13)	22)	31)	40)	49)	58)	67)	76)
	Same as before	5)	14)	23)	32)	41)	50)	59)	68)	77)
	Weaker	6)	15)	24)	33)	42)	51)	60)	69)	78)
Higher	Stronger	7)	16)	25)	34)	43)	52)	61)	70)	79)
	Same as before	8)	17)	26)	35)	44)	53)	62)	71)	80)
	Weaker	9)	18)	27)	36)	45)	54)	63)	72)	81)

Competitive Conditions in Individual Local Markets

Because competitive conditions vary widely from one local market to another, management must attend to individual market differences. It must not base plans and programs on overall magnitudes which often belie the market realities. Let us illustrate the errors that could result from regarding the firm's market as a single entity rather than as a large number of discrete and dissimilar parts.

Viewed nationally, a certain firm accounts for about 8 percent of total sales in its industry, while two other firms have substantially larger national market shares. However, the firm in question is fundamentally regional. In almost all the local markets in which it operates, its market share is between 25 percent and 40 percent and its brand is the largest single seller. Management should adopt marketing plans suitable for a major market factor.

A second firm has a large national market share, substantially larger than any other firm. Nevertheless, it does not have the largest share in more than 10 percent of the nation's markets. As a market reality, this firm is not a dominant firm; its rivals are not likely to regard it as a market leader and it will have only modest power in the marketplace.

Some aspects of a firm do transcend individual markets. Its production cost position relative to rivals often can be described accurately on an overall basis. But even then, its costs must be compared with those of the regional producers with which it competes. A firm's logistical costs almost always vary from market to market. Similarly, although the typical firm offers the same physical product in all local markets, it may represent top quality in some while in others regional producers may excel. It is prudent to assume great diversity rather than uniformity in local markets in almost every respect.

Table 14-5 includes the information which management requires to uncover competitive problems and opportunities in its individual markets. It contains three kinds of information: descriptors of changes in the market itself, indicators of the firm's position in the market, and information about individual rival firms.

It is mainly in the individual market analysis that management searches for vulnerable rivals and for its own vulnerabilities. Toward this end, management must determine what is evidence of vulnerability to inroads from rivals. It will then collect such evidence about rivals and itself. Indicators of vulnerability vary widely from industry to industry, as does the behavior by which firms can exploit their rivals' vulnerability.

Executives should differentiate general vulnerability from specific prize, specific product, and specific market vulnerability. In this section of the situation analysis, one is looking for evidence of general weakness in individual rivals—and in one's own position—that exists in particular local markets.

Table 14-5

FORM FOR DESCRIBING COMPETITIVE CONDITIONS IN MAJOR MARKETS

Major market	Description of individual market			Our position in market				Sales size of individual rivals			Usually aggressive activity	
	Growth =, +, −	Discipline H, M, L	Dominated? Yes, No	Market share	Size rank	Profit-ability	Distribution strength	Grow-ing	Stable	Declin-ing	Aggressor	Activity
N.Y. metro.												
Boston metro.												
D.C.—Baltimore metro.												
Detroit metro.												

Individual Prize Analysis

In conducting an individual prize analysis, the first task of the situation analyst is to select the prizes to study in detail; the second is to decide whether to study each one on an overall basis or to study local market by local market—or both.

Selection of prizes. What is vital for one firm in an industry may be far less so for another. Still, most producers of major appliances place a high premium on having strong distributors, brand preference based on perceived good quality of offerings, and a flow of product improvements. Package goods producers mainly seek strong brand image, shelf space and shelf position, and brand preference. Retail firms seek reputation for reliability, broad assortment, good service, and attractive values. The impression, perception, and image are usually quite as important as the reality.

Reporting on changes. A summary statement can usually be made to describe gains and losses with respect to every prize—for example, the number of distributors gained and lost by quality rating, the number of new product feature introductions by individual rivals during the previous year, or the changed preference ranking of individual brands. Executives take big risks when they base action programs or strategies on such summary statements. All too often, important developments are obscured or canceled out in global summaries.

In addition to summary descriptions of prize-related changes, the situation analyst should report on developments in individual markets. (Figure 14-1 presents a sample form that might be used for that purpose.) The selection of markets for close attention poses difficult problems for the situation analyst. (One would expect *operating* executives to pay attention to local difficulties and opportunities, but their concerns are different from and often not known to the situation analyst.) As a general rule, all the largest markets, clear problem markets, and the strongest markets should be included—plus a random sample of the remainder. The total time and money budget available will dictate the size of the sample.

In reviewing developments involving individual prizes, what developments should situation analysts record? If they observe only changes in factual circumstances they will describe what is old-hat and already known. Much more valuable would be symptoms of impending change, including (1) increased efforts by rivals to win the prize, (2) changed methods used to win it, and (3) changes in the apparent value of different prizes. (Prizes are often developed or strengthened, so their value must be reappraised periodically.) Such information is more valuable than actual changes in prize-ownership, but it is also more difficult to obtain.

Figure 14-1. Form for situation analysis.

Prize: Exclusive Distributors

Market: Pittsburgh, Pa.

1. Changes in identity of distributors in the market

   New distributors: (1) ———————— (2) ———————— Brands carried: (1) ———— (2)

   Distributors who left business: (1) ———————— (2) ———————— Brands carried: (1) ———— (2)

2. Significant changes in quality of established distributors

   Notable improvements: (1) ———————— (2) ———————— (3)

   Notable deteriorations: (1) ———————— (2) ———————— (3)

3. Switches in distributorships

Distributor	From brand	To brand	Apparent reason for switch
a.			
b.			
c.			

4. Firms actively trying to lure our distributor away

Firm	Method used	Effort expended
a.		
b.		
c.		

5. Our ranking of distributors: which ones we would most like to have

   a. ———————— b. ———————— c. ————————

Individual Rival Analysis

Every situation analysis made for competitive purposes includes a rival-by-rival description, with emphasis on changes since the preceding situation analysis. Our discussion of changes in the firm's position within its industry included a matrix (Table 14-4) that described changes in the position of rival firms also. That form dealt with the overall position of significant firms within the industry; we are also concerned with their position in individual markets. Attention was addressed to this issue in the individual market analyses described above. At some point, the situation analyst must put it all together.

One aspect of individual rival analysis that has not been discussed is the strong regional producer. Most studies of rivals focus on national producers; regional firms, which frequently are the most effective rivals where they operate, are consequently neglected in the formulation of strategy and marketing programs. Most firms would be wise to devote a special section of their situation analysis to regional rivals.

Discussions of the competitive ingredient of a marketing plan require a careful evaluation of rivals' resources, including an examination of their financial, managerial, technological, and distribution situation. In addition, close study should be made of personnel changes that might presage changes in behavior or strategy.

One ingenious approach to rival analysis calls for individual executives to be designated "G-2 Officers" who undertake to think like a particular rival. Thus, one executive might be asked to develop a marketing plan for the XYZ Corporation, another for the ABC Company—doing the very best to formulate the same plan as that company's management might produce. (The goal is not to formulate the best possible plan for that firm, but to "think the way they do.")

Large amounts of resources can be consumed in a rival-by-rival analysis. Consequently, the analyst will want to develop hypotheses about what changes reflect problems or opportunities for his firm; he will recognize that much of the information required about rivals is contained in individual market analyses, analyses of individual prizes, analyses of individual items in the product line, and in the general description of changed competitive conditions in the industry. Accordingly, he will restrict his rival-by-rival analysis mainly to such factors as personnel changes in top management, apparent changes in marketing strategy, overall financial position developments, and the rivals' activities in such other important areas as merger, acquisition, entry into foreign markets, and plant expansion in other industries.

Some firms regard an analysis of their few closest and strongest competitors as the totality of their competitive situation analysis. To serve that function, the individual rival analysis must be expanded to incorporate at least the most important local market, individual prize, and individual item in the product line developments. At present, descriptions of rivals focus on plant capacity, profitability, market share, cash flow, personnel, and strategy changes. Almost always, they virtually ignore individual market and individual prize developments.

ANALYSES OF INDIVIDUAL ITEMS IN THE PRODUCT LINE

It has been stressed repeatedly that individual firms in the same industry occupy dissimilar competitive positions; each of them, moreover, faces far more intense competition in some local markets than in others. Also, competition takes far different forms in some localities than in others. We now suggest another common complexity: some items in a firm's line will be under far more competitive pressure than other items. A firm's problems and opportunities often must be expressed in terms of individual items in the line, as well as particular prizes and designated local markets. The situation analysis should search out trouble spots and points of strength in the firm's line of offerings. Planners must be guided to those items that need support and informed about items which can provide such support.

Here again, the situation analyst must decide whether to examine each local market separately or settle for overall company experience. The answer is always the same: if major differences exist from market to market, the overall picture is distorted and no viable policy can be built upon it. Most companies find that major differences from local market to market arise from the effects of local and regional rivals. Consequently, local differences must be given close attention.

How might one best uncover the strengths and weaknesses in the product line? Performance relative to plan implies that the plan itself was soundly based. Other possibilities avoid that dubious assumption. Most useful is an indication of how the individual items sold compared to last year's sales; even more useful for some purposes is an examination of most recent sales experience relative to sales, say, six to nine months before—that is, recent sales trends for individual items. Such information is relatively easy to develop from the firm's records so that it usually is not necessary to study only a sample of markets (see Table 14-6).

In addition, the analysis of individual items in the product line should catalog the most important changes in product features, the firms that introduced them, and changes in suggested retail prices and in the differentials between the prices of individual items in the line. Particular attention

Table 14-6

FORM FOR ITEM-BY-ITEM ANALYSIS OF COMPETITIVE STRATEGY

Items	Sales Experience		Strongest competitive offerings				Weakest competitive offerings			
	This year vs. last year	End of year vs. beginning	#1	#2	#3	#4	#1	#2	#3	#4

should be paid to possible changes in distributor and retailer margins on individual items. Finally, the analysis should search out the product weaknesses of individual rivals—those with poor product performance as well as poor sales experience.

SUMMARY

The six sections of a thorough situation analysis should not be viewed as independent endeavors, though different individuals may prepare each one. The separate parts are different ways of looking at the same phenomenon—the turbulence and cross-currents of a modern market. It is hoped that the situation analyst will see important implications from a careful study of all the parts that are not apparent from any one of them.

The situation analyst might set himself the task of constructing a summary of the separate parts. His objective would be to identify the firms experiencing the greatest difficulties—and therefore presumably the most vulnerable—and those enjoying the greater success—and consequently the most formidable adversaries. In addition, the situation analyst might list the incipient developments that deserve close observation and even call for periodic reports on the more important of these.

Recognize that situation analyses need not be divided into the six sections described. Indeed, the special features of many industries will require added sections. Moreover, the six sections were not listed in the order in which they should generally be prepared. For parsimony and power, a different order is recommended. Usually, the best place to begin is the analysis of local markets; this should be followed by the prize analysis. The very last two sections to prepare are the rival-by-rival analysis and the competitive conditions in the industry. This order is proposed because the early analysis should provide inputs for the later ones. The recommended order suggests again that competition largely consists of what happens in local markets and to individual prizes.

A management that has completed a thorough situation analysis is ready to review its current competitive strategies and possibly formulate new ones. It also understands the competitive problems and opportunities that call for action. Before discussing the actions that firms can take to achieve their competitive objectives, we will present a procedure that may be used to develop an effective competitive strategy.

The Construction of a Competitive Strategy

Most managements possess a scheme for besting their rivals. Often it is not explicit; usually, it is short-run, and designed to help with exceptional market situations like the advent of a new rival, a competitor's particularly attractive new product feature, local price cutting, a product shortage, and the like. Effective strategies are valuable because they add impact to a firm's actions. They offer a logic for using resources and exploiting a firm's position so that its actions become exceptionally effective. A good strategy is equivalent to having additional resources. Little wonder that executives seek them. What is to wonder is why they do not do so more systematically and why they neglect long-run and enduring competitive strategies.

By a competitive strategy, we mean a logic, scheme, conception, or line of thinking for the attainment of a firm's competitive objectives. Our consideration here is limited to an enduring strategy—one intended to be effective for, say, three years or more. Competitive strategies should ordinarily contain both an offensive and defensive component.

Some strategies are very obvious and seem scarcely worthy of the name. For example, the strategy of doing everything better than rivals may be considered a nonstrategy strategy. Certainly, it represents the hard way of succeeding. On the other hand, firms may adopt ingenious schemes that incorporate novelty, excitement, humor, surprise, respect, and fear and produce favorable results even for firms with relatively meager resources and weak bargaining power. Clearly, management would be well advised to devise a competitive strategy that permits their firms to perform effectively against rivals who will themselves probably adopt a competitive strategy.

Is there a method, a more or less routine process, by which management can develop a competitive strategy, or are effective strategies arrived at only by inspiration? A method does exist for developing a competitive strategy, but it is not routine—an executive requires considerable experience and intelligence to employ it effectively. Although it may not produce an inspired result, it is likely to yield a sensible and effective strategy. Employed with imagination, it can produce a highly ingenious competitive strategy.

What then should management seek in a competitive strategy? Above all the strategy should work—it should enable a firm to achieve reasonable competitive objectives. Ordinarily, that will happen if the strategy has some of the following features:

It capitalizes on the firm's strengths and on its rivals' weaknesses.
It is not easily imitated or offset.
It is long-lasting.
It is consistent with what the firm has done in the past.
It takes account of the separate needs of ultimate customers, resellers, suppliers, and the firm itself.

The method to be described organizes and structures the executives' knowledge of feasible attractive *paths* that might enable the firm to attain its competitive objectives. It also systematizes the search for actions that would advance the firm along those paths. By providing structure and organization to executives' thoughts, the method produces the maximum benefit from what they know or can imagine. The chief steps in the procedure are:

- Identify all feasible attractive paths that might be followed to gain the firm's competitive objectives.
- Identify all feasible attractive paths leading to the paths that lead to these objectives.
- Select the best paths for the firm in question to follow, given its strengths and weaknesses and the constraints on its behavior.
- Select paths and actions that might be combined in ways that are reinforcing, consistent, and synergistic.

Let us be specific. The process starts with a hierarchy of objectives for the firm. The relationship among the different levels of the hierarchy is that of means and ends. Items listed on the third level, for example, represent all feasible attractive means known to the executive for achieving the items on the second level. Let us develop a hierarchy of objectives specifically for the purpose of devising a competitive strategy.

We start with the firm's ultimate objective, which we might describe as business success. We would define business success to include enduring high dividends and steadily increasing prices for the firm's securities. This essentially specifies what top management and the board of directors mean by business success.

On the next lower level we would list the means by which the firm might secure enduring high dividends and steadily increasing prices for its equities. These means clearly include earning high profits and possibly growth. On the next level we would indicate the means by which the firm might achieve high profits and growth. Clearly, the firm requires high revenues and low costs to achieve high profits.

On the next level we would list the feasible attractive paths that lead to high revenues and low costs. At this point we should focus particularly on items related to competition—to rivals, existing and potential. Following our earlier discussion, we would list sales growth and improved market discipline as our paths to high revenues. To obtain these, we must gain customers from rivals and prevent loss of customers to rivals, as well as learn from and cooperate with rivals.

To simplify our task, let us start another hierarchy with the competitive objective of gaining customers from rivals.

High-Level Aggressive Strategies

By what different means might a firm gain customers from its rivals? Two basically different, but consistent, approaches were suggested earlier: one is to offer ultimate customers better value—or what they perceive is better value; the other is to best rivals in the contest for "prizes." In effect, the second approach aims to gain ultimate customers in two steps, namely, by gaining subobjectives whose attainment then results in increased patronage by ultimate customers. Management will, either consciously or unconsciously, favor one approach over the other. This choice is one of the more important strategic decisions that the competitive strategist must make. There are other crucial decisions, exemplified by the following questions:

- What particular prizes will the firm seek, and in what geographic locations will they be sought?
- Will the firm seek to gain at the expense of selected vulnerable rivals or seek growth by taking small amounts of business from most of its rivals?
- Will it seek growth in particular geographic markets or in all of them?
- Will it endeavor to grow quickly or slowly?

- Under what circumstances will it try to take customers or prizes from rivals?
- By what methods will it try to take business or prizes from rivals?

Strategists ordinarily will have good reasons to select one alternative course of action over the others. Their reasons would represent some blend of logic concerning the results of past actions by their firm and other firms, and the particular strengths of their firm and of their closest rivals. The more alternatives the strategist identifies and the better these alternatives are, the better the outcome is likely to be.

The foregoing strategic choices may be derived either from a situation analysis or directly from the hierarchy. When one asks, "How can I take customers away from rivals?" a series of additional questions are immediately suggested: Which rivals? Where (in what local markets)? When (under what circumstances)? At what pace (gradually and almost imperceptibly or rapidly and markedly)? By what means? The possible answers to these questions can be combined in various ways to get literally hundreds of specific means to gain rivals' customers. Let us list some sample combinations.

One means of gaining customers at the expense of rivals would be to try to win Company Z's customers in Omaha during the height of the sales season by mounting a major sales promotion offensive. Another means would be to cultivate certain of Company B's customers in all major metropolitan markets when total demand for the product is at a cyclical peak by offering them a reduced price on "combination deals," but to do so at a slow pace so that the strategy would not be obvious. Still another means would be to try to take a little business from almost every rival at a gradual pace through the next year by providing speedier delivery to all dealers and substantially reducing the amount of imperfect merchandise.

As these illustrations suggest, a firm might employ different strategies against different rivals. Indeed, it can employ different means at different times against different targets in different places to gain customers at different rates. Sometimes problems of possible conflict in strategies arise, especially in measures taken to gain distributors and key retailers, who are often in active communication. The suspicion that others are receiving substantially better treatment is highly demoralizing to distributors and retailers and limits what a manufacturer might do to win them away from rivals.

We have carried the discussion far enough to confront some of the chief choices facing the strategist. However, to this point we have discussed only the firm's global competitive strategy—that is, its general competitive posture. Firms would also benefit from developing a competitive strategy for individual prizes and for individual markets. Ordinarily, such nonglobal strategies would represent the place to start the process of strategy development. When individual prize and individual local market strategies have been developed, executives are in a strong position to adopt a global competitive strategy. (In the interest of brevity, we will develop a sample strategy only for an individual prize and not for an individual local market. The method by which strategies for individual markets can be developed is precisely the same as that used in developing a global competitive strategy or a strategy for an individual prize.)

Aggressive Strategies for Gaining a Single Prize

Let us then construct a separate hierarchy of objectives for a single prize. In our illustration, we will seek a strategy for winning away highly valued distributors from a competitive line. Figure 14-2 presents such a strategy. Although the alternative means depicted in this hierarchy are selective rather than all-inclusive, the chart nevertheless illuminates the method. Six main paths are identified for winning a strong distributor away from a competitor; presumably, these are the very best available to the strategist's firm. Other possibilities were discarded as inappropriate.

Each of the six paths listed requires particular actions or subpaths. These are listed on the third level of the chart. It would be possible to extend the chart to another level, but little would be gained. The strategist now has before him, in clearly organized form, a set of paths he might elect to follow. Although the method clearly does not grind out a strategy, it helps extract the manager's view of the best alternatives available and the actions required to implement them. Once these are set down in a structured form, the selection of a strategy becomes easier and more valid.

After identifying potential strategies, the decision maker must select the most promising courses of action, given the particular strengths and weaknesses of the firm and its rivals. For example, if the firm's sales representatives are mature, experienced, diplomatic, and likeable, building close personal ties with distributors and retailers may be the most effective and attractive alternative. With a new, inexperienced sales force, on the other hand, other strategies may be preferable. Similarly, if most competitors suffered from heavy turnover among their sales representatives, the strategist might decide to invest substantial amounts of money and effort into building a stable sales force capable of winning and retaining the affection and loyalty of the firm's distributors.

The final step in the process of strategy development is to look for a way to give coherence or special meaning to one or more of the paths that have

Figure 14-2. A hierarchy for developing an aggressive competitive strategy for a single prize.

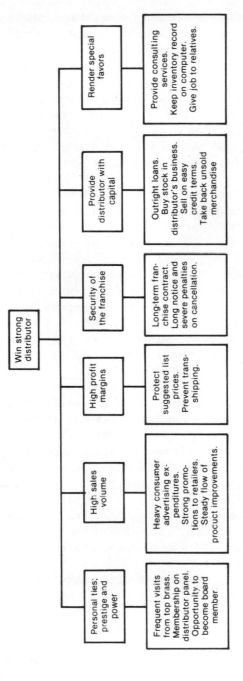

been mapped in the hierarchy. One strategy might simply consist of a decision about the amount of time and money devoted to each of the paths listed; that approach, though useful, amounts to an unsophisticated, piecemeal strategy. A more ingenious, integrated strategy the firm might adopt would be to develop the posture of a warm, friendly, loyal, helpful supplier to its distributors. Distributors would actually be treated like employees, be truly close to the supplier, and participate in some of the firm's decisions. They would not be treated solely as sources of profit for the manufacturer; personal and intangible values would get heavy weight from top management. That kind of posture could not be established quickly, but once made believable, it could represent a major asset to a firm in holding as well as gaining strong distributors.

Most of the items in the hierarchy treat distributors as if their sole objective were the maximization of profits. Insofar as that is in fact the main objective of many distributors, the proposed posture might not always be an effective strategy. No strategy will work well in all situations. A strategist ordinarily seeks distinctiveness and special effectiveness with the kinds of customers he values highly. In the hypothetical example, the supplier might prefer to deal with distributors who will not hound him for every possible little financial advantage but who will seek an enduring, trusting, and friendly business relationship.

Defensive Competitive Strategies

The strategy described was aggressive—that is, aimed at taking a prize from rivals. Firms also require strategies to defend what they hold. Figure 14-3 indicates some important paths in a defensive strategy for valued distributors. It reveals that a number of the paths that help to take distributors away also help to hold those already gained.

Winning a prize is only the first step, for a prize can easily be withdrawn. The recipient of a prize must not take for granted that he will forever be favored. He will want to demonstrate that he deserved to be favored and take any opportunities offered to develop close personal ties. Especially in this last respect, the prize recipient ordinarily holds a large advantage over those who seek to win the prize away.

We are now in the position of a competitive strategist who has explored strategies for the firm's main prizes and for its most important markets. That strategist also will know what strategy management has been pursuing in the recent past. The question to be addressed is, should the firm alter its competitive strategy? If so, how?

Again, the strategist would ordinarily search for combinations of sub-

Figure 14-3. A hierarchy for developing a defensive competitive strategy for a single prize.

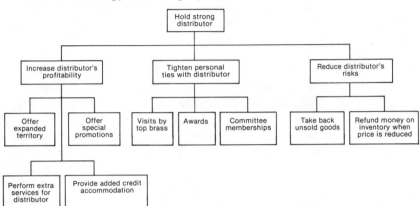

strategies that reinforce one another and that are consistent with the firm's past behavior; it would ordinarily not be wise to make a change in strategy to accommodate temporarily changed circumstances. Consistency is usually essential to achieve recognition and trust among ultimate customers as well as consistent execution within one's own organization and distributors. Usually, it takes a long time for an organization to assimilate a shift in thinking; until it does, some serious mistakes are likely to be made.

Competitor-Related Action Programs

Having discussed the development of competitive strategies for the firm as a whole and for the pursuit of individual prizes, we are ready to discuss competitor-related actions. The actions available to management cover a broad range, for they include everything a firm might do to gain or defend all prizes. It would not be feasible to list, let alone discuss, all competitor-related marketing actions. However, we can list the characteristics that make marketing actions attractive for competitive purposes; in so doing, we will also suggest what actions are particularly unattractive.

Some actions taken by a firm affect only a single rival while others affect many and possibly all. An intensive effort on the part of management to win the services of an important distributor away from another manufacturer will primarily affect that other manufacturer. In contrast, a major sales promotion composed of broadcast advertising, point-of-sales materials, and special incentives to salesmen will ordinarily affect all rivals (though not all of them equally) in the area in which the promotion takes place.

Similarly, some measures adopted by a firm are intended to exploit the weakness of a particular rival and to make major inroads into his position, in the belief that he is vulnerable and not able to retaliate effectively. Other measures are designed to improve a firm's market position by taking only trivial numbers of customers from all rivals. The expectation in the second case is that no rivals will feel impelled to retaliate since their losses were minor. Indeed, the action might pass unnoticed, especially if the market is expanding.

These illustrations highlight two essential characteristics of competitor-related behavior: the selectivity-directionality of the action and the concentration or diffusion of the action's effect. But other characteristics also deserve the attention of an executive designing programs of marketing action. In particular, the following features are usually desirable in actions taken in order to gain a competitive advantage:

- Highly directional—can be focused on a single rival.
- A small or modest threat to rivals—they do not threaten major injury and thus will not provoke a major and emotional counterblow.
- Not easily imitated—it would require considerable time and skill to duplicate the aggressive action and even then it would not be identical. (Price actions can be duplicated exactly; almost no others can be.)
- Reversible—the action can be withdrawn without embarrassment or injury if a decision is made to do so.
- Implemented speedily—it can be put into effect almost as quickly as one can make a phone call or print up a new price list.
- Quick to have impact—it is readily perceived and takes effect immediately.
- Not requiring major outlays in advance of its taking effect—the action is paid for more or less concurrently with the receipt of its benefits.
- Not very risky—it does not make the firm vulnerable to a counterploy by rivals; cannot be misinterpreted and, as a consequence, give rise to a major response.
- Does not need to be consistent with other actions taken.
- Not likely to create problems of credibility—it is essentially independent of other actions by the firm.
- Not likely to boomerang even if executed poorly.
- Diffused in its effects on rivals—it takes a little from many rivals.

Competitor-related actions can be classified usefully according to their target. Are they designed to influence ultimate customers? Resellers? If so, at what level of distribution? (Retailers, distributors, brokers, salesmen?) Suppliers? Government regulators? These classifications are very general, but a few relatively specific observations would be in order.

Price—the main action considered by economic theorists—is unique among the many actions available to management. It is immediately perceived, is almost perfectly imitable, is speedily implemented, threatens major and very prompt impact, and is paid for as sales are made (in the form of lower profit margins) rather than in advance. Moreover, price reductions may prove irreversible but price increases usually can be retracted without great difficulty; the nature of a price change is easily comprehended; it cannot be focused on a single rival, and changes in price usually affect more than one party to the business process—that is, different layers of resellers as well as ultimate customers. Some other competitor-related actions are relatively private, or can be kept so. The seller can often disguise or misrepresent the motive for his actions, direct them at only one target, and make the action effective for a stated short period.

In summary, management has a wide choice of actions that might be taken to influence one or more different targets. In specific cases, management will ordinarily pick the "victim"—a vulnerable rival—and then select the prizes it will try to win away from it and where to do so. After that has been decided, management will find its range of choice sharply restricted. Still, it will ordinarily have options and will select those whose characteristics meet its needs. Sometimes the most effective action is also the most risky; or it must be paid for in advance; or it cannot be directed solely at the intended target.

The effectiveness with which management deals with competition depends to a considerable degree upon the wisdom with which it selects the actions to employ. As a general rule, management should favor those actions that it uses most skillfully.

Management of Competitive Problems Below Top Management

Up to this point, we have discussed competitive problems as they confront top management and planners. But executives well below the top face serious competitive problems. Let us now view competition from the perspective of senior and subsenior executives who are responsible for functions like purchasing, warehouse operations, the purchase of advertising media, personnel, customer service, executive development, and the like.

Executives at this level and their subordinates seek prizes of some kind for their firm. Presumably their firm already holds some prizes that they must retain. Thus, their task is to obtain and retain prizes and to do so at low cost. More specifically, they must do the following:

• Identify the prizes for which they contend with other firms, and identify those firms by name and the particular local markets and specific prizes for which they are competing. For example, "we shall try to win the Ace Distributing Corporation away from the ABC Corporation in St. Louis." Or "we must resist the efforts of the King Corporation to lure the Crown Distributor in Atlanta away from our line."

• Assess the capabilities of their firm to gain and to retain the specific prizes for which they are responsible. For example, "we offer our distributors a less attractive profit opportunity than do the ABC Corporation and the XYZ Company, but compare favorably with all other major producers. Before we can match those two rivals, we must build up our brand preference by consistent and substantial advertising effort—including attractive point of sale materials."

• Develop a repertoire of behaviors by which their firm may mount an attack on the prizes for which they are responsible and for resisting such attacks from others. They should learn and create a variety of programs by which they can gain prizes and defend them against others.

• Monitor developments related to the prizes for which they are responsible. Much of the earlier discussion in this chapter applies here, for example, the need for market discipline, the danger of retaliation, and the recognition that prizes may impose unduly high cost.

Perhaps the most serious error made in the study of competition is to assume it occurs only on the highest level—in major price and promotional moves. Competition takes place on many levels in the organizational hierarchy and for many prizes. A firm's success depends largely on how each of these competitive domains is managed.

Summary and Conclusions

Competition is the foremost threat to every firm's prosperity and even to its very survival. Competition is no vague abstract set of market forces. For almost every management, it denotes identifiable rivals who seek the very prizes that it seeks. Management must formulate plans, strategies, and programs of action to cope effectively with its competitors. It must lose no more prizes to rivals than it wins away from them.

Actually, most managements seek to grow; a majority seek steadily larger market shares—an impossible goal. Some seek to dominate their particular market niches. All firms would gain from an interrelated set of attitudes and behaviors, here termed market discipline, which mainly denotes farsightedness and forbearance—the ability to resist the temptation to take a sure quick profit at the expense of a less certain diminution of profits.

Most writings about competition have adopted a social or public policy viewpoint; executives get very little guidance from those writings or from the models of formal economic theory. They must develop a deep understanding of market forces from personal experience and interchange with their colleagues. Individual industries differ enormously in the form and intensity of competition. Individual firms within an industry experience very different competitive pressures and respond to them in varied ways.

One of the most fruitful views of market competition is as a contest among firms for a very large number of prizes—subobjectives—each of which contributes toward the winning of patronage from ultimate customers. Firms can grow and prosper by protecting themselves against loss of business to rivals and by determining which of their rivals are vulnerable and taking action to grow at their expense.

In drawing up competitive plans and strategies, management must first determine where it stands competitively at present. To establish its position, management requires a thorough—but not completely so—situation analysis. Such an analysis would review developments in six spheres: in the competitiveness of the industry, in the firm's position within its industry, in the firm's position in individual markets, its experience in gaining the prizes most essential to its prosperity, changes in the resources and position of rival firms, and the problems and opportunities of the individual items in its product line.

Management requires a competitive strategy on several levels: an overall strategy for its firm against other firms on a global level, and separate strategies for the winning of individual prizes. It may also adopt a strategy about the kinds of markets in which it will concentrate its resources and those it will avoid or cultivate only on a minimum level because of their extreme competitiveness. Among the key strategic choices management must make are the following: should it mainly strive to win the patronage of ultimate customers directly or concentrate on winning subprizes? Should it strive mainly to win new customers away from rivals or to reduce its losses to rivals while gaining the same number of new customers? Should it adopt aggressive measures that would gain only small amounts from many rivals or seek to gain large amounts from a vulnerable rival?

The numerous prizes sought by management, the great variation in competitive conditions from market to market, the varying reception of individual items in a firm's product line all suggest the large number of executives who bear some responsibility for the firm's competitive standing. Many executives below top management rank must be able to identify the prizes that the firm can win, appraise the value of those prizes, devise actions that are likely to win them, and find means of retaining the prizes won.

Chapter 15

THE PREPARATION OF PROPOSALS FOR ACTION

E XECUTIVES make some important and difficult decisions quickly, with little data search or discussion with colleagues. Frequently, no written record remains of such decisions. Far more usually, the most important and difficult decisions of senior executives do, and should, take the form of written proposals to top management.

Objectives of Project Proposals

Written proposals mainly aim to inform others thoroughly so that they can review a recommended action or reach an independent valid judgment on some vital matter; that is, they permit the reader, should he so desire, to virtually make the decision for himself and not take anything on faith. In addition, written proposals usually suggest how to carry out the proposed action effectively; proposals link decision with action. Observe that the purpose of such proposals is *not* to persuade others to accept the recommendations.

What should such written proposals contain? What posture should the author adopt? To what publics should the author address his thoughts? What should the author avoid? On what level should the proposal be written?

Most of these questions answer themselves if one is clear about the objectives of the report. If, as was suggested, the objectives are to inform others and thus enable them to reach a valid judgment and also assist them to carry out a proposal, then the report should include everything required to achieve these ends. Most of all, the author must assure the readers that he has considered and examined everything that deserved attention thoroughly and objectively. Completeness and thoroughness are valued highly by those who receive reports for they occupy a painful dependent position. They need reassurance that the author has done his work carefully, especially if large sums or risks are at stake. Partly to meet such dependency needs, authors of reports might be wise to include some material that is interesting and satisfies general background curiosity, even though it contributes virtually nothing to the conclusions reached.

A proposal for action has other objectives than to enable the recipients of the report to reach a conclusion. It has an important defensive goal, for example. In the future it might be used to defend recommendations that turned out badly. In addition, it can serve as proof of responsible management—evidence of thoroughness and imaginativeness. If things do not turn out well, but management was aware of potential dangers and appraised them prudently, they will receive relatively little blame— though no way is known for completely avoiding blame.

A proposal should also prod and stimulate its readers to suggest ways of overcoming difficulties and of capitalizing on opportunities. It should motivate others to make contributions; consequently, the author might pose some questions to those who receive the proposal.

The proposal should also help those for whom it was prepared to take action to carry out the recommendations made. Accordingly, it might propose assignments of responsibilities, recommend an organization for the project, and suggest a timetable. In addition, it might call for particular controls to insure that errors are caught early.

Those submitting proposals often feel obliged to win acceptance for their proposals, if they regard them as meritorious; they may do so "for the good of the firm." They unconsciously become advocates, even salesmen. Many assume that they know far better than those who review the proposal what should be done. Not infrequently, they try to insure acceptance of their proposals by omitting possible pitfalls or negative contingencies and by underestimating some costs.

Those preparing proposals are usually far better informed than those who receive their proposals about the factual aspects of their proposals. (If they prepare their proposal well, the gap between the preparers and readers will not be very large.) However, those who pass on proposals almost invariably can add something of value—if nothing more than an independent confirmation of the views of the author. Usually, they can relate the proposal to other opportunities the firm possesses; they can make an independent assessment of the firm's capabilities to perform tasks implied by the proposal. As suggested, they usually can contribute additional ideas—new alternatives and embellishments of suggestions included in the report. In short, they represent a resource—a source of added input—which can strengthen the proposal. Accordingly, a proposal should be written in a manner calculated to elicit a maximum of useful input. Those preparing the report should not feel obliged to think of everything and to claim that they have done so. On the other hand, they are obliged at least to think of everything that would occur quickly to most intelligent people. As suggested, they should demonstrate thoroughness and completeness as far as possible; where they have not been thorough, they are wise to make that fact clear so that those reviewing the report can concentrate their attention on those points.

Objectivity is another important characteristic highly valued in a proposal. Failure to mention difficulties and risks is guaranteed to undermine the confidence of those receiving a report, even on scores where the report is objective and valid. It is not proposed that a proposal exaggerate the pitfalls and risks of a proposal, but it should certainly set them out clearly. Almost nothing of value is free of any risk; those preparing a proposal do not owe their supervisors any foolproof gold-plated projects. They do owe them an honest, objective, and careful evaluation, however.

The Parties to a Project Proposal

In a project proposal, the author communicates with several distinct publics. He should never lose sight of the groups to whom he is addressing his report.

THE AUTHORS

The report writer may represent a committee, which could have been active and contributing but more often is neither. He must make clear for whom he speaks.

The author would also do well to make clear just what level of competence he claims for himself and the amount of effort that he devoted to the report. He would be very unwise to exaggerate either point. He should indicate how many man-hours were spent by persons with what, if any, competence to make a study of this particular subject.

THE SEPARATE AUDIENCES OF A PROJECT PROPOSAL

No one of a project proposal's several distinct audiences is all-important. The author should aim to inform all of them by writing essentially different reports for each, though all are served by certain common elements.

One audience is the very busy executive who is frustrated by and impatient with detail. This audience wants to get the essential facts and ideas. Often it wants details about some particular issue, but each individual wants details about different things. At the opposite extreme is an audience that is often far less influential than the first in determining whether the proposal will be approved but quite important in carrying it out. This audience frequently demands more detail than anyone should require to meet the organization's needs. Other audiences include those who believe they will be injured if the report's recommendations are adopted; and those who wish to discredit the author of the report for either personal or professional reasons.

Suggested Structure for a Multi-Audience Report

Every sizable project proposal should begin with a specific recommendation and a brief summary. The purpose of the summary is to provide readers with a model which will illuminate the subsequent sections of the report. The summary should be written with that specific purpose in view and should not degenerate into a compression of much information into minimum space. The summary should present the rationale of the proposal.

THE SUMMARY

The summary should be no longer than the busiest audience will tolerate—rarely should it exceed two single-spaced pages and usually it should be about half that size. It should start with what specifically is being proposed followed by its rationale. For example:

> It is proposed that we change our distribution arrangements in those 11 markets where we have exclusive distributors with overlapping territories as quickly as feasible—and in every case within one year. This proposal aims to eliminate the conflict among distributors, some instances of excessive price competition, and, above all, to end the disquiet of some of our distributors who fear that others will be placed in their territory. This proposal should entail only modest costs to repurchase merchandise and should require minimal top-management time. Its ultimate effects are expected to be almost a 1 percent reduction in overhead costs and a moderate increase in sales, but the rise in sales is not expected until about a year after the changeover occurs.

Beyond the recommendation and its general rationale, the summary should list the key points that support the recommendation. Usually, it is best to state these as "propositions" and accompany them by reference to the pages in the report where the point is developed. These propositions should be stated in a manner that is self-explanatory. The reader should not need to turn to the pages listed in order to understand the point. For example:

> Numerous complaints were received from distributors during the last six months about overlapping territories. These came from distributors in all 11 markets where such overlaps exist. (p. 2)
>
> The major complaints mainly related to suspected secret price cutting (p. 3) and insufficient sales volume to support a distributor. (pp. 4–6)
>
> Other complaints appear less serious, in financial terms, but cause great resentment and even some hostility toward us. (pp. 6–9)

Even the audience that is deeply interested in full detail benefits greatly from such a summary. But the chief beneficiary is usually the author, who will generally discover instances of disorganization, disproportionate treatment of topics, and even some omissions.

THE BODY OF THE REPORT

The body of the report is addressed to the not-so-busy members of the audience. It tells most, but not all, of what the author knows. It is selective and simplified. The proposed contents of the body of the report include:

- An indication of all the issues that top management must consider.
- The elements that determine the outcome of the contemplated action.
- The main contingencies on which the outcome depends.
- The worst things that might happen.
- What is to be gained and what must be given up by adopting the proposal.
- The alternative actions that received consideration.

THE FOOTNOTES

The report should include footnotes. These are mainly for those who have doubts about the methods and the sources and who look for alternate explanations to the ones accepted by the author. Footnotes should reassure readers of the thoroughness with which the author prepared the report, allay doubts, and forestall criticism. The footnotes should generally err in the direction of telling the reader more than he wants to know.

APPENDIXES

Most project proposals should include appendixes. These should be directed to three different audiences:

1. Those in disagreement with the report who will try to find fault with the proposal by arguing that the author did not make a careful study or made superficial or erroneous interpretations of the facts.
2. Those who will be expected to carry out the proposal—these persons should receive guidance from the author that is above and beyond what would be obvious to any intelligent executive. In the course of preparing his report, an author often hears and thinks of things that could help the people asked to put a proposal into effect.
3. Technicians to whom the report might be given for an objective evaluation—they will want to know the methodology employed and see the basic data on which the conclusions rest. These persons might be expected, however, to speak personally to those who have prepared the report. Still, technical back-up adds greatly to the credibility of a report and serves as a deterrent to those who might otherwise attempt to "shoot down" the author.

Some danger results from overengineering a project proposal. The author should maintain some sense of proportion between the weightiness of the project and the weight of the document which proposes it. If one must err, almost always it should be in the direction of providing strong back-up material, as long as the summary and the body of the report are clear, brief, and even spritely.

INDEX